Restoring Financial Stability

Founded in 1807, John Wiley & Sons is the oldest independent publishing company in the United States. With offices in North America, Europe, Australia, and Asia, Wiley is globally committed to developing and marketing print and electronic products and services for our customers' professional and personal knowledge and understanding.

The Wiley Finance series contains books written specifically for finance and investment professionals as well as sophisticated individual investors and their financial advisors. Book topics range from portfolio management to e-commerce, risk management, financial engineering, valuation, and financial instrument analysis, as well as much more.

For a list of available titles, visit our web site at www.WileyFinance.com.

Restoring Financial Stability

How to Repair a Failed System

VIRAL V. ACHARYA
MATTHEW RICHARDSON

WILEY

John Wiley & Sons, Inc.

Published by John Wiley & Sons, Inc., Hoboken, New Jersey.
Published simultaneously in Canada.

For general information on our other products and services or for technical support, please contact our Customer Care Department within the United States at (800) 762-2974, outside the United States at (317) 572-3993 or fax (317) 572-4002.

Wiley also publishes its books in a variety of electronic formats. Some content that appears in print may not be available in electronic books. For more information about Wiley products, visit our web site at www.wiley.com.

Library of Congress Cataloging-in-Publication Data:

Restoring financial stability : how to repair a failed system / Viral V. Acharya and Matthew Richardson, editors.
     p.   cm.—(Wiley finance series)
  Includes bibliographical references and index.
  ISBN 978-0-470-49934-4 (cloth)
    1. Finance—United States.   2. Financial crises—Government policy—United States.
  3. Banks and banking—United States.   4. Financial services industry—United States.
  5. United States—Economic conditions—2001–   I. Acharya, Viral V.   II. Richardson, Matthew, 1964–
   HG181.R37   2009
   339.50973—dc22   2009004115

Printed in the United States of America

10 9 8 7 6 5 4 3

To Manjiree

—V.V.A.

To my best friend and love of my life, Julie, and our three wonders, Jack, Charlie, and Lucas.

—M.R.

Contents

Foreword

As 2008 was drawing to a close, we were reflecting on the dramatic and often unprecedented events of the past year in financial markets and the broader economy. Nothing like this had occurred in our lifetimes. In our academic world, few events have had as much potential for providing us and our colleagues with a rich source of raw material for good research and teaching for a long time to come. This is the ultimate teachable moment, and it is essential to teach it. We were in the middle of a financial and economic hurricane that was certain to leave behind massive financial and economic damage. It will eventually blow over, as all hurricanes do, but it is not too early to begin to think about what changes to the system can mitigate the damage and, it is hoped, make future financial storms less likely.

With one of the largest and best faculties in the world focused on finance, economics, and related disciplines—academics deeply rooted in their respective disciplines and also heavily exposed to the practices of modern financial institutions—we thought that the financial crisis provided a unique opportunity to harness our collective expertise and make a serious contribution to the repair efforts that are getting under way. We convened a small group of interested faculty, the idea caught on, and we decided to execute this project. All faculty members in the relevant disciplines at the Stern School of Business were invited to participate if they had the time and the interest, and 33 colleagues did so (participants are listed at the end of this volume).

Next, key topics related to the crisis and its resolution were identified, and individual teams of authors set to work. As a common format we used the white paper. Each starts by discussing the nature of the problem, where things went wrong, and where we are today, and then goes on to outline what options are available to repair the immediate damage and prevent a recurrence at the least possible cost to financial efficiency and growth, and offers a recommended course of action with respect to public policy or business conduct. Each white paper (many of which are substantially more definitive than we initially envisaged) is accompanied by a short, easily accessible Executive Summary, published separately in New York University Salomon Center's academic journal *Financial Markets, Institutions & Instruments* (Blackwell, 2009). Each white paper was intensively debated both formally and informally among the group over six weeks or so, although no attempt was made to enforce uniformity of views.

This has been a unique opportunity to bring our cumulative expertise to bear on an overarching set of issues that will affect the national and global financial landscape going forward. We know that the repair process in the months and years to come will be highly politicized, and that special interests of all kinds will work hard to affect the outcomes. We also know that some of those entrusted with the repair have also been responsible for some of the damage. So we present here a set of views that are at once informed, carefully considered and debated, independent, and focused exclusively on the public interest.

THOMAS F. COOLEY, Dean
INGO WALTER, Vice Dean
New York University Stern School of Business

New York, New York
February 2009

Acknowledgments

First and foremost, we would like to thank all the faculty who participated in the writing of the white papers. We started this process in early November and completed the majority of the project by late December. Many of the faculty put a tremendous amount of time into this endeavor without really any type of reward at all. Special thanks should go to Anthony W. Lynch, Thomas Philippon, Rangarajan K. Sundaram, and Ingo Walter, who were involved and played a primary role in a number of white papers.

We benefited and were influenced by discussions on the overall theme with a number of co-authors, as well as academic colleagues and practitioners who do not appear in the book, especially Franklin Allen, Yakov Amihud, Sreedhar Bharath, Jacob Boudoukh, Darrell Duffie, Julian Franks, Douglas Gale, Anurag Gupta, Max Holmes, Timothy Johnson, Jeff Mahoney, Ouarda Merrouche, Holger Mueller, Eli Ofek, Matthew Pritzker, Raghuram Rajan, Orly Sade, Hyun Shin, Glen Suarez, Suresh Sundaresan, Richard Sylla, Vikrant Vig, S. "Vish" Viswanathan, and Tanju Yorulmazer.

Finally, special thanks need to be given to our PhD students, especially Hanh Le for proofreading and Farhang Faramand for research assistance, and New York University Salomon Center administrators Mary Jaffier and Robyn Vanterpool. And, of course, to Les Levi, Anjolein Schmeits, and Myron Scholes for reading the book cover to cover and giving many valuable comments that greatly improved the work.

VIRAL V. ACHARYA
MATTHEW RICHARDSON

A Bird's-Eye View

The Financial Crisis of 2007–2009: Causes and Remedies

Viral V. Acharya, Thomas Philippon,
Matthew Richardson, and Nouriel Roubini

The integration of global financial markets has delivered large welfare gains through improvements in static and dynamic efficiency—the *allocation* of real resources and the *rate* of economic growth. These achievements have, however, come at the cost of increased systemic fragility, evidenced by the ongoing financial crisis. We must now face the challenge of redesigning the regulatory overlay of the global financial system in order to make it more robust without crippling its ability to innovate and spur economic growth.

P.1 THE FINANCIAL CRISIS OF 2007–2009

The financial sector has produced large economic efficiencies because financial institutions, which play a unique role in the economy, act as intermediaries between parties that need to borrow and parties willing to lend or invest. Without such intermediation, it is difficult for companies to conduct business. Thus, systemic risk can be thought of as widespread failures of financial institutions or freezing up of capital markets that can substantially reduce the supply of capital to the real economy. The United States experienced this type of systemic failure during 2007 and 2008 and continues to struggle with its consequences as we enter 2009.

When did this financial crisis start and when did it become systemic?

The financial crisis was triggered in the first quarter of 2006 when the housing market turned. A number of the mortgages designed for a subset of the market, namely subprime mortgages, were designed with a balloon interest payment, implying that the mortgage would be refinanced within a short period to avoid the jump in the mortgage rate. The mortgage refinancing presupposed that home prices would continue to appreciate. Thus, the collapse in the housing market necessarily meant a wave of future defaults in the subprime area—a systemic event was coming. Indeed, starting in late 2006 with Ownit Mortgage Solutions' bankruptcy and later on April 2, 2007, with the failure of the second-largest subprime lender, New Century Financial, it was clear that the subprime game had ended.

While subprime defaults were the root cause, the most identifiable event that led to systemic failure was most likely the collapse on June 20, 2007, of two highly levered Bear Stearns–managed hedge funds that invested in subprime asset-backed securities (ABSs). In particular, as the prices of the collateralized debt obligations (CDOs) began to fall with the defaults of subprime mortgages, lenders to the funds demanded more collateral. In fact, one of the funds' creditors, Merrill Lynch, seized $800 million of their assets and tried to auction them off. When only $100 million worth could be sold, the illiquid nature and declining value of the assets became quite evident. In an attempt to minimize any further auctions at fire sale prices, possibly leading to a death spiral, two days later Bear Stearns injected $3.2 billion worth of loans to keep the hedge funds afloat.

This event illustrates the features that typify financial crises—a credit boom (which leads to the leveraging of financial institutions, in this case, the Bear Stearns hedge funds) and an asset bubble (which increases the probability of a large price shock, in this case, the housing market). Eventually, when shocks lead to a bursting of the asset bubble (i.e., the fall in house prices) and trigger a process of deleveraging, these unsustainable asset bubbles and credit booms go bust with the following three consequences:

1. The fall in the value of the asset backed by high leverage leads to margin calls that force borrowers to sell the bubbly asset, which in turn starts to deflate in value.
2. This fall in the asset value now reduces the value of the collateral backing the initial leveraged credit boom.
3. Then, margin calls and the forced fire sale of the asset can drive down its price even below its now lower fundamental value, creating a cascading vicious circle of falling asset prices, margin calls, fire sales, deleveraging, and further asset price deflation.

Even though Bear Stearns tried to salvage the funds, the damage had been done. By the following month, the funds had lost over 90 percent of their value and were shuttered. As we know now, this event was just the tip of a very large iceberg that had already been created.

Coincident with the fate of these funds, there was a complete repricing of all credit instruments, led by the widening of credit spreads on investment grade bonds, high yield bonds, leverage loans via the LCDX index, CDOs backed by commercial mortgages via the CMBX, and CDOs backed by subprime mortgages via the ABX.[1] This led to an almost overnight halt on CDO issuance. As an illustration, Figure P.1 graphs an increase of over 200 basis points (bps) in high yield spreads between mid-June and the end of July 2007 and an almost complete collapse in the leveraged loan market.

Although it is difficult to tie the credit moves directly to other markets, on July 25, 2007, the largest, best-known speculative trade, the carry trade in which investors go long the high-yielding currency and short the

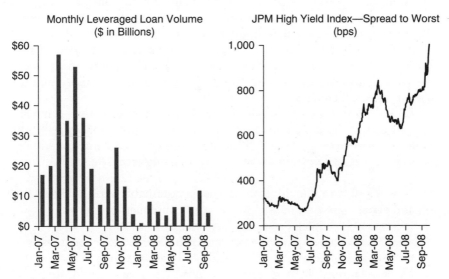

FIGURE P.1 Leveraged Finance Market (January 2007 to September 2008)

These graphs show the monthly leveraged loan volume and the spread on the yield to worst on the JPMorgan High Yield Index over the period January 2007 to September 2008. The yield to worst on each bond in the index is the lowest yield of all the call dates of each bond.

Source: S&P LCD, JPMorgan.

low-yielding one, had its largest move in many years. Specifically, being long 50 percent each in the Australian dollar and New Zealand kiwi and short 100 percent in Japanese yen lost 3.5 percent in a single day. The daily standard deviation over the previous three years for this trade had been 0.6 percent. It was, in short, a massive six standard deviation move. It is now widely believed that hedge fund losses in the carry trade, or perhaps a shift in risk aversion, led to the next major event—the meltdown of quantitative, long-short hedge fund strategies (value, momentum, and statistical arbitrage) over the week of August 6, 2007. A large liquidation the previous week in these strategies most likely started a cascade that caused hedge fund losses (with leverage) on the order of 25 to 35 percent before recovering on August 9.

The subprime mortgage decline had truly become systemic.

And then it happened. For over a week, there had been a run on the assets of three structured investment vehicles (SIVs) of BNP Paribas. The run was so severe that on August 9, BNP Paribas had to suspend redemptions. This event informed investors that the asset-backed commercial papers (ABCPs) and SIVs were not necessarily safe short-term vehicles. Instead, these conduits were supported by subprime and other questionable credit quality assets, which had essentially lost their liquidity or resale options.

BNP Paribas' announcement caused the asset-backed commercial paper market to freeze, an event that most succinctly highlights the next major step to a financial crisis, namely the lack of transparency and resulting counterparty risk concerns.

Consider the conduits of BNP Paribas. For several years, there had been huge growth in the development of structured products, ABCPs and SIVs being just two examples. However, once pricing was called into question as subprime mortgages defaulted, the conduit market faced:

- New exotic and illiquid financial instruments that were hard to value and price.
- Increasingly complex derivative instruments.
- The fact that many of these instruments traded over the counter rather than on an exchange.
- The revelation that there was little information and disclosure about such instruments and who was holding them.
- The fact that many new financial institutions were opaque with little or no regulation (hedge funds, private equity, SIVs, and other off-balance-sheet conduits).

Given that there was little to distinguish between BNP Paribas' conduits and those of other financial institutions, the lack of transparency on what financial institutions were holding and how much of the conduit loss would get passed back to the sponsoring institutions caused the entire market to shut down. All short-term markets, such as commercial paper and repurchase agreements (repo), began to freeze, only to open again once the central banks injected liquidity into the system.

Private financial markets cannot function properly unless there is enough information, reporting, and disclosure both to market participants and to relevant regulators and supervisors. When investors cannot appropriately price complex new securities, they cannot properly assess the overall losses faced by financial institutions, and when they cannot know who is holding the risk for so-called toxic waste, this turns into generalized uncertainty. The outcome is an excessive increase in risk aversion, lack of trust and confidence in counterparties, and a massive seizure of liquidity in financial markets. Thus, once lack of financial market transparency and increased opacity of these markets became an issue, the seeds were sown for a full-blown systemic crisis.

After this market freeze, the next several months became a continual series of announcements about subprime lenders going bankrupt, massive write-downs by financial institutions, monolines approaching bankruptcy, and so on. The appendix at the end of this Prologue provides a time line of all major events of the crisis.

While the market was learning about who was exposed, it was still unclear what the magnitude of this exposure was and who was at risk through counterparty failure. By now, banks had stopped trusting each other as well and were hoarding significant liquidity as a precautionary buffer; unsecured interbank lending at three-month maturity had largely switched to secured overnight borrowing; the flow of liquidity through the interbank markets had frozen; and lending to the real economy had begun to be adversely affected.

Two defining events in the period to follow confirmed that these counterparty risk concerns were valid. These were the rescue of Bear Stearns and the bankruptcy of Lehman Brothers. We discuss the systemic risk concerns raised by these events in turn.

There was a run on Bear Stearns, the fifth-largest investment bank, during the week of March 10, 2008. Bear Stearns was a prime candidate; it was the smallest of the major investment banks, had the most leverage, and was exposed quite significantly to the subprime mortgage market. On that weekend, the government helped engineer JPMorgan Chase's purchase of Bear Stearns by guaranteeing $29 billion of subprime-backed securities, thus preventing a collapse. Bear Stearns had substantive systemic risk, as it had a high degree of interconnectedness to other parts of the financial system. In particular, its default represented a significant counterparty risk since it was a major player in the $2.5 trillion repo market (which is the primary source of short-term funding of security purchases), the leading prime broker on Wall Street to hedge funds, and a significant participant—on both sides—in the credit default swap (CDS) market. Its rescue temporarily calmed markets.

In contrast, as an example of systemic risk that actually materialized, consider the fourth-largest investment bank, Lehman Brothers. Lehman filed for bankruptcy over the weekend following Friday, September 12, 2008. In hindsight, Lehman contained considerable systemic risk and led to the near collapse of the financial system. Arguably, this stopped—and again, just temporarily—only when the government announced its full-blown bailout the following week.

The type of systemic risk related to Lehman's collapse can be broken down into three categories:

1. The market's realization that if Lehman Brothers was not too big to fail, then that might be true for the other investment banks as well. This led to a classic run on the other institutions, irrespective of the fact that they were most likely more solvent than Lehman Brothers. This led to Merrill Lynch selling itself to Bank of America. The other two institutions, Morgan Stanley and Goldman Sachs, saw the cost of their five-year CDS protection rise from 250 basis points (bps) to 500 bps and from 200 bps to 350 bps (respectively), from Friday, September 12, to Monday, September 15, and then to 997 bps and 620 bps (respectively) on September 17.
2. The lack of transparency in the system as a whole:
   - Collateral calls on American International Group (AIG) led to its government bailout on Monday, September 15. Without the bailout, its exposure to the financial sector through its insuring of some $500 billion worth of CDSs on AAA-rated CDOs would have caused immediate, and possibly catastrophic, losses to a number of firms.
   - One of the largest money market funds, the Reserve Primary Fund, owned $700 million of Lehman Brothers' short-term paper. After Lehman's bankruptcy, Lehman's debt was essentially worthless, making the Reserve Primary Fund "break the buck" (i.e., drop below par), an event that had not occurred for over a decade. This created uncertainty about all money market funds, causing a massive run on the system. Since money market funds are the primary source for funding repos and commercial paper, this was arguably the most serious systemic event of the crisis. The government then had to guarantee all money market funds.

3. The counterparty risk of Lehman:
   - As one illustration, consider its prime brokerage business. In contrast to its U.S. operations, when Lehman declared bankruptcy, its prime brokerage in the United Kingdom went bankrupt. This meant that any hedge fund whose securities were hypothecated by Lehman was now an unsecured creditor. This led to massive losses across many hedge funds as their securities that had been posted as collateral disappeared in the system.
   - As another illustration, in the wake of Lehman's failure, interbank markets truly froze, as no bank trusted another's solvency; the entire financial intermediation activity was at risk of complete collapse.

What the Lehman Brothers episode revealed was that there really is a "too big to fail" label for financial institutions. We will argue that this designation is incredibly costly because it induces, somewhat paradoxically, a moral hazard in the form of a race to become systemic, and, when a crisis hits, results in wealth transfers from taxpayers to the systemic institution.

The next section presents a requiem for the shadow banking sector—how the run propagated from the nonbank mortgage lenders to independent broker-dealers and then all the way to money market funds and corporations reliant on short-term financing. Section P.3 discusses in greater detail the root causes of the crisis. Sections P.4 and P.5 describe (respectively) the basic principles of regulation we propose in order to reduce the likelihood of systemic failure within an economy such as that of the United States, and the principles of a bailout when the crisis hits. Section P.6 discusses why such regulation will be effective only if there is reasonable coordination among different national regulators on its principles and implementation.

P.2 REQUIEM FOR THE SHADOW BANKING SECTOR

Before we proceed to understanding the root causes of the financial crisis of 2007 to 2009, it is important to stress that this was a crisis of traditional banks and, more important, a crisis of the so-called shadow banking sector—that is, of those financial institutions that mostly looked like banks. These institutions borrowed short-term in rollover debt markets, leveraged significantly, and lent and invested in longer-term and illiquid assets. However, unlike banks, they did not have access until 2008 to the safety nets—deposit insurance, as well as the lender of last resort (LOLR), the central bank—that have been designed to prevent runs on banks. In

2007 and 2008, we effectively observed a run on the shadow banking system that led to the demise of a significant part of the (then) unguaranteed financial system.

This run and demise started in early 2007 with the collapse of several hundred nonbank mortgage lenders, mostly specialized in subprime and Alt-A mortgages, and continued thereafter in a series of steps that we list in the following pages. When the market realized that these institutions had made mostly toxic loans, the wholesale financing of these nonbank lenders disappeared, and one by one, hundreds of them failed, were closed down, or were merged into larger banking institutions. Given the extent of poor underwriting standards, this collapse of mortgage lenders included even some that had depository arms, such as Countrywide—the largest U.S. mortgage lender—which was acquired under distressed conditions by Bank of America.

The second phase of the shadow banking system's demise was the collapse of the entire system of structured investment vehicles (SIVs) and conduits that started when investors realized that they had invested in very risky and/or illiquid assets—toxic CDOs based on mortgages and other credit derivatives—thus triggering the run on their short-term ABCP financing. Since many of these SIVs and conduits had been offered credit enhancements and contingent liquidity lines from their sponsoring financial institutions, mostly banks, while they were *de jure* off-balance-sheet vehicles of such banks, they became *de facto* on balance sheet when the unraveling of their financing forced the sponsoring banks to bring them back on balance sheet.

The third phase of the shadow banking system's demise was the collapse of the major U.S. independent broker-dealers that occurred when the run on their liabilities took the form of the unraveling of the repo financing that was the basis of their leveraged operations. Bear Stearns was the first victim. After the Bear episode, the Federal Reserve introduced its most radical change in monetary policy since the Great Depression—the provision of LOLR support via the new Primary Dealer Credit Facility (PDCF)[2]—to systemically important broker-dealers (those that were primary dealers of the Fed). Even this LOLR did not prevent the run on Lehman, as investors realized that this support was not unconditional and unlimited—the conditions for an LOLR to be able to credibly stop *any* banklike run. The decision to let Lehman collapse then forced Merrill Lynch, next in line for a run, to merge with Bank of America. Next, the two other remaining independent broker-dealers, which after the creation of the PDCF were effectively already under the supervisory arm of the Fed, were forced to convert into bank holding companies (allowing them—if willing—to acquire more stable insured deposits) and thus be formally put under supervision and regulation of the Fed. In fact, in a matter of seven months the Wall Street system of independent broker-dealers had collapsed.

The demise of the shadow banking system continued with the run on money market funds. These funds were not highly leveraged but, like banks, relied on the short-term financing of their investors. These investors could run if concerned about funds' liquidity or solvency. Concerns about solvency were first triggered by the Reserve Primary Fund "breaking the buck," as it had invested into Lehman debt. Like the Reserve fund, many of these money market funds, which were competing aggressively for investors' savings, were promising higher than market returns on allegedly liquid and safe investment by putting a small fraction of their assets into illiquid, toxic, and risky securities. Once the Reserve fund broke the buck, investors panicked because they did not—and could not—know which funds were holding toxic assets and how much of them were held. Given the banklike short-run nature of their liabilities and the absence of deposit insurance, a run on money market funds rapidly ensued. This run on a $3 trillion industry, if left unchecked, would have been destructive, as money market funds were the major source of funding for the corporate commercial paper market. Thus, when the run started, the Federal Reserve and the Treasury were forced to provide deposit insurance to all the money market funds to stop such a run, another major extension of the banks' safety nets to nonbank financial institutions.

The following phase of the shadow banking system's demise was the run on hundreds of hedge funds. Like other institutions, hedge funds' financing was very short-term since investors could redeem their investments in these funds after short lockup periods; also, given that the basis of their leverage was short-term repo financing, their financing fizzled out as primary brokers disappeared or cut back their financing to hedge funds. These runs were amplified by the crowded nature of many of the hedge fund strategies.

The next phase of the demise of the shadow banking system may be the coming refinancing crisis of the private equity–financed leveraged buyouts (LBOs). Private equity and LBOs are highly leveraged in their operation, but they tend to have longer-maturity financing that reduces, but does not eliminate, the risk of a refinancing crisis; it only makes it a slow-motion run. The existence of "covenant-lite/loose" clauses and pay-in-kind (PIK) toggles further allows LBO firms to postpone a refinancing crisis. But the large number of leveraged loans that are coming to maturity in 2010 and 2011—when credit spreads would have most likely massively widened—suggests that many of these LBOs may go bust once the refinancing crisis emerges. While some of the LBO firms may only require financial restructuring, it is likely that the process of restructuring will result in substantial economic losses in some cases.

The drying up of liquidity and financial distress did not spare other financial institutions such as insurance companies and monoline bond insurers that had aggressively provided insurance to a variety of toxic credit derivatives. Some of these, American International Group (AIG) in particular, which had sold over $500 billion of such insurance, went bust and had to receive a government bailout. Others, such as monoline bond insurers, eventually lost their AAA ratings. While not subject to a formal run and collapse as they had longer-term financing via the insurance premiums, the loss of the AAA rating meant that they had to post significant additional collateral on many existing contracts and were unable to provide new insurance. Their business model collapsed as a result.

Runs on the short-term liabilities caused problems even for traditional banks and for nonfinancial corporations. By the summer of 2007 and following the collapse of Lehman, there were traditional bank runs that put significant pressure on likely insolvent banking institutions such as IndyMac, Washington Mutual (WaMu), and Wachovia. Since at that stage deposits in the United States were insured up to just $100,000, only about 70 percent of deposits were insured. Uninsured deposits accounted for about $2.6 trillion of the $7 trillion of deposits in Federal Deposit Insurance Corporation (FDIC)–insured institutions. Concerns about the solvency of U.S. banking institutions peaked in the summer of 2008 following the failure or near failure of Indy Mac, WaMu, and Wachovia. The lack of active interbank lending, which manifested in the very high London Interbank Offered Rate (LIBOR) spreads and bank hoarding of liquidity, and the risk to uninsured deposits (including a substantial amount of large cross-border lines) led to concerns about a generalized bank run. The policy authorities responded to the possibility of a bank run by formally extending deposit insurance from $100,000 to $250,000 and effectively providing an implicit guarantee even to uninsured deposits (these remained significant at about $1.9 trillion) via resolution of distressed banks that would not involve any losses for uninsured deposits. The creation of new government facilities to guarantee for a period of time any new debt issued by financial institutions also provided a significant public safety net against the risk of a roll-off of maturing liabilities of the financial sector.

Other facilities created by the Fed further expanded indirectly its lender of last resort support even to foreign banks and primary dealers that did not operate in the United States (and that thus did not have access to the discount window and the new facilities). In particular, the large swap lines upon which the Fed agreed with a number of other central banks effectively allowed other central banks to borrow dollar liquidity from the Fed and then relend such dollar liquidity to their domestic financial institutions that were facing a dollar liquidity shortage because of the roll-off of their dollar liabilities. These swap lines were both a form of lender of last resort support of non-U.S. banks and a form of foreign exchange intervention to prevent the excessive appreciation of the U.S. dollar that such a demand for dollar liquidity by foreign banks was triggering.

Finally, the risk of a run on short-term liabilities did not even spare the corporate sector. In the fall of 2008, and especially after the collapse of Lehman, the ability of corporate firms, in particular those employing commercial paper financing, to roll over their short-term debt was severely impaired. The deepening of the credit crunch and the incipient run on money market funds—the main investors in such commercial paper—led to a sharp roll-off of this essential form of short-term financing that was funding the corporate sector's working capital requirements. The risk now became one of solvent but illiquid firms' risking a default on their short-term liabilities as the consequence of their inability to roll over short-term debt induced by the sequence of market freezes just described. The U.S. policy authorities responded to this unprecedented risk with—again—an unprecedented action: A new facility was created for the Fed to purchase commercial paper from the corporate sector.

As a consequence of this run or near run on the short-term liabilities of shadow banks, commercial banks, and even corporate firms, policy makers adopted massive new and hitherto unexplored roles as providers of liquidity to a very broad range of institutions. Usually central banks are lenders of last resort; but in the financial crisis of 2007, the Fed became the lender of first and only resort: Since banks were not lending to each other and were not lending to nonbank financial institutions, and financial firms were not even lending to the corporate sector, the Fed ended up backstopping the short-term liabilities of banks, nonbank financial institutions, and nonfinancial corporations.

It is difficult to quantify the effect the financial crisis in the summer of 2007 had on the recession that started in December 2007 and is working its way through 2009. This is especially true given that a large number of households lost a majority of their wealth when housing prices started their steep downward trend in 2006. In other words, the recession may well have occurred even if the financial crisis had not taken root. But most would agree that the near collapse of the financial system in the fall of 2008 has had severe consequences for the economy. The losses that highly leveraged financial institutions faced led to a significant credit crunch that exacerbated the asset price deflation and led to lower real spending on capital goods—consumer durables and investment goods—that has triggered the overall economic contraction. It is, however, a vicious circle. Deleveraging and credit crunches have both financial and real consequences: They trigger financial losses and they can trigger an economic recession that worsens financial losses for debtors and creditors, and so on.

With this requiem for the shadow banking sector (in fact, for most of the financial sector!), it is useful to organize our thinking around the various causes of the underlying instability in the financial sector which led to this vicious circle.

P.3 CAUSES

There is almost universal agreement that the fundamental cause of the crisis was the combination of a credit boom and a housing bubble. By mid-2006, the two most common features of these so-called bubbles, the spreads on credit instruments and the ratio of house prices to rental income, were at their all-time extremes. Figures P.2 and P.3 graph both these phenomena, respectively.

There are two quite disparate views of these bubbles.

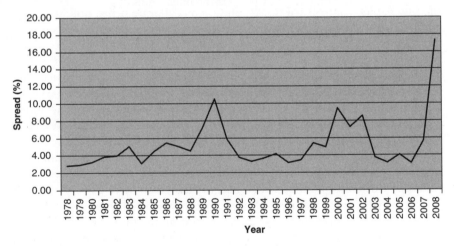

FIGURE P.2   Historical High Yield Bond Spreads, 1978–2008

This chart graphs the high yield bond spread over Treasuries on an annual basis over the period 1978 to 2008. The lowest point of the graph from June 1, 2006, onward, not visible due to the annual nature of the data, is 260 basis points on June 12.

Source: Salomon Center, Stern School of Business, New York University.

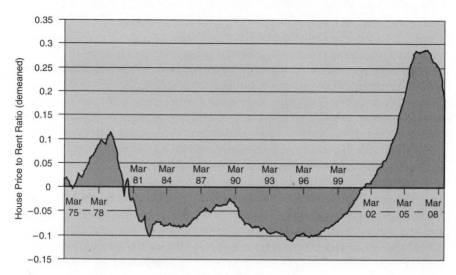

FIGURE P.3 House Price to Rent Ratio, 1975–2008

This chart graphs the demeaned value of the ratio of the Office of Federal Housing Enterprise Oversight (OFHEO) repeat-sale house price index to the Bureau of Labor Statistics (BLS) shelter index (i.e., gross rent plus utilities components of the CPI). Because of demeaning, the average value of this ratio is zero.

Source: Authors' own calculations, OFHEO, BLS.

The first is that there was just a fundamental mispricing in capital markets—risk premiums were too low and long-term volatility reflected a false belief that future short-term volatility would stay at its current low levels. This mispricing necessarily implied low credit spreads and inflated prices of risky assets. One explanation for this mispricing was the global imbalance that arose due to the emergence and tremendous growth of new capitalist societies in China, India, and the eastern bloc of Europe. On the one side, there were the consumer-oriented nations of the United States, Western Europe, Australia, and so forth. And on the other side, there were these fast-growing, investment- and savings-driven nations. Capital from the second set of countries poured into assets of the first set, leading to excess liquidity, low volatility, and low spreads.

The second is that mistakes made by the Federal Reserve (and some other central banks) in the past decade may have been partially responsible. In particular, the decision of the Fed to keep the federal funds rate too low for too long (down to 1 percent until 2004) created both a credit bubble and a housing bubble. In other words, with an artificially low federal funds target, banks gorged themselves on cheap funding and made cheap loans available. In addition to easy money, the other mistake made by the Fed and other regulators was the failure to control the poor underwriting standards in the mortgage markets. Poor underwriting practices such as no down payments; no verification of income, assets, and jobs (no-doc or low-doc or NINJA—no income, jobs, or assets—mortgages); interest-only mortgages; negative amortization; and teaser rates were widespread among subprime, near-prime (Alt-A), and even prime mortgages. The Fed and other regulators generally supported these financial innovations.

There may be some truth to both views. On the one hand, credit was widely available across all markets—mortgage, consumer, and corporate loans—with characteristics that suggested poorer and poorer loan quality. On the other hand, both the credit boom and the housing bubble were worldwide phenomena, making it difficult to pin the blame only on the Fed's policy and lack of proper supervision and regulation of mortgages.

As we now know, a massive shock to one of the asset markets, most notably housing, led to a wave of defaults (with many more expected to come) in the mortgage sector. In terms of magnitude, the drop in housing prices from the peak in the first quarter of 2006 to today is 23 percent (see Figure P.3). Therefore, at first glance one might presume that mere loss of wealth might explain the severity of the crisis. However, the United States went through a similarly large shock relatively recently without creating the same systemic effects: The high-tech bubble in U.S. equity markets led to extraordinary rates of return in the late 1990s, only to collapse in March 2000. As a result, the NASDAQ fell 70 percent over the next 18 months (up until 9/11). The ensuing collapse of the dot-coms, the sharp fall in real investment by the corporate sector, and the eventual collapse of most high-tech stocks triggered the U.S. recession of 2001 and the extraordinary wave of defaults of high yield bonds in 2002. Yet there was no systemic financial crisis.

Why has the housing market collapse of 2007 been so much more severe than the dot-com crash of 2001, or, for that matter, the market crash of 1987 or any of the other crashes that have punctuated financial history (perhaps with the exception of the Great Depression)?

There are four major differences with respect to this current crisis.

First, unlike the Internet bubble, the loss in wealth for households in this crisis comes from highly leveraged positions in the underlying asset (i.e., housing). In fact, given the current price drop, the estimate is that 30 percent of all owner-occupied homes with a mortgage have negative equity, and that figure may become as high as 40 percent if home prices drop another 15 percent. Since homes are the primary assets for most households, this means that

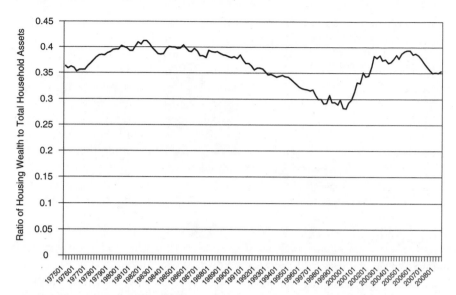

FIGURE P.4   Housing Wealth/Total Household Assets, 1975–2008

This chart graphs the ratio of housing wealth (owner-occupied and tenant-occupied owned by households) divided by total household assets.

Source: Federal Reserve Flow of Funds.

a significant number of households are essentially broke, leading the way for the surge in mortgage defaults, especially at the subprime and Alt-A levels.

Figure P.4 provides estimates of the importance of household wealth as a fraction of total household assets. As can be seen from the figure, the number is economically significant, varying from 30 percent to 40 percent over the period from 1975 to 2008, with 35 percent being the ratio in the third quarter of 2008. Figure P.5 adds consumer leverage to the mix and shows the extraordinary jump in consumer debt as a fraction of home value. Specifically, this ratio went from 56 percent in 1985 to 68 percent in 2005 and finally to 89 percent in late 2008. We are standing on the precipice.

It did not help that the majority of mortgages, the 2/28 and 3/27 adjustable rate mortgages (ARMs), were basically structured to either refinance or default within two or three years, respectively, making them completely dependent on the path of home prices and thus systemic in nature. In any event, independent of other activity in the financial sector, this shock to household wealth necessarily had greater consequences for the real economy than the burst of the technology bubble in 2000.

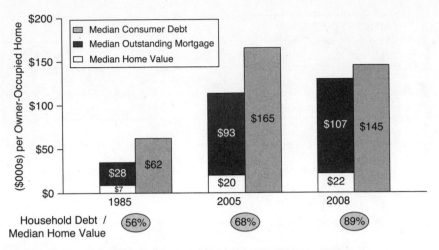

FIGURE P.5   Household Debt/Home Values, 1985, 2005, 2008

This chart graphs estimates of household debt over home values of the median household. Specifically, the median value of outstanding mortgage principal amount of owner-occupied units and the consumer credit per household were derived from the U.S. Census Bureau and Federal Reserve Flow of Funds. The 2008 median home value was adjusted from the fourth quarter 2005 value using the S&P/Case-Shiller National Home Price Index.

Source: U.S. Census Bureau, Federal Reserve Flow of Funds, S&P/Case-Shiller Index.

Moreover, while the focus has been primarily on the mortgage sector, and in particular on the market for subprime mortgages, the problems run much deeper. Individuals and institutions gorged on credit across the economy. Figure P.6 shows that, as of 2007, there was over $38.2 trillion of nongovernment debt, only 3 percent of which is subprime. Other breakdowns include 3 percent worth of leveraged loans and high yield debt, 25 percent corporate debt, 7 percent consumer credit, 9 percent commercial mortgages, and 26 percent prime residential mortgages. Compared to the past 15 years, the underlying capital structure of the economy appears much more levered and its assets much less healthy. For example, in December 2008, 63 percent of all high-yield bonds traded below 70 percent of par, compared to the previous high of around 30 percent discount during the blowout in 2002. The current state of the union is not for the fainthearted!

The second, and related, difference is that over the past several years, the quantity and quality of loans across a variety of markets has weakened in two important ways. In terms of quantity, there was a large increase in

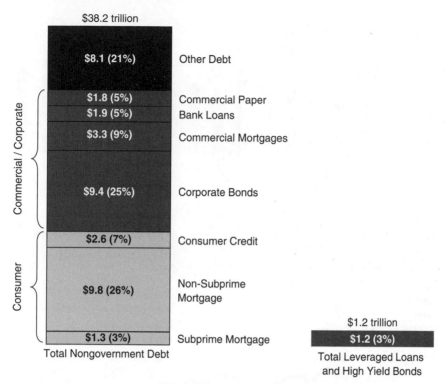

FIGURE P.6   Total Nongovernment U.S. Debt, 2008

This chart shows the components of total U.S. nongovernment debt in 2008. Specifically, the calculations exclude government-issued debt such as Treasury securities, municipal securities, and agency-backed debt.

Source: Federal Reserve Flow of Funds, International Swaps and Derivatives Association (ISDA), Securities Industry and Financial Markets Association (SIFMA), Goldman Sachs, U.S. Treasury.

lower-rated issuance from 2004 to 2007. As an example, Figure P.7 graphs the number of new issues rated B– or below as a percentage of all new issues over the past 15 years. There is a large jump starting in 2004, with an average of 43.8 percent over the next four years compared to 27.8 percent over the prior 11 years.

Perhaps even more frightening is the fact that historically safe leveraged loans are a substantially different asset class today. This is because historically these loans had substantial debt beneath them in the capital structure. But leveraged loans over the past several years were issued with little capital structure support. Their recovery rates are going to be magnitudes lower. To see this, Figure P.8 graphs the prices of the LCDX series 8 from the

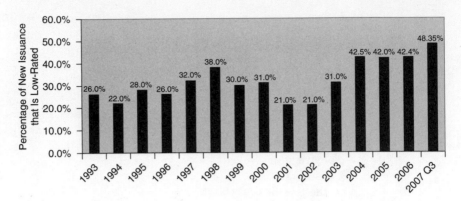

FIGURE P.7   Quality of New Debt Issuance, 1993–2007

This chart graphs total new issues rated B– or below as a percentage of all new issues over the period 1993 to the third quarter of 2007.

Source: Standard & Poor's Global Fixed Income Research.

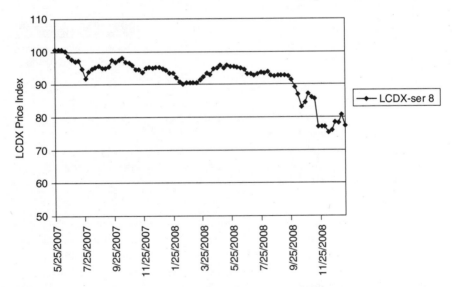

FIGURE P.8   LCDX Pricing, May 2007 to January 2009

This chart shows the series 8 of the LCDX index from May 22, 2007, to January 22, 2009. The LCDX index is a portfolio credit default swap (CDS) product composed of 100 loan CDSs referencing syndicated secured first-lien loans.

Source: Bloomberg.

end of May 2007 through January 2009. The index initially paid a coupon of 120 basis points over a five-year maturity and comprised 100 equally weighted loan credit default swaps (CDSs) referencing syndicated first-lien loans. Once the crisis erupted in late June 2007, the prices of the LCDX began to drop. By January 2009 it was at unprecedented low levels, hovering around 75 cents on the dollar.

Moreover, many of these loans were issued to finance leveraged buyouts (LBOs). Over this same period, the average debt leverage ratios grew rapidly to levels not seen previously. Thus, even in normal times, many of the companies would be struggling to meet these debt demands. In a recessionary environment, these struggles will be amplified. Figure P.9 illustrates this point by graphing the leverage ratios of LBOs over the past decade or so both in the United States and in Europe.

In terms of quality, there was also a general increase in no-documentation and high loan-to-value subprime mortgages, and "covenant-lite" and PIK toggle leveraged loans. As an illustration, Figure P.10 charts various measures of loan quality in the subprime mortgage area, starting from 2001 and going through 2006. As is visible from the graphs, there were dramatic changes in the quality of the loans during this period.

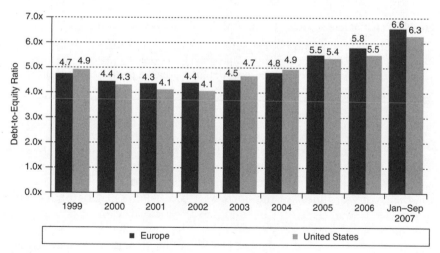

FIGURE P.9   Leverage Ratio for LBOs, 1999–2007

This chart graphs the average total debt leverage ratio for LBOs in both the United States and Europe with earnings before interest, taxes, depreciation, and amortization (EBITDA) of 50 million or more in dollars or euros, respectively. The chart covers the period from 1999 to 2007.

Source: Standard & Poor's LCD.

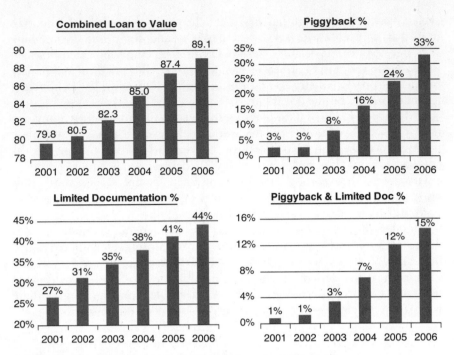

FIGURE P.10   Deteriorating Credit Quality of Subprime Mortgages

These four charts graph various measures of the quality of subprime mortgages, including loan-to-value ratios, percent of piggyback loans, and percent of loans with limited documentation. These are estimated over the period 2001–2006.

Source: LoanPerformance, Paulson & Co.

One explanation for deteriorating loan quality is the huge growth in securitized credit. This is because the originate-to-distribute model of securitization reduces the incentives for the originator of the claims to monitor the creditworthiness of the borrower, because the originator has little or no skin in the game. For example, in the securitization food chain for U.S. mortgages, every intermediary in the chain was making a fee; eventually the credit risk got transferred to a structure that was so opaque even the most sophisticated investors had no real idea what they were holding. The mortgage broker; the home appraiser; the bank originating the mortgages and repackaging them into MBSs; the investment bank repackaging the MBSs into CDOs, CDOs of CDOs, and even CDOs cubed; the credit rating agencies giving their AAA blessing to such instruments—each of these intermediaries was earning income from charging fees for their step of the intermediation process and transferring the credit risk down the line. The reduction in quality of the loans and lack of transparency of the securitized structure added to the fragility of the system.

The shock to housing (and resulting defaults) and the aforementioned fragility of this system of securitized loans certainly implied significant losses in the portfolios of investors. But the whole point of securitization is precisely that by transferring credit risk from lenders to investors, the risks will be spread throughout the economy with minimal systemic effect. This leads to the third, and most important, reason for why the financial crisis occurred.

Credit transfer *did not* take place in the mortgage market and, even when intended in the leverage loan market, banks got caught holding up to $300 billion of leveraged loans when the market collapsed in late July 2007. The reality is that banks and other financial institutions maintained a significant exposure to mortgages, MBSs, and CDOs. Indeed, in the United States about 47 percent of all the assets of major banks are real estate related; the figure for smaller banks is closer to 67 percent. Thus, instead of following the originate-to-distribute model of securitization which would have transferred credit risk of mortgages to capital market investors, banks and broker-dealers retained, themselves, a significant portion of that credit risk across a variety of instruments. Indeed, if that credit risk had been fully or at least substantially transferred, such banks and other financial intermediaries would not have suffered the hundreds of billions of dollars of losses that they have incurred so far and will have to recognize in the future.

Why did banks take such a risky bet? At the peak of the housing bubble in June 2006, one can compare the spreads from the tranches of subprime MBSs (as described by the ABX index) to similarly rated debt of the average U.S. firm. Specifically, the spreads are 18 basis points (bps) versus 11 bps for AAA-rated securities, 32 bps versus 16 bps for AA-rated, 54 bps versus 24 bps for A-rated, and 154 bps versus 48 bps for BBB-rated.

Consider the AAA-rated tranche. According to estimates from Lehman Brothers, U.S. financial institutions (e.g., banks and thrifts, government-sponsored enterprises [GSEs], broker-dealers, and insurance companies) were holding $916 billion worth of these tranches. Note that these financial firms would be earning a premium most of the time and would face losses only in the rare event that the AAA-rated tranche of the CDO would get hit. If this rare event occurred, however, it would almost surely be a systemic shock affecting all markets. Financial firms were in essence writing a very large out-of-the-money put option on the market. Of course, the problem with writing huge amounts of systemic insurance like this is that the firms cannot make good when it counts—hence, this financial crisis. Put simply, financial firms took a huge asymmetric bet on the real estate market.

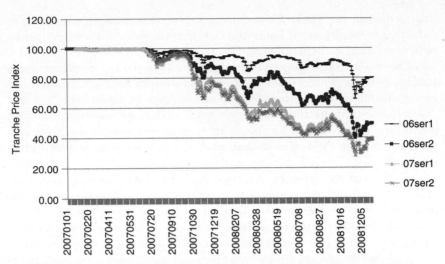

FIGURE P.11   Subprime Mortgage AAA Tranche Pricing, 2007 and 2008

This chart shows the AAA tranche of the ABX index of the 2006 and 2007 first and second half of the year series from January 1, 2007, to December 31, 2008. The ABX index is an index of 20 representative collateralized debt obligations (CDOs) of subprime mortgages. The AAA tranche represents an initial equally weighted portfolio of these same tranches of each CDO.

Source: Markit.

To get some understanding of how hard these tranches have been hit, Figure P.11 graphs the various AAA-rated ABX index series from their initiation to the end of 2008. Specifically, we graph the prices of the AAA tranche of the ABX index of the 2006 and 2007 first and second half of the year series from January 1, 2007, to December 31, 2008. The ABX index is an index of 20 representative collateralized debt obligations (CDOs) of subprime mortgages, and the AAA tranche represents an initial equally weighted portfolio of these same tranches of each CDO. These indexes are initially priced at par, and one can see that the 2006 series stayed around that level until late July 2007 when the crisis started. Depending on the series, the tranches are now selling at from 40 cents to 80 cents on the dollar. Putting aside issues specific to the pricing of the ABX, at the current prices in Figure P.11 and given the aforementioned $916 billion, losses to the financial sector range from $550 billion to $183 billion on their holdings of the AAA tranches of mortgage-backed securities alone.

Finally, the fourth difference is that the potential losses from these bets were greatly amplified through the use of more and more leverage by financial firms. These firms got around capital requirements in various ways. For commercial banks, setting up off-balance-sheet asset-backed commercial paper (ABCP) conduits and structured investment vehicles (SIVs)—with recourse to their balance sheets through liquidity and credit enhancements—allowed them to move the so-called AAA assets in such a way as would not incur most of the capital adequacy requirement.

Investment banks added leverage the old-fashioned way by persuading the SEC in August 2004 to amend the net capital rule of the Securities Exchange Act of 1934. This amendment allowed a voluntary method of computing deductions to net capital for large broker-dealers. This alternative approach allowed the investment banks to use internal models to calculate net capital requirements for market- and derivatives-related credit risk. In theory, the amendment also called for greater scrutiny by the SEC. It effectively allowed big investment banks to lever up as much as they wanted.

Still, why take the risky *asymmetric* bet?

We believe there are three possibilities:

1. The first is governance. The system of compensation of bankers and agents within the financial system is characterized by moral hazard in the form of "gambling for redemption." The typical agency problems between a financial firm's shareholders and the firm's managers/bankers/traders are exacerbated by the way the latter have been compensated. Because a large fraction of such compensation is in the form of cash bonuses tied to short-term profits, and because such bonuses are one-sided (positive in good times and at most zero when returns are poor), managers/bankers/traders have a huge incentive to take larger risks than warranted by the goal of shareholders' long-run value maximization.

2. The second is that explicit and implicit government guarantees across the financial system lead to moral hazard. These guarantees remove the discipline normally imposed by depositors on commercial banks, and by debt holders on government-sponsored enterprises (GSEs) and "too-big-to-fail" financial institutions. Because these claimants are convinced of the government's guaranty function, they require a low cost of debt. Hence, the implicit guarantees, if mispriced by governments, provide the firm with an incentive to take risk and leverage.

3. The third is that, even with good governance and no guarantees from the government, the financial firm might still take the risky asymmetric bet. Each firm might maximize its risk/return profile even though such behavior exerts substantive negative impact elsewhere in the financial system. In other words, given the incompleteness of financial contracts at varying levels, financial firms did not internalize the full impact of their decisions on the rest of the system and the economy.

Whatever the reasons, and they may have differed across firms, we believe that the combination of leverage and the fact that financial firms chose *not* to transfer the credit risk (even though they pretended to do so) is the root cause of the financial crisis.

Stepping back from the experience of the current crisis, and looking forward, it is clear that the issue of financial stability remains central to assessments of the financial development of a country, and not only with respect to the current experience. Indeed, the experience of the past few decades in both emerging markets and advanced economies shows the pervasiveness of financial crises. These crises—signals of financial instability and the failure of the proper working of the financial system—have important economic and financial consequences, and usually lead to severe economic contractions that may either be short-lived or persist over time. If the real effects persist, the long-run potential and actual growth rate of an economy may be significantly lowered, negatively affecting long-term welfare.

Financial crises are also expensive, since they are associated with significant bankruptcies among households, corporate firms, and financial institutions, with all the ensuing social deadweight losses from debt restructurings and liquidations. An additional cost of these crises is that they cannot be privately resolved; that is, the crises require government intervention. Given that lack of government intervention is not credible, this creates moral hazard exacerbating the original problem. The fiscal costs of bailing out distressed borrowers (households, firms, and financial institutions) therefore end up being very high—often well above 10 percent of gross domestic product (GDP). Thus, persistent and severe financial instability, as measured by the pervasiveness and severity of financial crises, is a signal of failure of the financial system: failure to properly allocate savings to worthy investment projects and failure of corporate governance.

Of course, in a market economy, some degree of bankruptcy is a healthy sign of risk taking. A financial system so stable that no bankruptcy would ever occur indicates low risk taking and diminished entrepreneurship. The absence of somewhat risky—but potentially high-return—investment projects ultimately decreases long-term economic growth. There is a substantial difference, however, between occasional bankruptcies of firms, households, or banks—bankruptcies that are healthy developments in flexible and dynamic market economies—and a systemic banking or corporate crisis where a large number of financial institutions or corporations go bankrupt because of unfettered risk-taking incentives.

Therefore, regulation needs to balance risk taking and innovation against the likelihood of a systemic crisis. In our opinion, a primary reason to regulate systemic risk is the presence of externalities between institutions. By its very nature, systemic risk is a negative externality imposed by each financial firm on the system. Since each individual firm is clearly motivated to prevent its own collapse but not that of the system as a whole, the private market may not be able to solve this problem. The analogous example is of a firm that pollutes and can cause a negative externality on those affected. Such a firm is often regulated to limit the pollution or taxed based on the externality it causes.

So when a financial firm considers holding large amounts of illiquid securities (i.e., CDOs), or concentrates its risk into particular ones (e.g., subprime-based assets), or puts high amounts of leverage on its books (as a way to drive up supposedly safe excess returns), it has the incentive to manage its own risk/return trade-off, provided decision makers are properly compensated. But even in this unlikely case, the firm has no specific incentive to consider the spillover risk its own leverage and risk taking imposes on other financial institutions. This externality is further amplified when many of the financial firms face similar issues. Of course, if firms fail individually, other healthy firms can readily buy them, or even otherwise take up most of their lending and related activities. Thus, real losses primarily arise when firms fail together and cannot be readily resolved, but are important to the economy—as are banks due to their intermediation activities. In such joint failure cases, financial firms know they are likely to be bailed out, and this gives them incentives to end up here in the first place.

In the next section, we suggest a series of principles and proposals for regulatory reform to minimize these issues in future.

P.4 EFFICIENT REGULATION: PRINCIPLES AND PROPOSALS

In order to provide a framework for efficient regulation of the financial sector based on sound economic principles, we reiterate the four important themes that have been intertwined in producing this trenchant crisis. While the following discussion overlaps to an extent with the preceding one, its goal is to establish the core set of issues and the linkages between them and reinforce how they combined into a lethal mixture risking the financial stability and real-sector output of our economies. These four themes are:

1. Risk-taking incentives at banks and financial institutions.
2. Mispriced guarantees awarded to the financial sector.
3. Increasing opaqueness of the financial sector and resulting counterparty risk externality.
4. Focus of regulation on institution-level risk rather than on aggregate or systemic risk.

Risk-Taking Incentives at Banks and Financial Institutions

Given their inherently high leverage and the ease with which the risk profile of financial assets can be altered, *banks and financial institutions have incentives to take on excessive risks*. Ordinarily, one would expect market mechanisms to price risks correctly and thereby ensure that risk taking in the economy is at efficient levels. However, there are several factors—some novel and some traditional—that have ruled out such efficient outcomes.

On the novel front, financial institutions have become large and increasingly complex and opaque in their activities. This has weakened external governance that operates through capital markets (accurate prices), market for corporate control (takeovers), and boards. Coincident with this, and to some extent a corollary to this, has been the fact that financial risks at these institutions are now increasingly concentrated in the hands of a few high-performance profit/risk centers. Employees (bankers, traders) in charge of these centers have skills in creating, packaging and repackaging, marking to market, and hedging financial securities. Since the skills are largely fungible across institutions, these employees have exerted tremendous bargaining power in their institutions and gotten themselves rewarded through highly attractive, short-term compensation packages that provide them significant cash bonuses for short-run performance and what has proven to be effectively "fake alpha."

Financial institutions therefore need strong internal governance, which is easier to adopt as a principle than to put into practice. No one institution or its board can change the compensation expectations alone. Were they to institute new and more appropriate incentive packages together with stronger risk-control management, they would lose their best traders to the competitors. The inefficiency is thus due to a coordination problem among financial institutions, and has manifested in the form of weak risk controls, innovation activity aimed purely at regulatory arbitrage, excessive leverage, and the so-called search for yield, which is just a polite way of describing the practice of shifting assets to riskier and illiquid ones.

Mispriced Guarantees Awarded to the Financial Sector

Are the governance failures by themselves sufficient to cause a crisis of the magnitude we have seen? Most likely not. The issues have been exacerbated by the traditional factor of *ill-designed and mispriced regulatory guarantees*—ill-designed in that the accordance of the too big to fail (TBTF) guarantee to the large, complex financial institutions (LCFIs) has led to consolidation of all sorts of financial activities under the same umbrella, and mispriced in the sense that guarantees such as TBTF and deposit insurance have not been appropriately priced.

Government guarantees are a double-edged sword. They are aimed ex post at limiting risks from institutional failures to the rest of the system. TBTF and deposit insurance were conceived to limit the risks of contagious runs on financial institutions. However, ex ante they blunt the edge of market discipline that such runs impose. Hence, to substitute for such market discipline, it is critical that guarantees be priced correctly and supplemented with regulatory supervision. This has, however, not been the case.

For example, the GSEs have access to implicit government guarantees and are perhaps too big to fail (at least within a short period of time, especially in a crisis), but have been indulging in financial investments in securities such as CDOs based on subprime and Alt-A mortgages. This fails any smell test as far as moral hazard induced by government guarantees is concerned. In yet another important example, large depository institutions have paid no deposit insurance premium to the Federal Deposit Insurance Corporation (FDIC) for the past several years under the economically flawed argument that the FDIC fund has been extremely well-capitalized since 2000 relative to the size of deposits it insures. This has meant that a number of banks have paid little, if anything, for deposit insurance in the past several years, and are enjoying this subsidy to finance all sorts of securities activities, such as market making in CDS contracts.

Increasing Opaqueness and Resulting Counterparty Risk Externality

While there are four types of institutions with different regulation and guarantee levels—commercial banks, broker-dealers (investment banks), asset management firms, and insurance companies—mispriced guarantees to any one type can wreak havoc in the modern financial sector in a pervasive manner. This is because of the *counterparty risk externality* that has largely been unregulated. There are three aspects that have contributed to this externality.

First, the incentive to get too big to fail pushes institutions toward the LCFI model, the regulatory structure for which has yet to be fully articulated. The coarseness of regulation of such institutions has allowed the unregulated sectors—primarily, the so-called shadow banking sector and hedge funds—to thrive. Financial institutions have innovated ways by which they can take exposure to unregulated risk taking (for example, through prime brokerage activity) and temporarily park their assets off balance sheet (for example, in the form of asset-backed conduits and SIVs) so as to get regulatory capital relief and take on additional risks. The sheer magnitude of this activity—especially with respect to the shadow banking sector—and its recourse to the financial sector have meant that systemically important pockets can easily develop in the financial system but without any regulatory oversight or scrutiny.

Second, innovations for sharing credit risk such as credit default swaps (CDSs) and collateralized debt and loan obligations (CDOs and CLOs), which have the potential to serve a fundamental risk-sharing and information role in the economy, were designed to trade in opaque, over-the-counter (OTC) markets. While such trading infrastructure is generally beneficial to large players and has some benefits in terms of matching trading counterparties, its opacity—especially in terms of counterparty exposures—is a serious shortcoming from the standpoint of financial stability during a systemic crisis. If financial institutions take on large exposures in such markets (for example, commercial banks with access to mispriced deposit insurance encourage the growth of a large insurer providing credit protection), then the failure of a large institution can raise concerns about solvency of *all* others due to the opacity of institutional linkages.

And third, regulated institutions as well as their unregulated siblings have fragile capital structures in that they hold assets with long-term duration or low liquidity but their liabilities are highly short-term in nature. While commercial banks are not subject to large-scale runs due to deposit insurance and central bank lender of last resort support, the other institutions are, and indeed, many of them, most notably Bear Stearns and Lehman Brothers, as well as a number of managed funds in the money market and hedge fund arena, did experience wholesale runs during the crisis. And, importantly, commercial banks, too, are subject to localized runs in the wholesale funding and interbank markets if they are perceived to have exposure to institutions experiencing large-scale runs.

Thus, the growth in size of financial institutions, along with their linkages and their fragility, has raised the prospect of extreme counterparty risk concerns. When these concerns have manifested, financial institutions have themselves been unable to fathom how losses from a large institution's failure would travel along the complex chains connecting them. The result has been complete illiquidity of securities held primarily by these institutions (such as credit derivatives) and a paralysis of interbank markets, and, in turn, of credit intermediation for the whole economy. It is important to realize that what superficially may appear to be a problem of illiquidity of a class of assets and markets may well be a symptom of the deeper issues of excessive leverage and risk taking, and the resulting insolvency of financial institutions fueled at least in part by mispriced guarantees.

Financial institutions, left to private incentives, do not and will not internalize this potentially severe counterparty risk externality.

Focus of Regulation on Institution-Level Rather Than Aggregate or Systemic Risk

One would think that prudential bank regulation, primarily capital requirements, aimed at constraining financial leverage and risk should be focused on such externalities so as to curb the risks to the financial sector and the economy at large. However, *current regulation is focused not on systemic risk but rather on the individual institution's risk*. This design is seriously flawed. Such regulation encourages financial institutions to pass their risks in an unfettered manner around the system and to unregulated entities. As they reduce their individual risks, financial institutions are awarded with a lower capital requirement, which gives them the license to originate more risk, possibly aggregate in nature. This new risk gets passed around in the system as well, and we end up with a financial sector in which any individual institution's risk of failure appears low to the regulator, but either it is hidden in the unregulated sector or all of it is aggregate—in either case, systemic in nature. Thus, instead of penalizing behavior that leads to excessive systemic risk, current regulation appears to be rewarding it.

While the counterparty risk externality may itself be sufficient to create high prospects of a systemic crisis, mispriced guarantees and ill-designed prudential regulation heighten the prospects even further. The effect of poor regulation of even just one type of institution (GSEs, for example) can lead to mispricing of risk in transactions between this type and the rest of the financial sector. Given the ease with which financial risks can now be transferred, the germ that causes the outbreak of a systemic crisis can arise from *any* part of the system.

Viewed in this light, the lethal mixture just described has the potential to start soon after a systemic crisis if bailout packages adopted to rescue the system are also mispriced and encourage institutions to be too big to fail.

Principles for Repairing the Financial Architecture

Since we deal with bailout-related recommendations in the next part of this overview, we focus here on the overarching principles for prudential regulation that arise from these four themes and offer the most salient examples of each. The individual chapters flesh out the proposals and thinking behind them in greater detail; they also cover more specific regulatory issues that are not listed here (such as mortgage lender contracts, rating agencies, hedge funds, and fair value accounting); and Table P.1 at the end of this section summarizes our full set of main proposals.

1. Improved governance and compensation practices to curb excessive leverage and risk taking. In order to improve the internal governance of the large, complex financial institutions (LCFIs), regulators should get LCFIs to coordinate on the adoption of long-term performance assessment and compensation, not just for senior management but also for their high-performance (risk-taking) profit centers. In particular, the regulators should insist on:

- Greater disclosure and transparency of compensation packages and assessment criteria.
- Longer stock holding periods and stricter forfeiture rules; for example, failed senior executives and traders who are ejected might confront a minimum holding period for the shares they take with them.
- A bonus/malus approach to compensation, which represents a multi-year structure where good performances accumulate in a bonus pool used to subtract bad performances in future, not to be cashed out as and when the pool is augmented but only in a staggered manner over time.

And, to implement these changes, regulators should adopt a convoy approach wherein they employ suasion to get the most important LCFIs to agree on a basic code of best practices for compensation based on the aforementioned principles and over time get other LCFIs to follow. To this end, regulators should not hesitate to use their current leverage over the financial sector (which has arisen because of the bailout packages).

2. Fair pricing of explicit government guarantees and ring-fencing their access in some cases. Providing unpriced or mispriced guarantees to one set of institutions can readily travel through a chain of contracts to even unregulated parts of the financial sector, giving rise to systemic crisis from potentially any part of the financial system. To avoid such an outcome, regulators should price guarantees correctly and, where they are being patently abused, restrict the scope of guaranteed institutions. In particular,

- Regulators should revisit the practice of reducing (or not charging) deposit insurance premiums when the FDIC fund becomes well capitalized. Such guarantees should be priced fairly—based on institution-level risk and health (leverage, capitalization)—and for such pricing schemes to limit moral hazard associated with guarantees, the premiums should be collected on a continual basis.

- Given the sheer size of government-sponsored enterprises (GSEs) and their potential linkage through the risk-transfer mechanism, the investor function of the GSEs should be shut down. The primary function of the implicitly guaranteed GSEs was to securitize assets; this is what they should do. In other words, their scope should be limited to securitization activities so that guarantees are not exploited for risk-taking activities such as speculation in mortgage-backed assets. Killing regulatory arbitrage at these mammoth institutions may well be a significant step to financial stability.

3. Better transparency to reduce the counterparty risk externality. First, regulators should separate the economic role played by derivatives and financial transactions from shortcomings in their trading infrastructure. There is little merit in shutting down these markets (for example, short selling) altogether, even during crises. However, the counterparty risk concerns arising due to the opaque nature of OTC derivatives need to be addressed. In particular:

- Large, standardized markets such as credit default swaps (CDSs) and related indexes should be traded on centralized counterparties-cum-clearinghouses or exchanges.
- Smaller, less standardized markets such as in collateralized debt and loan obligations (CDOs and CLOs), which also pose significant counterparty risk concerns, should have at the least a centralized clearing mechanism so that the clearing registry is available to regulators to assess contagion effects of a large institution's failure.
- OTC markets can continue to remain the platform through which financial products are innovated; but, to give these markets an incentive to move to a centralized registry and eventually to a clearinghouse, there should be an explicit regulator in charge of (1) enforcing higher transparency in OTC markets, possibly in the form of bilateral information on net exposures with some time delay, and (2) providing infrastructure for enforcement relating to insider trading and market manipulation practices.
- In order to implement these changes, the regulator may simply have to play the coordinating role—possibly requiring some firmness with large players—to move trading on to centralized trading infrastructures. Also, the global nature of these markets may require a certain degree of international coordination between regulators, especially when timely counterparty information is required.

Second, the regulators should require banks and financial institutions to report their off-balance-sheet activities in a more transparent fashion, especially with details on contingencies and recourse features of these activities.

More generally, though, regulatory supervision needs to broaden its focus.
In particular:

- Regulation that focuses narrowly on just one performance metric
  of banks will be easy to game. The current regulatory focus is on
  a single ratio (capital to suitably risk-weighted assets). Regulators
  should take a more rounded approach that examines bank balance
  sheets as equity or credit analysts would, relying on several aspects
  (such as loans to deposits, insured deposits to assets, holdings of
  liquid treasuries and OECD government bonds relative to assets,
  etc.). Using this broader set of data, regulators should create an
  early warning system that raises a flag when further investigation
  is needed and that is alert to ways in which regulatory arbitrage activities would show up in off-balance-sheet transactions and choice of
  organizational form.

4. **Prudential regulation of large, complex financial institutions based
on their systemic risk contribution to the financial sector or the economy.**
Current financial sector regulations seek to limit each institution's risk seen
in isolation; they are not sufficiently focused on systemic risk. As a result,
while individual firms' risks are properly dealt with in normal times, the
system itself remains, or is induced to be, fragile and vulnerable to large
macroeconomic shocks. We advocate that financial regulation be focused on
limiting systemic risk, and we propose a new set of prudential regulations
to achieve this goal. In particular,

- There should be one regulator for supervision of the LCFIs (say, the
  Federal Reserve) in charge of the prudential regulation of systemic
  risk. This regulator would be in a position to perform the tasks outlined under our first three proposals.
- The regulator should first assess the systemic risk posed by each firm.
  The assessment would be based on individual characteristics (leverage, asset quality); on measures of complexity and connectedness
  (that define large, complex financial institutions); and on statistical
  measures.
  - We propose that the regulator should estimate the contribution
    of each firm to the downside risk of the economy, applying at a
    macroeconomic level the standard risk management tools routinely
    employed within financial firms to manage firm-level risk. These
    tools include value at risk, expected loss, stress tests, and macroe-
    conomic scenario analysis. These tools would allow the regulator
    to detect the systemic risk of one institution or of a group of insti-
    tutions.
- The overall systemic risk assessments would then determine the regulatory constraints imposed on individual firms. In particular, each firm

TABLE P.1 Systemic Risk Causes and Proposals for Regulatory Reform

	Systemic Risk and Transparency	
	Issue	Solution
Causes of the Financial Crisis		
Loan Origination	Subprime loans were unwittingly structured as hybrid ARMs in such a way that they would systemically default or refinance around the reset dates.	Albeit costly, the only way to ensure no systemic default is that each borrower should be able to cover the interest. We therefore support recent amendments to Regulation Z (Truth in Lending).
Securitization of Loans	(1) Growth in market for and quality of subprime loans depended on securitization, leading to lenders having no skin in the game, and (2) financial institutions ignored a securitization business model of credit risk transfer and held on to large amounts of asset-backed securities (ABSs).	Securitization involving institutions with government guarantees should force lenders to have skin in the game. We make several suggestions.
Leverage Game	Banks created off-balance-sheet conduits to increase their leverage ratios; deregulation allowed broker-dealers to do the same.	Regulation should (1) focus on more than one metric to make capital ratios less easy to game, and (2) look at aggregate risk.
Rating Agencies	No built-in accountability, making it possible to inappropriately sanction AAA ratings of ABSs way down the chain of securitization.	We provide two proposals for increasing competition and reducing the conflict of interest between rating agencies and firms.
Governance	Similar governance across investment and commercial banks allowed ABS desks to essentially write a huge volume of out-of-the-money puts on systemic events.	Explicit/implicit guarantees need to be priced correctly. Employ suasion to get the most important LCFIs to agree on a basic code of best practices for compensation.
Fair-Value Accounting	In illiquid and disorderly markets, fair-value accounting may cause feedback effects that increase overall risk of the system.	Keep fair-value accounting. The cure is worse than the disease. We make several suggestions to deal with the illiquidity problem.

(Continued)

TABLE P.1 *(Continued)*

	Systemic Risk and Transparency	
	Issue	Solution
OTC Derivatives	Bilaterally set collateral and margin requirements in OTC trading do not take account of the counterparty risk externality that each trade imposes on the rest of the system, allowing systemically important exposures to be built up without sufficient capital to mitigate associated risks.	Large, standardized markets such as credit default swaps and related indexes should trade on centralized counterparty clearinghouses or exchanges. Smaller, less standardized markets (e.g., CDOs and CLOs) should have a centralized clearing mechanism available to the regulator.
Short Selling	Should short selling be blamed for the rapid decline in the stock prices of financial firms, thus leading to banklike runs?	Short selling should generally not be banned. It is crucial for generating price discovery.
Financial Institutions		
Explicit Guarantees (Deposit Institutions, GSEs)	Because some institutions have government guarantees, they are subject to moral hazard. It manifested itself here with these institutions taking large asymmetric bets on the credit, and especially the housing, markets.	Price the guarantees to market as carefully as possible and do not return the insurance fees if the events do not occur. When the guarantees are not priced (as with the GSEs), the regulator should get rid of them.
Implicit Guarantees (Too-Big-to-Fail LCFIs)	The TBTF mantra leads to a similar moral hazard problem. Moreover, the complexity of the organizations highlights transparency issues and thus counterparty risk.	Create a systemic risk regulator that specializes in LCFIs. Also, systemic risk should be priced and taxed as an externality.
Unregulated Managed Funds (Hedge Funds)	These funds act as financial intermediaries but are subject to banklike runs, causing instability in the system. During the crisis, runs took place in both the conduit and money markets.	If hedge funds do not fall into the LCFI class, only light regulation is required, primarily in the form of greater transparency to the regulator. We make suggestions for preventing banklike runs.

would pay for its own systemic risk contribution. This charge could take the form of capital requirements, taxes, and required purchase of insurance against aggregate risk.

- Capital requirements would introduce a charge for a firm's assets based on their systemic risk contribution. This would be a "Basel III" approach; or,
- Taxes could be levied based on systemic risk contribution of firms and used to create a systemic fund. This would be an FDIC-style approach but at a systemic level. It would have the added benefit of reducing the incentives for financial institutions to become too big to fail; or,
- Systemic firms could be required to buy insurance—partly from the private sector—against their own losses in a scenario in which there is aggregate economic or financial sector stress. To reduce moral hazard, the payouts on the insurance would go to a government bailout fund and not directly into the coffers of the firm. This would allow for price discovery by the private sector, enable the regulator to provide remaining insurance at a price linked to the price charged by the private sector, and lessen the regulatory burden to calculate the relative price of systemic risk for different financial firms.

With this discussion of guidelines for prudential regulation of the financial sector in future, we now turn to issues relating to crisis management and public interventions.

P.5 DESCRIPTION OF PUBLIC INTERVENTIONS TO STABILIZE THE FINANCIAL SYSTEM AND ASSESSMENT OF THEIR EFFICACY

When credit and asset price bubbles go bust, they result in significant real economic costs and they can create or amplify recessions. They also impose serious costs to the governments that must bail out overextended borrowers and/or lenders. These bailouts lead to higher fiscal deficits and public debt. Financial crises are, however, to some extent unavoidable. No matter how sound our future regulations become, financial crises will occur most likely in a newer guise. It is therefore crucial for contingency plans to be prepared based on some broad principles that typify most crises. In that respect, we have much to learn from the current crisis and regulatory responses to it.

The regulatory response to the crisis can be broken down into two stages, logically or chronologically: first, the liquidity provision by central banks, and second, the government bailout or rescue packages. We review these for the United States, then provide a framework for assessing their efficacy, and finally, present our recommendations for future interventions.

Brief Overview of the Federal Reserve's Lending Operations since August 2007

Table P.2 describes the various liquidity tools used by the Federal Reserve since August 2007 to address the first stage of the crisis:

As a first step, the Fed expanded its lending to depository institutions. Eligible depository institutions used to borrow from the discount window on an overnight basis and at a penalty rate. The Fed extended the maximum term for borrowing to 30 days in August 2007, and then to 90 days in March 2008, and it reduced the penalty spread from 100 basis points (bps) to 50 bps, and then to 25 bps. Since this was not sufficient to provide long-term liquidity, the Fed created the Term Auction Facility (TAF) in December 2007 to auction term funds to depository institutions.

In late March 2008, following the collapse of Bear Stearns, the Fed expanded the range of institutions with access to its facilities. It created the Primary Dealer Credit Facility (PDCF) to provide overnight loans to primary dealers, and the Term Securities Lending Facility (TSLF) and TSLF Options Program (TOP) to promote liquidity in Treasury and other collateral markets. PDCF is comparable in its design to the discount window, while TSLF is comparable to TAF.

As the crisis entered its deepest stage (to date) with the failure of Lehman Brothers in September 2008, the Fed announced the Asset-Backed Commercial Paper Money Market Mutual Fund Liquidity Facility (AMLF) to extend loans to banking organizations to purchase asset-backed commercial paper from money market mutual funds.

In October 2008, the Fed introduced the Money Market Investor Funding Facility (MMIFF) to provide liquidity to U.S. money market investors, and the Commercial Paper Funding Facility (CPFF) to provide a liquidity backstop to U.S. issuers of commercial paper. The MMIFF provides senior secured funding to a series of special purpose vehicles to facilitate a private-sector initiative to finance the purchase of certificates of deposit (CDs), bank notes, and financial commercial paper from money market mutual funds. In contrast, the CPFF finances the purchase of highly rated unsecured and asset-backed commercial paper.

Finally, in November 2008, the Federal Reserve created the Term Asset-Backed Securities Loan Facility (TALF) to help market participants meet the

TABLE P.2 Liquidity Tools Employed by the Federal Reserve since August 2007

Facility	Acronym	Goal	Functioning	Audience	Interest Rate or Price	Quantity	Collateral or Eligible Assets	Frequency	Maturity	History
Open Market Operations, System Open Market Account	OMO, SOMA	Implement monetary policy	Repo, lending or purchase of GC securities	Primary dealers	Determined by auction	Determined by SOMA manager	General collateral (GC): obligations of U.S. Treasury, some agencies, and some agency pass-throughs (MBS)	Daily (weekly for LT repo)	Overnight (LT repo 14-day)	Monetary policy tool in normal times
Discount Window (Primary Credit Program)	DW	Provide short-term liquidity to depository institutions	Direct borrowing of reserves against collateral	Depository institutions	Fixed premium over target fed funds rate (25 bps since March 2008)	Limited only by available collateral	Very broad: obligations of states, government, and GSEs; CMOs; ABS; corporate bonds; money market instruments; real estate, consumer, commercial, and agricultural loans	Daily	Up to 90-day (initially overnight)	Modified in August 2007

(Continued)

TABLE P.2 (Continued)

Facility	Acronym	Goal	Functioning	Audience	Interest Rate or Price	Quantity	Collateral or Eligible Assets	Frequency	Maturity	History
Term Auction Facility	TAF	Provide medium-term liquidity to depository institutions	Direct borrowing of reserves against collateral	Depository institutions	Stop-out rate determined by auction (with minimum bid rate above OIS rate)	Fixed in advance ($150 billion since October 2008)	Very broad: obligations of states, government, and GSEs; CMOs; ABS; corporate bonds; money market instruments; real estate, consumer, commercial, and agricultural loans.	Biweekly	28-day and 84-day	Introduced in December 2007
Primary Dealer Credit Facility	PDCF	Provide short-term liquidity to primary dealers	Direct borrowing of securities	Primary dealers	Same as DW	Limited only by available collateral	GC plus investment grade corporate	Daily	Overnight	Established in March 2008
Term Securities Lending Facility	TSLF	Provide medium-term liquidity to primary dealers	Exchange GC securities from SOMA against eligible securities	Primary dealers	Determined by auction	Fixed in advance	OMO collateral plus AAA RMBS, CMBS, agency CMOs, and other ABS	Weekly	28-day	Established in March 2008
Asset-Backed Commercial Paper Money Market Mutual Fund Liquidity Facility	AMLF	Restore liquidity to the ABCP markets	Borrow funds from the AMLF to fund the purchase of eligible ABCP	DI, BHC, branch of foreign bank	Primary credit rate on the initiation date of the loan	Depends on size of ABCP	ABCP must be rated not lower than A1, F1, or P1 by at least two nationally recognized statistical rating organizations (NRSROs)	When necessary	120-day	Established in September 2008

38

Facility	Abbrev.	Goal	Mechanism	Eligible	Rate/Terms	Quantity	Requirements	Maturity	End date	Established
Commercial Paper Funding Facility	CPFF	Provide a liquidity backstop to U.S. issuers of commercial paper	Finance the purchase of unsecured ABCP	U.S. issuers of commercial paper	Unsecured commercial paper at 100 bps spread to the overnight index swap (OIS) rate; asset-backed commercial paper at 300 bps spread to the OIS rate	The issuer's outstanding paper cannot exceed its 2008 maximum	The commercial paper must be rated at least A-1/P-1/F1 by a major nationally recognized statistical rating organization (NRSRO)	Maturity of the commercial paper	4/30/09	Established in October 2008
Money Market Investor Funding Facility	MMIFF	Provide liquidity to U.S. money market investors	Senior secured funding to SPVs	Money market investors	Primary credit rate	Quantity should be at most 15% for a single institution. Total limit will be $540 billion	U.S. dollar-denominated CDs and commercial paper of highly rated financial institutions with maturity of 90 days or less	7–90 days	4/30/09	Established in October 2008
Purchase of Obligations from GSEs		Reduce mortgage costs for U.S. borrowers	Purchase obligations of Fannie, Freddie, and FHLB by creating reserves	Primary dealers	Auction	Program to purchase up to $100 billion		Weekly		Announced in November 2008

credit needs of households and small businesses by supporting the issuance of asset-backed securities (ABSs) collateralized by student loans, auto loans, credit card loans, and loans guaranteed by the Small Business Administration (SBA). It also announced a program to purchase obligations from Fannie Mae, Freddie Mac, and the Federal Home Loan Banks.

Brief Overview of the Bailout since September 2008

Within six months of the failure of Bear Stearns in mid-March, the economic outlook worsened progressively. Output and consumption fell. House prices collapsed, and the quality of mortgage-backed securities deteriorated. It gradually became clear that liquidity facilities, at least by themselves, were not resolving the financial crisis. On September 7, 2008, the Federal Housing Finance Agency (FHFA) announced that it was placing Fannie Mae (Federal National Mortgage Association) and Freddie Mac (Federal Home Loan Mortgage Corporation) into conservatorship. The government bailed out the large insurer American International Group (AIG) on September 16.[3] This signaled the beginning of the full-fledged bailout phase of the crisis.

On September 19 the U.S. Treasury offered temporary insurance to money market funds, and proposed a Troubled Asset Relief Program (TARP) whereby the government would purchase illiquid assets from financial institutions. The bailout plan, renamed the Emergency Economic Stabilization Act of 2008, was initially rejected in the House of Representatives (205 for the plan, 228 against) on Monday, September 29. The Senate's version of the bailout plan[4] passed 74 to 25 on October 1, and finally the House of Representatives passed the Emergency Economic Stabilization Act 263-171. The initial bailout plan was never implemented, and essentially abandoned in November 2008. No clear plan has yet been laid out to deal with the housing crisis.

The three main features of the bailout (as of December 2008) had been:

1. A loan-guarantee scheme administered by the FDIC.
2. A compulsory bank recapitalization scheme undertaken by the United States.
3. The CPFF and TALF described earlier as part of the Fed facilities.

Framework to Assess the Regulatory Interventions

How do we assess the efficacy of these regulatory responses? At a purely empirical level, the new regulatory measures were supposed to thaw the frozen money and credit markets. They did not do so. Therefore, they have not been successful. Of course, there may not have been a viable solution, given the depth of the problems. Nevertheless, the following framework helps understand some of the reasons behind this failure with the caveat that its effects may yet be unfolding in the economy.

In general, steps of the government intervention to stabilize a financial system in a severe crisis can be broken down into various components. Conceptually, it is useful to distinguish two stages:

1. **Systemic liquidity stage.** In this stage, the monetary authority, the only credible lender of last resort (LOLR) in the economy, provides liquidity against collateral to prevent liquidity problems from morphing into widespread financial distress. All liquidity crises share three fundamental properties that drive the response of monetary authorities:
   1. The horizon of financiers and lenders shortens, so it becomes difficult to borrow at longer maturities.
   2. Lenders accept fewer securities as collateral.
   3. Lenders accept fewer institutions as counterparties, even for secured lending, since their own precautionary motives for holding liquidity become stronger.
      Any nonsystemic insolvency in this phase is resolved following standard procedures such as private-sector resolution or corrective action procedures of the deposit insurance provider, such as the Federal Deposit Insurance Corporation (FDIC).
2. **Systemic solvency stage.** If the liquidity crisis threatens to turn into a systemic solvency crisis where lenders refuse to lend to any other institution except overnight and that too at extraordinarily high rates, then a larger intervention—a bailout—is needed to rescue the system. The bailout itself has two stages:
   1. **Short-term stabilization.** The focus here is on the financial sector. The goal is to act quickly to prevent a complete collapse of the financial system. The tools used in the past crises as well as in the current one are generally loan guarantees (or more broadly, debt guarantees) and recapitalization. The critical issues in how these tools work relate to the pricing of the guarantees and capital injection, and the decision to make participation voluntary or compulsory.
   2. **Long-term solution.** The focus here is on the macroeconomy, not simply the financial sector. A plan must be offered to limit economic malaise, not just financial distress, and return the system to normality. In the current crisis, the solution involves limiting deadweight losses from foreclosures, and dealing with the debt overhang of CDOs and other instruments on balance sheets of (potentially insolvent) financial institutions.

In practice, the various stages overlap, and it is not always possible to draw clear-cut lines between providing liquidity and bailing out the system, but the distinctions just outlined are useful in framing the discussion. Indeed, an important issue is that excessive liquidity provision to the financial system can prolong solvency issues, and, should fundamentals worsen, this procrastination can lead to a deeper financial and economic crisis.

Under this framework, we offer an assessment of each phase of regulatory response to the current crisis.

Assessment of the Fed's Response to the Liquidity Stage

The number of new lending facilities (and the complexity of their acronyms!) seems to suggest that the Fed was largely improvising. Indeed, given the complexity of the crisis, its speed, and its unexpected nature, improvisation was perhaps both unavoidable and to an extent necessary. Despite the complexity, however, there is some coherent logic behind the creation of the various facilities. This logic can most readily be seen by referring to the characteristics of liquidity crises outlined at the beginning of this section: excessive shortening of horizons of investors and lenders, and drastic reductions in the range of acceptable collateral and counterparties.

Indeed, one can map the actions taken by the Fed to expand liquidity in three dimensions: time, collateral, and counterparties. Starting from its core activities of lending short-term reserves to depository institutions, the Fed has progressively introduced new facilities to provide liquidity at a longer horizon, expand the range of securities it accepts as collateral, and expand the range of institutions that can benefit from liquidity provisions.

Providing liquidity is part of the Fed's role as a lender of last resort, but it is not meant to resolve a systemic solvency crisis. In practice, however, the lines between liquidity provision and outright bailout can be difficult to draw. This was the case when, in March 2008, the Federal Reserve Bank of New York provided an emergency loan to Bear Stearns and brokered its sale to JPMorgan Chase. Similarly, CPFF and TALF are as much part of a bailout as they are part of liquidity provision.

Blurring the lines between providing liquidity to sound institutions and artificially keeping insolvent firms alive is the one chink in the armor of the Fed's response to the liquidity crisis. Indeed, providing too much liquidity can have the perverse effect of prolonging a solvency crisis. On this front, the Fed's new strategy lacks the conditionality needed to keep an undercapitalized bank (or firm) from using its facilities.[5]

We recommend that to separate the illiquidity problem from that of insolvency, the LOLR facilities, much like the private lines of credit made by banks to borrowers, adopt material adverse change (MAC) clauses. With such clauses, the Fed's supervisory role feeds back to its lending role and banks/firms that do not raise sufficient capital in time or are patently insolvent are denied liquidity and resolved or restructured as appropriate.

Overall, though, the Fed appears to have responded reasonably well to the liquidity crisis subject to this important caveat.

Assessment of the Government Bailout Package

It is relatively more difficult to see a coherent logic behind the U.S. Treasury's actions and the design of bailout packages. Clearly, given the magnitude of the problems and the urgent need for some solutions, a certain improvisatory quality entered into the Treasury's actions as well. Increasingly, however, these actions have taken the form of a discretionary approach (that is, ad hoc or institution by institution) rather than a principles-based one. Moreover, the final plan appears to be providing a large transfer of wealth from the taxpayers to the financial sector without significant returns and without a resolution of the credit crunch at hand.

In brief, in the analysis to follow, we identify several key elements. The first is the appropriate sequencing of the government's actions with respect to the bailout. The second is that, while massive recapitalization needs to take place because the sector is close to insolvency, we must do it in a way that isolates the banks' accumulated bad assets from their ongoing operations. Moreover, high-risk borrowers must pay higher rates than others. Finally, the ultimate goal of the bailout of the financial system should be to strengthen viable banks and quickly dispose of those that are already bankrupt.

Initially, TARP proposed using complex auctions to buy back mortgage-backed securities and provide short-term stability. While partly sound in its underlying appeal, this proposal had several shortcomings in its exact implementation:

- First, since exact details of its implementation were not fully spelled out, TARP cost one month of time before loan guarantees (debt guarantees, more generally) and recapitalizations were announced. While four weeks is normally not a crucial time frame, during a systemic crisis where the situation worsens day by day, it constituted a significant delay.
- Second, the initial failure of TARP led to the erroneous conclusion—including from a large body of academics—that TARP was not necessary or was simply infeasible in the first place (even though asset-restructuring vehicles or good-bank/bad-bank separations have featured in most, if not all, severe financial crises of the past). When the Treasury

announced in November 2008 that it was dropping its initial plan entirely, it reignited the financial turmoil, thereby illustrating the expectation that such a plan would have been a valuable part of the long-term rescue plan.

- Third, while TARP's initial focus on the illiquid, hard-to-value assets on the bank's balance sheet was a step toward a long-term solution to the crisis, it ignored an essential root cause, namely the issue of mortgage defaults and foreclosures. In principle, the two issues seem fraught with equal difficulty—toxic assets with difficulty of valuation and mortgages with difficulty of legalities.
- Finally, a strategic opportunity was missed. If the Treasury had implemented the short-term solution (loan guarantees and recapitalization) immediately, it would not have been necessary to provide the details of the long-term plan right away. The announcement of a credible long-term plan would probably have been sufficient to restore investors' confidence in the financial system and, importantly, also in its policy makers, as long as the plan presented the correct diagnostic.

The rapidly unfolding nature of the crisis in September 2008 was perhaps as difficult to master for policy makers as for market participants. Once Lehman Brothers was allowed to fail, accusations multiplied that the Treasury had potentially ignited a crisis of confidence. In this context, the subsequent regulatory response can be best characterized as having signs of panic written on it. Nevertheless, from an objective standpoint, it is useful to highlight the aforementioned strategic and technical limitations of the Treasury's actions since this can help avoid such mistakes in future.

The revised plan of the Treasury did have the appropriate short-term focus. However, the program seems to fall short on two dimensions.

1. The first is that by adopting a one-size-fits-all approach, it is too generous to the financial industry (especially to a small set of institutions, for example, Goldman Sachs and Morgan Stanley, whose credit risk was substantially higher than that of others); is too costly for taxpayers; and lacks an exit plan. As just one illustration of this giveaway, our estimates suggest that the loan guarantee scheme has essentially transferred between $13 billion and $70 billion of taxpayer wealth to the banks by charging a flat fee of 75 basis points per annum to all banks regardless of their credit risk.

2. The second is that the compulsory nature of the loan guarantee and recapitalization schemes has made it more difficult for the market to distinguish sound institutions from troubled ones. The U.S. scheme has

therefore encouraged banks to become increasingly reliant on government guarantees until the crisis fully abates. The lack of sufficient information generation by the market in the meanwhile is likely to slow down a transition away from government guarantees. Also, because these guarantees exist for three years, the concern is that a new round of moral hazard problems will likely arise, especially because guarantees are not priced fairly.

Interestingly, all these features are in striking contrast to the UK scheme, which appears to be fairly priced, mostly voluntary, reliant on market information, and suitable for smooth transition from guarantees to markets in due course.

The Missing Piece: The Housing Market

Dealing with the housing crisis as a part of the long-term solution is critical for at least two reasons. The welfare losses from the housing crisis are large: On top of the distress of displaced families, the average cost of foreclosure is 30 to 35 percent of the value of a house, and foreclosed houses have negative externalities on their neighborhood. Moreover, mortgage default losses are at the heart of the financial crisis since default losses are concentrated in the "first loss" equity and mezzanine tranches of CDOs—the risk that banks never transferred to markets. This interconnection between mortgages and the balance sheets of financial firms is such that stabilizing the housing market would also help stabilize the economy as a whole.

Unfortunately, the plans put forward to address the mortgage crisis are not properly designed. We argue that existing approaches to loan modification—for instance, the Hope for Homeowners from the Federal Housing Administration (FHA), or the FDIC plans—do not balance the incentives of the borrowers and the lenders. On the one hand, some are too lenient with delinquent borrowers and give them perverse incentives to stop making payments. On the other hand, some programs propose restructuring the loans with no write-down of principal and with a balloon payment due at the end, which is at best a temporary solution.

We instead advocate using shared appreciation mortgages (which are part of the FHA plan). Shared appreciation restructurings offer a debt-for-equity swap whereby, in return for modifying the loan, the borrower must give up some of the future appreciation in the value of the property. Designed properly, this would discourage borrowers from seeking modifications if they can continue to pay their mortgage. In addition, Congress should address the legal barriers to modifying securitized loans—for instance, by invoking a standard such as "a good-faith effort to advance the collective interests of holders."

And, Where Should the Bailout Stop?

The massive U.S. government bailout originally intended for the financial industry has now spread to the nonfinancial sector, and the government is bailing out car manufacturers. This is partly the fault of the financial bailout itself, which was too generous to the financial industry. Unfortunately, history and political economy considerations suggest that ad-hoc government interventions to bail out industries are a recipe for long-run economic stagnation, as they prevent the Darwinian evolution whereby better firms survive and worse ones are weeded out. This does not mean, however, that the government should stay on the sidelines.

We argue that government interventions should be based on a consistent set of principles to avoid becoming excessively politicized or captured by interest groups. We present four broad principles:

1. First, the market failure must be identified.
2. Second, the intervention should use efficient tools.
3. Third, the costs for the taxpayers should be minimized.
4. And finally, government intervention should not create moral hazard.

Consider the case of General Motors (GM). Based on the four principles, there is indeed a case for government intervention in favor of GM, but this intervention should not be a giveaway bailout. The market failure that we identify is the disappearance of the debtor-in-possession (DIP) market because of the financial crisis. This provides a rationale for government intervention (first principle). To be efficient, the reorganization should be thorough, and therefore likely to be lengthy. This is why it should take place under Chapter 11 of the Bankruptcy Code (second principle). To minimize the costs to the taxpayers, the government should provide *only* DIP financing (directly or through private financial institutions), because DIP loans are well protected (third principle). Finally, reorganization in bankruptcy should not reward bad management and therefore minimize moral hazard (fourth principle).[6]

Overall Recommendations for Future Interventions

Our overall recommendations for short-term and long-term regulatory interventions during a crisis in future are summarized in Table P.3.

TABLE P.3 Regulatory Recommendations for Government Intervention

Goal	Provide liquidity	Prevent collapse	Offer long-term solution
Horizon	Very short (days)	Short (weeks)	Long (months)
Tools	Lending facilities, but conditional on bank quality	Resolve insolvent banks Guarantee bank debt Inject equity in healthy ones	Buy back risky assets Restructure loans (e.g., mortgages in this crisis)
Actors	Federal Reserve	Fed, FDIC, Treasury	Treasury, FDIC, private buyers

The following principles could be useful for regulators in such direct government intervention:

- Maximize efficiency by being clear about short-run and long-run objectives and corresponding regulatory tools.
- Avoid one-size-fits-all approach in charging for bailout packages, and as corollaries to this overall principle:
  - Rely on market prices wherever available.
  - Reward more those institutions that performed well relative to those that did not.

And, finally, take advantage of the leverage offered by the bailout to review incentive systems within institutions that may have led to the crisis in the first place; in particular, wherever feasible, replace management and pass on losses to shareholders and uninsured creditors.

P.6 THE NEED FOR INTERNATIONAL COORDINATION

It is clear that many of the policy recommendations we have put forward may be ineffective or their edge blunted if there is little international coordination among central banks and financial stability regulators. This issue is important; although cross-border banking and financial flows have expanded in scale, much of bank supervision remains national. And, while there is some consensus on prudential aspects of regulation such as capital requirements and their calculation, there is hardly any consensus on how much forbearance regulators show toward their national banks, how they should share the burden of bailing out global financial institutions, and so on.

Complications that could arise from lack of coordination among national regulators are many. Here are six examples:

1. Suppose that deposit insurance guarantees are priced fairly in the United States but commercial banking counterparts in the United Kingdom pay no premium whatsoever. This would affect the competitiveness of the U.S. banks—at least relative to those UK banks that are global players—and thereby give them incentives to lobby for lower premiums, forcing the U.S. regulators to be lenient as well, and giving rise to moral hazard issues in both sets of countries.

2. While the United States sets up a centralized clearing platform for OTC credit derivatives, say regulators in Europe do not enforce such a requirement. Then, the large players will simply move their trading offices to such credit havens to enjoy the benefits of OTC trading. The result would be that lack of transparency that manifested as counterparty risk externality in the current crisis would be an issue again when a crisis hits the financial sector in the future.

3. Suppose that the Federal Reserve adds conditionality to its terms for lender of last resort facilities, requiring that highly leveraged institutions raise sufficient capital in order to be eligible for borrowing against illiquid collateral, but central banks in other parts of the world do not require that such criteria be met. Then, a global financial firm, based primarily in the United States, could simply access liquidity from these other central banks, rendering ineffective the purpose of conditionality in the Fed LOLR.

4. Similarly, if large, complex financial institutions (LCFIs) are subject to a systemic risk charge (say, in the form of a higher capital requirement), then some jurisdictional coordination is necessary for implementing the charge. How would a national regulator acquire the rights to tax a financial entity that is not formally a part of its jurisdiction? If each country is implementing some form of LCFI tax on its players, the outcome would lead to far fewer distortions than otherwise.

5. Next, consider the bailout packages put in place in October 2008. The U.S. package, as we have discussed, adopted a one-size-fits-all pricing for the loan guarantees, whereas the UK package, being overall more market-based, relied on each institution's perceived risk in the CDS market in the preceding 12 months. This immediately led to the UK banks lobbying their regulators to soften the terms of their bailout package, even though from the standpoint of sound economic principles, the UK scheme is the more desirable one.

6. Finally, a striking historical example is the repeal of Glass-Steagall Act (in fact, its gradual erosion since the mid-1960s) in the United States, which allowed commercial banks, investment banks, and insurance

firms to operate under a single umbrella. While the United States had enforced this Act since 1933, very few other countries had. This meant that as financial markets became more global, the U.S. commercial banks started looking increasingly uncompetitive relative to the universal banks of Europe. Lobbying efforts followed, and repeal was inevitable. Many academics had questioned the Act in the first place on the basis of synergies between lending and underwriting activities.

In hindsight, however, it seems that a financial architecture where deposit insurance is provided *only* to commercial lending and securities underwriting, but not for speculation in highly risky securities activity, has several advantages: It limits the scope of regulation and therefore also of its follies; it limits linkages from the unregulated sector to the regulated (insured) sector and reduces the counterparty risk externality; and it reduces the ex post pressure on regulators to bail out even unregulated institutions, since they would no longer be "too connected to fail." Such a separation of financial activities is once again being revisited at the Bank of England, and more generally in Europe, as a possible way of insulating credit intermediaries and the payments and settlements system from securities activities. But it may be untenable in a global financial architecture unless there is coordination among national regulators: The separated entities will most likely be less profitable than their universal counterparts abroad.

All these examples suggest that a "beggar thy neighbor" competitive approach to regulation among central banks and financial stability groups in different countries, or their failure to coordinate even without any explicit competitive incentives, will lead to a race to the bottom in regulatory standards. This will end up conferring substantial guarantees to banks and financial institutions and give rise to excessive leverage and risk taking in spite of imposing substantial regulation in each country. Such an outcome needs to be avoided.

It appears to us that most regulators would find our overarching principles (pricing guarantees and bailouts fairly, requiring transparency in derivatives that connect financial institutions, avoiding the provision of liquidity to insolvent institutions) reasonably convincing. Once such agreement is reached, it is possible that individual countries will implement slightly different variants of each principle. But the coordination of overall approach will minimize the arbitrage in which financial institutions can engage by shopping for the most favorable jurisdiction. This, in turn, will ensure that the desired objectives of each individual country's financial stability plans are not compromised altogether.

Will such coordination necessarily arise? And, if yes, what form will it take?

Unfortunately, the nations of the world do not have a very good track record at creating international policy makers with significant cross-national powers. It is somewhat unlikely that an international financial sector regulator with significant power over markets and institutions will emerge right away; countries are not willing to surrender their national authority over decision making, especially during a crisis. Perhaps complete centralization is not necessary and may even be undesirable, especially since coordination has gradually increased in the past 20 years and most likely will increase going forward. Basel II provides an important precedent. No matter what one thinks of the Basle II product, the process by which the Basel Committee crafted an international consensus with a common set of rules and got countries to adhere to these rules (without any direct authority over them) has been an important achievement. The Bank for International Settlements (BIS)—which houses the Basel Committee—has gained valuable experience in setting such standardized rules and definitions for financial institutions. In fact, there is a new player on the scene as well—the Financial Stability Form (also housed at BIS) established in 1999 by the G7 countries. It has issued several reports detailing specific recommendations for strengthening and standardizing financial regulation.

Our recommendation to achieve such international coordination is thus to exploit this experience using the following three steps:

1. Central banks of the largest financial markets (say G7) should convene first to agree on a broad set of principles for regulation of banks. Each central bank should play the role of a regulator in charge of supervising and managing the systemic risk of large, complex financial institutions (LCFIs). By playing this role, the central banks would be able to agree on a common agenda of identifying the LCFIs.
2. Central banks should agree at this convention on the overarching set of principles for prudential regulation of LCFIs and for crisis management and interventions. The principled approach we have presented in this book may be a useful starting point.
3. Next, central banks should present a joint proposal with specific recommendations to their respective treasuries or national authorities, seek political consensus for an international forum such as the Financial Stability Forum or a committee of the BIS to coordinate an ongoing discussion and implementation of the commonly agreed regulatory principles, and monitor their acceptance and application.

A commitment to such a process will generate a willingness to take the outcome seriously and, it is hoped, pave the way for international coordination on well-rounded policies that balance growth with financial stability as efforts get under way to repair national financial architectures.

APPENDIX: TIME LINE OF CRISIS

Date	Event
March 5, 2007	HSBC Holdings announces one portfolio of purchased subprime mortgages evidenced much higher delinquency than had been built into the pricing of these products.
April 22, 2007	Second-largest subprime lender, New Century Financial, declares bankruptcy.
June 22, 2007	Bear Stearns pledges a collateralized loan to one of its hedge funds but does not support another.
July 25, 2007	Carry trade experiences a six standard deviation move.
Aug. 6, 2007	Beginning of much publicized quant hedge fund meltdown.
Aug. 9, 2007	BNP Paribas suspends calculation of asset values of three money market funds exposed to subprime and halts redemptions. AXA had earlier announced support for its funds.
Aug. 9, 2007	European Central Bank (ECB) injects €95 billion overnight to improve liquidity. Injections by other central banks.
Aug. 17, 2007	Sachsen LB receives bailout from German savings bank association. Run on Countrywide.
Aug. 17, 2007	Federal Reserve approves temporary 50 basis points reduction in the discount window borrowing rate, extends term financing, and notes it will "accept a broad range of collateral."
Sep. 14, 2007	Bank of England announces it has provided a liquidity support facility to Northern Rock.
Sep. 17, 2007	Following a retail deposit run, the chancellor announces a government guarantee for Northern Rock's existing deposits.
October 2007	Citi, Merrill Lynch, and UBS report significant write-downs.
Nov. 8, 2007	Moody's announces it will reestimate capital adequacy ratios of U.S. monoline insurers/financial guarantors.

Date	Event
Nov. 20, 2007	Freddie Mac announces 2007 Q3 losses and says it is considering cutting dividends and raising new capital.
Dec. 10, 2007	UBS announces measures to address capital concerns following further write-downs.
Dec. 12, 2007	Joint Bank of England, Federal Reserve, ECB, Swiss National Bank (SNB), and Bank of Canada announcement of measures designed to address pressures in short-term funding markets. Actions taken by the Federal Reserve include the establishment of a temporary Term Auction Facility (TAF).
Dec. 20, 2007	Bear Stearns announces expected 2007 Q4 write-downs.
Jan. 11, 2008	Bank of America confirms purchase of Countrywide.
Jan. 14–18, 2008	Announcements of significant 2007 Q4 losses by Citi and Merrill Lynch, among others.
Jan. 15, 2008	Citi announces it is to raise US$14.5 billion in new capital.
Jan. 24, 2008	Société Générale reveals trading losses resulting from fraudulent trading by a single trader.
Feb. 7, 2008	Auctions for auction rate securities begin to fail. Six days later, 80 percent of these auctions fail, starting a complete freeze in these markets.
Feb. 11, 2008	American International Group (AIG) announces its auditors have found a "material weakness" in its internal controls over the valuation of the AIGFP super senior credit default swap portfolio.
Feb. 17, 2008	UK government announces temporary nationalization of Northern Rock.
Mar. 11, 2008	Federal Reserve announces the introduction of a Term Securities Lending Facility, and Bank of England announces it will maintain its expanded three-month long-term repo against a wider range of high-quality collateral.
Mar. 14, 2008	JPMorgan Chase & Co. announces that it has agreed, in conjunction with the Federal Reserve Bank of New York, to provide secured funding to Bear Stearns for an initial period of up to 28 days.
Mar. 16, 2008	JPMorgan Chase & Co. agrees to purchase Bear Stearns. Federal Reserve provides US$30 billion nonrecourse funding.

Date	Event
Mar. 16, 2008	Federal Reserve announces establishment of Primary Dealer Credit Facility.
Apr. 21, 2008	Bank of England launches its Special Liquidity Scheme (SLS) to allow banks to swap temporarily their high-quality mortgage-backed and other securities for UK Treasury bills.
May 2, 2008	Coordinated announcement from the Federal Reserve, ECB, and SNB regarding further liquidity measures.
June 2008	MBIA and Ambac lose their AAA ratings from the Nationally Recognized Statistical Rating Organizations (NRSROs).
June 16, 2008	Lehman Brothers confirms a net loss of US$2.8 billion in Q2.
July 11, 2008	Closure of U.S. mortgage lender IndyMac.
July 13, 2008	U.S. Treasury announces a rescue plan for Fannie Mae and Freddie Mac.
July 15, 2008	U.S. Securities and Exchange Commission (SEC) issues an emergency order to enhance investor protection against "naked short selling."
July 30, 2008	Federal Reserve announces the introduction of an 84-day Term Auction Facility in addition to its existing 28-day loans. The ECB and SNB announce they will provide 84-day U.S. dollar liquidity in addition to their existing operations with a maturity of 28 days.
Sep. 7, 2008	Fannie Mae and Freddie Mac are taken into conservatorship.
Sep. 15, 2008	Lehman Brothers files for bankruptcy. Bank of America announces purchase of Merrill Lynch.
Sep. 16, 2008	U.S. government provides emergency loan to AIG of US$85 billion in exchange for a 79.9 percent stake and right to veto dividend payments.
Sep. 16, 2008	Reserve Primary Fund "breaks the buck" due to its holdings of Lehman Brothers debt. Begins a run on money market funds.
Sep. 17, 2008	Bank of England extends drawdown period for SLS.
Sep. 18, 2008	Announcement of coordinated central bank measures to address continued elevated pressures in U.S. dollar short-term funding markets. Bank of England concludes a reciprocal swap agreement with the Federal Reserve.
Sep. 18, 2008	FSA announces regulations prohibiting short selling of financial shares.

Date	Event
Sep. 19, 2008	U.S. Treasury announces temporary guarantee program for the U.S. money market mutual funds (MMMFs). The Federal Reserve Board announces it will extend nonrecourse loans to banks to finance purchases of asset-backed commercial paper from MMMFs.
Sep. 19, 2008	SEC prohibits short selling in financial companies. Bans follow from a number of European regulators.
Sep. 20, 2008	U.S. Treasury announces draft proposals to purchase up to US$700 billion of troubled assets (Troubled Asset Relief Program).
Sep. 21, 2008	The Federal Reserve approves transformation of Goldman Sachs and Morgan Stanley into bank holding companies.
Sep. 23, 2008	Announcement that Berkshire Hathaway is to invest US$5 billion in Goldman Sachs.
Sep. 25, 2008	JPMorgan Chase & Co. buys the deposits, assets, and certain liabilities of Washington Mutual bank.
Sep. 29, 2008	Bradford & Bingley is nationalized by UK government. Abbey buys its branches and retail deposit book.
Sep. 29, 2008	Belgian, Dutch, and Luxembourg governments announce they will invest €11.2 billion in Fortis.
Sep. 29, 2008	Federal Reserve increases swap lines to foreign central banks.
Sep. 29, 2008	Announcement of Citi's intention to acquire the banking operations of Wachovia in a transaction facilitated by the Federal Deposit Insurance Corporation (FDIC), protecting all depositors (under the systemic risk exception of the FDIC Improvement Act of 1991).
Sep. 30, 2008	Irish government announces deposit guarantee. Other governments follow with extensions to deposit guarantees.
Oct. 3, 2008	U.S. House of Representatives passes US$700 billion government plan to rescue the U.S. financial sector (having voted against an earlier version of the plan on September 29, 2008).
Oct. 3, 2008	FSA raises the limit of the deposit guarantee to £50,000 (with effect from October 7, 2008).
Oct. 3, 2008	Wells Fargo and Wachovia agree to merge in a transaction requiring no financial assistance from the FDIC.

Date	Event
Oct. 3, 2008	Dutch government acquires Fortis Bank Nederland (Holding) N.V.
Oct. 6, 2008	German authorities announce package to save Hypo Real Estate.
Oct. 7, 2008	The Icelandic government takes control of Glitner and Landsbanki, which owns Icesave.
Oct. 7, 2008	Federal Reserve announces the creation of the Commercial Paper Funding Facility.
Oct. 8, 2008	Coordinated interest rate cuts of 50 basis points (including the Bank of England, the Federal Reserve, and the ECB).
Oct. 13, 2008	Further details of the UK support package are released.
Oct. 13, 2008	Members of the euro zone announce measures to provide their banks with capital funding. Further coordinated action to provide U.S. dollar liquidity.
Oct. 14, 2008	U.S. government announces Capital Purchase Program of up to US$250 billion.
Oct. 21, 2008	Federal Reserve Board announces the creation of the Money Market Investor Funding Facility.
Nov./Dec. 2008	Many hedge funds put up gates and suspend withdrawals as unprecedented redemption notices come in.
Nov. 10, 2008	The U.S. government modifies its bailout of AIG as the insurance company buckles as market conditions deteriorate.
Nov. 13, 2008	The announcement by the U.S. Treasury that funds from the TARP would not be used to buy distressed assets has a negative impact on the U.S. LCFIs and share prices fall substantially.
Nov. 23, 2008	The U.S. Treasury and FDIC announce a rescue package for Citigroup, which includes guaranteeing $306 billion of impaired RMBS and CMBS assets.
Nov. 25, 2008	The Federal Reserve announces that it will purchase up to $500 billion of agency MBSs, as well as buy up to $100 billion of agency unsecured debt.
Nov. 25, 2008	The Federal Reserve announces the creation of the Term Asset-Backed Securities Loan Facility (TALF) whereby up to $200 billion will be lent to holders of "new and recently originated" AAA ABSs backed by consumer and small business loans. The Treasury will provide $20 billion of credit protection via TARP funds

Date	Event
	to the Federal Reserve Bank of New York, which will be running the TALF.
Dec. 12, 2008	Bernard Madoff is arrested for allegedly carrying out a Ponzi scheme through Madoff Securities. U.S. investigators report losses to the scheme could total approximately $50 billion.
Dec. 16, 2008	The federal funds target rate is cut from 1 percent to a range of 0 to 0.25 percent, its lowest level on record dating back to 1954.
Dec. 19, 2008	The Bush administration agrees to lend $13.4 billion of TARP funds to GM and Chrysler in exchange for an agreed restructuring plan.

Source: Bank of England.

NOTES

1. The ABX, LCDX, and CMBX indexes are portfolios of credit default swaps based respectively on tranches of 20 subprime mortgage pools, 100 equally weighted loan credit default swaps referencing syndicated first-lien loans, and tranches of 25 commercial mortgage-backed securities.
2. Primary dealers are banks and securities brokerages that trade in U.S. government securities with the Federal Reserve System. As of September 2008, there were 19 primary dealers. Lehman Brothers and Bear Stearns used to be primary dealers.
3. The Fed created a credit facility for up to US$85 billion in exchange for 80 percent of equity and the right to suspend dividends.
4. The plan was modified to expand bank deposit guarantees to $250,000 and to include $100 billion in tax breaks for businesses and alternative energy.
5. One reason for such lack of conditionality could have been that the lack of a consistent response to the solvency crisis from its regulatory counterparts forced the Fed to play the dual role of LOLR and solvency regulator.
6. Specifically, we advocate a massive DIP loan to GM in bankruptcy. The current bailout plan would offer less of a breathing space to GM and imply more job cuts in the short run than our proposed bankruptcy/DIP financing plan. The DIP loan would allow the restructuring to take place over 18 to 24 months, whereas the bailout would be barely sufficient to avoid liquidation in 2009. To further limit the ripple effects of GM's bankruptcy, the government should also consider backstopping warranties and spare parts availability, even if the reorganization fails.

PART ONE

Causes of the Financial Crisis of 2007–2009

Matthew Richardson

There is almost universal agreement that the fundamental cause of the financial crisis was the combination of a credit boom and a housing bubble. It is much less clear, however, why this combination led to such a severe crisis.

The common view is that the crisis was due to the originate-to-distribute model of securitization, which led to lower-quality loans being miraculously transformed into highly rated securities by the rating agencies. To some extent, this characterization is unfortunately true. That is:

- There was a tremendous growth in subprime loans. Many of these loans were highly risky and only possible due to the clever creation of products like 2/28 and 3/27 adjustable rate mortgages (ARMs).
- Moreover, this growth in subprime lending was only possible due to the ability of securitization to pass on the credit risk of loans faced by the lender to the end user investor in asset-backed securities (ABSs).
- The end user was willing to invest only because the rating agencies had rubber-stamped a large portion of these securities as AAA by creating a chain of complex structured products.

Chapter 1, "Mortgage Origination and Securitization in the Financial Crisis," looks at these issues in detail and lays out principles and proposals for future regulation. Of course, while this chapter focuses on the mortgage market and—in particular—on subprime loans, the discussion holds more generally. There was a plethora of cheap loans made throughout the economy, and many of the same issues of deteriorating loan quality are at play in these other markets. Credit card debt, car loans, "covenant-lite" corporate bonds, and leveraged loans for leveraged buyout (LBO) transactions were all trading at historically low spreads over risk-free bonds. Like the past fate of the subprime market, many of these loans are now facing increasing default rates. For example, default rates on credit card debts may rise to 10 percent in 2009, which is double the 5 percent average of the past 10 years. Car loan delinquencies are on the rise, and financial economists (e.g., NYU Stern School's Edward Altman) forecast corporate bond delinquencies to double from around 4 percent in 2008 to 8.5 to 9 percent in 2009. The same argument made in Chapter 1 that an increase in securitization reduced screening and monitoring efforts for the lenders in the mortgage market could be made in these other markets as well.

The subprime market, however, has one unique feature relative to these other credit markets. The loans were unwittingly structured to be systemic in nature. To understand this point, note that the majority of subprime loans were structured as hybrid 2/28 or 3/27 ARMs. These loans offered a fixed teaser rate for the first few years (i.e., two or three years) and then adjustable rates thereafter, with a large enough spread to cause a significant jump in the rate. By design, therefore, these mortgages were intended to default in a few years or to be refinanced assuming that the collateral value (i.e., the house price) increased. Because these mortgages were all set around the same time, mortgage lenders had inadvertently created an environment that would lead to either a systemic wave of refinancings or one of defaults.

The growth in structured products across Wall Street during this period was staggering. While residential mortgage-related products were certainly a large component, so too were asset-backed securities using commercial mortgages, leveraged loans, corporate bonds, student loans, and so forth. For example, according to Asset-Backed Alert, securitization worldwide went from $767 billion at the end of 2001 to $1.4 trillion in 2004 to $2.7 trillion at the peak of the bubble in December 2006. It has fallen dramatically over the past few years, with the drop being over 60 percent from the third quarter of 2007 to the third quarter of 2008. A common feature of most of these structures was that the rating agencies sanctioned the products (and their credit risk) by providing ratings for the different tranches within these securities. It is very clear that the greatest demand for these products came through the creation of the AAA-rated tranches that would appeal to a host of potential investors. Since the rating agencies described the tranche ratings as comparable to other rating classes, their role in this process cannot be overlooked. To this end, Chapter 3, "The Rating Agencies: Is Regulation the Answer?" describes the history of how the rating agencies were formed, their role in the current crisis, and suggestions with respect to future regulation.

Nevertheless, we believe that, although the originate-to-distribute model of securitization and the rating agencies were clearly important factors, the financial crisis occurred because financial institutions did not follow the business model of securitization. Rather than acting as intermediaries by transferring the risk from mortgage lenders to capital market investors, these institutions themselves took on this investment role. But unlike a typical pension fund, fixed income mutual fund, or sovereign wealth fund, financial firms are highly levered institutions. Given regulatory oversight, how did the major financial firms manage to do this, and perhaps more important, why did they do it?

Chapter 2, "How Banks Played the Leverage Game," addresses the former question. Specifically, in order to stretch their capital requirements, commercial banks set up off-balance-sheet asset-backed commercial paper (ABCP) conduits and structured investment vehicles (SIVs), where they transferred some of the assets they would have otherwise held on their books. ABCPs and SIVs were funded with small amounts of equity and the rolling over of short-term debt. These conduits had credit enhancements that were recourse back to the banks. Investment banks, however, did not have to be so clever. Following the investment banks' request in the spring of 2004, in August of that year the SEC amended the net capital rule of the Securities Exchange Act of 1934. This amendment effectively allowed the investment banks to lever up, albeit with potentially more scrutiny by the SEC.

With now much higher leverage ratios, financial firms had to address the likely increase in their value at risk. The firms found relief by switching away from loans into investments in the form of AAA-rated tranches of collateralized debt obligations (CDOs) and collateralized loan obligations (CLOs). These highly rated CDOs and CLOs had a significantly lower capital charge. In fact, about 30 percent of all AAA asset-backed securities remained *within* the banking system, and if one includes ABCP conduits and SIVs that had recourse, this fraction rises to 50 percent.

Why asset-backed securities? At the peak of the housing bubble in June 2006, AAA-rated subprime CDOs offered twice the premium on the typical AAA credit default swap of a corporation. Therefore, financial firms would be earning a higher premium most of the time; by construction, losses would occur only if the AAA tranche of the CDO got hit. If this rare event occurred, however, it would almost surely be a systemic shock affecting all markets. In effect, financial firms were writing a large number of deeply out-of-the-money put options on the housing market. Of course, the problem with writing huge amounts of systemic insurance like this is that the firms cannot make good when it counts—hence, the financial crisis.

CHAPTER 1

Mortgage Origination and Securitization in the Financial Crisis

Dwight Jaffee, Anthony W. Lynch, Matthew Richardson, and Stijn Van Nieuwerburgh

1.1 INTRODUCTION: THE U.S. MORTGAGE MARKET

There are three main types of mortgages: fixed rate mortgages (FRMs), adjustable rate mortgages (ARMs), and hybrids. ARMs have an adjusting interest rate tied to an index, whereas hybrids typically offer a fixed rate for a prespecified number of years before the rate becomes adjustable for the remainder of the loan. Mortgage loans fall into two categories, prime and nonprime. We discuss each category in turn.

Prime Mortgages

There are three main types of prime mortgages. Loans that conform to the guidelines used by Fannie Mae and Freddie Mac for buying loans are known as conforming loans. The guidelines include a loan limit, currently $417,000 for one-family loans, and underwriting criteria on credit score (FICO score), combined loan-to-value ratio and debt-to-income ratio. Loans that roughly conform to all the guidelines for a conforming loan except the loan limit are known as jumbo loans. The interest rate charged on jumbo mortgage loans is generally higher than that charged on conforming loans, most likely due to the slightly higher cost of securitizing such loans without the implicit government guarantee that backs conforming-loan mortgage-backed securities (MBSs). The third type of prime mortgages is FHA/VA loans. FHA loans are insured by the Federal Housing Administration (FHA) and may be issued by federally qualified lenders. The FHA primarily serves people who cannot afford a conventional down payment or otherwise do not qualify for private mortgage insurance. VA loans are guaranteed by the Department of Veterans Affairs and are available to veterans and military personnel. FHA/VA loans are also regarded as conforming loans.

Nonprime Mortgages

There are three main types of nonprime mortgages. Although there is no standardized definition, subprime loans are usually classified in the United States as those where the borrower has a credit (FICO) score below a particular level and whose rate is much higher than that for prime loans. Alt-A loans are considered riskier than prime loans but less risky than subprime loans. Alt-A borrowers pay higher rates than prime borrowers but much lower rates than subprime borrowers. With an Alt-A loan, the borrower's credit score is not quite high enough for a conforming loan, or the borrower has not fully documented his or her application, or there is something a little out of the ordinary with the deal. Lender criteria for Alt-A vary, with credit score requirements being the most common area of variance. Finally, a home equity loan (HEL) or home equity line of credit (HELOC) is typically a second-lien loan. A HELOC loan differs from a conventional mortgage loan in that the borrower is not advanced the entire sum up front, but uses a line of credit to borrow sums that total no more than the agreed amount, similar to a credit card and usually with an adjustable rate. In contrast, a HEL is a one-time lump-sum loan, often with a fixed interest rate.

Securitization

Securitization in the mortgage market involves the pooling of mortgages into mortgage-backed securities (MBSs) in which the holder of these securities is entitled to some fraction of all the interest and principal paid out by the portfolio of loans. Some of these securities are straight pass-throughs, while others are collateralized mortgage obligations (CMOs) or collateralized debt obligations (CDOs) in which the pools are tranched and cash flows get paid out according to some priority structure. The size of the residential mortgage market in the United States is well over $10 trillion, with over 55 percent of it being securitized. Interestingly, after explosive growth in the 1980s with the development of mortgage-backed pass-throughs and CMOs, the fraction of securitization has held relatively constant since the early 1990s, hovering between 50 percent and 60 percent.

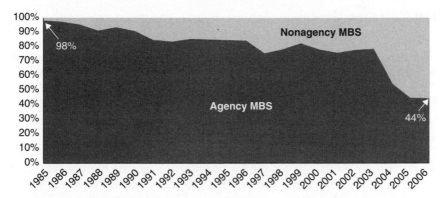

FIGURE 1.1   Nonagency Securitized Mortgage Issuance, 1985–2006

This chart presents the percentage of securitization issuance coming from nonagency mortgage-backed securities (MBSs). Nonagency MBSs include private-label jumbo, Alt-A, and mortgage-related ABSs.

Source: FDIC, UBS, PIMCO.

Government-sponsored enterprises (GSEs) purchase and securitize mortgages. While GSEs are privately funded, their government sponsorship implies a presumption that their guarantor function is fully backed by the U.S. government. There are three GSEs: the Federal National Mortgage Association (Fannie Mae); the Federal Home Loan Mortgage Corporation (Freddie Mac); and the Federal Home Loan Bank (FHLB) system consisting of 12 regional banks. The contribution of the GSEs to securitization of mortgages is startling. In the early 1980s, agency MBSs represented approximately 50 percent of the securitized market, by 1992 a 64 percent share, and by 2002 a 73 percent share.

However, after 2002, the mortgage market and, in particular, the securitization market changed dramatically, with nonagency MBSs representing 15 percent in 2003, 23 percent in 2004, 31 percent in 2005, and 32 percent in 2006 of the total securities outstanding. In fact, in terms of new issuance of MBSs, the share of nonagency securitization was for the first time larger than that of agency-backed securitization, reaching 56 percent in 2006. A considerable portion of this issuance consisted of subprime and Alt-A loans. Figure 1.1 illustrates these points.

1.2 SOME SALIENT FACTS

In this section, we describe some of the important characteristics of the mortgage market and securitization of this market over the period 2001 to 2007.

The Mortgage Market

There has been enormous growth in nonprime mortgages. Table 1.1 reports data on the size of the U.S. mortgage market from 2001 to 2006. Nonprime mortgage originations (subprime, Alt-A, and HELOCs) were more than $1 trillion annually in 2004, 2005, and 2006. They rose as a share of total originations from 14 percent in 2001 to 48 percent in 2006. Many of these subprime loans were adjustable rate loans, due to be reset in the period 2007–2009, which may be part of the reason for the foreclosure crisis.

The quality of mortgages has declined considerably over the past five years. From 2002 to 2006, loan-to-value ratios increased dramatically in all three major loan categories (prime, Alt-A, and subprime), while the prevalence of loans with full documentation decreased dramatically. At the same time, debt-to-income ratios increased dramatically only for prime loans, while FICO scores were largely unaffected in all major loan categories. The following numbers are taken from Zimmerman (2007) and the data source is Loan Performance data.

- There has been substantial growth in the average *combined loan-to-value* (CLTV) ratio of loans in all three major loan categories. For prime ARMs, this ratio has increased from 66.4 percent in 2002 to 75.3 percent in 2006, while for Alt-A ARMs, it has increased from 74.3 percent in 2002 to 85.0 percent in 2006. Finally, for subprime ARMs, this ratio has increased from 81.2 percent in 2002 to 86.7 percent in 2006.
- There has been dramatic growth in the fraction of loans whose *CLTV exceeded 80 percent* in all three major loan categories. For prime ARMs, the fraction has increased from 4.1 percent in 2002 to 26.2 percent in 2006, while for Alt-A ARMs, it has increased from 20.8 percent in 2002 to 55.5 percent in 2006. Finally, for subprime ARMs, it increased from 46.8 percent in 2002 to 64.0 percent in 2006.
- There has been dramatic growth in the fraction of loans that are *interest only* in all three major loan categories. For prime ARMs, the fraction has increased from 46 percent in 2002 to 91 percent in 2006, while for Alt-A ARMs, it has increased from 26 percent in 2002 to 87 percent in 2006. For subprime ARMs, the fraction has increased from 1 percent in 2002 to 20 percent in 2006.
- There have been substantial declines in the fraction of loans that have *full documentation* in all three major loan categories. For prime ARMs, the fraction has declined from 56.0 percent in 2002 to 33.6 percent in 2006, while for Alt-A ARMs, it has declined from 29.3 percent in 2002 to 19 percent in 2006. For subprime ARMs, the fraction has declined from 66.9 percent in 2002 to 54.6 percent in 2006.

TABLE 1.1 U.S. Mortgage Market Originations, 2001–2006 ($ Amounts in Billions)

	Conforming	Jumbo	FHA/VA	Subprime	Alt-A	HELOCs	Total	ARMs	Refinance	Prime	Nonprime	% Nonprime
2001	$1,280	$450	$175	$120	$ 60	$130	$2,215	$ 355	$1,298	$1,905	$ 310	14%
2002	1,711	576	176	185	67	170	2,885	679	1,821	2,463	422	15
2003	2,460	650	220	310	85	220	3,945	1,034	2,839	3,330	615	16
2004	1,210	510	130	530	185	355	2,920	1,464	1,510	1,850	1,070	37
2005	1,090	570	90	625	380	365	3,120	1,490	1,572	1,750	1,370	44
2006	990	480	80	600	400	430	2,980	1,340	1,345	1,550	1,430	48

Source: Inside Mortgage Finance.

- There has been substantial growth in the *average debt-to-income ratio* of households holding prime ARMs but more modest growth for those holding Alt-A ARMs and subprime ARMs. While the ratio for prime ARMs has increased from 31.0 percent in 2002 to 37.2 percent in 2006, it was 35.4 percent in 2002 and 38.3 percent in 2006 for Alt-A ARMs and it was 40.0 percent in 2002 and 42.1 percent in 2006 for subprime ARMs.
- There has been little change in the fraction of loans with FICO scores less than 700 in all three major loan categories. For prime ARMs, the fraction was 20.7 percent in 2002 and 19.5 percent in 2006, while for Alt-A ARMs, it was 46.4 percent in 2002 and 44.2 percent in 2006. For subprime ARMs, the fraction was 93.4 percent in 2002 and 91.8 percent in 2006. Demyanyk and Van Hemert (forthcoming) show that FICO scores on subprime loans actually went up.

The patterns for fixed rate mortgage loans over the same five-year period are similar, except that prime FRMs contain a much larger fraction of full-documentation loans.

Loan quality continued to decline in 2007. According to a survey by the National Association of Realtors, the median down payment on home purchases was 9 percent in 2007, down from 20 percent in 1989. Twenty-nine percent of buyers put no money down. And many borrowed more than the price of the home to cover closing costs.

Prior to the current situation, the U.S. economy witnessed an unprecedented boom in home values. Between June 1996 and June 2006, the Case-Shiller house price index for the 10 largest metropolitan areas in the United States almost tripled from 77.8 to 226.3, a growth rate of 17 percent per year. From the peak of June 2006 until September 2008, the index fell from 226.3 to 173.3, a decrease of 23.4 percent. The broader 20-city index and nationwide indexes from different sources showed similar declines of 21.8 percent and 21.0 percent. The decline was moderate at first and concentrated in a few regional markets such as Miami and Las Vegas. However, over the last 12 months, the decline has accelerated (−18.6 percent) and spread to all regions. Not a single one of the 20 largest regions saw its house prices increase over the last year, and only Charlotte and Dallas saw a decline of less than 5 percent. House prices are now back at 2004 values. Supporting this picture, Federal Reserve Flow of Funds data show that aggregate residential real estate wealth increased from $10 trillion to $21.8 trillion over the 1996–2006 period, an increase of almost $200,000 in housing wealth per homeowner. Residential wealth then peaked at $22.4 trillion in the third quarter of 2007 and has since fallen back to $21.4 trillion in the third quarter of 2008.

As house prices have dropped, the number of loan originations has fallen in 2007 and 2008. The number of loan originations fell 25 percent in 2007 to 3.5 million, according to data released under the Home Mortgage Disclosure Act. According to the Mortgage Bankers Association, loan originations fell 22 percent in November 2008 compared to November 2007.

Simultaneously, mortgage delinquencies and defaults have started to mount. Delinquencies on the GSE portfolio (Freddie Mac and Fannie Mae) almost tripled from 0.48 percent in 1999 to 1.15 percent in 2007. Data from the Mortgage Bankers Association show that at the end of 2007, 2.56 percent of all prime fixed rate mortgages and 5.51 percent of all prime adjustable rate mortgages were delinquent. The corresponding foreclosure rates were 0.55 percent and 2.59 percent, up from 0.40 percent and 0.88 percent at the end of 2002. Subprime delinquencies (60 to 90 days late) are much higher and stand at 11.6 percent at the end of 2007, according to CreditSights.

Finally, based on Mortgage Bankers Association data, Table 1.2 lists the largest mortgage originators in 2007 as well as their market shares. There has been substantial consolidation in the mortgage origination business over the past 10 years. The share of the top three originators nearly doubled from 19.4 percent in 1998 to 36.6 percent in 2007. This trend accelerated in 2008 when several large mortgage originators such as Countrywide, Washington Mutual, and Wachovia were taken over by Bank of America, JPMorgan Chase, and Wells Fargo, respectively, and several others, such as IndyMac, disappeared.

TABLE 1.2 Largest Mortgage Originators

Name	2007 Rank	2007 Market Share
Countrywide	1	16.8%
Wells Fargo	2	11.2
Chase Home Finance	3	8.6
Citi/CitiMortgage	4	8.1
Bank of America	5	7.8
Washington Mutual	6	5.7
Wachovia	7	4.0
Residential Capital	8	3.9
IndyMac	9	3.2
SunTrust	10	2.4
Total Top 10		71.7%

Source: Mortgage Bankers Association data.

Securitization

Coincident with the underlying growth in nonprime mortgages (see Table 1.1) and, in particular, subprime mortgages, there was a surge in securitizations of subprime mortgages. Table 1.3 reports data on the relative size of the subprime origination and securitization market from 2001 to 2006. Over this period, subprime originations tripled from $190 billion to $600 billion annually, going from a market share of 8.6 percent to 20.1 percent. More important to the current financial crisis, however, is the fact that the proportion of securitization went from 50.4 percent to 80.5 percent. In other words, almost all the subprime mortgages ended up in a structured product.

The benefits of securitization are well understood. It allows for a credit risk transfer from the originators of the loans to capital market investors willing to hold the risk, thus allowing the particular market for credit to expand. In theory, the balance sheet of the bank or mortgage lender is no longer an impediment to the loan being made. If (a big if) the potential incentive problems between originators, securitizers, and investors have been minimized through contracting, then large amounts of securitization are evidence that capital markets may actually be working.

Table 1.4 lists the largest issuers of collateralized debt obligations (CDOs), primarily made up of nonprime residential mortgage-backed securities (RMBSs) and commercial mortgage-backed securities (CMBSs), from 2004 to 2008. The table is organized by the top 12 firms based on the year 2007 and lists their total issuance in billions of dollars and their market shares. Several observations are in order. First, across all the major CDO players, there was a remarkable growth in CDO issuance over the period through 2007, mirroring the aggregate results given in Table 1.3. Second, in each period, the top five firms took approximately 40 percent of the market share, so that the issuance was concentrated in just a few institutions.

TABLE 1.3 Subprime Origination and Securitization, 2001–2006 ($ Amounts in Billions)

	Total	Subprime	Share %	Subprime MBS	% Securitized
2001	$2,215	$190	8.6%	$ 95	50.4%
2002	2,885	231	8.0	121	52.7
2003	3,945	335	8.5	202	60.5
2004	2,920	540	18.5	401	74.3
2005	3,120	625	20.0	507	81.2
2006	2,980	600	20.1	483	80.5

Source: Inside Mortgage Finance, Gorton (2008).

TABLE 1.4 Book Runners of Worldwide CDOs, 2004–2008
($ Amounts in Billions / % Market Share)

	2004 $ / %	2005 $ / %	2006 $ / %	2007 $ / %	2008 (thru Sept.) $ / %
Citigroup	7 / 5.6	27 / 12.5	40 / 8.3	40 / 9.7	5 / 6.9
Merrill Lynch	16 / 12.5	27 / 12.4	54 / 11.3	38 / 9.3	5 / 6.4
Deutsche Bank	12 / 9.4	9 / 4.6	31 / 7.5	31 / 7.7	12 / 15.7
Barclays	0 / 0.0	17 / 7.9	18 / 3.7	28 / 6.8	2 / 2.6
Wachovia	11 / 8.3	15 / 6.8	24 / 4.9	24 / 5.9	2 / 2.8
Goldman Sachs	7 / 5.7	13 / 6.0	33 / 6.9	24 / 5.8	5 / 6.1
ABN Amro	0 / 0.0	3 / 1.3	5 / 1.0	23 / 5.6	1 / 1.9
UBS	8 / 6.3	7 / 3.2	22 / 4.6	20 / 4.8	0 / 0.0
Lehman Brothers	6 / 4.5	11 / 4.9	17 / 3.6	18 / 4.5	18 / 23.6
JPMorgan	7 / 5.4	9 / 4.1	22 / 4.5	18 / 4.4	3 / 3.7
Bear Stearns	7 / 5.5	12 / 5.8	25 / 5.1	16 / 3.9	0 / 0.0
Bank of America	4 / 3.4	10 / 4.6	23 / 4.7	15 / 3.8	2 / 2.0

Source: Asset-Backed Alert.

Third, the list of firms is a who's who of the current financial crisis: Many of the firms either went bust (e.g., Bear Stearns, Lehman Brothers, and Wachovia) or suffered huge write-downs that led to significant government intervention (e.g., Merrill Lynch, Citigroup, and UBS). Fourth, while it is well documented that the CDO market collapsed in the summer of 2007, the 2008 column shows just how severe the shutdown was. Among these 12 firms, CDO issuance dropped from $314 billion in 2006 to $295 billion in 2007 to just $55 billion in 2008.

As can be seen from Table 1.4, commercial and investment banks were the primary financial intermediaries in the securitization market for subprime-based structured products such as CDOs. Depending on the tranche, fees on CDOs vary from 0.4 to 2 percent. Clearly, it was a very profitable business. The business model for securitization, however, is that the securitizing institutions act as intermediaries in the process and not as investors, otherwise defeating the purpose of the credit risk transfer rationale for securitization. This issue is discussed in the next section.

1.3 WHAT WENT WRONG?

One of the major scapegoats for the financial crisis is the "originate-to-distribute" model of securitization. That is, securitization allowed mortgage lenders (mortgage banks or brokers working on their behalf) to pass through the loans and so reduced their incentive to screen and monitor the mortgage loans. It reduced their "skin in the game." As the previous section demonstrates, lending standards slipped considerably in the five years leading up to the crisis. There are a number of careful academic papers that argued the case that securitization did indeed lead to a reduction in loan quality—for example, Dell'Ariccia, Igan, and Laeven (2008); Mian and Sufi (forthcoming); Berndt and Gupta (2008); and Keys, Mukherjee, Seru, and Vig (2008).

While this evidence cannot be ignored, the case against securitization is not so straightforward. Mortgage lenders do have "skin in the game" to the extent that a considerable portion of their income derives from mortgage servicing. For example, Countrywide (the largest originator according to Table 1.2) suffered huge write-downs from the loss of mortgage servicing rights as the crisis unfolded (Gorton 2008). On the securitization front, while the banks received large securitization fees, they also faced risk holding on to all the loans during the securitization process. This process lasts anywhere from two to four months. Finally, on the contractual side, as Gorton (2008) points out, a catastrophic decline in mortgage underwriting standards would have led to an increase in first payment defaults. These defaults, however, tend to get pushed back to originators in order to align incentives.

The other commonly cited culprit is predatory lending. There is no doubt that mortgage lenders sold very sophisticated products to unsophisticated investors who may not have understood what they were buying. Option-adjusted ARMs are just one example of the many complex products that were offered to households. The more sophisticated products were the ones that earned mortgage brokers the highest fees, creating perverse incentives. It is widely reported that these lenders often did not explain the risk of increases in payments upon termination of an initially low teaser rate, or an interest rate reset due to changing market interest rates. Sometimes they even failed to inform mortgage customers of the availability of government-subsidized home loans that offered lower rates than the subprime products they were offering, even though the customers were eligible. These sophisticated products were sometimes predatory. Often mortgage lenders did not insist on complete documentation. The failure to obtain complete documentation coupled with the predatory nature of many of these mortgages compromised the ability of many borrowers to pay. It is unclear at the current time what proportion of the subprime loans fall into this predatory category, but it will clearly end up playing its part in the overall analysis.

The immediate explanation for the rash of defaults and foreclosures in 2007 and 2008 was the fact that the vast majority of the loans made were 2/28 and 3/27 hybrid ARMs. These loans fix the initial interest rate at some teaser level for the first two (2/28) or three (3/27) years below what the borrower would pay for a fixed rate mortgage. After the initial period, the interest rate then floats based on a variable base rate (i.e., LIBOR,

Treasury bill rate, etc.) plus a significant margin (e.g., 6 percent). This jump in rate gives borrowers an incentive to refinance their mortgage before the reset date albeit at a cost due to prepayment penalties. Otherwise, without some jump in the borrower's income, it becomes difficult for the borrower to make the payments. Refinancing of the mortgage, however, is possible only if the house has appreciated in value. Therefore, the majority of subprime loans were predicated on the assumption that the housing market would appreciate (see Gorton 2008; Ashcraft and Schuermann 2008). Thus, it is not surprising that there was a wave of defaults when home prices started to fall in the summer of 2006. This is an example of how predatory lending can create systemic risk if the resulting defaults occur at or around the same time.

In this context, the two unanswered questions are:

1. Would lenders have made these risky loans (i.e., would a subprime market have existed) if securitization had not been available?
2. Did borrowers understand that they were essentially taking a short-horizon gamble on the housing market?

These are important questions, but answers to them will not by themselves explain the financial crisis. With massive defaults of subprime mortgages, one would have thought there would be two important outcomes. The first is that the portfolios of investors worldwide would be reduced in value. However, if these portfolios were well diversified, the effect would be a few percent here or there. After all, the size of the subprime and Alt-A markets was around $2 trillion, a significant but not overwhelming number. The second effect would be an economic downturn. Because the majority of a household's wealth is tied up in a leveraged asset (i.e., their home), a shock to the housing market essentially wipes out the equity of the homeowner (especially one of the nonprime sort). This wealth shock would presumably affect spending patterns that would then ripple throughout the economy. But the drop in worldwide investor wealth and the ongoing recession do not explain the financial crisis.

The financial crisis occurred because financial institutions did not follow the business model of securitization. Rather than acting as intermediaries by transferring the risk from mortgage lenders to capital market investors, they became the investors. They put "skin in the game." But unlike your typical pension fund or fixed income mutual fund, financial firms are highly levered institutions. In theory, they can take on leverage only because the risk of their underlying assets is low through hedging and intermediation.

Table 1.5 lists the entities that were holding the various types of mortgage debt early in 2008 and how much of each type of debt they were holding. The table illustrates how financial institutions had become the investors in several ways. First, the overall exposure of the financial sector (i.e., banks,

TABLE 1.5   Holders of Mortgage Debt, 2008 ($ Amounts in Billions)

	Loans	HELOCs	Agency MBSs	Nonagency AAA	CDO Subord.	Non-CDO Subord.	Total	
Banks and Thrifts	$2,020	$ 869	$ 852	$ 383	$ 90		$ 4,212	39%
GSEs and FHLB	444		741	308			1,493	14%
Broker-Dealers			49	100	130	24	303	3%
Financial Guarantors		62			100		162	2%
Insurance Companies			856	125	65	24	1,070	10%
Overseas			689	413	45	24	1,172	11%
Other	461	185	1,175	307	46	49	2,268	21%
Total	2,925	1,116	4,362	1,636	476	121	10,680	
	27%	10%	41%	15%	4%	1%		

Source: Lehman Brothers, Krishnamurthy (2008).

broker-dealers, monolines, and insurance companies) to real estate was $5.8 trillion worth of mortgages. This was a majority of the mortgage market. Second, while some of this can be explained by banks holding whole loans, the surprising fact is that banks held $1.325 trillion worth of securitized loans. Coupled with broker-dealers and the GSEs, there was $2.644 trillion held by highly levered institutions. Third, only $1.642 trillion of these MBSs were agency-backed, that is, of the prime loan type. Fourth, of the AAA-rated CDOs (backed by nonprime loans), a majority was held by the banks, GSEs, and broker-dealers, specifically $791 billion worth or approximately 48 percent. This is the exact opposite of what should take place with securitization. Finally, the majority of exposure to the subordinated tranches of the CDOs was also held by banks, broker-dealers, and the monolines with $320 billion of $476 billion in total. The overall exposure might be even bigger, because these numbers do not include over-the-counter (OTC) derivatives. These derivatives may also have led to one-sided exposure, as was the case with AIG.

It is a puzzle why so many financial institutions took such a large gamble on real estate, thereby putting their own firms and, as it turns out, the system at risk. By holding on to such large amounts of the AAA-rated, non-agency-backed CDOs, these firms were for all economic purposes writing deep out-of-the-money put options on the housing market. That is, the firms writing these options would receive a premium in most states of the world, and, in the rare event of massive defaults (i.e., a severe housing shock and/or recession), would be on the hook for them. Of course, if the event were to occur, it is not clear that firms could cover the roughly $1 trillion exposure. This is not hindsight. The marketplace certainly priced the AAA securities this way. For example, at the peak of the housing market in June 2006, a comparison of the relevant spreads from the tranches of subprime MBSs (as described by the ABX index) to the average U.S. firm for a given rating shows for AAA-rated 18 basis points (bps) versus 11 bps, AA-rated 32 bps versus 16 bps, A-rated 54 bps versus 24 bps, and BBB-rated 154 bps versus 48 bps (Ashcraft and Schuermann 2008).

We present three possible explanations for why financial firms took the gamble. The first possibility is that there was poor governance within financial firms. The creation of structured product groups, and their meteoric success through the combination of fees and continued premiums from retaining these products, gave these groups a free hand to take big asymmetric bets.[1] The second possibility is that, because many of the firms had an explicit guarantee on their short-term debt (i.e., deposit insurance) and an implicit guarantee from being too big to fail, their funding costs for these types of risky investments were lower than they would have otherwise been. Thus, the AAA-rated security was the most attractive investment opportunity given (1) their capital and risk constraints and (2) artificially cheap funding sources. The third possibility is that the financial firms did not fully understand the nature of the loans they were securitizing because (1) they didn't fully appreciate how securitization had eroded loan quality, and (2) a lack of transparency about the quality of the loans meant they did not realize their mistake. Consequently, when housing prices started dropping, these institutions did not realize that the value of their MBS positions was declining dramatically and so did not unwind their positions in a timely fashion before the losses got too big.

Was securitization therefore really at fault? It clearly was the vehicle by which housing risk got transferred from those making the loans to the balance sheets of financial institutions. But this was an anathema to how it was supposed to work.

Arguably, the type of securitization that was performed has made the crisis much worse than it would have been even with the bank failures that we are seeing. There is so much complexity and therefore so little transparency with the securitized products that the effect of the crisis has been amplified. To understand the nature of the complexity, consider Figure 1.2, which shows in further detail how subprime loans work their way through the structuring process. A portfolio of subprime mortgages is pooled into a residential mortgage-backed security (RMBS). The RMBS has five tranches;

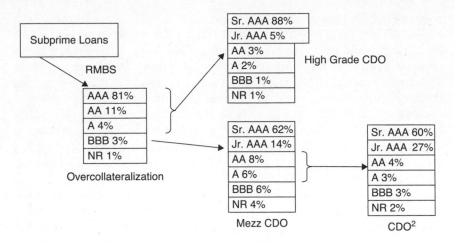

FIGURE 1.2   The Securitization Process of Subprime Mortgage Loans
Source: UBS (2007), Gorton (2008).

the priority of the tranches is based on seniority in terms of allocating default losses, ranging from the most protected tranche (AAA) down to the least protected one (BBB). At each point in the structure, the rating agency would determine the rating based on its assessment of each loan's default probability and, in theory, the correlation across defaults. Note that the top 96 percent of the cash flows go to a high grade CDO, which then splits into six tranches of different rating classes. The next 3 percent of the cash flows goes toward a mezzanine CDO, which in turn splits into six classes of different priorities. But it doesn't stop there. The middle 14 percent of this mezzanine CDO is structured into another CDO, which again is broken into six classes, the top 60 percent of which is the senior AAA tranche. The game was to try to generate as many AAA rated securities as possible. In this example, the original fraction of AAA-rated securities in the RMBS was 81 percent, while at the end of the securitization process, it was 91.93 percent. Knowing that there is now a significant probability of widespread defaults, the question is whether the market can price or understand the senior and junior tranches of the AAA CDO^2.

In the heat of this financial crisis, it is difficult for financial markets to operate if there is a lack of transparency. This is due to (1) agents not being able to price these complex CDOs and (2) uncertainty about who is holding them. Without being able to assess the solvency of the financial firms within the system, there is a complete lack of trust and confidence in counterparties, a spike in the overall level of risk aversion, and marketwide freezes without any source of liquidity.

1.4 PRINCIPLES

What should be the principles behind regulatory reform of the mortgage origination and securitization markets? We present a set of principles that can point to effective regulation and that guide the proposals we suggest in the next section.

Choice is good, but predatory lending is bad. It is important that households continue to have access to an array of mortgage products. Different households, by virtue of where they are in the life cycle and the properties of their labor income risk, will prefer different contracts. They should have at least this choice. But complicated contracts that offer no benefits and only confusion need to be prohibited. There is clearly a tension between providing mortgage customers with choice and innovation, and at the same time protecting them from predatory lending practices. Developing concrete proposals to promote choice while limiting predatory lending practices should be a policy priority.

Standardization is good; it promotes liquidity in the mortgage-backed securities market because standardization makes the securities easier to value. So while we need choice, the need for liquidity in the mortgage-backed securities market may be a reason to limit the menu of loans that can be securitized. The rule should be: If the pools of loans of a given type are not large enough to create a liquid market, then the mortgage-backed security should not be created. Standardization also limits abuse. The proliferation of products makes it more difficult to regulate mortgage products effectively. A smaller menu of options may facilitate more timely and effective oversight by regulators.

At the same time, nonstandard contracts can add value because of the inherent heterogeneity of mortgage customers along important dimensions like labor income profile and financial sophistication. The rationale for the new products with low initial payments that were created in the period from 2002 to 2006 was that they promoted home ownership for households previously excluded from home ownership. This was especially true for low-income households and for households with no regular paycheck (e.g., freelance workers).

Home ownership has many advantages, such as promoting the development of stable and safe neighborhoods. But it also has its costs, such as the reduction of household mobility, which makes labor markets less efficient. It is a controversial question whether the advantages of increasing the home-ownership rate from its current value of two-thirds outweigh the costs. But whatever the answer, a household's ability to obtain a mortgage loan should depend on the value of its entire human capital, not just its current labor income. It is important to develop proposals for how banks can offer nonstandard products that are not predatory in nature without compromising the liquidity of the mortgage-backed securities market.

Loan originators and mortgage brokers need to have an incentive to internalize the externalities created by the deadweight costs associated with defaults and foreclosures. Making sure mortgage customers understand fully the terms of all loan products offered to them helps these customers to internalize the costs that they bear in the event of default or foreclosure. Including provisions for efficient renegotiation and reorganization of a loan in event of default can reduce the deadweight costs of foreclosure but can also make it more difficult to securitize the loan.[2] So there is a trade-off. The nature of the provisions is likely to be important.

1.5 PROPOSALS

Given the previous discussion of how mortgage origination and securitization may have contributed to the crisis (Section 1.3) and the principles developed in Section 1.4 for future regulation, we suggest the following policies.

Predatory Lending

The recent amendments to Regulation Z (Truth in Lending) by the Federal Reserve Board are a big step in the right direction of protecting consumers from predatory practices among mortgage banks and brokers in the subprime space. According to a press release by the Board of Governors on July 14, 2008, the amendments add four key protections for a newly defined category of "higher-priced mortgage loans." The rule's definition of "higher-priced mortgage loans" will capture virtually all loans in the subprime market, but generally exclude loans in the prime market. To provide an index, the Federal Reserve Board will publish the "average prime offer rate," based on a survey currently published by Freddie Mac. A loan is higher-priced if it is a first-lien mortgage and has an annual percentage rate that is 1.5 percentage points or more above this index, or 3.5 percentage points if it is a subordinate-lien mortgage. The new protections are delineated as follows:

- A lender is prohibited from making a loan without regard to a borrower's ability to repay the loan from income and assets other than the home's value. A lender complies, in part, by assessing repayment ability based on the highest scheduled payment in the first seven years of the loan. To show that a lender violated this prohibition, a borrower does not need to demonstrate that it is part of a "pattern or practice."

- Creditors are required to verify the income and assets they rely on to determine repayment ability.
- Any prepayment penalty is banned if the payment can change in the initial four years. For other higher-priced loans, a prepayment penalty period cannot last for more than two years.
- Creditors are required to establish escrow accounts for property taxes and homeowner's insurance for all first-lien mortgage loans.

Because flexibility and choice are valuable, it is important that the first two protections are construed literally and are not used to restrict the combinations of income and assets that creditors are allowed to find acceptable.

Standardization

Households should be offered an array of standardized products. Conforming loans should include, at the very least, a 30-year ARM with annual resetting of the rate, a 15-year FRM, a 30-year FRM, and a 5/25 hybrid with a fixed rate for the first five years and then an adjustable rate for the remaining 25 years of the loan. In addition to the current conforming loan criteria, it would be in the best interest of systemwide financial stability to place an upper limit on the loan-to-value ratios for these loans (e.g., 80 percent).

For households that do not qualify for a conforming loan because the loan is too big (jumbo mortgages) or their credit score is too low (Alt-A and subprime mortgages), the same effort toward standardization ought to be made. Households should also have access to nonstandardized products. These products should be designed to benefit a wide array of households that differ in terms of their age (stage of the life cycle) and labor income risk. These nonstandardized products should be subject to additional regulatory vetting to ensure no predatory lending.

Securitization

As they were in the past, loan originators should be able to securitize any of these standardized conforming mortgage products in the form of mortgage-backed securities.[3] The markets for these mortgage-backed securities would be expected to be very liquid. The ease of securitization would make these products attractive for originators. This benefit will result in lower interest rates on mortgages for households and wider availability of mortgage credit in general. Loan originators should not be allowed to fully securitize (and pass on the risk to others of) any nonconforming loan. Moreover, the heterogeneity in nonstandardized products makes them unlikely candidates for securitization due to concerns about illiquidity in the markets for the mortgage-backed securities that these products would be backing.

The question is whether regulation should compel originators of nonconforming loans to have "skin in the game," given that this may have been a factor in the current crisis. There are a number of ways to align the incentives of originators, securitizers, and investors:

- One could compel mortgage originators to hold a fraction of each loan on their balance sheets, thus giving them the proper incentives to screen and monitor borrowers. Alternatively, in order to reduce the number of loans that originators should be compelled to hold, one could *randomly* determine which loans the originators must hold in full. Either way, reducing the fraction of loans that must be held reduces the cost incurred by the originator, which in turn lowers the interest rates that borrowers have to pay.
- Many mortgage lenders are not banking institutions and may not have a source of sustained capital, such as deposits. Another possibility would be to have the origination fee of the lenders be amortized over some period of the loan. Thus, if default occurs within a certain period of time (i.e., before the end of the amortization period), the originator would receive only a portion of the fee.
- The mortgage lender would not be able to sell the mortgage servicing rights. Servicing of mortgages typically commands a 0.50 percent fee and thus gives the lender an incentive to choose good loans and monitor them accordingly. Currently, the majority of major lenders do in fact service the loans.

Of course, securitization firms and asset-backed security (ABS) investors have the incentive to enter into contracts with lenders that achieve these goals. In general, there will be a trade-off between the amount of discipline imposed on the lender and the interest rate and the fraction of the principal of the loan that flows to the investor. At first glance, it is not readily clear why the government needs to get involved. One reason why is if the full costs of poor-quality loans are not being borne totally by the holders of the MBSs that these loans back (because their holdings of these MBSs cause systemic risk).

Another reason for government intervention is that many of the parties in the marketplace for securitized products (at least for mortgage-related securities) have some type of guarantee from the U.S. government: the implicit guarantee on the GSEs, the explicit guarantee on deposits by the FDIC for deposit institutions, or the very implicit guarantee of being too big to fail that large, complex financial institutions (LCFIs) have. As long as one of these guaranteed entities is active in the securitization process—as either a lender, a securitizer, or an investor—incentives will be distorted. For example, the investor in prime MBSs that are guaranteed by the GSE does not care per se about the quality of the loan, because the principal will be paid regardless. Alternatively, if the investor is an FDIC-insured institution, then external discipline to not take on risky loans is diminished. Therefore, one possible proposal is that financial firms with government guarantees should only securitize or purchase nonconforming loans that have been originated by lenders with "skin in the game" of the sort described earlier. If the loan does not satisfy this criterion, it is still possible for it to be securitized, just not involving government-guaranteed firms anywhere in the securitization chain.

Conforming Loan Limits

According to provisions of the Housing and Economic Recovery Act of 2008 (HERA), the conforming national loan limit is set each year based on changes in average home prices over the previous year, but cannot decline from year to year. We support this calculation of the conforming national loan limit. People who want to buy a house today should not be penalized relative to those who wanted to buy last year, just because house prices have gone up.

At the same time, a case can be made for abolishing the conforming loan limit altogether. In particular, as long as the current GSE criteria on combined loan-to-value ratio, credit score, and debt-to-income ratio are satisfied, a jumbo loan is probably not much riskier than a conforming loan, an assertion that is supported by the fact that the rate on jumbo loans is typically only slightly higher than the rate on conforming loans. However, the implicit government guarantee associated with an MBS being backed by conforming loans makes conforming loans easier to securitize than nonconforming loans. To the extent that the fee charged by the GSE is less than the full value of the implicit guarantee, there is a subsidy for borrowers whose loans are conforming. And so removing the loan limit changes the amount of the subsidy as a function of the amount borrowed. Thus, there may be welfare-policy reasons for the conforming loan limit that are unrelated to any issue of systemic risk and that provide a rationale for leaving the conforming loan limit in place.

Even given the possibility of welfare-policy reasons for conforming loan limits, we also support the GSEs' mandate under the government's economic stimulus package to purchase loans beyond the conforming national loan limit in high-cost areas. People should not be penalized because they live in an area with high property values, especially since those areas typically are some of the most productive areas. Under the stimulus package, loans originated in 2008 and the second half of 2007 are subject to loan limits equal to the maximum of the conforming national limit, which is currently $417,000, and the "high-cost" area limit of 125 percent of the local price median, up to a maximum of $729,750. For 2009, the Federal Housing Finance Agency (FHFA) has set loan limits for high-cost areas equal to 115 percent of local median house prices, and the amount borrowed cannot exceed $625,500, 150 percent of the national limit. Thus, the conforming loan limit for 2009 is set equal to the maximum of the current general loan limit of $417,000 and 115 percent of the median home price in that metropolitan area or $625,500, whichever is smaller. We call for the GSEs' mandate to purchase loans beyond the conforming national loan limit in high-cost areas to become a permanent mandate. We also support tying the conforming high-cost area limits to regional house price indexes. Since 125 percent of the median house price seems quite conservative, we favor that number over the more stringent 115 percent that has been adopted for next year. Finally, we support the abolition of the maximum dollar cap on the loan, since it penalizes people who live in high-cost areas.

Mortgage Brokers

Independent mortgage brokers selling mortgages on commission should have a fiduciary duty of disclosure to their mortgage customers that compels them to disclose the availability of any government-subsidized home loans that the household is eligible for, and to describe fully the terms and conditions of any product that they offer to them. As discussed earlier, brokers should be compelled to receive only a fraction of their sales fee up front. The rest of the fee should be paid out over the following several years and only as long as the loan payments are current. A similar principle is already used for insurance brokers. There should be tighter supervision on the certification of licensed brokers. Certification may require additional financial education and ethics guidelines.

Households

While this involves the application of federal versus states laws, a dialogue should be started as to whether households should suffer harsher penalties in the event of default or foreclosure. In particular, the impact of default or foreclosure on a household's credit availability could be harsher. A first channel is to increase the length of time a default or foreclosure stays on a borrower's credit report. Another channel available to make penalties harsher is to strengthen the lender's ability to recover the debt from the household's other assets in the event of default and/or foreclosure (recourse). While strengthening recourse would unambiguously increase the collateral value of the mortgage, it may adversely affect the liquidity of the underlying mortgage-backed securities, particularly in the nonprime space. Giving lenders recourse to the borrower's other assets may make nonconforming mortgages more difficult to value because of increased uncertainty about the recovery rate, which now depends on the wealth of the borrower, in event of foreclosure.

Loan Agreements

Loan agreements should be required to include provisions for efficient renegotiation and reorganization of the loan in event of default. Provisions should be designed with an eye to their impact on the ease with which the loans can be securitized.[4]

1.6 CONCLUSION

One of the major catalysts for the current financial crisis was the spate of defaults and foreclosures in 2007 and 2008. And the two big reasons for all the defaults and foreclosures were the downturn in house prices coupled with a dramatic decline in the quality of mortgage loans. Loan quality declined in large part because of an unintended consequence of securitization—namely, that mortgage lenders did not bear the costs of these declines in loan quality, and so did not care about them. The financial crisis occurred because financial institutions did not follow the business model of securitization. Rather than acting as intermediaries by transferring the risk from mortgage lenders to capital market investors, they became the investors. We argue that securitization is still a valuable tool for the mortgage market because it allows loans to be offered at lower rates than they otherwise could be. Consequently, standardization is valuable because it facilitates securitization.

At the same time, it is important that mortgage lenders have an incentive to internalize the deadweight costs associated with defaults and foreclosures. This can be done by spreading their fees over time and making them hold a fraction of loans. To minimize the fraction of loans that lenders need to hold, the loans to be held could be randomly selected. Just as important, mortgage lenders need to help borrowers to internalize these deadweight costs by helping them to understand exactly what their obligations are under any loan offered to them. Last, the availability of nonstandard contracts allows the mortgage industry to accommodate heterogeneity across borrowers, which is valuable. However, nonstandard contracts are not good candidates for securitization, because securities backed by nonstandard contracts are difficult to value, and so markets for these securities are likely to be illiquid. Moreover, nonstandard contracts need to be subject to additional regulatory vetting to ensure they are not predatory.

NOTES

1. See Chapter 7, "Corporate Governance in the Modern Financial Sector," and Chapter 8, "Rethinking Compensation in Financial Firms."
2. An unintended problem with securitization is that it inhibits the ability of households and banks to renegotiate the loans since by then the loans have been sliced and diced through the system.
3. See Chapter 4, "What to Do about the Government-Sponsored Enterprises?"
4. For a discussion as to which provisions should be included, see Chapter 16, "Mortgages and Households."

REFERENCES

Ashcraft, Adam, and Til Schuermann. 2008. Understanding the securitization of the subprime mortgage credit. Federal Reserve Bank of New York staff reports.

Berndt, Antje, and Anurag Gupta. 2008. Moral hazard and adverse selection in the originate-to-distribute model of bank credit. Working paper.

Dell'Ariccia, Giovanni, Deniz Igan, and Luc Laeven. 2008. Credit booms and lending standards: Evidence from the subprime mortgage market. Working paper.

Demyanyk, Yuliya, and Otto Van Hemert. Forthcoming. Understanding the subprime mortgage crisis. *Review of Financial Studies*.

Gorton, Gary. 2008. The panic of 2007. Yale working paper.

Keys, Benjamin, Tanmoy Mukherjee, Amit Seru, and Vikrant Vig. 2008. Did securitization lead to lax screening? Evidence from subprime loans. EFA 2008 Athens Meetings Paper.

Krishnamurthy, Arvind. 2008. The financial meltdown: Data and diagnoses. Northwestern working paper.

Mian, Atif, and Amir Sufi. Forthcoming. The consequences of mortgage credit expansion: Evidence from the 2007 mortgage default crisis. *Quarterly Journal of Economics*.

UBS. 2007. Market commentary (December 13).

Zimmerman, Thomas. 2007. How did we get here and what lies ahead? UBS Lunch and Learn.

CHAPTER 2

How Banks Played the Leverage Game

Viral V. Acharya and Philipp Schnabl

If there is one conclusion that analysts of the financial crisis all agree upon, it is that high bank leverage has made the crisis far worse. But how could excessive leverage be built up in a sector that is so heavily regulated? In this paper we show that banks used *credit risk transfer* mechanisms to get around regulatory requirements. Credit risk transfer mechanisms are supposed to transfer assets off bank balance sheets onto other investors in the economy, but instead banks exploited credit transfer mechanisms for regulatory arbitrage and increased their *effective* leverage and exposure to aggregate risk by availing of such mechanisms. In the process, they exposed themselves to the risk that a significant economy-wide shock would be sufficient to rapidly wipe out their capital base.

The regulatory arbitrage undertaken by banks took two principal forms. First, banks set up off-balance-sheet asset-backed commercial paper (ABCP) conduits, and sister concerns such as structured investment vehicles (SIVs). ABCP conduits held assets the banks would have otherwise held on their books, and banks provided *liquidity enhancement* and *credit enhancement* to these conduits. These enhancements implied that the investors in conduits had recourse to banks in case the quality of the assets deteriorated. Such enhancements were treated as capital-light in existing capital requirements, allowing five times higher leverage ratios off the balance sheet than on the balance sheet.

Second, banks exploited the fact that they could also get capital relief by simply switching away from loans into investments in the form of AAA-rated tranches of CDOs and CLOs, which again had a significantly lower capital charge. As a result, about 50 percent of all AAA asset-backed securities remained *within* the banking system. Indeed, banks that had greater activity in ABCP conduits and had greater capital-light investments suffered the greatest losses and equity price declines during the crisis.

Can such regulatory arbitrage be prevented in future? There are at least two simple recommendations toward this objective. First, any regulation that focuses narrowly on just one performance metric of banks is easy to game. The current regulatory focus on a single ratio (capital to suitably risk-weighted assets) should be made more robust by expanding it to a more rounded approach that examines bank balance sheets as equity or credit analysts would, relying on several key indicators (such as loans to deposits, insured deposit to assets, holdings of liquid treasuries and OECD government bonds relative to assets, etc.). Second, bank regulation has to focus more on aggregate risk to the economy instead of the risk of failure of individual institutions. The focus on aggregate risk should ensure that credit risk is truly passed to investors outside the banking system rather than transferred between institutions within the banking system.

2.1   CREDIT RISK TRANSFER AND BANK LEVERAGE

If there is one conclusion that analysts of the subprime crisis all agree upon, it is that leverage of financial institutions matters. The period from 2003 to 2007 was characterized by loose monetary policy and readily available liquidity in the developed countries (partly due to the savings glut in other parts of the world). During this period, banks built up significantly high levels of leverage and lent "down the quality curve." There is now robust academic evidence suggesting that it was the ability to securitize assets that led to the deterioration of subprime lending decisions.[1]

Taken literally, credit risk transfer mechanisms such as securitization should simply transfer assets off bank balance sheets onto other investors in the economy, and not necessarily lead to increased bank leverage or risk. Nevertheless, it appears that in the buildup to the subprime crisis, banks increased their *effective* leverage and exposure to aggregate risk precisely by availing themselves of such mechanisms. In the process, they exposed themselves to the risk that a significant economy-wide shock would be sufficient to rapidly wipe out their capital base. Indeed, this risk materialized starting with an increase in delinquencies on subprime mortgages in 2006 and 2007 and the subsequent house price collapse. A painful process of deleveraging ensued, rendering illiquid several markets (such as the market in asset-backed securities, rollover debt finance, and credit derivatives) that had appeared reasonably liquid just a year before and were deemed especially suitable for risk transfer within the financial system.

This sequence of events from (apparent) credit risk transfer to the freezing up of markets that had a short-run burst of liquidity prompts the question as to how excessive leverage and aggregate risk could be built up in a financial sector that is so heavily regulated. In particular, how and why did capital adequacy requirements fail in their stated job of limiting bank leverage and risk? The answer is simple: While credit risk transfer may have economic merit as a risk-transfer tool, its dark side is that many of its incarnations may have been clever innovations of the financial sector to arbitrage regulation. Such regulatory arbitrage took two principal forms: first, the setting up of asset-backed commercial paper (ABCP) conduits (and sister concerns such as SIVs) by banks, and, second, the significant retention by banks of AAA-rated asset-backed securities.

On the first front, banks set up off-balance-sheet ABCP conduits where they transferred some of the assets they would have otherwise held on their books; the conduits were funded with a sliver of equity and the rest in rollover finance in the form of asset-backed commercial paper. In addition, banks provided liquidity enhancement and credit enhancement to these conduits. These enhancements implied that the investors in conduits had recourse to banks in case the quality of assets deteriorated. Put simply, investors would return the assets back to the bank once they suffered a loss. Importantly, such enhancements were treated as capital-light in existing Basel rules for calculating risk-weighted capital requirements, most notably that liquidity facilities of less than one year maturity had less than 20 percent of capital requirement compared to the one if assets were on the bank balance sheet. As banks rolled out more and more ABCP conduits, they increased their short-term liabilities but their effective or contingent leverage remained in the shadow banking system. What is more, they got capital freed up to originate more assets, generally of lower quality.

On the second front, banks exploited the fact that they could also get capital relief by simply switching away from loans into investments in the form of AAA-rated tranches of CDOs and CLOs, which again had a significantly lower capital charge. Indeed, about 30 percent of all AAA asset-backed securities remained *within* the banking system, and if one includes ABCP conduits and SIVs as effectively being parts of the banking system, then this fraction rises to 50 percent. While AAA-rated securities should have low absolute risk levels, the fact that newer assets originated by banks were "down the quality curve" was ignored and thus their ratings were overly generous. Even in the absence of such ratings failures, in pursuit of regulatory capital relief banks were taking on significant aggregate risks. For example, an AAA-rated mortgage-backed security would again be significantly capital-light relative to holding mortgages on one's books. So banks passed their mortgage parcels around in the system. Did banks simply not understand that AAA-rated tranches on housing assets were "economic catastrophe bonds" (to borrow a recent academic phrase)? While this is possible, the short-run regulatory arbitrage from holding such tranches most likely caused banks to ignore their fundamental economic risk.

Not surprisingly, banks that had greater activity in ABCP conduits and had greater capital-light investments (paradoxically, these were safer banks as per regulatory standards) suffered the greatest losses and equity price declines during the crisis. Can such arbitrage be prevented or its incidence reduced? What policy lessons, if any, are to be learned from the sudden emergence and collapse of the shadow banking system and credit risk transfer activities?

There are at least two simple, and yet novel, lessons. First, any regulation that focuses narrowly on just one performance metric of banks will fall into the box-ticking trap and be easy to game. The current regulatory focus on a single ratio (capital to suitably risk-weighted assets) should be made more robust by expanding it to a more rounded approach that examines bank balance sheets as equity or credit analysts would, relying on several indicators (such as loans to deposits, insured deposit to assets, holdings of liquid treasuries and OECD government bonds relative to assets, etc.) to create an early warning system that raises a flag when further investigation is needed. The second lesson is to understand the aggregate risk component of risk transfer vehicles, and more broadly, of bank balance sheets. Isolated failures of credit intermediaries are not a problem for economies per se; but systemic failures of many credit intermediaries are. This intuitive observation suggests that regulation designed to make banks individually safer may encourage excessive credit risk transfer that makes aggregate crises more severe. Bank regulation needs to be reformed and focused more on aggregate risk to the economy rather than a single capital ratio tied to individual bank risks.

The remainder of this paper discusses in more detail how banks used credit risk transfer mechanisms to reduce regulatory capital without shrinking their risk exposure. The first part focuses on ABCP conduits, and the second part analyzes the use of securitization. The paper concludes with specific recommendations on how to reform bank regulation to avoid regulatory arbitrage in the future.

2.2 ASSET-BACKED COMMERCIAL PAPER CONDUITS

Asset-backed commercial paper (ABCP) conduits are one example of how banks used credit risk transfer mechanism to increase leverage. ABCP conduits are shell companies that hold financial assets such as corporate loans, trade receivables, student loans, credit card receivables, or mortgages. Typically, conduits hold only AAA-rated securities or unrated assets of similar quality. Conduits have no employees or headquarters, and the conduit management is outsourced to an administrator, typically a commercial bank that sets up the conduit in the first place. The administrator runs the conduit's day-to-day activities, which consist of managing the asset portfolio according to prespecified investment guidelines and issues asset-backed commercial paper to finance the conduit assets. Often the administrator invests in assets that have been generated by the administrator itself or assets generated by clients of the administrator.

One of the most important characteristics of conduits is the extensive recourse to bank balance sheets. This characteristic distinguishes conduits from other shell companies that hold financial assets but have no recourse to bank balance sheets (e.g., collateralized debt obligations). What does *recourse* mean? In its simplest form, recourse is the institutional arrangement through which risks of the conduit get transferred back to the commercial bank setting up the conduit; thus, under the scenario of losses to conduits' assets, assets that were off-balance-sheet for the commercial bank effectively become on-balance-sheet again, undoing the credit risk transfer that resulted in the setting up of the conduit. Such recourse to balance sheets is based on two separate arrangements between conduits and large commercial banks or other large financial institutions.

First, conduits contract with banks to insure against liquidity risk. This insurance is called liquidity enhancement and provides a backup credit line or commitment to repurchase nondefaulted assets in case a conduit cannot roll over maturing commercial paper (CP).[2] In most cases, liquidity enhancement is provided by the conduit administrator itself. Second, conduits contract with large financial institutions to insure against credit losses. This credit insurance is called credit enhancement and covers credit losses on conduit assets. Typically credit insurance is provided by the conduit administrator alone or jointly with other financial institutions. In addition, conduits are structured as bankruptcy-remote companies in the sense that their legal charter prevents them from declaring bankruptcy without drawing upon available liquidity and credit enhancement. Box 2.1 explains the overall conduit structure in the context of Solitaire Funding Limited, a conduit set up by HSBC Holdings PLC.

From the perspective of a commercial paper investor—the creditor of the conduit—the structure provides three separate lines of defense against nonrepayment. First, conduits own highly rated assets to satisfy investor claims. Second, if the assets in the conduit have not defaulted but the assets are insufficient to cover investor claims, conduits can draw on liquidity enhancement to repay investors. Third, if assets are defaulted, conduits can

BOX 2.1   SOLITAIRE FUNDING LIMITED

Solitaire Funding Limited is a conduit founded and administered by HSBC Holdings. In January 2007, Solitaire had assets worth US$20.5 billion. US$9.8 billion (48 percent) of conduit assets were in asset-backed residential mortgages, US$3.0 billion (15 percent) in asset-backed commercial mortgages, US$2.8 billion (15 percent) in asset-backed student loans, and the remainder in CDOs and other asset-backed securities. US$14.1 billion (69 percent) of conduit assets were backed by assets in the United States, US$4.9 billion (24 percent) backed by assets in the United Kingdom, and the remainder by assets in other countries. About 98 percent of the assets in the portfolio were rated Aaa and the remainder was not rated.

On the liabilities side, Solitaire issued asset-backed commercial paper (ABCP) worth US$20.8 billion. US$14.1 billion (68%) of commercial paper was issued in the United States and the remaining US$6.7 billion (32%) was issued in Europe. The maturity structure and yield of the commercial paper is not available, but market data suggests that commercial paper has a median maturity of 30 days and the average yield is a few basis points above the federal funds rate. The conduit does not publish data on equity, but for a conduit of its size the estimated equity is US$62 million, which equals 0.3 percent of total conduit assets.

The main risks associated with Solitaire remain with HSBC and other financial institutions. HSBC provides a liquidity guarantee to repurchase nondefaulted assets if Solitaire fails to roll over commercial paper (liquidity enhancement). The definition of default is not available, but the industry standard is that assets are considered defaulted if they are downgraded below investment grade. With respect to the value of the assets, the conduit is insured against credit losses of up to US$185 million (credit enhancement). The identity of the insurers is not available but accompanying documentation suggests that the credit insurance was provided jointly by HSBC and bond insurer Ambac.

draw on credit enhancement to cover credit losses. In addition, commercial paper has very short maturities such that CP investors can react relatively quickly to changes in the value of conduit assets. If CP investors believe that the risk of nonrepayment increases, they simply do not roll over maturing commercial paper. In this case, the conduit typically either draws on its liquidity and credit enhancement (i.e., banks take assets on their balance sheet) or contracts additional liquidity or credit enhancement from banks. Only if both options fail does the conduit default, and CP investors then satisfy their claims from the proceeds of selling conduit assets.

In monitoring conduits, CP investors often rely on rating agencies. Almost all CP issued by conduits has the highest Prime 1 rating by at least two rating agencies. When a conduit is set up, rating agencies work with the conduit administrator to ensure that the conduit has enough liquidity and credit enhancement to satisfy the criteria for the highest rating. As market conditions worsened throughout the recent crisis and CP investors became unwilling to roll over maturing CP, ratings agencies put pressure on conduits to increase liquidity and credit enhancement or face downgrades otherwise. As discussed later, the conduits most under pressure were the ones with the least amount of liquidity and credit enhancement.

The economic rationale for setting up conduits has always been to reduce capital requirements imposed by bank regulation, constituting a classic example of financial innovation that is pioneered by banks to unwind a constraining regulation. If high-quality assets are held on balance sheets, Basel I capital regulation requires banks to hold up to 8 percent of asset values as equity capital, the exact capital required being based on the assets' risk weight. From the bank's perspective, equity capital is costly to issue and also lowers effective leverage and risk taking, and thus banks pursue a variety of strategies to reduce regulatory capital requirements. Conduits are one way to economize on equity capital, because banks are not required to hold equity capital for conduit assets but instead need to hold equity against liquidity and credit enhancement provided to conduits. However, capital requirements for liquidity enhancement are only 0.8 percent of asset value—that is, in the best case just *one-tenth* of the requirement. Capital requirements for credit enhancement are somewhat larger but sufficiently low such that banks have lower total capital requirements for financing high-quality assets via conduits relative to holding them on bank balance sheets. The recent Basel II capital regulation reduces some of the difference in capital requirements between on-balance-sheet and off-balance-sheet financing but does not completely eliminate it.

As a result of this capital regulation, many commercial banks have set up conduits. Figure 2.1 plots total asset-backed commercial paper outstanding from January 2006 to December 2008. Before the recent crisis, total commercial paper issued in the United States grew from US$866 billion in January 2006 to US$1,222 billion in August 2007. On August 9, 2007, BNP Paribas suspended the calculation of the net asset value of three money market funds that had invested in asset-backed commercial paper. The effect on the markets was catastrophic. It caused the asset-backed commercial paper market to effectively freeze. The resulting rollover risk that was imposed on a

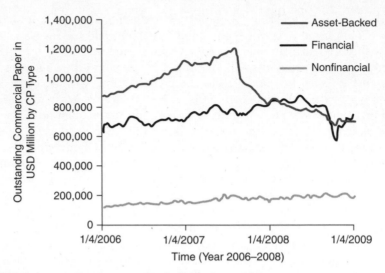

FIGURE 2.1   Decline in Asset-Backed Commercial Paper

Note: Data does not include euro ABCP; includes ABCP issued by CDOs.
Source: Federal Reserve Board.

large number of ABCP conduits and SIVs, which now would have had to be taken back on bank balance sheets due to recourse, caused interbank lending rates to skyrocket as well. There were two aspects that led to such a sharp effect: first, the large extent to which banks had parked such contingent liabilities in the shadow banking world of conduits and SIVs, and second, the opaqueness of these structures, which meant banks were themselves unsure of who would be hit by what kind of losses if the ABCP market experienced permanent rollover risk. As a result of the crisis, asset-backed commercial paper dropped to US$797 billion by January 2008 and only stabilized after banks increased explicit recourse to bank balance sheets by providing further credit enhancement. On September 17, Lehman went bankrupt and as a result many conduits again experienced difficulties issuing commercial paper. The Federal Reserve devised several policies in response to stabilize the market. On September 18, the Federal Reserve guaranteed investment in money market mutual funds, which are the main investors in asset-backed commercial paper. On October 27, the Federal Reserve started a new liquidity facility that directly purchases asset-backed commercial paper.

The impact on banks of this decline in asset-backed commercial paper depends on the structure of the liquidity and credit enhancement provided to conduits. On this front, there are, broadly speaking, three types of conduits to consider. The first type is *fully supported* conduits, which have liquidity enhancement that covers the entire amount of commercial paper outstanding and credit enhancement that covers all assets in the conduit. Hence, fully supported conduits have *full recourse* to the bank balance sheet. In January 2007, there were 79 fully supported conduits with total commercial paper outstanding of US$245 billion or 19.9 percent of total ABCP. To the best of our knowledge, there has not been a single fully supported conduit that has declared bankruptcy throughout the economic crisis. Either fully supported conduits have continued to issue commercial paper or administrators have taken back their assets on the bank balance sheets.

The second type is *partially supported* conduits, which have liquidity enhancement that covers the entire commercial paper outstanding and partial credit enhancement that covers a fixed proportion of the assets. The extent of partial credit enhancement depends on the underlying assets and averages about 7 to 10 percent of total assets. In addition, many assets have asset-specific credit enhancement in the form of either overcollateralization or credit insurance. Hence, if conduit assets experience a sudden decline in credit losses exceeding total credit enhancement, it is possible that the conduit does not have enough resources to repay commercial paper investors. In January 2007, there were 234 partially supported programs with total commercial paper outstanding of US$889 billion or 72.4 percent of total ABCP. To the best of our knowledge, only four partially supported conduits have declared bankruptcy throughout the economic crisis and were unable to fully repay their investors. Instead, conduit administrators of partially supported conduits usually either take back assets onto bank balance sheets or extend balance sheet recourse by strengthening credit enhancement. Either way, the partially supported conduits effectively have close to full recourse to bank balance sheets. Box 2.2 illustrates this point through the recourse implementation on Grampian Funding, a large conduit set up by Bank of Scotland (HBOS).

The third type is *structured investment vehicles* (SIVs), which have only partial liquidity and credit enhancement. The extent of liquidity and credit enhancement varies depending on the underlying assets and averages about a quarter of assets. Commercial paper investors have recourse to bank balance sheets up to the amount of partial enhancement. In order to offset the lower amount of liquidity and credit enhancement, SIVs typically issue other liabilities such as medium-term notes (MTNs) and subordinated capital notes. The amount of CP is usually roughly equivalent to the amount of liquidity enhancement. In January 2007, there were 55 SIVs with total commercial paper outstanding of US$93 billion or 7.4 percent of total asset-backed commercial paper. In contrast to other conduits, CP outstanding is significantly smaller than total conduit assets

BOX 2.2   GRAMPIAN FUNDING

Grampian Funding is a large conduit administered by the Bank of Scotland (HBOS) with total commercial paper outstanding of US$27 billion in January 2007. HBOS provides liquidity support for 100 percent of CP outstanding. In February 2008, Grampian announced that it had added Repo Facilities with HBOS to provide further liquidity support. In June 2008, Grampian announced that HBOS increased credit enhancement from US$1.2 billion to US$4 billion. Importantly, throughout the crises at least 98.6 percent of assets held by Grampian were rated A3 or higher. As long as assets are rated above investment grade, HBOS is required to provide liquidity support, which means that throughout the crisis CP investors had full recourse to the balance sheet of HBOS. However, the average credit quality of conduit assets deteriorated over time and Grampian had to reduce its asset holdings. It is likely that Grampian had difficulties issuing CP and HBOS therefore decided to take some assets back on its balance sheet, while extending more credit enhancement for the remaining assets in the conduit. Hence, Grampian's liquidity and credit enhancement were effectively sufficient such that CP investors had full recourse to the balance sheet of HBOS throughout the crisis.

because of other liabilities such as MTNs and subordinated capital notes. In January 2007, total conduit assets were about US$400 billion.

SIVs were heavily affected by the economic crisis. By June 2008, either SIVs had defaulted, the administrator had taken assets back on the balance sheet, or the administrator was in the process of restructuring the assets. Importantly, even though SIVs had only partial enhancement, the vast majority of assets in SIVs were taken back on the bank balance sheets. This result is striking since the partial enhancement was structured in order to limit bank exposure to liquidity and credit risk. Instead, it appears that partial enhancement was sufficient to force banks to take back conduit assets. Hence, even SIVs that were structured to limit the impact on banks effectively provided recourse to bank balance sheets (a prime example being over $50 billion of such investments taken back by Citigroup on its balance sheet during the crisis).

In short, effectively all conduits have recourse to the bank balance sheet. Importantly, limitations on liquidity and credit enhancement were largely ineffective in the sense that across all conduit structures banks were forced

TABLE 2.1 Ten Largest Conduit Administrators by Size ($ Amounts in Billions)

	Conduits		Administrator			
	#	CP	Assets	Equity	CP/Asset	CP/Equity
Citibank	23	$93	$1,884	$120	4.9%	77.4%
ABN Amro	9	69	1,000	34	5.3	201.1
Bank of America	12	46	1,464	136	3.1	33.7
HBOS	2	44	1,160	42	3.8	105.6
JPMorgan Chase	9	42	1,352	116	3.1	36.1
HSBC	6	39	1,861	123	2.1	32.1
Société Générale	7	39	1,260	44	3.1	87.2
Deutsche Bank	14	38	1,483	44	2.6	87.8
Barclays	3	33	1,957	54	1.7	61.5
WestLB	8	30	376	9	8.0	336.6

Notes: January 2007, administrator merged for all subsidiaries associated with bank administrator, not necessarily liquidity/credit risk provider. Bank variables from Bankscope; selected largest bank with banking groups (usually bank holding company), dropped nonbanks and corporates.

to take back assets or to extend more recourse to bank balance sheets by strengthening credit enhancement. Either way, commercial paper investors benefited from extensive recourse to bank balance sheets.

To assess the impact of bank balance sheet recourse on banks, Table 2.1 provides statistics on conduit administrators. The identity of the conduit administrator is a good proxy for the financial institution that provides liquidity and credit enhancement to the conduit. The table lists the identity of the 10 largest conduit administrators measured by total CP outstanding as of January 2007. The list is restricted to conduit administrators that are banks, because nonbank administrators lack the financial strength to support a conduit and purchase liquidity and credit enhancement from banks (in January 2007, 8 out of the 10 largest administrators were banks).

As shown in Figure 2.2, banks with more exposure to ABCP conduits prior to August 2007 experienced larger declines in share prices after the crisis. ABCP exposure is measured as the ratio of total ABCP of bank-administered conduits relative to total bank equity prior to August 2007. For example, this ratio is less than 40 percent on average for JPMorgan Chase, Bank of America, and HSBC (banks that have weathered the crisis substantially better than most), compared to moderately high ratios for ING Bank, Barclays, and KBC Bank and very high ratios for Citigroup, HBOS, and Fortis. Put simply, these latter banks had effectively taken on substantial

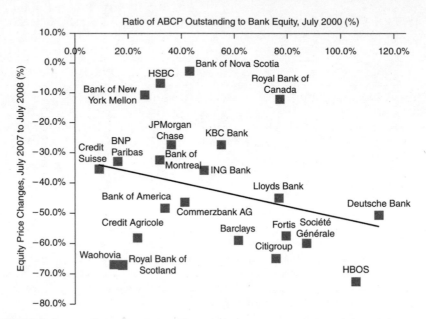

FIGURE 2.2   Bank Equity Price Change and Exposure to ABCP Conduits

Source: Authors' own calculations based on Moody's, Bankscope, and Bloomberg data. Sample is restricted to 35 largest bank administrators of ABCP conduits for which share price and balance sheet data are available. Exposure is measured as the ratio of total bank-sponsored ABCP over bank equity; banks with exposure of more than 200 percent are excluded (those are almost all German Landesbanken). Change in share prices is measured as the relative change from July 2007 to July 2008.

economic leverage through these conduits, as the contingency that would trigger a recourse to their balance sheets was far more likely given the CP/equity ratio of their conduits; this leverage was, however, *not* reflected in their regulatory leverage or risk-weighted assets since the conduits were highly rated and recourse features or capital structure of conduits had not received careful attention until the crisis.

2.3 BANK BALANCE SHEETS AND RISK-WEIGHTED ASSETS

Figure 2.3 shows the trend in size of assets of the top 10 publicly traded banks relative to the trend in the size of their *risk-weighted assets* where the risk weights are based on those employed by the Basel capital requirements.

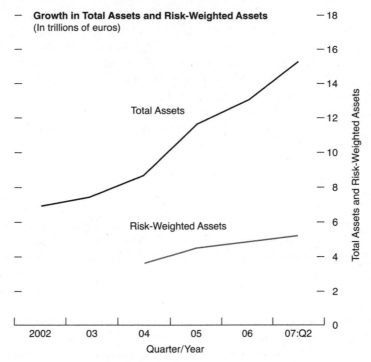

FIGURE 2.3   Trends in Bank Assets, Nature of Assets, and Leverage

Source: International Monetary Fund (2008).

Briefly, most banks in the United States employ Basel I weights to comply with capital adequacy requirements, whereas European banks employ Basel II schemes. While the distinction between the two will become clearer later on, for now risk-weighted assets can simply be understood as a regulatory assessment of the risk of bank assets. What Figure 2.3 shows is that while bank balance sheets grew twofold between 2004 and 2007 Q2, the regulatory assessment of risk-weighted assets grew at a far more sluggish pace. Put another way, banks were deemed by regulatory assessment to have been investing in relatively safer assets over this period.

The widening gap between total assets and risk-weighted assets reflects the expansion of the share of assets that carried low risk weights according to the Basel bank regulation. Two key factors contributed to the widening gap. First, banks increased their trading and investment activities (e.g., asset-backed securities, hedging) over this period. The capital weights of these instruments were typically lower than loans because the instruments were typically highly rated by a rating agency.

Second, under the International Financial Reporting Standards (IFRS) some banks started to consolidate a portion of their exposure to asset-backed commercial paper conduits. Since banks continued to compute capital requirements as if the assets were off-balance-sheet, the consolidation resulted in a much larger increase in total assets relative to risk-weighted assets. Overall, the regulatory requirements under both Basel I and Basel II regulation did not constrain this asset growth. In fact, according to standard bank capital ratios most banks appeared well-capitalized. The banks showed on average a Tier 1 capital to risk-weighted assets ratio of 7 to 9 percent, which is about twice as large as the regulatory minimum of 4 percent (International Monetary Fund 2008).

How do we know that these trends reflected regulatory arbitrage? This is based on evidence in Figure 2.4. Consider ranking banks by their ratio of total assets to risk-weighted assets. Risk weights are close to one for the relatively risky assets like corporate loans and close to zero for safer holdings such as government mortgages and mortgage-backed assets, and short-term lines of credit provided for liquidity enhancement to firms and other borrowers (including banks' own conduits and SIVs, as we will see shortly). Thus, a *high* ratio of total assets to risk-weighted assets should signal the bank as being relatively *safe*. Importantly, this is true only providing that the risk weights are in fact suitable for the true risk of different investments.

Figure 2.4 plots the share price reaction of different banks during the period July 2007 to March 2008 as a function of the ratio of total assets to

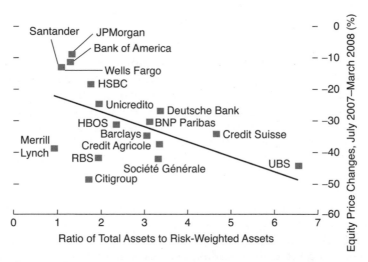

FIGURE 2.4   Bank Stock Performance and Regulatory Leverage

Source: International Monetary Fund (2008).

risk-weighted assets. Alas, somewhat disturbingly for Basel capital requirements, the relationship is sharply negative. Banks such as JPMorgan Chase,
Bank of America, Santander, and Wells Fargo that emerged ex post to be the
stronger banks had ratios close to one, whereas banks that have performed
the worst (most notably UBS) had the highest ratios.

What explains the relationship between the decline in share price and
the extent of regulatory arbitrage via ABCP exposure or investments in
highly rated securities? One explanation is that this was simply a bad draw
and that relatively safer assets turned out to suffer the biggest losses. In this
view of the world, JPMorgan and the like were indeed the riskier banks but
ex post turned out to be lucky. The second explanation, the one that we
find is supported by the evidence presented so far, is that the Basel capital
requirements were simply gamed by banks that had high ratios of total assets
to risk-weighted assets. They were indeed much less safe than their capital
requirements showed them to be, ended up holding less capital than was
suitable for their true risk profile, and therefore suffered the most during
the crisis.

In fact, from the perspective of the aggregate risk of the banking system, there was little risk transfer to investors outside the banking system.
Table 2.2 shows that of all the AAA-rated asset-backed securities created
in the process of risk transfer, as much as 30 percent was simply parceled
out by banks to each other; about 20 percent was sitting in conduits and
SIVs (but given the recourse features, this belonged to banks for most part
as well); and the rest was distributed among other market participants,
mainly money market funds, hedge funds, and credit funds. The picture that
emerges is thus the following: What started as pure regulatory arbitrage
and gave banks substantial regulatory capital relief became over time banks'

TABLE 2.2 Asset-Backed Securities'
Exposure Concentrations

Type of Institution	% Buyer of AAA ABS
Banks	30%
Conduits	12
SIVs	8
Hedge Funds	2
Money Market Funds	26
Credit Funds	17
Others	5

Source: Financial Times, July 1, 2008.

preferred investment strategy. As long as asset prices (mainly house prices) kept rising, the equity cushion of risk transfer vehicles remained uneroded or even expanded, and banks, whose capital budgeting has become increasingly short-term in nature,[3] kept generating additional profits with the freed-up capital. The true risk of this business strategy manifested itself when the housing bubble burst—and the rest is well known.

Why did such risk-taking remain unfettered? While there are multiple reasons, two of them are more critical than others. First, as explained earlier, there was a regulatory failure in that Basel capital requirements were effectively gamed and the gravity of this arbitrage activity was simply not recognized by policy makers. This is important because in a world with deposit guarantees and other implicit subsidies, market discipline imposed by bank runs is effectively outsourced to regulatory supervision and intelligence. When that fails, levered institutions can undertake value-destroying, risky strategies.

Second, in our opinion, regulatory assessment of risks requires a conceptual reorientation. Thus far, Basel requirements have aimed for charging a tax for the total risk of an asset. A moment of reflection reveals that what regulators ought to care about is the aggregate risk contribution of an asset (or bank balance sheet, more broadly). The AAA-rated risk transfer assets and vehicles were a way of betting on aggregate risk. In academic parlance, these are now referred to as "economic catastrophe bonds":[4] They are low in risk overall, but their risk is aggregate in nature; in fact, it arises only in aggregate crashes. It is attractive for banks to undertake such assets since during aggregate or systemic stress, when their risks materialize, banks are explicitly or implicitly guaranteed: there are "too big to fail" guarantees in place, and even if they are not explicit, it is difficult for reasons of political economy as well as efficiency not to bail out the banking sector in such times.

2.4 WAYS TO COUNTER REGULATORY ARBITRAGE AND AGGREGATE RISK SHIFTING

We discuss elsewhere in this book[5] how banks should be charged for the aggregate risk they take on based on their aggregate risk exposure, which would depend on their size, leverage, as well as concentration of exposures. Before we conclude, we list our policy recommendations that would help minimize the risk of regulatory arbitrage.

The overall principle is simple: Regulation should not be narrowly focused on a single ratio from the bank balance sheet such as capital requirement. An analyst, investing private money, would rarely assess the health of an institution based on just one number from the balance sheet. It would be more prudent for regulators to regularly assess individual and collective bank health based on a variety of different aspects of their balance sheets, and indeed based on market indicators. Additional ratios to examine would be loans-to-deposits ratio, deposits-to-assets ratio, liquidity-to-assets ratio (measured only through stress-time liquidity, that is, Treasuries and OECD government bonds), and so on. As we illustrated earlier, the recent regulatory arbitrage produced reductions not only in risk weights but also in deposits-to-assets ratios and gave rise to relatively flat loans-to-deposits ratios. This combination flags a warning signal that warrants further scrutiny of activities that led to it. In terms of market indicators, the recent evidence has shown that credit default swap fees for financials as well as financial commercial paper spreads had been experiencing a steady rise through most of early 2007. These are valuable market indicators that depositors, in the absence of government insurance, would rely on to impose discipline on banks. Regulators need to effectively play the role of such market discipline and thus avoid its narrow, box-ticking implementation. Banks clearly played the leverage game well, at significant costs to the economy and in some cases even to themselves. It is time for policy to rethink and reinvent.

NOTES

1. For empirical evidence on the decrease in asset quality during credit booms, see Dell'Ariccia, Igan, and Laeven (2008); Keys, Mukherjee, Seru, and Vig (2008); Mian and Sufi (forthcoming); and Demyanyk and Van Hemert (forthcoming).
2. Liquidity enhancement is similar to backup credit lines provided to corporations that issue unsecured commercial paper.
3. See Chapter 7, "Corporate Governance in the Modern Financial Sector."
4. See the discussions in Chapter 1, "Mortgage Origination and Securitization in the Financial Crisis"; Chapter 8, "Rethinking Compensation in Financial Firms"; and Coval, Jurek, and Stafford (forthcoming).
5. See Chapter 13, "Regulating Systemic Risk."

REFERENCES

Coval, Joshua, Jakub Jurek, and Erik Stafford. Forthcoming. Economic catastrophe bonds. *American Economic Review*.

Dell'Ariccia, Giovanni, Deniz Igan, and Luc Laeven. 2008. Credit booms and lending standards: Evidence from the subprime mortgage market. Working Paper 08/106, International Monetary Fund.

Demyanyk, Yuliya, and Otto Van Hemert. Forthcoming. Understanding the sub-prime mortgage crisis. *Review of Financial Studies*.

Keys, Benjamin, Tanmoy Mukherjee, Amit Seru, and Vikrant Vig. 2008. Did securitization lead to lax screening? Evidence from subprime loans. EFA 2008 Athens Meetings Paper.

International Monetary Fund. 2008. International Monetary Fund Global Financial Stability Report (April).

Mian, Atif, and Amir Sufi. Forthcoming. The consequences of mortgage credit expansion: Evidence from the 2007 mortgage default crisis. *Quarterly Journal of Economics*.

CHAPTER 3

The Rating Agencies

Is Regulation the Answer?

Matthew Richardson and Lawrence J. White

3.1 BACKGROUND

The three major credit rating agencies in the United States—Moody's, Standard & Poor's, and Fitch—played a central role in the recent housing bubble and then in the subprime mortgage debacle of 2007–2008. The successful sale of the mortgage-related debt securities that had subprime residential mortgages and other debt obligations as their underlying collateral depended crucially on these agencies' initial ratings on these securities. When house prices ceased rising and began to decline, these initial ratings proved to be excessively optimistic—especially for the mortgages that were originated in 2005 and 2006—and the mortgage bonds collapsed, bringing the rest of the U.S. financial sector crashing down as well. As a consequence of this central role, a significant amount of policy attention has recently focused on the rating agencies and whether changes in regulation could forestall such behavior in the future.

Credit rating agencies are firms that offer judgments about the creditworthiness of bonds—specifically, their likelihood of default—that have been issued by various kinds of entities, such as corporations, governments, and (most recently) securitizers of mortgages and other debt obligations.[1] Those judgments come in the form of ratings, which are usually a letter grade. The best-known scale is that used by Standard & Poor's and some other rating agencies: AAA, AA, A, BBB, BB, and so forth (with pluses and minuses, as well).[2]

The lenders in credit markets, including investors in bonds, are always trying to ascertain the creditworthiness of borrowers. Credit rating agencies are one potential source of such information for bond investors—but they are far from the only potential source. Nevertheless, because of some important quirks of financial regulatory history, the rating agencies have acquired a central position in the market for information about the creditworthiness of bonds. An understanding of that history is crucial for understanding how the credit rating agencies attained such a central role.

In 1909 John Moody offered the first publicly available rating on corporate bonds.[3] Poor's Publishing Co. followed in 1916; the Standard Statistics Co. began issuing ratings in 1922.[4] The Fitch Publishing Co. began its ratings in 1924.[5] The standard business model for these rating agencies was that they sold their ratings to investors (i.e., an "investor pays" model).

In the 1930s bank regulators began to require that banks' bond investment decisions should heed the agencies' ratings on those bonds. Most important, in 1936 the Office of the Comptroller of the Currency (OCC), the regulator of nationally chartered banks, required that the bonds held by banks must be "investment grade,"[6] as determined by the rating agencies.[7] This rule is still in place today.

During the next few decades, the 50 state insurance regulators began to link the capital requirements of insurance companies to the ratings on the bonds that the companies held in their portfolios.

Notice that these regulatory requirements were, in essence, an outsourcing—a delegation—of the regulators' safety judgments to a group of third-party rating firms. Note also that this outsourcing greatly enhanced the rating agencies' role in the bond markets, since major participants in the bond markets—banks and insurance companies—were forced to heed their ratings; and because these major participants were required to heed these particular ratings, other bond market participants would want to know these agencies' ratings as well.

In the early 1970s the standard business model of the rating agencies changed from the "investor pays" model that had been in place since 1909 to an "issuer pays" model, whereby the issuer pays fees to the rating agency for the rating.[8]

In 1975 the Securities and Exchange Commission (SEC) decided that it wanted broker-dealers to maintain adequate capital levels and that, like the other financial regulators' earlier requirements, those capital levels should be geared to the ratings on the bonds in the broker-dealers' portfolios. The SEC, however, realized that there had never been a clear statement by regulators as to which credit rating agencies' ratings should be heeded. So as to forestall the possibility that a bogus rating agency's ratings might be used for regulatory purposes, the SEC established (as part of its broker-dealer capital requirements) a wholly new regulatory category—nationally recognized statistical rating organization (NRSRO)—and immediately grandfathered Moody's, S&P, and Fitch into the category. Other financial regulators soon adopted the NRSRO category as applicable to their requirements with respect to bond ratings and their regulated financial institutions.[9]

Once again the role of the credit rating agencies in the bond markets was enhanced.

Over the next 25 years the SEC designated only four more firms as NRSROs.[10] But mergers among the entrants and with Fitch caused the number of NRSROs at year-end 2000 to decline to the original three. It was clear that the SEC had created a barrier to entry into the credit rating business, since the NRSRO designation was crucial for a credit rater to gain widespread attention by bond market participants.

In the wake of the Enron bankruptcy in November 2001, the media discovered that the three NRSROs had maintained investment grade ratings on Enron's debt until five days before the bankruptcy. Congressional hearings followed, yielding a more widespread recognition of the NRSRO process than had generally been true before then. As part of the Sarbanes-Oxley Act of 2002, the SEC was required to issue a report on the credit rating industry. It duly did so, but the report simply raised a series of questions rather than addressing the issues of the SEC's barriers to entry or the enhanced role of the credit rating agencies in the bond markets that the financial regulators since the 1930s had fostered and that the SEC's NRSRO framework had strengthened.

In early 2003 the SEC designated a fourth NRSRO (Dominion Bond Rating Services, a Canadian firm), and in early 2005 it designated a fifth NRSRO (A.M. Best, a specialist on insurance companies' obligations). Having become impatient with the SEC's sluggishness and opacity in NRSRO designations, Congress passed the Credit Rating Agency Reform Act (CRARA), which was signed into law in September 2006. The Act specifically instructed the SEC to cease being a barrier to entry, specified the criteria that the SEC should use in designating new NRSROs, insisted on transparency in the designation process, and provided the SEC with some limited abilities to oversee the incumbent NRSROs—but specifically forbade the SEC from influencing the ratings or the business models of the industry.

Since the passage of the legislation, the SEC has designated five additional NRSROs—two Japanese rating firms (Japan Credit Rating Agency, and Rating and Information, Inc.) and three smaller U.S.-based firms (Egan-Jones, Lace Financial, and Realpoint)—so that the total number of NRSROs currently is 10. Table 3.1 provides a full list of the NRSROs and their dates of formation.

TABLE 3.1 Current Nationally Recognized Statistical Rating Organizations (NRSROs) and Their Year of Designation by the Securities and Exchange Commission (SEC)

Current NRSROs	Year of Designation
Moody's	1975
Standard & Poor's	1975
Fitch	1975
Dominion Bond Rating Services	2003
A.M. Best	2005
Japan Credit Rating Agency	2007
Rating and Information, Inc.	2007
Egan-Jones	2007
Lace Financial	2008
Realpoint	2008

Source: White (2006), SEC press releases.

3.2 WHAT IS THE PROBLEM?

As the history just recounted indicates, financial regulation (starting in the 1930s) has mandated that the rating agencies be the central source of information about the creditworthiness of bonds in the U.S. financial markets. Reinforcing this centrality was the SEC's creation of the NRSRO category in 1975 and the SEC's subsequent protective entry barrier around the incumbent NRSROs, which effectively ensured the dominance of Moody's, S&P, and Fitch.[11] Finally, the industry's change to the "issuer pays" business model in the early 1970s[12] meant that potential problems of conflicts of interest were sure to arise.

The potential conflict of interest in the "issuer pays" model typically arises whenever an issuer has alternative NRSROs to which it can turn. Thus if a bond issuer believes that rating agency X is going to give its bonds a less favorable rating than will rating agency Y (and that bond buyers will attach equal credibility to the ratings of both raters), then the issuer will bring its bond rating business to the latter rating firm; in turn, the former rating firm will have an incentive to loosen its rating standards so as to re-attract issuers.[13] Moreover, even without this trolling for higher ratings, there is not much market accountability for the NRSROs. Their incentives to compete, and therefore to provide the best and most comprehensive analysis (which is costly to them), are subdued. In other words, suppose the rating agencies were producing rudimentary and low-quality analysis of tranches of subprime securitized mortgage pools (i.e., collateralized debt obligations

[CDOs]). Was there an incentive for one of the agencies to deviate, invest in talent, and improve the analysis? It is not clear that there was.

That the rating agencies were thrust by financial regulation into the center of the bond markets tended to exacerbate this problem. If a bond purchaser (such as a bank) is required to heed the ratings of NRSROs, then its incentive to search out other sources of information about the creditworthiness of bonds is greatly diminished. Further, if (subsequent to issuance) the bond markets realize that the rating offered by a NRSRO is too optimistic, which causes the markets to reprice the bond downward and thus increase its yield, then a bank that wishes to increase its risk profile can invest in that higher-yielding (but riskier) bond but can still appear to be adhering to its regulator's safety standards because of the NRSRO's (excessively optimistic) rating.

Though this problem was present in the rating agency business from the early 1970s onward, the relative transparency of the companies and governments being rated and the rating agencies' regard for their long-run reputations apparently served to keep the problem in check. The complexity and opaqueness of the mortgage-related securities, however, created new opportunities and irresistible temptations.[14] Further, the rating agencies were much more involved in the creation of these mortgage-related securities, since it was the agencies' decisions as to what kinds of mortgages and other collateral would earn what levels of ratings for what sizes of tranches of these securities that determined the levels of profitability of these securitizations.

In order to understand this better, consider the typical CDO structure shown in Figure 3.1.

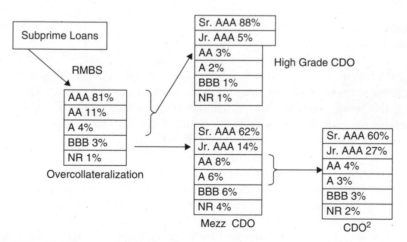

FIGURE 3.1 The Securitization Process of Subprime Mortgage Loans
Source: UBS (2007), Gorton (2008).

Here a portfolio of subprime mortgages is pooled into a residential mortgage-backed security (RMBS). The RMBS has five tranches; the priority of the tranches is based on seniority in terms of allocating default losses, ranging from the most protected tranche, AAA, down to the least protected one, BBB. At each point in the structure, the rating agency would determine the rating based on their assessment of each loan's default probability and, in theory, the correlation across defaults. Note that the top 96 percent of the cash flows go to a high grade CDO that splits into six tranches of different rating classes, while the bottom 3 percent goes toward a mezzanine CDO, which in turn splits into six classes of different priorities. But it doesn't stop there. The middle 14 percent of this mezzanine CDO is structured into another CDO that again is broken into six classes, the top 60 percent of which is the senior AAA tranche. The game was to try to generate as many AAA-rated securities as possible.

Theoretically, the tranches of the original RMBS are simply combinations of options on default losses where the strike rates are determined by the priority claims. Because these options are quite sensitive to default correlations, the tranches are difficult, but not impossible, to value. Once these claims, however, get restructured into additional CDOs, the problem becomes one of compound options (i.e., options on options) and huge amounts of leverage. It is well known and easy to show that these compound options are much more sensitive to the underlying model's assumptions. That is, model misspecification is arguably at least as important as actual realizations of defaults. Given the meaning of an AAA rating, both from a regulatory point of view as well as an investor's, it is surprising that the rating agencies would even attempt to rate the mezzanine CDOs and CDO^2s. That the rating agencies became a scapegoat for the financial crisis is therefore not necessarily undeserved.

There is a second pervasive phenomenon of the major credit rating agencies: their delays in adjusting their ratings to reflect the changed financial circumstances of the rated security or its issuer. It has been widely observed that the rating agencies tend to change their ratings only after the bond markets have already recognized the changed circumstances, especially with respect to downward adjustments (the Enron ratings that were mentioned earlier are poster children for this phenomenon).

The same conflicts—the agencies' fears of alienating issuers, who may not reengage the agency for the issuer's next set of bonds—may be part of the story. But there's at least one more component: The rating agencies have traditionally professed to be "rating through the cycle"—that is, they don't try to provide a minute-by-minute assessment but instead offer a longer-term view that looks past cyclical variations.[15] In this context, a rating agency will be slow to identify a secular trend, since there will always be a delay in perceiving that any particular movement isn't just the initial part of a reversible cycle but instead is a sustained movement (downward or upward).

In the context of the "issuer pays" model, it would appear that a monopoly rating structure would be better than a competitive structure, since it is the availability of competitive alternatives that allows the issuer to play off one rater against another.[16] However, even within a monopoly construct, the issuer would still have an incentive to tempt the rating agency with a higher fee if the agency would deliver a more favorable rating. Also, a monopoly construct would have the usual problems of rent extraction (especially since issuers need ratings in order to get their bonds into financial institutions' portfolios), as well as the problem of incentives for the monopoly rating agency to maintain the accuracy of ratings or to develop and implement new ideas with respect to ratings methodologies or technologies.

In their defense of their "issuer pays" model, the major rating agencies have argued (e.g., in congressional hearings) that the "investor pays" model also has potential conflicts. At the time of issuance, investors would prefer lower ratings (since they will then receive higher yields), as would the short sellers of any other security of the issuing company. At the time of possible subsequent changes in a security's rating, investors who already hold the bonds would favor upgrades and disfavor downgrades, while short sellers would prefer the opposite. Nevertheless, these potential conflicts seem much less severe than those for the "issuer pays" model.

The major credit rating agencies also point out that the "issuer pays" model has the advantage of rapid dissemination of the rating information, whereas the "investor pays" model would require some lag in the general dissemination of an agency's ratings. However, the advantages of speedy dissemination are muted if the accuracy of those ratings is compromised.

3.3 PRINCIPLES AND REGULATION PROPOSALS

The appropriate public policy actions depend importantly on what one perceives as the fundamental problem vis-à-vis the credit rating agencies and also on one's confidence in the ability of regulators to devise effective remedies. If the problem is perceived to be the "issuer pays" business model and one has confidence in the ability of the SEC to craft sensible remedial regulations, then the appropriate course of action might be more regulation. However, if the problem is perceived to be the regulatory actions that required that a small set of credit rating agencies be placed at the center of the bond markets, then the appropriate course of action may be a rolling back of those regulations that mandated the prominence of these rating agencies.

Fixing the Issuer Pay Model

The discussion in Section 3.2 argued that the potential conflict of the "issuer pays" model is that it leads to an overestimate of a firm's or a structured product's rating and, perhaps less nefariously, lower-quality work. If the "issuer pays" model is considered to be the problem and one has confidence in the SEC's ability to craft remedial regulations, then the appropriate course of action is more regulation.[17] For example, in December 2008, the SEC instituted a number of new rules addressing conflict of interest prohibitions, including not being able to rate debt they helped structure, not allowing analysts to be involved in fee negotiations, and not being able to receive gifts exceeding $25 from the firms they are rating. Additional rules address disclosure and documentation of the ratings and how they were constructed. The new rules did not, however, regulate the fees paid by issuers to the rating agencies, or even ban the payment of fees by issuers to the rating agencies, which would effectively ban the "issuer pays" model.[18]

It is not clear that the regulation to date gets at the heart of the problem. One could imagine more intrusive regulation, but it seems inevitable that such regulation would reduce the flexibility of the rating industry and could discourage innovation and creativity in business models and in developing better ways of assessing the default probabilities of bonds.

Competition among rating agencies should be a good thing, leading to innovation and higher-quality research. There is, however, a problem with putting this competition into practice. On the one hand, in the "issuer pays" model, the competition can lead to inflated ratings because the company chooses who should rate its securities. On the other hand, in the "investor pays" model where incentives should be aligned, there is a free rider problem, and it is not clear how the free market can solve it.

To correct the competition problem within the "issuer pays" model, the SEC could place limits on the competition that occurs among the rating agencies. For example, it could create a centralized rating agency that gets paid by the firms it rates, but is not beholden to them. Since the rating agency is the only game in town, the firm would pay some designated fee to the agency, the agency would rate the bond or structured debt product, and the investor could then act on that information. Of course, the lack of competition would stifle innovation, and it is not clear what the path would be to high-quality research.

An alternative structure that appears more promising would be for the SEC to create a department that houses a centralized clearing platform for rating agencies. It would work as follows: First, a company that would like some debt rated goes to the centralized clearing platform. Depending on the attributes of the security (i.e., type of debt, complexity of firm and issue, whether other debt outstanding is already rated, etc.), there would be a flat fee. Second, the centralized clearing platform chooses, from a sample of approved rating agencies, which agency will rate the debt. While this choice could be random, a more systematic choice process could enhance competition. The choice would be based on the agency's experience at rating this type of debt, some historical perspective on how well the agency rates this type of debt relative to other rating agencies, past audits of the rating agency's quality, and so forth. Third, for the fixed fee, the rating agency would then go ahead and rate the debt.

This model has several advantages: First, because the issuer still pays, the free rider problem of the "investor pays" system is avoided. Second, because the agency is chosen by the regulating body, there is no conflict of interest with the firm it is rating. Third, because this choice can be based on some degree of excellence, it provides the rating agency with incentives to invest resources, innovate, and perform high-quality work. The problem, of course, is that one has to have faith that the regulator (i.e., the centralized platform) can adequately choose the rating agency. There will be many Type I and II errors made, as it might take time for poor rating agencies to be identified and occasionally good rating agencies to be dropped.

Deregulation of the NRSROs

Recall that it is financial regulation—by bank regulators, insurance company regulators, pension fund regulators, and the SEC—that thrust the rating agencies into the center of the bond markets, by requiring that the rating agencies be the source of the bond markets' information on creditworthiness. The SEC's NRSRO construct specified which particular rating agencies should be the focus of the bond markets' attention; and the SEC's use of the NRSRO category as a barrier to entry into the bond rating business forced the bond market participants to heed the ratings of only a few—in essence, three—major rating agencies.

It should not be surprising that, with this secure market, the three major rating agencies could grow complacent and sloppy; and the potential conflicts of the "issuer pays" model that all three had adopted surely didn't help matters. Although—thanks to pressures from Congress and then the passage of the CRARA in 2006—the SEC has ceased being a barrier to entry and there are now 10 NRSROs rather than just the three NRSROs of eight years ago, the legacy of the three-firm oligopoly persists. Of the seven entrants of the past eight years, one is based in Canada, two are based in Japan, one is an insurance company rating specialist, and three are small U.S.-based firms. Moody's, S&P, and Fitch continue to dominate the industry.

Rather than trying to fix the business model through SEC regulation (and risking the mistakes and inflexibility that could follow), an alternative route would be to withdraw the regulations that have forced the rating agencies to be at the center of the bond markets. In essence, the financial regulators that have mandated that their financial institutions heed the NRSROs in bond portfolio decisions should withdraw those requirements—withdraw the delegation of safety judgments that the regulators made in the past. Instead, regulators should place the responsibility for maintaining a safe portfolio of bonds directly on the financial institution.

The regulatory goal should still be that regulated financial institutions maintain safe bond portfolios. But the burden would be directly on the financial institution to justify its choice of bonds to its regulator. This defense could reside in original research. Or it could involve a trusted adviser—which could be a rating agency or any other advisory service that the institution found trustworthy. Regardless of the form of defense, the regulator should insist that the institution has a sound, reasoned basis for its bond choices.[19]

Regulated financial institutions would thus be free to take advice from sources that they considered to be most reliable—based on the track record of the adviser, the business model of the adviser (including the possibilities of conflicts of interest),[20] the other activities of the adviser (which might pose potential conflicts),[21] and anything else that the institution considered relevant. Again, the institution would have to justify its choice of adviser to its regulator. But, subject to that constraint, the bond-advisory information market would be opened to new ideas—about business models, methodologies, and technologies—and new entry in a way that has not been true since the 1930s.

Although the "issuer pays" and "investor pays" business models for rating agencies are the two current contenders, they may not be the only possibilities. Because the combination of financial safety regulation and the SEC's NRSRO construct effectively forced bond market participants to heed the ratings of only a handful of rating agency incumbents (who originally embodied an "investor pays" model and then switched to an "issuer pays" model in the early 1970s), the bond markets have not really had a chance to explore alternatives.

The following list of additional potential models should be considered to be a blue-sky set of possibilities; and there may well be further possibilities that creative entrepreneurs could conjure:

- A hybrid model, whereby both issuers and investors pay fees to the rating agency.[22]

- An "advertiser pays" model, whereby the rating information is provided with advertising attached, and the advertising covers the cost of the informational content.
- A loss leader model, whereby an information conglomerate produces and gives away rating information as an inducement for users to buy its other informational services.
- A joint venture model, whereby major buy-side financial firms (such as major investment banks) would form a collectively financed joint venture to produce ratings.

With this burden-on-the-institution regulatory model adopted by financial regulators, the SEC could eliminate the NRSRO category and designation, since the bogus rating firm problem would be the responsibility of the individual financial regulators.

Though this system could create a tremendous amount of innovation and thus high-quality research, the problem is that there is still the possibility to free ride on others. Moreover, without the NRSRO designation, it may not be worthwhile for the firm to hire a rating agency to rate it, or, alternatively, if it does hire such a firm, the system may be back to the old equilibrium—that is, the issuer pays, and the investor just uses those ratings to justify its holdings to the regulator. In addition, similar to the first proposal, having the institution justify its own ratings research adviser periodically to the regulator may be burdensome on the regulatory organization. However, banks and other depository institutions are now subject to periodic mandatory examinations by regulators, and routine examinations of the banks' bond portfolios could and should take place alongside the routine examinations of their loan portfolios. Similar examinations of the bond portfolios of other regulated financial institutions seem like a natural development (unless one is content to stay with the model of delegating those safety decisions to the NRSROs, which lies at the center of the current difficulties).

The Timing Question

As mentioned earlier, the rating agencies provide ratings through the cycle, so their adjustments tend to be stale. Is this a problem, and, if so, is there a regulatory role? Certainly, for securities with some type of secondary market, it is somewhat irrelevant. For example, during the current crisis, the first sign of trouble in the subprime market was revealed through the pricing of the ABX indexes (i.e., portfolios of CDOs of subprime mortgages), and the credit default swaps (CDS) market judged the quality of financial firms' bankruptcy prospects in a remarkably prescient way. Presumably, for highly illiquid securities where there may be no price discovery, the solutions just offered would be helpful for enhancing the discovery of default likelihood.

Poor quality of the ratings aside, the rating agencies, however, did play an important role during the current crisis with respect to the timing of ratings adjustments. Upon downgrading a slew of subprime-backed CDOs, various financial institutions faced margin calls either contractually or for regulatory reasons. This more than likely helped create the liquidity spiral and intense price pressure on these securities.[23] This in turn made the rating agencies question the potential solvency of the financial institutions themselves. For example, it is generally understood that the expected downgrade of AIG was going to trigger capital calls that the company could not meet; hence, the government's intervention. In an environment where ratings play such an important role in determining margin calls, it is clear that continual adjustments of ratings can cause havoc. Any suggestions to change the "ratings through the cycle" methodology must look at the financial environment as a whole, and be careful not to have regulation lead to unintended consequences. The current model, therefore, of price discovery coming from securities markets, with staggered ratings adjustments, may actually be sensible.

3.4 CONCLUSION

The rating agency conundrum is not an easy one to tackle. The core problem is one of competition, either with the "issuer pays" model of competing to the lowest common denominator (i.e., highest rating) or with a more open business model setting of having too little innovation given the special NRSRO status.

There is an obvious fix that gives the SEC expanded regulatory control by matching the rating agencies to the issuer. The issuer still pays all the fees, the rating agencies now have no conflict of interest, and competition can thrive if the regulator chooses the agency based on performance. A regulator going the route of solving the rating agency problem by fixing the apparently defective "issuer pays" business model is understandable. However, the realization that past financial regulation may well be responsible for the central and enhanced role that the rating agencies have played in the bond markets leads to another possible course of action: to withdraw the regulations that have forced the bond markets to rely almost exclusively on the rating agencies and thus to open the bond information advisory market to the possibility of new ideas and new entry in a way that has not been true since the 1930s. The regulatory goal of maintaining safe bond portfolios in financial institutions could still be achieved through the placement of responsibility for defending their bond choices directly on the financial institutions.

Policy makers should consider the alternatives carefully before proceeding.

NOTES

1. Overviews of the credit rating industry can be found in, for example, Cantor and Packer (1995); Partnoy (1999, 2002); Sylla (2002); and White (2002, 2002–2003, 2006, 2007).
2. For short-term obligations, such as commercial paper, a separate set of ratings is used.
3. Moody's company was acquired by Dun & Bradstreet in 1962; Moody's was spun off as a freestanding company in 2000.
4. The two companies merged, to become Standard & Poor's, in 1941; in 1966 that company was absorbed into McGraw-Hill, where it remains today.
5. Fitch merged with a British rating firm, IBCA, in 1997 and is now a subsidiary of FIMILAC, a French business services conglomerate.
6. On the S&P rating scale, investment grade is BBB– or higher.
7. In the event of differences of opinion among the rating agencies, at least two must rank the bond as investment grade; see Partnoy (1999, 688; 2002, 71).
8. The reasons for this change in business model have not been established definitively. Some candidate explanations include: (1) The early 1970s was the era when high-speed photocopy machines became commonplace, and the rating agencies may have feared that bond investors' photocopying of the agencies' ratings manuals would significantly reduce their revenues. (2) The agencies may have belatedly realized that the issuers needed ratings in order to get their bonds into banks' and insurance companies' portfolios, and photocopying wouldn't interfere with charging the issuers. (3) The bankruptcy of the Penn-Central Railroad in 1970 rattled the bond markets and may have caused issuers to be willing to pay the credit raters to vouch for their creditworthiness (although investors' willingness to pay to discover which issuers were more creditworthy should also have increased). (4) In two-sided markets, such as the bond information market, the determination of which side of the market will pay fees is an idiosyncratic matter.
9. The Department of Labor, as the regulator of defined-benefit pension funds under the Employee Retirement Income Security Act (ERISA) of 1974, began requiring the use of NRSROs' ratings in the 1970s. And the SEC relied on the NRSRO category in the early 1990s when it established safety criteria for the commercial paper held by money market mutual funds.
10. In addition, the SEC was remarkably opaque in its designation process. It never established criteria for what would constitute a NRSRO and never established a formal application and review process.

11. We should hasten to add that economies of scale and brand name reputation certainly also contributed to the size and market share of the three major rating agencies. The rating industry was never going to be a commodity business, with hundreds (or thousands) of small producers, akin to wheat farming or textiles. Nevertheless, the financial regulatory history recounted in the preceding section surely contributed heavily to the dominance of the three major rating agencies.

12. The three smaller U.S.-based NRSROs, however, maintain "investor pays" models.

13. Skreta and Veldkamp (2008) show that, even in the absence of deliberate rating shading by raters, excessively optimistic ratings can arise as a consequence of random error in the rating of complex (i.e., hard to rate) securities and the ability of issuers to choose the most favorable rating among those that are presented to them by raters. This ability of the issuer to select the most favorable rating might itself be considered to be a conflict of interest.

14. The Skreta and Veldkamp (2008) model predicts that just the increase in complexity of the mortgage-related securities would have been enough to generate wider (symmetric) errors by the rating agencies and thus greater optimism in the ratings that the issuers would choose.

15. See, for example, Altman and Rijken (2004, 2006). Investors apparently prefer stable ratings, so that they are not rebalancing their portfolios in response to changes that subsequently prove to be temporary. But they also want timely ratings, which induces the same trade-offs of cycle versus trend that are noted in the text. A policy of rating through the cycle also reduces the instances in which the rating agency will be seen to have been wrong in its judgments. And the policy reduces the agency's need for analyst resources.

16. Also, in the Skreta and Veldkamp (2008) model, more competitors lead to a wider range of estimates and thereby to a greater opportunity for the issuer to pick a more optimistic rating.

17. The SEC proposed a set of regulations along these lines in June 2008; see the SEC's File No. S7-13-08, issued June 16, 2008.

18. Since the CRARA forbids the SEC from taking actions that would affect the business models of the rating agencies, this last action would require new legislation.

19. The SEC proposed regulations along these lines in July 2008; see the SEC's File No. S7-17-08, S7-18-08, and S7-19-08, issued July 1, 2008.

20. In this alternative route, an "issuer pays" model for rating agencies is still possible. If investors are able to ascertain which agencies provide reliable bond ratings, then they would be willing to pay higher prices (and accept lower yields) on the bonds that are rated highly by these agencies. In turn, issuers should want to hire the recognized-to-be-reliable agencies since the issuers will thereby be able to pay lower interest rates on the bonds that they issue.

21. Under this alternative route, we could conceive of the possibility of major investment banks' offering bond creditworthiness advice to investors and erecting sufficiently resilient Chinese walls to convince the investor (and, in the event that the investor is a regulated financial institution, the investor's regulator) of the reliability of the advice.

22. After all, the rating market, like other information markets, is a two-sided market. If newspapers can collect payments from both advertisers and readers, why can't a rating agency collect fees from both issuers and investors?
23. See Chapter 9, "Fair Value Accounting."

REFERENCES

Altman, Edward I., and Herbert A. Rijken. 2004. How rating agencies achieve rating stability. *Journal of Banking & Finance* 28 (November): 2679–2714.

Altman, Edward I., and Herbert A. Rijken. 2006. A point-in-time perspective on through-the-cycle ratings. *Financial Analysts Journal* 62 (January–February): 54–70.

Cantor, Richard, and Frank Packer. 1995. The credit rating industry. *Journal of Fixed Income* 5 (December): 10–34.

Gorton, Gary. 2008. The panic of 2007. Yale working paper.

Partnoy, Frank. 1999. The Siskel and Ebert of financial markets: Two thumbs down for the credit rating agencies. *Washington University Law Quarterly* 77 (3): 619–712.

Partnoy, Frank. 2002. The paradox of credit ratings. In *Ratings, rating agencies, and the global financial system*, ed. Richard M. Levich, Carmen Reinhart, and Giovanni Majnoni, 65–84. Boston: Kluwer.

Skreta, Vasiliki, and Laura Veldkamp. 2008. Ratings shopping and asset complexity: A theory of ratings inflation. Working Paper #EC-08-28, Stern School of Business, New York University, October.

Sylla, Richard. 2002. An historical primer on the business of credit ratings. In *Ratings, rating agencies, and the global financial system*, ed. Richard M. Levich, Carmen Reinhart, and Giovanni Majnoni, 19–40. Boston: Kluwer.

UBS. 2007. Market commentary (December 13).

White, Lawrence J. 2002. The credit rating industry: An industrial organization analysis. In *Ratings, rating agencies, and the global financial system*, ed. Richard M. Levich, Carmen Reinhart, and Giovanni Majnoni, 41–63. Boston: Kluwer.

White, Lawrence J. 2002–2003. The SEC's other problem. *Regulation* 25 (Winter): 38–42.

White, Lawrence J. 2006. Good intentions gone awry: A policy analysis of the SEC's regulation of the bond rating industry. Policy Brief #2006-PB-05, Networks Financial Institute, Indiana State University.

White, Lawrence J. 2007. A new law for the bond rating industry. *Regulation* 30 (Spring): 48–52.

Financial Institutions

Matthew Richardson

In the depths of the Great Depression, Congress passed the Glass-Steagall Act (officially called the Banking Act of 1933). The act had two main features, namely the creation of the Federal Deposit Insurance Corporation (FDIC) for insuring bank deposits, and the separation of banking functions, most notably commercial and investment banking. The main motivation for this separation was that investment activities can be risky and thus threaten the deposit base of an institution. It was not until 50 or so years later that Glass-Steagall got chipped away as commercial banks argued the need for universal banking in a more global and less regulated capital market. In fact, Glass-Steagall was officially repealed in the Gramm-Leach-Bliley Act in November 1999.

Even with the existence of Gramm-Leach-Bliley, commercial banks are subject to much greater regulation and supervision than nondepository institutions. As a result of this regulatory arbitrage, a considerable amount of financial intermediation is now performed by the so-called shadow banking system. This shadow banking system includes investment banks, insurance companies (including the monolines), and managed funds, such as hedge funds, money market funds, structured investment vehicles (SIVs), asset-backed commercial paper (ABCP) conduits, and so forth. As made clear by the current crisis, however, the shadow financial system is not without its own risks. For example, as with Bear Stearns, Lehman Brothers, and American International Group (AIG), nondepository institutions can be systemic. In addition, because these financial institutions invest in long-term and

117

illiquid securities funded with liquid short-term notes, they are subject to runs on their assets. In fact, the shutdown of the commercial paper market in August 2007, the near bankruptcy of Bear Stearns in March 2008, and the run on the money market system in September 2008 all came about through a run on the assets of one particular institution in each case, namely Bear Stearns, BNP Paribas' SIVs, and the Reserve Primary Fund, respectively.

Nevertheless, because the problems that arose in the current crisis may have been caused by the fact that some institutions receive government guarantees (e.g., deposit institutions and government-sponsored enterprises [GSEs]),[*] one argument may be to go back to a world of Glass-Steagall. That is, by severely limiting the guaranteed institutions and their purview, many of the distortions in the market would get rooted out. Investment banks would no longer have to stretch to compete with government-backed institutions. This could be pushed even further and break financial institutions into four groupings: commercial banks, broker-dealers, asset management, and insurance. This deserves some thought. Policy considerations aside, however, three obstacles are that (1) in a global financial system, this would have to be coordinated internationally(which would seem unlikely);[†] (2) in the complex financial architecture, it is often not clear what product would belong in which grouping; and (3) putting aside the point that government guarantees distort all participants' behaviors, many of the problems in the current crisis actually emerged from the shadow banking system.

In this part of the book, we look at three different types of financial institutions, each with varying degrees of government guarantees. The two main conclusions of our analysis are:

1. Government guarantees (e.g., deposit insurance and being considered too big to fail), to the extent they are necessary, need to be priced accordingly. Otherwise, severe distortions throughout the entire system can take place.
2. Systemic risk needs to be regulated and priced to minimize the externality it imposes on the system.

With respect to the first conclusion, providing unpriced or mispriced guarantees to one set of institutions can very readily travel through a chain of contracts to even unregulated parts of the financial sector, giving rise to a crisis due to a shock from unexpected parts. To avoid this, the regulators should price the guarantees correctly and, where they are patently

---

[*]See Part One of this book, "Causes of the Financial Crisis of 2007–2008."
[†]See Chapter 18, "International Alignment of Financial Sector Regulation."

being abused, restrict the scope of guaranteed institutions. The most glaring illustration of this point is provided in Chapter 4, "What to Do about the Government-Sponsored Enterprises?" In particular, because the FDIC at least attempts to price its guarantees, we focus on a set of institutions, namely Fannie Mae and Freddie Mac, that receive government guarantees without any real price. These guarantees impose huge costs on the system, most importantly through the moral hazard they create. Those costs manifested themselves in the current financial crisis. Therefore, the investor function of the GSEs should be shut down. The current setup leads to froth in the marketplace such as the support for weak Alt-A and subprime loans, and—even more serious—systemic risk due to the moral hazard problem of the GSEs taking risky bets. The GSE firms should continue the mortgage guarantee and securitization programs for conforming mortgage loans. To reduce the moral hazard problem, however, the programs should now operate within government agencies, in a format parallel to the current Federal Housing Administration (FHA) and successful Government National Mortgage Association (GNMA or Ginnie Mae) programs.

With respect to the second conclusion, current financial sector regulations seek to limit each institution's risk seen in isolation; they are not sufficiently focused on systemic risk. As a result, while individual firms' risks are properly dealt with in normal times, the system itself remains, or is induced to be, fragile and vulnerable to large macroeconomic shocks. In Chapter 5, "Enhanced Regulation of Large, Complex Financial Institutions," we consider financial firms that may or may not have explicit guarantees, but certainly have implicit ones through the "too big to fail" policy. The chapter traces back the history of large, complex financial institutions (LCFIs), the current regulatory environment, and a regulatory structure recently proposed by the U.S. Treasury. We propose an alternative framework that creates and empowers a dedicated regulator for LCFIs. This would require that LCFIs be identified as such and subjected to an enhanced level of regulation to ensure their safety and soundness. Using information collected in this role, the LCFI regulator will be able to more accurately price the government guarantee that inevitably underpins LCFIs. This can enable setting a fair baseline insurance cost or premium that is linked to the asset size and institution-specific risk attributes of individual LCFIs, coupled to surcharges based on measurable systemic risk exposures.

As described earlier, the financial crisis of 2007–2009 has been a crisis not only of traditional banks but also of the shadow banking system—financial institutions that mostly looked like banks, as they borrowed liquid and short-term, leveraged a lot, and lent and invested in longer-term and illiquid ways, but, unlike banks, did not have access to the safety nets (deposit insurance and the lender of last resort role of the central bank) that prevent runs on banks until 2008. Thus, in 2007–2009 we effectively observed a run on the shadow banking system that led to the demise of a significant part of this system. These runs have taken place on nonbank mortgage lenders, on structured investment vehicles (SIVs) and asset-backed commercial paper (ABCP) conduits, on money market funds, on the major broker-dealers that fit into the LCFI category, and most recently on hedge funds.

The last chapter of this section, "Hedge Funds in the Aftermath of the Financial Crisis," looks at these institutions as an example of the shadow banking system. That is, we focus on hedge funds because they are mostly unregulated and receive little or no support from the U.S. government. We argue that hedge funds play an important role in financial markets, primarily as a liquidity provider. Because they receive no guarantees, it is not clear why hedge funds need to be regulated. The exceptions are: (1) some hedge funds may be large enough (or interconnected enough) to produce systemic risk, (2) there should be some degree of transparency for sufficiently large hedge funds, resulting in the availability of information about both their asset positions and leverage levels at the regulator level, and (3) somewhat more controversially, the regulator should try to alleviate the possibility of runs on the system.

CHAPTER 4

What to Do about the Government-Sponsored Enterprises?

Dwight Jaffee, Matthew Richardson, Stijn Van Nieuwerburgh, Lawrence J. White, and Robert E. Wright

4.1 BACKGROUND

The Federal National Mortgage Association (FNMA), nicknamed Fannie Mae, was founded in 1938 in the wake of the Depression to provide liquidity and aid to the mortgage market. It became a government-sponsored enterprise (GSE) in 1968, turning over its purely governmental responsibilities to the Government National Mortgage Association (GNMA, Ginnie Mae). Shortly after, the Federal Home Loan Mortgage Corporation (FHLMC, Freddie Mac) was formed to compete with Fannie Mae to create a more efficient secondary market for mortgages. While not explicit, there has always been the presumption that the guarantor function of these government-sponsored enterprises, Fannie Mae and Freddie Mac, had full backing of the U.S. government. Indeed, this implicit relationship was reinforced when the Federal Housing Finance Authority (FHFA) placed the GSEs into conservatorship during the financial crisis of September 2008.

The question is: What should the government do with the GSEs in the long run?

The GSEs serve a primary function, namely to purchase and securitize mortgages. Within this function, the securitized mortgages are sold off to outside investors. In addition, the GSEs hold some of the purchased mortgages as investments, and, in theory, help provide liquidity to the secondary market by repurchasing the mortgage-backed securities (MBSs). Their size

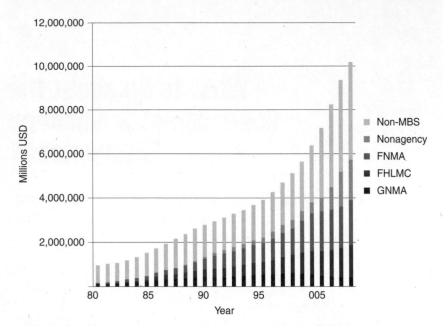

FIGURE 4.1 The Mortgage-Backed Securities Market and the Government-Sponsored Enterprises

This chart presents the size of the residential mortgage market over the past 25 years, separated by nonsecuritized mortgages and mortgage-backed securities, broken down by nonagency and the various agencies.

Source: PIMCO.

and importance for the market for residential mortgages is undisputed. Figure 4.1 graphs the growth of the mortgage market from 1980 to 2006 in millions of dollars. The chart breaks down each year into securitized mortgages—GNMA (Ginnie Mae), FHLMC (Freddie Mac), FNMA (Fannie Mae), and nonagency—plus nonsecuritized mortgages of one- to four-family residential homes.

4.2 SECURITIZATION

The size of the residential mortgage market is well over $10 trillion, with over 55 percent of it being securitized. Interestingly, after explosive growth in the 1980s with the development of mortgage-backed pass-throughs and collateralized mortgage obligations (CMOs), the fraction of securitization has held relatively constant since the early 1990s, hovering between

50 and 60 percent. The contribution of the GSEs to securitization in the mortgage-backed securities (MBS) market is startling. In the early 1980s, they represented approximately 50 percent of the securitized market, the other 50 percent being Ginnie Mae, with a total amount outstanding of $124 billion in 1982. By 1992, this amount had increased to $982 billion and a 64 percent share (the other 27 percent being Ginnie Mae and 9 percent being nonagency firms); and, by 2002, the amount outstanding was $2.774 trillion and a 73 percent share (14 percent being Ginnie Mae, and 13 percent nonagency).

The securitization of the mortgage market is one of the great stories of financial innovation. Prior to securitization, mortgage credit was much more local.[1] Community banks and other local lenders used their superior knowledge of borrowers to issue mortgages but only to those with collateral. Unable to diversify away idiosyncratic and regional risks, and finding it difficult to attract deposits from other parts of the country, the mortgage market was somewhat limited in its size. This is unfortunate because, in a perfectly functioning capital market, the borrower should pay the mortgage rate that just reflects the term structure, the prepayment option, the probability of defaulting on the mortgage, and the market risk premium associated with default, but not diversifiable risk premiums.[2] What securitization does is make sure these risk premiums reflect just aggregate risks (such as those due to aggregate housing price collapse and/or economic downturns) by selling the risks to a broad marketplace. The market for MBSs essentially faces a flat demand curve, and, thus, all that matters are its cash flows and priced risks.

In particular, in the securitized world of GSEs, mortgage originators can offer pools of newly originated and qualifying mortgages, which are evaluated by the GSEs using proprietary loan evaluation tools. As compensation for the guarantees, the GSEs charge a fee as a percentage of the outstanding loan balance, which historically has been about 0.20 percent (that is, 20 basis points) annually. The MBSs are then sold to third-party investors, who hold them till maturity. If any of the underlying mortgages become delinquent or default, the guarantee requires that the GSEs provide timely payment of all interest and principal. The GSE charters further require that the firms hold capital equal to 0.45 percent (45 basis points) of their outstanding MBSs to backstop their guarantees. For most of their history, losses on insured mortgages never approached the 20-basis-point guarantee fee, so the MBS business was both safe and profitable, generating returns on equity of about 15 percent annually.

Of course, securitization is not without potential costs.[3] Specifically, the loans in the securitization program suffer from the adverse selection problem of lenders having no skin in the game. Because lenders have more information than investors about the quality of loans, lenders will have incentives to hold the good loans and sell off the poor-quality ones. Without some type of optimal contracting, investors realize the misaligned incentives and demand higher mortgage rates. Furthermore, even if lenders do not have higher-quality information about the loans, they have no incentive to intermediate, through either evaluating or monitoring the loans. There is considerable evidence that this was a serious problem for the subprime loan market.[4] In particular, this evidence strongly links lower lending standards to disintermediation, such as the existence of new large lenders and securitization of the market.

It is not clear, however, that these lax standards carried through to the GSE-conforming loans. It would not be observable from mortgage rates. With GSE-backed mortgages, investors are relatively indifferent to this issue due to the government's implicit backstop of the GSEs. Thus, this cost is passed on to taxpayers. To mitigate this cost, the GSEs audit and evaluate the approved lenders for mortgage defaults. Moreover, the mortgages must conform to certain quality standards, such as size, loan-to-value ratio, payment-to-income ratio, and borrower credit quality, which make the adverse selection issues only matter at the margin. It remains an open question whether adverse selection of loans is a problem for the GSEs.

As mentioned earlier, while the GSEs perform the bulk of the securitization ($3.5 trillion outstanding in 2006), nonagency securitization (i.e., excluding the GSEs and Ginnie Mae) exploded recently, growing from 13 percent in 2002 to 32 percent in 2006. Much of this increase was due to the resecuritization of subprime and Alternative-A (Alt-A) mortgages (i.e., mortgages that did not conform to the GSE standards) into collateralized debt obligations (CDOs).[5] Figure 4.2 shows that the growth of subprime securitization went from 1 percent of the market in the mid-1990s to over 13 percent a decade later. While the financial crisis generally can be pinned on an abundance of seemingly cheap credit available across the housing, consumer, and corporate markets, it is clear that ground zero for the crisis was the shock to housing prices, the actual and expected default rates in the subprime area, and the collapse in subprime-backed CDOs, held (and surprisingly so) in great numbers at financial institutions. The chart illustrates that the market had grown large in a very short period of time.

4.3 THE GSEs' MORTGAGE INVESTMENT STRATEGY

At first glance, it is hard to argue that the GSEs played a dominant role in the current crisis. While this is certainly true with respect to securitization, it is less clear this is the case with respect to their other primary function, namely investing in mortgages and retaining those portfolios on their balance sheets.

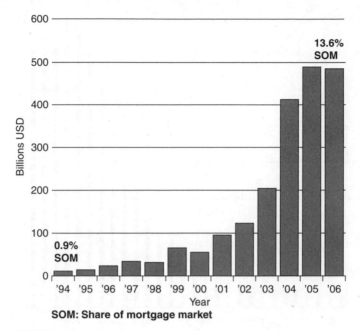

FIGURE 4.2   Subprime Securitization, 1994–2006

This figure presents the percentage share subprime securitization has of the mortgage market.

Source: Lehman Brothers.

The motivation for the GSEs' purview in purchasing mortgages is to provide liquidity and help support the market for MBSs. To understand how large an investor they are in the mortgage market, the GSEs' portfolios represent as much as 20 percent of all outstanding U.S. mortgage securities, the current size being about $1.4 trillion for the two firms. Figure 4.3 graphs the sizes of the mortgage portfolios of the GSEs through time, including a breakdown between prime and nonprime assets (i.e., subprime and Alt-A) starting in 2004. As can be seen from the figure, there was tremendous growth in the GSEs' mortgage book during the 1990s. While the GSEs roughly maintained a 20:1 debt-to-equity ratio throughout this period, the size of the portfolios placed much more systemic risk on the system. Available since 2004, the figure also shows that nonprime holdings of the GSEs were $190 billion, $247 billion, $259 billion, and $217 billion respectively from 2004 to 2007. Since the size of the nonprime market is approximately $2.2 trillion, this means the GSEs represent an alarming 10 percent of the entire nonprime market.

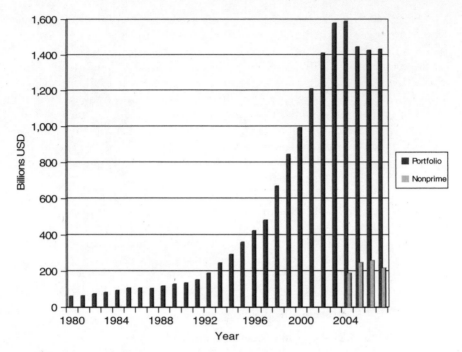

FIGURE 4.3   GSEs' Retained Mortgage Portfolios

This figure reports the size of the GSEs' retained portfolios of mortgages over the past 25 years, including a breakdown into nonprime mortgages (since 2004).

Source: The GSEs' reports to Congress.

How was it possible for the GSEs to grow such large mortgage portfolios?

These portfolios are primarily funded by issuing GSE bonds—called "agency bonds"—for which investors have presumed an implicit Treasury guarantee. The financial markets, therefore, treated their debt as almost risk-free, so that they were able to borrow at rates that were about 0.40 percent lower than their stand-alone finances would have justified. Given that they face a statutory capital requirement of 2.5 percent of their retained portfolio assets, this means that $1 of GSE equity supports $40 of earning assets, a leverage ratio that would be the envy of even the most aggressive investment banks and hedge funds. However, in addition to holding all the risks of possible default by mortgage borrowers, the retained portfolios additionally create significant interest rate and liquidity risks for the GSEs due to the particular strategies employed by the firms in managing these portfolios.

From the GSEs' perspective, given the access to cheap debt due to the implicit government guarantee, their incentive was to leverage up as much as possible to take advantage of the "regulatory arbitrage." The profitability of the retained portfolios arises from the spread equal to the interest rates earned on the mortgage assets minus the interest rates paid on the agency bonds. This spread often exceeded 1 full percentage point annually, creating a return on capital around 25 percent annually, a level more than double that of most successful financial firms. Given this high profit margin, the firms had incentive to grow the portfolios at a fast pace and generally did so, as seen in Figure 4.3. They also had an incentive to expand the profit margin by taking on riskier portfolio positions.

One basic strategy was to use short-term debt to fund long-term mortgage assets, a version of riding the yield curve. While this generally expanded profits, it exposed the firms to losses from large interest rate changes or from a liquidity crisis, the latter arising if capital market investors became unwilling to roll over the firms' maturing debt. The GSEs tried to hedge their interest rate risk via the swaps market. Even if their models, however, matched the durations of their assets and liabilities, their exposure to model misspecification and large interest rate moves put the franchises at risk given their degree of leverage. A second and more recent strategy, again quite visible from Figure 4.3, was to invest in subprime and Alt-A mortgages. These mortgages offered exceptionally high interest rates, but of course also created a much greater risk of credit losses. Moreover, to reduce some of this credit risk, the GSEs bought the so-called AAA tranche of the subprime- and Alt-A-backed CDOs, pocketing the spread but still nevertheless exposing themselves to liquidity shocks and sharp economic downturns. Putting nonprime holdings aside, it is not clear that the GSEs had enough capital to survive the massive housing price declines where even prime loans go under water and borrowers default.[6]

The structure of the GSEs leads to the classic moral hazard problem. Having a private institution backed by the government in this way was a recipe for disaster.[7] Given the description of the GSEs' investment strategy, which may have been optimal from their own singular viewpoint, there is little doubt that the GSEs would eventually fail. In normal, well-functioning capital markets, debtholders impose market discipline and shareholders would not be able to take such risky (and possibly) negative net present value bets. Here, because the debt was essentially guaranteed, debt holders were indifferent to the investment policies of the GSEs. Moreover, the government backstop also exacerbated the adverse selection problem of the loans because the investors cared less about the loan quality than they would have otherwise. This led the GSEs to become a greater vehicle for bad loans.

4.4 THE FINANCIAL CRISIS OF 2007–2009

As is clear now, the GSEs had two clear, negative influences on the financial system. The first, and possibly more controversial in its effect, was their investments into the subprime and Alt-A areas. As Figure 4.3 shows, by 2007, as a percentage of their own outstanding mortgage portfolio, over 15 percent was invested in nonprime assets. This amount represented 10 percent of the entire market for these assets. While not the only institutional culprit, it is reasonable to assume that the mere size of the GSEs created froth and excess liquidity in the MBS market, especially with respect to the troublesome 2005–2007 vintages. This is the period when the GSEs greatly expanded their portfolios (i.e., from $190 billion in 2004 to the peak $259 billion in 2006). The moral hazard gave the GSEs the incentive to purchase CDOs even when other investors were less willing to do so. Figure 4.4 shows the growth of the CDO market for mortgages quarter by quarter during this period.

The second, and more important, effect was to introduce systemic risk into the system and therefore add to the growing financial crisis. This systemic risk came in three forms.

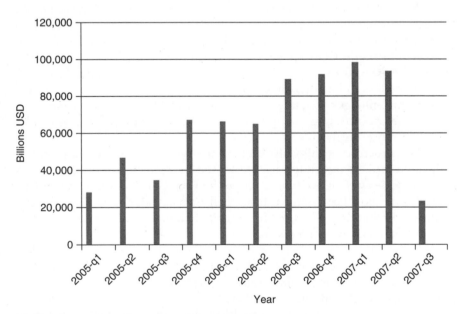

FIGURE 4.4 Size of Mortgage CDO Market

This figure reports the issuance of mortgage-backed CDOs since 2005.

Source: Securities Industry and Financial Markets Association (SIFMA).

First, by owning such a large (and levered) portfolio of relatively illiquid MBSs, failure of the GSEs would have led to a fire sale of these assets that would infect the rest of the financial system holding similar assets. To the extent that the MBS market is one of the largest debt markets, the fire sale could have brought other financial institutions down, similar to what actually happened with the subprime CDOs.

Second, as one of the largest investors in capital markets, the GSEs presented considerable counterparty risk to the system, similar in spirit to Long-Term Capital Management (LTCM) in the summer of 1998, and to the investment banks and some insurance companies during this current crisis. While often criticized for not adequately hedging the interest rate exposure of their portfolios, the GSEs were nevertheless major participants in the interest rate swaps market. Figure 4.5 shows the growth of swaps and derivatives positions through the years. As the figure shows, by 2007, the total notional amount of swaps and OTC derivatives was $1.38 trillion and $523 billion, respectively. Failure of GSEs would have led to the winding down of large quantities of swaps with the usual systemic consequences.

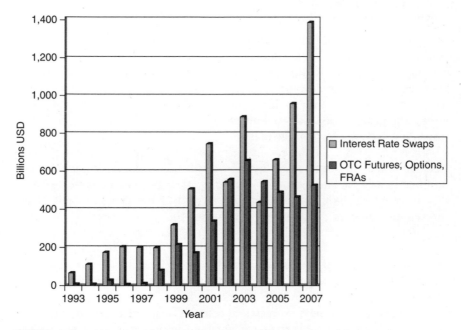

FIGURE 4.5   GSEs' Holdings of Financial Derivatives—Notional Amounts

This figure reports the size of the GSEs' holdings of financial derivatives since 1993.

Source: The GSEs' reports to Congress.

Third, the failure of the GSEs would have disrupted the firms' ongoing MBS issue/guarantee business, with major consequences for the U.S. mortgage markets. In the context of the evolving subprime mortgage crisis, with virtually no ongoing private mortgage investment activity, the result would likely have been a systemic failure of the U.S. mortgage system with obvious dire consequences for the real economy. Thus, the government had no choice but to place the firms in conservatorship and to implement various Treasury loan and equity backstops using its authority under the newly passed Housing and Economic Recovery Act of 2008.

The causes of the conservatorship imposed on the GSEs on September 7, 2008, were expanding credit losses and expected losses on their retained mortgage portfolios, primarily from their subprime and Alt-A positions. As a result of the losses, the firms violated, or soon would have violated, their capital requirements, and they had no likely prospect to raise new capital. As a further consequence, investors became increasingly reluctant to roll over the firms' maturing debt, raising the prospect of an immediate bankruptcy.

4.5 ON REGULATORY REFORM OF THE GSEs

Regulatory reform of the GSEs has been a continuing quest for most of the firms' history, and with a notable, even remarkable, lack of success. The primary case for regulatory reform has always been based on the systemic risks that the firms pose for the U.S. mortgage and financial markets due to the severe moral hazard problems that exist. But in the absence of an actual crisis, the firms always deterred any serious action. The lobbying power of the GSEs in this regard is legendary.

It is now clear, of course, that the fears of a systemic meltdown were all too accurate, and that the GSE model—combining a public mission with an implicit guarantee and a profit maximizing strategy—is untenable.

In thinking about the appropriate reform of the GSEs in light of the preceding statement, it is useful to consider the possible path a mortgage might take to reach outside investors. Once the mortgage is originated, Figure 4.6 considers a series of questions: (1) should it be securitized? (2) if securitized, should the principal and interest be guaranteed? and (3) if guaranteed, should the guarantor be the government or a private institution? Answers to these questions help suggest the appropriate reform.

With respect to the first question, calculations derived from Figure 4.1 show that 56 percent of the current outstanding mortgages are securitized, representing roughly $5.7 trillion. This means that $5.7 trillion worth of default and interest rate risk has been spread through the worldwide economy.

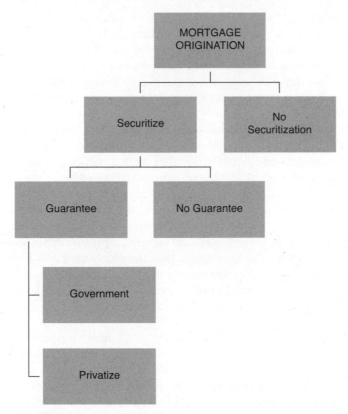

FIGURE 4.6 Mortgage Path

This figure traces the possible path of a mortgage from origination to possible securitization, to be potentially guaranteed, and to be guaranteed by the government or privately.

It seems hard to believe that this quantity of assets could be placed as whole loans within the banking and mortgage lending sectors. Securitization does not come without costs. However, as mentioned previously, securitization leads to an adverse selection problem because lenders have an incentive to keep the good loans and pass along the poor loans to the securitization firms. The GSEs alleviate this problem by tracking the default rates of their lenders. The repetitive nature of these actions reduces the inherent adverse selection. Of course, if few defaults occur due to the economic and rising home prices, then it may be difficult to evaluate the quality of the audits under different economic conditions and declining home prices. An alternative solution would be for the securitizing firm to demand that the lenders have skin in the game by requiring them to either (1) hold some fraction of the mortgage loan on their balance sheets or (2) take their origination fee over the life of the loan, or clawed back in case of default. As an aside, the life insurance industry fixed a similar problem by spreading payments out over five or more years, thereby providing originators with an incentive to assess credit risk.

With respect to the second question, there is room for securitization both with and without guarantees. Computations from Figure 4.1 show that approximately 68 percent of the MBS market is agency-backed, whereas 32 percent is nonagency. Of course, some of the nonagency mortgage debt is guaranteed by private mortgage insurers, but some is not. With respect to the agency-guaranteed market, there exists a $4 trillion investment community that has been built over the past 40 years, which focuses on interest rate and prepayment risk as opposed to default risk. This investment community was developed under the assumption that the mortgage pools have implicit government guarantees. A substantial amount of human capital (i.e., knowledge and training) and number of investment networks are devoted to this product. Taking guarantees away would cause a deadweight loss to all this invested capital so far.

In the nonguarantee market, borrowers take out a mortgage with lenders that would pass on the loans to securitization firms that would then package and sell the loans via CDOs to outside investors. These loans could be tranched in such a way that, for all intents and purposes, there would exist a guaranteed part and a nonguaranteed part, and clienteles of investors would choose one or the other. This, of course, is what happened during the current crisis for CDOs of subprime and Alt-A loans. One of the problems with the current period is that, because the market grew so rapidly, an investment community analogous to the agency-backed market had not yet fully developed.

To better understand today's CDO market for nonprime loans, it is useful to refer to the sequence of innovations through which the securitization of mortgages has developed. Ginnie Mae introduced the first single-class MBS in 1968. The cash flow from the mortgages was passed through to the investors who held prorated shares of the total mortgage pool. In the mid-1980s, the securitization of nongovernment, and thus risky, mortgages began. The key innovation here was a multiclass structure—hence the term *structured finance*—with the junior tranche facing the first loss position if mortgages did default. These securities were initially called collateralized mortgage obligations (CMOs). The CMO market took single-class MBS pass-throughs and broke them into different tranches of prepayment and interest rate risk. As can be seen from Figure 4.7, the market expanded rapidly,

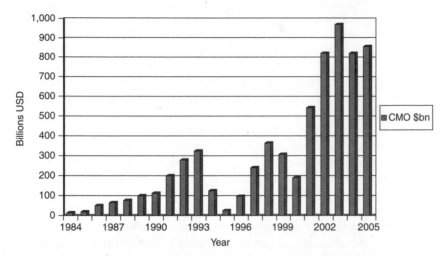

FIGURE 4.7 History of Collateralized Mortgage Obligation (CMO) Issuance

This figure shows the history of CMO issuance of agency mortgage-backed securities from 1984 through 2005.

Source: Inside Mortgage Finance.

only to all but disappear in the mid-1990s. Very similar to the current crisis, two features explained the CMO collapse. First, there was a large shock to the market—in this case, prepayments. Second, the market had become overly complex, with some CMOs having 100 tranches or more. As can be seen from the figure, however, the CMO market gradually recovered to become an important part of the MBS market. The lesson is that it takes time for financial innovation to reach its full potential. The important component is an investment community that, through experience and new expertise, is able to fully understand the new market.

The final innovation was the CDO, which is a securitized product built up from a series of tranches from already-issued multiclass MBSs. For example, a CDO might consist of the B-rated mezzanine tranche from 20 existing MBSs. This provides a potential benefit of diversification, and is the reason that a CDO can have an AAA tranche even though the underlying components are all, say, single B. This diversification benefit depends critically on the correlation of losses among the underlying tranches. For example, if the correlation is 1.0, then there is no diversification benefit at all, and the entire issue should be rated single B. The CDOs were issued on the expectation of relatively low correlations, but the actual results have been just the opposite.

Nevertheless, even if the growth area in the MBS market is via nonguaranteed securitization, the $4+ trillion guaranteed market is just too large to cull. The final question (3), then, is whether the guaranteed market could be completely privatized. There are several obstacles to privatization.

First, private institutions are not good insurers against systemic risk. By definition, systemic risk occurs very infrequently. That is, most of the time the payoff is zero or small, but on a rare occasion the payoff is very large. Insurers, however, have to be able to cover, so it requires them to have considerable capital for relatively small expected values. Second, given this point, is there any way to credibly signal that the government would not bail out these private institutions in times of a crisis? If not, then these private institutions fall into the existing moral hazard trap of the GSEs. Third, if the government could credibly signal no bailout, then these private institutions fall into the regulatory environment being discussed elsewhere in this report. Specifically, the government can impose time-varying capital requirements (via fees on systemic risk) that would reduce the aggressiveness of private institutions. Of course, in reducing but not eradicating counterparty risk, is that enough to satisfy the well-developed market for government backed mortgages? Can a counterparty failure and thus losses in the guaranteed portion (i.e., presumably to investors in mortgage-backed securities) (1) induce a systemic collapse in other asset prices, leading to a death spiral throughout the system, or (2) lead to a collapse of the mortgage market and a credit crunch for creditworthy home buyers? Circumstantial evidence suggests that in a severe crisis it may be only the government-backed loans that can be sold.

The preceding analysis suggests three points:

1. The current GSE model failed in the current crisis, and will almost surely fail again if left untouched. Failure imposes severe costs on the financial system and the real economy.
2. There is a need to maintain the current investor base for guaranteed MBSs. The reason is that it takes many years to build an investor clientele, whether through marketing or the human capital buildup of experience and knowledge, which is difficult to duplicate.
3. The private market for MBSs is important for developing future innovation, in particular, as conditions change.

4.6 SPECIFIC PROPOSALS

In this subsection, we make specific proposals with respect to the GSE's securitization, guarantor, and investment roles in the mortgage market.

Securitization

The obvious solution is for the GSE firms to continue the mortgage guarantee and securitization programs for conforming mortgage loans. To reduce the moral hazard problem, however, the programs would now operate within government agencies, in a format parallel to the current Federal Housing Administration (FHA) and GNMA programs. By most accounts, the existing FHA/GNMA programs provide a highly useful model because they represent a long-standing, stable, and successful framework for supporting the housing market through mortgage guarantees and MBS issues. The new program will charge its borrowers actuarially based insurance fees, in exactly the same manner as the FHA. The loans would need to conform much to the same standards of the current GSEs (i.e., mortgage size, down payment, interest coverage, credit score, and so on). Just like the FHA, the goal of the program is for it to be self-supporting and require no government appropriations. This way, the securitization of guaranteed mortgages, with all its investors already in place, would run almost as is yet without systemic risk.

A reasonable question is how well a government agency can handle the adverse selection of the mortgage lenders. While it is no doubt true that the government agency has less incentive than the private market, and thus is less able to find market solutions to problems, the government can install second-best practices. Among these practices, the FHA already conducts audits of its mortgage lenders, which in a repetitive environment will reduce the adverse selection. Furthermore, for those banks and mortgage lenders to participate in the program, the government entity could require banks/mortgage lenders to (1) hold a fraction of the loan on their own books, and/or (2) amortize the mortgage fee over the life of the loan or receive only a fraction of the loan if it defaults.

Private Guarantors

Parallel to the government market, there will exist a private market. Specifically, much like there is now, there will be three distinct securitization markets, consisting of jumbo, Alt-A, and subprime mortgages, respectively. These mortgages may or may not be guaranteed by the private firm. If guaranteed by the securitizing firm, or a private insurer such as the Morgan Guaranty Insurance Corporation (MGIC), AIG's United Guaranty Corporation, and the like, these firms would be subject to the capital requirement restrictions to avoid systemic risk.[8] Due to the negative externality of systemic risk, one may expect that the nonguaranteed market would eventually dominate. This current period notwithstanding, as investors learn and develop expertise, this securitized mortgage market would innovate and provide market solutions to changing conditions.

It will be a tougher road for the private guarantee market. On the one hand, one might expect the private market to dominate, as it would probably be more efficient at solving the adverse selection problems inherent in securitization than would a specified set of government rules that can be gamed. On the other hand, in order to avoid systemic risk, the capital requirements may be too imposing or create too much fracture in the guaranteed MBS market, especially for conforming loans. Only time will tell, though the past century and a half of experience from the guaranteed private securitization of mortgages does not bode well.

Mortgage Portfolio

The final action will be to essentially shut down the investor function of the GSEs. As discussed earlier, the current setup leads to froth in the marketplace, such as the support for weak Alt-A and subprime loans, and, even more serious, systemic risk due to the moral hazard problem of the GSEs taking risky bets. The obvious solution is to spin off the retained mortgage portfolios—mortgage assets, bond liabilities, and net worth—to the GSE shareholders, and to transform these entities into the equivalent of mortgage REITs or hedge funds. These entities would also receive the intellectual capital of the GSEs, covering their proprietary software for evaluating loan quality, techniques for hedging interest rate risk, and similar items. The spin-off would thus fully respect the property rights of the GSE investors. The new private-sector entities would have no links in any form to the federal government. The disassociation would be credible, since there would be no issues of safety and soundness and no form of regulatory oversight other than with respect to new regulation of asset management firms that might pose systemic risk. Furthermore, the new firms would no longer be constrained by the limitations of the GSE charters. They would thus be allowed, for the first time, to originate mortgages directly. A similar path to privatization was taken earlier by Sallie Mae—the student loan government-sponsored enterprise—and it prospered for many years based on its new power to originate student loans.

NOTES

1. The securitization of mortgages in the United States was not a 1970 (and later) development. Rather, there were six attempts between 1870 and 1940 to securitize the system. Most of these attempts were private programs that essentially failed due to either (1) adverse selection problems at the loan level if defaults were not guaranteed, and thus poor loan underwriting standards, or (2), if guarantees were provided, undercapitalization of the insurers of default. See Snowden (1995). Of course, both of these reasons ring true in the current subprime crisis.

2. While it is difficult to quantify what these premiums might be, it should be noted that $5.7 trillion in securitized mortgages represents over twice the total market capitalization of all publicly traded financial institutions, and over 80 percent of the $7.1 trillion in deposits of FDIC commercial banks and savings institutions.
3. See Chapter 1, "Mortgage Origination and Securitization in the Financial Crisis."
4. For example, see Dell'Ariccia, Igan, and Laeven (2008); Berndt and Gupta (2008); Keys, Mukherjee, Seru, and Vig (2008); and Mian and Sufi (forthcoming).
5. Alt-A mortgages are usually considered somewhere between the aforementioned GSE conforming loan standards denoted as prime and the subprime ones. While subprime loans usually have borrowers with (1) weak credit and poor debt-to-income ratios, (2) mortgages with high loan-to-value ratios, and (3) possibly poor documentation, the Alt-A type borrower usually has a much stronger profile, albeit not across all the preceding factors to conform to GSE standards.
6. The delinquency rate for GSE prime mortgages hovered around 0.60 percent between 1985 and 1995, reached a low point of 0.48 percent in 1999, and has increased each year thereafter, reaching to 1.16 percent in 2007 and most probably much higher in 2008.
7. This point has been made repeatedly in the academic literature; for example, see Jaffee (2003), Frame and White (2005), and Lucas and McDonald (2006), among others.
8. See Chapter 13, "Regulating Systemic Risk."

REFERENCES

Berndt, Antje, and Anurag Gupta. 2008. Moral hazard and adverse selection in the originate-to-distribute model of bank credit. Working paper.

Dell'Ariccia, Giovanni, Deniz Igan, and Luc Laeven. 2008. Credit booms and lending standards: Evidence from the subprime mortgage market. Working paper.

Frame, W. Scott, and Lawrence J. White. 2005. Fussing and fuming over Fannie and Freddie: How much smoke, how much fire? *Journal of Economic Perspectives* 19:159–184.

Jaffee, Dwight. 2003. The interest rate risk of Fannie Mae and Freddie Mac. *Journal of Financial Services Research* 24:5–29.

Keys, Benjamin, Tanmoy Mukherjee, Amit Seru, and Vikrant Vig. 2008. Did securitization lead to lax screening? Evidence from subprime loans. EFA 2008 Athens Meetings Paper.

Lucas, Deborah, and Robert L. McDonald. 2006. An options-based approach to evaluating the risk of Fannie Mae and Freddie Mac. *Journal of Monetary Economics* 53:155–176.

Mian, Atif, and Amir Sufi. Forthcoming. The consequences of mortgage credit expansion: Evidence from the 2007 mortgage default crisis. *Quarterly Journal of Economics*.

Snowden, Kenneth. 1995. Mortgage securitization in the United States: Twentieth century developments in historical perspective. Chapter 8 in *Anglo-American financial systems: Institutions and markets in the twentieth century*, ed. Michael Bordo and Richard Sylla. New York: Irwin Professional Publishers.

CHAPTER 5

Enhanced Regulation of Large, Complex Financial Institutions

Anthony Saunders, Roy C. Smith, and Ingo Walter

5.1 WHAT ARE LARGE, COMPLEX FINANCIAL INSTITUTIONS?

Large, complex financial institutions (LCFIs) can be defined as financial intermediaries engaged in some combination of commercial banking, investment banking, asset management, and insurance, whose failure poses a systemic risk or externality to the financial system as a whole. This externality can come through multiple forms, including an informationally contagious effect on other financial institutions, a depressing effect on asset prices, and/or a reduction in overall market liquidity. The key factors that define LCFIs are size, complexity, and financial interrelatedness. LCFIs present special boundary problems in regulation by crossing traditional (historic) and functional lines, and in many cases cutting across national domains on both financial and regulatory fronts. LCFIs are always likely to be considered too important to fail because of potential financial system externalities relating to their failure.

This chapter discusses the evolution of LCFIs, surveys alternative approaches to their regulation, and recommends the adoption of a single, separate LCFI regulator, while utilizing a separate functional regulatory apparatus for all other financial institutions. We argue that the LCFI regulator should be focused exclusively on those institutions viewed as imposing systemic risk on the financial system.

5.2 WHERE DID THEY COME FROM?

Large, complex financial institutions (LCFIs) began to appear in the post-1984 period, following the failure of Continental Illinois Bank & Trust Co. The decade 1984–1994 involved heavily restrained operations on the part of major banks in the United States. Passage of the Riegle-Neal Interstate Banking and Branching Efficiency Act of 1994, and the broadening of banks' powers to include securities activities using regulatory exemptions to Section 20 of the Glass-Steagall provisions of the Banking Act of 1933, fundamentally altered the playing field. These regulatory changes greatly expanded the power of banks to spread their activities both geographically and functionally. As a result, many banks were consolidated with others to provide a more stable, cost-effective business platform with larger market shares. Such platforms were thought to be necessary in order for larger U.S. commercial banks to be able to compete with European and Japanese rivals. These foreign-based firms had taken up increased market share while U.S. banks were under regulatory restraints on the growth of their assets and nonbanking activities. They were also less able to compete effectively in the capital market, which had emerged as a principal source of both working capital and long-term finance for U.S. and international corporations. Table 5.1 shows the volume of nongovernmental financing in global capital markets—comprising the flow of transactions for which all wholesale financial intermediaries must compete—for the period 1997–2007.

To improve the ability of banks to compete in providing capital market services, the 1933 Glass-Steagall legislation was repealed in 1999 and replaced by the Gramm-Leach-Bliley Financial Services Modernization Act, which expanded not only banks' securities powers but also their ability to enter into insurance and other financial services businesses, and vice versa. Some of the largest U.S. banks moved vigorously and successfully to build significant market share in investment banking by offering favorable lending terms in exchange for commitments to include them in underwriting and mergers and acquisitions (M&A) advisory work. Meanwhile, certain large insurance companies (Equitable Life, Prudential) acquired investment banking units to engage in capital market activities (subsequently selling these units after not being able to manage them effectively), and other insurers (AIG, Allianz) became engaged in the writing and selling of credit and other derivatives contracts.

The activities of the larger banks—including some additional large-scale mergers with other banks and the acquisition of investment banking businesses by commercial banks—led to enhanced competition in global capital markets, and a rising (and ultimately leading) market share for U.S. banks in underwriting bonds and stocks. (See Table 5.2.) These activities

TABLE 5.1 Nongovernment Capital Market Activity, 1997–2007 ($ Amounts in Billions)

	2007	2006	2005	2004	2003	2002	2001	2000	1999	1998	1997
U.S. Domestic New Issues											
U.S. MTNs	$ 0.0	$ 159.4	$ 56.0	$ 143.6	$ 370.6	$ 357.0	$ 429.2	$ 372.8	$ 397.9	$ 308.6	$ 284.7
Investment Grade Debt	2,235.9	2,056.6	1,828.2	2,086.8	2,323.6	1,944.1	1,851.5	1,579.6	1,195.8	504.2	726.1
Collateralized Securities	1,274.0	1,690.1	1,812.4	1,394.8	1,359.1	1,154.2	841.1	479.0	559.0	560.9	378.0
High Yield Debt	119.3	95.5	100.8	141.0	147.5	77.1	109.0	70.3	108.7	149.9	125.3
Municipal Debt	349.3	248.3	201.6	264.4	331.5	346.1	320.8	204.0	219.3	279.7	214.8
Total Debt	$3,978.3	$ 4,249.9	$3,999.0	$4,030.6	$4,532.3	$3,878.5	$3,551.6	$2,705.7	$2,480.7	$1,803.3	$1,728.9
Preferred Stock & Convertibles	98.8	72.0	44.5	52.1	93.1	66.5	137.9	87.6	68.3	74.5	91.3
Common Stock	188.1	155.4	161.3	170.1	121.1	117.8	128.6	206.9	171.9	114.8	120.1
Total Equity	$ 286.9	$ 227.4	$ 205.8	$ 222.2	$ 214.2	$ 184.3	$ 266.5	$ 294.5	$ 240.2	$ 189.3	$ 211.4
Total U.S. Domestic	$4,263.4	$ 4,477.3	$4,204.8	$4,252.8	$4,764.5	$4,062.8	$3,818.1	$3,000.2	$2,720.9	$1,992.6	$1,940.3
International Issues											
Euro MTNs	32.9	872.1	600.4	609.9	514.2	390.9	484.0	440.2	607.8	598.0	420.0
Euro Investment Grade Debt	3,274.8	3,436.4	2,269.2	1,979.2	1,641.6	1,044.5	910.3	779.8	815.5	553.4	573.4
Euro Collateralized Securities	1,107.5	1,066.0	505.8	341.6	243.7	146.8	130.8	78.9	103.4	60.6	65.6
Euro High Yield Debt	148.3	179.7	101.9	102.6	66.4	32.6	34.0	50.6	46.1	41.0	40.7
International Equity	415.3	209.4	114.2	151.9	59.4	53.7	82.8	98.9	181.0	74.1	75.0
Total International	$4,978.8	$ 5,763.6	$3,591.5	$3,185.2	$2,525.3	$1,668.5	$1,641.9	$1,448.4	$1,753.8	$1,327.1	$1,174.7
Worldwide Total	$9,244.2	$10,240.9	$7,796.3	$7,483.0	$7,271.8	$5,731.3	$5,460.0	$4,448.6	$4,474.7	$3,319.7	$3,115.0
Global Syndicated Bank Loans	$5,246.1	$ 4,531.9	$4,008.8	$3,076.0	$2,166.3	$1,860.2	$2,359.0	$1,789.2	$1,750.0	$1,223.0	$1,265.8

Data: Thomson Financial Securities Data, *Investment Dealers Digest*, author calculations. MTN—medium-term note.

TABLE 5.2 Global Wholesale Finance League Tables, 2006–2007

Firm	Rank 2007	Rank 2006	Syndicated Bank Loans	Global Debt	Global Equity	M&A Advisory	Total	Market Share
Citigroup	1	1	$ 614,544.9	$ 222,046.1	$ 26,790.7	$1,371,842.0	$ 2,235,223.7	15.3%
JPMorgan	2	2	599,466.2	172,753.6	31,312.4	1,354,604.3	2,158,116.5	14.8
Goldman Sachs & Co.	3	3	187,192.8	95,668.8	26,194.6	1,641,452.4	1,950,508.6	13.4
Morgan Stanley	4	4	83,464.7	136,896.8	27,010.3	1,453,944.3	1,701,316.1	11.7
UBS	5	8	89,240.7	134,809.1	38,534.9	1,322,059.6	1,584,644.3	10.9
Deutsche Bank AG	6	6	197,044.7	277,988.5	20,998.3	988,123.9	1,484,155.4	10.2
Credit Suisse	7	7	145,659.2	130,356.5	57,489.2	1,085,771.9	1,419,276.8	9.7
Merrill Lynch	8	5	85,686.9	169,870.2	52,340.5	1,101,362.8	1,409,260.4	9.7
Lehman Brothers	9	9	101,722.8	108,987.4	25,748.0	991,082.5	1,227,540.7	8.4
BNP Paribas SA	10	11	197,258.8	118,376.3	3,712.0	396,048.6	715,395.7	4.9
Lazard	11	16				713,105.1	713,105.1	4.9
Banc of America Securities LLC	12	10	366,496.6	70,605.9		258,230.7	695,333.2	4.8
Rothschild	13	18				654,769.3	654,769.3	4.5
ABN Amro	14	15	110,289.9	129,810.3	9,738.3	380,848.8	630,687.3	4.3
Royal Bank of Scotland Group	15	14	244,486.0	163,799.4		145,032.5	553,317.9	3.8
HSBC Holdings PLC	16	12	88,142.1	119,900.1	4,804.5	314,931.3	527,778.0	3.6
Société Générale	17	21	103,468.4	98,365.8		259,393.7	461,227.9	3.2
Barclays Capital	18	13	193,040.8	220,179.4			413,220.2	2.8
Calyon	19	20	131,430.6	72,118.8		114,910.2	318,459.6	2.2
RBC Capital Markets	20	24	54,886.9	36,404.9	5,302.5	214,715.6	311,309.9	2.1
Greenhill & Co., LLC	21	—				292,111.4	292,111.4	2.0
Macquarie Bank	22	—			7,300.3	282,265.6	289,565.9	2.0
Wachovia Corp.	23	19	119,960.1	31,973.9		74,005.2	225,939.2	1.6
Gresham Partners	24	—				209,412.5	209,412.5	1.4
Santander Global Banking	25	—	31,801.3			168,260.2	200,061.5	1.4
Industry Total			**$5,246,054.9**	**$3,148,618.0**	**$458,424.7**	**$5,722,739.6**	**$14,575,837.2**	**100%**

Data: Thomson Financial Securities Data, *Investment Dealers Digest*, author calculations.

were increasingly aggressive and driven by the need to capture important corporate mandates, greatly increasing the risk exposures that banks were willing to take on their own books. Further, like their investment banking competitors, the banks increasingly relied on proprietary trading revenues as competitive pressure eroded intermediation margins. Some also expanded off-balance-sheet activities in swaps and other derivatives as well as special-purpose, off-balance-sheet structured investment vehicles (SIVs) as a then-perceived profitable way of circumventing regulatory capital requirements and expanding their overall leverage.

5.3 THE BIG BALANCE SHEET BUSINESS MODEL

The largest banks (having evolved into LCFIs) announced their commitment to a "big balance sheet" business model that would enable them to dominate wholesale finance, command large market shares, and substantially increase the contribution to total profit of nonlending businesses. LCFIs' expansive efforts over two decades were principally aimed at persuading investors that they were capable of high rates of profit growth (15 to 20 percent annual increases in earnings per share) and that such prospective growth rates could justify high price-earnings multiples for their stock (15 to 20 times earnings).

The LCFIs, however, proved unable to deliver on these claims. In the 2000–2002 recession that followed the collapse of Enron, WorldCom, and numerous high-tech firms, the leading banks reported heavy losses from loan and securities write-offs and class action litigation, as well as fines and penalties imposed by regulators. These losses largely offset the cumulative wholesale and investment banking profits the LCFIs had earned since the 1999 repeal of Glass-Steagall. As a result, their price-earnings ratios dropped into the single digits, bringing pressure on some LCFIs to increase earnings from whatever sources were available, so as to demonstrate to the market that the business model remained intact and that their stock prices would return to higher levels. Several LCFIs vigorously pursued the origination, underwriting, syndication, and warehousing of mortgage-backed securities and corporate loans, as well as credit derivatives, as ways to boost earnings. As a result, when the markets turned down in 2007 and 2008—which most LCFIs were late to recognize—substantial realized and unrealized losses were incurred that required significant additional capital to be raised (see Table 5.3).

By this time, the population of LCFIs had grown to include historically specialized investment banks (such as Merrill Lynch) and insurance companies (such as AIG), all of which met as competitors in the derivatives,

TABLE 5.3   Major Wholesale Banks Write-Downs and Exposures, Q2-2008

EQUITY (US$bn)	UBS Investment Bank		Credit Suisse		Deutsche Bank		JPMorgan	
	2Q08	12/31/06	2Q08	12/31/06	2Q08	12/31/06	2Q08	12/31/06
Equity Attr. to Shareholders	43.5	40.5	35.8	21.3	50.3	43.3	127	115.8
Write-Downs (US$bn)	2Q08	Cumulative	2Q08	Cumulative	2Q08	Cumulative	2Q08	Cumulative
Leveraged Loans[a]	0.2	0.5	0.1	2.8	0.3	3.9	0.7	3.1
Total Subprime[b]	1.1	22.4	(0.5)	4.4	0.3	0.3	0.4	2.2
Other MBS/ABS	3.4	18.7	0.5	1.9	2.9	5.9		1.4
Total MBS/ABS Write-Downs	4.5	41.1	(0.1)	6.3	3.2	6.2	0.4	3.6
Total	4.7	41.6	0.0	9.1	3.5	10.0	1.1	6.7
Exposures (US$bn)	2Q08		2Q08		2Q08		2Q08	
Leveraged Loans	6.8		14.0		38.3		18.9	
U.S. Subprime Exposure[c]	6.7		1.9		2.9		1.9	
U.S. Alt-A Exposure	6.4		1.1		5.9		10.6	
U.S. Prime Exposure	6.1		0.7				8.9	
Other MBS/ABS Exp.	11.8		2.7					
CMBS Exposure	6.5		14.7		16.7		11.6	
Total MBS/ABS Exposure	37.5		21.1		25.5		33.0	
Total	44.3		35.1		63.8		51.9	

Source: Competitor second-quarter result announcements and pre-announcements, transcripts, broker's notes, 10-Q filings. *Data:* UBS AG.
[a] Net of hedges and underwriting fees.
[b] Net of hedges.
[c] Exposure net of hedges (except for LEH) or monoline insurance.

wholesale lending, and securities markets. Like bank-based LCFIs, the non-bank LCFIs had also become very large and complex institutions. Figure 5.1 illustrates the degree of complexity that may characterize LCFIs, regardless of their historic industry origins.

The 2007–2009 global financial crisis demonstrated repeated instances of LCFIs that lost control of their risk management functions after having committed themselves to unusual degrees of leverage and other business practices on and off the balance sheet to ramp up earnings but which at the time jeopardized their institution's safety and soundness, ultimately imposing a high level of risk on the financial system as a whole. This generalization applied equally to LCFIs originating in commercial banking, insurance, and investment banking. There is no evidence, based on recent asset-related losses, that one cohort performed better than another in the context of the current financial crisis. All types of LCFIs contributed to placing the financial system and consequently the real economy at severe risk. However,

	Citi		Merrill Lynch		Morgan Stanley		Goldman Sachs		Lehman Brothers	
2Q08	12/31/06	2Q08	12/31/06	2Q08	12/31/06	2Q08	12/31/06	2Q08	12/31/06
109	118.8	21.1	35.9	33.4	34.3	39.7	32.7	19.3	18.1
2Q08	Cumulative	2Q08	Cumulative	2Q08	Cumulative	2Q08	Cumulative	2Q08	Cumulative
0.4	4.2	0.3	1.9	0.5	2.3	0.8	2.8	0.4	1.3
6.0	32.5	6.9	34.2	0.4	8.8			2.0	3.6
0.9	2.5	0.7	2.3	0.3	2.1		1.0	1.7	2.8
6.9	34.9	7.6	36.5	0.7	10.9	0.0	1.0	3.7	6.4
7.3	39.1	8.0	38.3	1.2	13.2	0.8	3.8	4.1	7.7
2Q08		2Q08		2Q08		2Q08		2Q08	
24.2		7.5		22.3		11.0		11.5	
22.5		8.3		0.3		1.8		3.4	
16.4		1.5		2.4		4.7⎤			
		33.7⎤				8.5⎦		10.2	
		7.4⎦		4.3				11.3	
45.1		14.9		6.4		17.0		29.4	
84.0		65.8		13.4		32.0		54.3	
108.2		73.3		35.7		43.0		65.8	

intermediaries that relied exclusively on wholesale market financing for their trading positions were disadvantaged against those able to access retail deposits, and therefore bank-based LCFIs were more resistant to runs on funding sources.

5.4 IS THERE VALUE IN LCFIs?

The rise of LCFIs as competitors in global markets should imply that beneficial scale, operating efficiency, and scope effects, as viewed from the private welfare perspective of the shareholder, outweigh their corresponding costs. On the contrary, however, various academic studies suggest that, while LCFIs may have important efficiency advantages, there is little convincing evidence of either economies of scale or scope due to the greater size or activity range among banking and financial firms. Moreover, there is credible evidence of a significant holding-company discount in broad-gauge LCFIs as

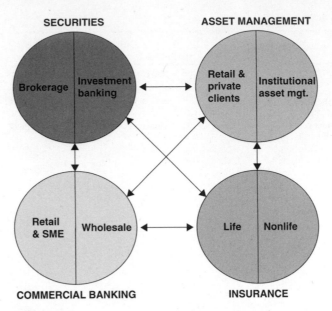

FIGURE 5.1 The Complexity of Large, Complex Financial Institutions

compared to the stand-alone value of their various businesses, as has often been the case for industrial conglomerates.

The key issue is that the risk exposures of LCFIs can trigger externalities on the rest of the financial system, thereby creating social costs of failure far exceeding private costs. But, since all LCFIs are inside the "too big to fail" boundary, implicit bailout guarantees may well have been sufficient to shift the competitive balance in their favor, thereby supporting their growing importance in the U.S. financial system.

5.5 BROADENING OF LCFI BAILOUT GUARANTEES

The broadening of LCFI bailout guarantees in 2008 includes the Federal Reserve's absorption of risk in JPMorgan Chase's acquisitions of Bear Stearns and Washington Mutual and public funding infusions into AIG.[1] It also includes use of the first $125 billion in Troubled Asset Relief Program (TARP) funding to acquire government equity holdings in Citigroup, Goldman Sachs, Wells Fargo, JPMorgan Chase, Bank of America–Merrill Lynch, Morgan Stanley, State Street, and Bank of New York–Mellon, all of them LCFIs. Conversion of Morgan Stanley, Goldman Sachs, American Express, CIT Financial, and possibly others to bank holding companies was clearly designed to get them inside the TBTF boundary and have access to government-provided and potentially underpriced implicit and explicit guarantees. Wells Fargo's acquisition of Wachovia, Bank of America's acquisition of Countrywide and Merrill Lynch, and PNC Financial Services Group's acquisition of National City represent further strengthening of the role of LCFIs in the U.S. financial system, albeit always with explicitly government-guaranteed retail deposits as part of the capital structure.[2] Finally, the $306 billion bailout of Citigroup in November 2008 emphasized just how failure-proof LCFIs are.

The Fed and the Treasury appear to be actively encouraging consolidation among U.S. financial intermediaries and expanding the size of LCFIs as an essential tool in ongoing financial stabilization efforts. In the process they appear to be promoting the consolidation of smaller financial intermediaries with existing LCFIs. In effect, they are engineering a financial system that favors a much greater role for LCFIs, and a potential expansion of the future TBTF guarantee pool. It remains to be seen whether this represents real progress in balancing stability along with efficiency and competitiveness in the U.S. financial system, or whether it encourages creation of large financial oligopolies that are as difficult to manage as they are to regulate—all of them with explicit and implicit TBTF guarantees and wholesale socialization of risk.

5.6 THE REGULATORY CHALLENGE

The government's numerous emergency actions to date have been relatively ad hoc, aimed at containing recurring financial crises. These actions were supplemented by the submission of a longer-term regulatory reform proposal (the "Blueprint") by the Treasury Department. This proposal, which has not been acted upon as yet, represents a studied view of the key regulatory problems of the financial system and possible regulatory and structural remedies. Other proposals have come from a variety of sources, including proposals and declarations by the G7 and G20 groups of countries and the EU finance ministers.

There seems to be an emerging consensus that serious regulatory weaknesses exist relating to LCFIs that urgently need to be corrected. The challenge is to identify those dimensions of the regulatory infrastructure that need correction, together with the means of doing so, in ways that do not unnecessarily depreciate the competitive and innovative effectiveness of the global capital markets and the financial system as a whole.

Considering the Alternatives

Six regulatory alternatives are available for consideration:

1. *Retention of the historic regulatory structure.* The regulatory structure has been based on industry segments—commercial banking, investment banking, insurance, and asset management. In the United States, this involves mainly the Federal Reserve, the Office of the Comptroller of the Currency (OCC), the Commodity Futures Trading Commission (CFTC), and the Securities and Exchange Commission (SEC), as well as state insurance regulators, all implementing banking, insurance, and securities laws as they have evolved over time.

2. *Functional regulation by type of activity.* The regulatory structure can be altered to create a commercial banking regulator (including responsibility for deposit insurance), a securities regulator, a national insurance regulator, and an asset management regulator. LCFIs would be cross-regulated based on their specific activity domains. (See Figure 5.2.)

3. *A single regulator.* Models of unified regulation exist in the United Kingdom (Financial Services Authority—FSA), Singapore (Monetary Authority of Singapore—MAS), and elsewhere. In the former case the monetary authority (Bank of England) is theoretically (if not practically) confined exclusively to the conduct of monetary policy, but of necessity works closely with the regulator. The single regulator may be organized according to financial function, business practices, or other criteria.

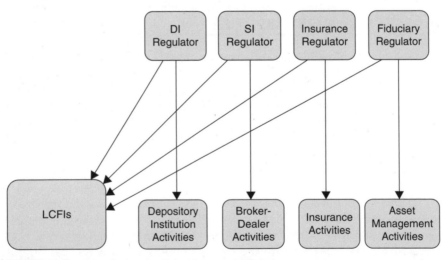

FIGURE 5.2 Regulation by Function or Activity

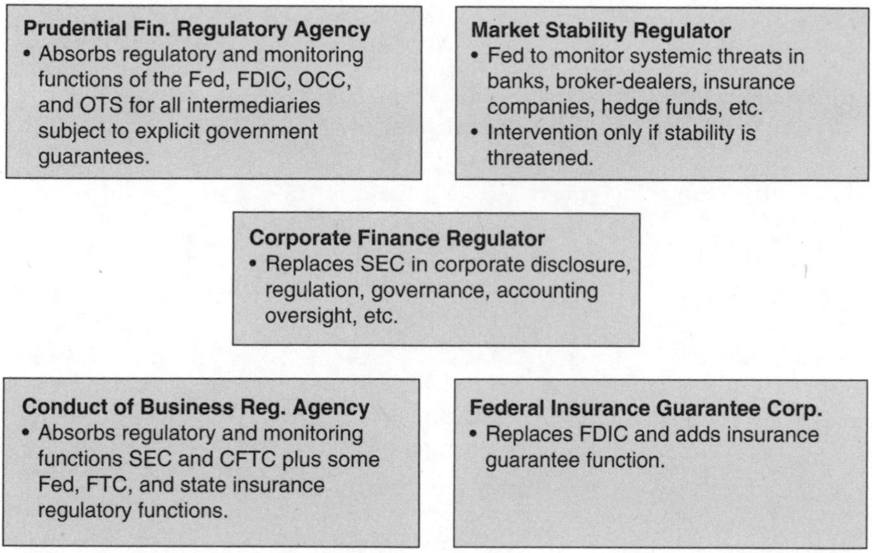

Prudential Fin. Regulatory Agency	Market Stability Regulator
• Absorbs regulatory and monitoring functions of the Fed, FDIC, OCC, and OTS for all intermediaries subject to explicit government guarantees.	• Fed to monitor systemic threats in banks, broker-dealers, insurance companies, hedge funds, etc. • Intervention only if stability is threatened.

Corporate Finance Regulator
• Replaces SEC in corporate disclosure, regulation, governance, accounting oversight, etc.

Conduct of Business Reg. Agency	Federal Insurance Guarantee Corp.
• Absorbs regulatory and monitoring functions SEC and CFTC plus some Fed, FTC, and state insurance regulatory functions.	• Replaces FDIC and adds insurance guarantee function.

FIGURE 5.3 Redesigning the Financial Regulatory Architecture—U.S. Treasury

4. *Regulation by objective.* The principal targets of regulation (e.g., market stability in order to minimize systemic risk, prudential regulation to prevent institutional collapse) could be defined using a combination of market discipline, insurance, and guarantees (as practiced, for example, in Australia and the Netherlands), alongside business conduct regulation to protect consumers and investors by assuring transparency and a level playing field in financial markets.

5. *Modified regulation by objectives.* This is best represented by the 2008 U.S. Treasury plan. It involves creation of successors to the current U.S. regulatory structure consisting of five agencies—a prudential financial regulatory agency, a market stability regulator, a corporate finance regulator, a conduct of business regulator, and a guarantee agency covering bank deposits and insurance contracts. This approach would apply to all financial institutions, whether or not they are considered TBTF (see Figures 5.3 and 5.4).

6. *A single separate LCFI regulator.* This would create a dedicated regulator for those institutions viewed as imposing systemic risk exposure upon the financial system, and separate functional regulators for so-called non-LCFIs. (See Figure 5.5.)

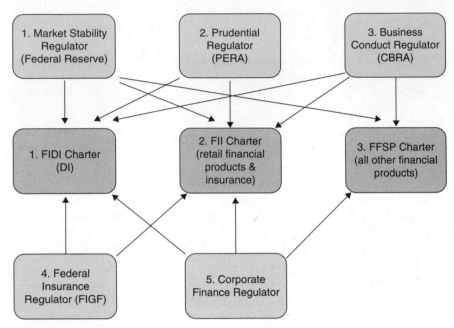

FIGURE 5.4 Treasury Proposals: Regulation by Type of Charter

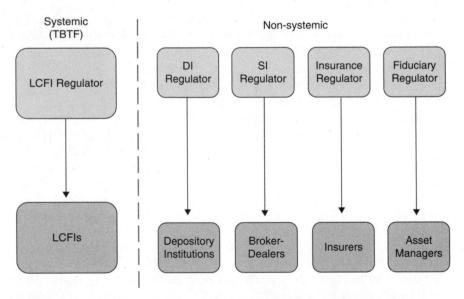

FIGURE 5.5 Saunders, Smith, and Walter (SSW) Proposal: Regulation by Function

Framework for the LCFI-Specific Enhanced Regulation System

We would advocate the sixth option, representing an alternative regulatory structure that involves separate regulation of LCFIs that are too big to fail—the Saunders, Smith, and Walter (SSW) proposal. Non-systemic-risk institutions whose failure would not impose serious externalities on the financial system would be regulated by authorities focusing on their core financial functions. Each regulator would specialize in its own regulatory domain and ultimately develop deep expertise both in its specific functional area and in the institutions that focus on that domain. This regulatory specialization would allow a certain degree of granular "fitness and properness" to be incorporated into the regulatory process.

Systemic (or TBTF) institutions would be the sole domain of a special LCFI regulator. This regulator would encompass all of the constituent functional areas of the existing system, and at the same time be familiar with the consequences and the complex interlinkages between the various financial activities of LCFIs that could lead to potential systemic risks. The regulator would also serve as an efficient collector and transferor of information within the institution with respect to exposures in particular activity areas. This structure is likely to be more successful than other alternatives in capturing key risk exposures and their interrelationships within these massive organizations, as well as the kinds of risk management failures and governance problems that characterize the ongoing financial crisis. Finally, and most important, the LCFI regulator, using information collected in this role, will be able to more accurately price any explicit or implicit guarantees provided to LCFIs. For example, a base insurance or guarantee premium might be set—one that is linked to the asset size and non-systemic-risk attributes of the LCFI—with additional surcharges based on measurable systemic risk exposures.[3]

We believe the SSW proposal may dominate the alternatives for the following five reasons:

1. The financial regulatory structure that currently exists, in our view, is adequate for controlling activities of regulated entities other than LCFIs, which need special attention because they are invariably TBTF. Regulating LCFIs is much more complex, and must involve powers not normally ceded to financial regulators to force compliance with safety and soundness and competition measures, even at the expense of growth and profitability objectives. Without this power, the LCFIs would only be subjected to additional private regulatory costs without any assurance that the public was being better protected from systemic risk. These

enhanced powers need not be applied to other types of regulated entities, and the skill sets required for enhanced LCFI regulation will be different from those of the functional regulators.

2. Complexity requires unique insight into the structure of LCFIs. Risks that surface in one domain of their activities can trigger risks in one or more other domains. At issue here is the need for integrated regulatory risk control by an enhanced regulator.

3. LCFI corporate governance requires sound general understanding of risk exposures. This combines reliance on appropriate models with a solid dose of common sense. Recent events have exposed potentially serious lapses among boards of directors in their duties of care and loyalty. Interactions with, and the monitoring of, a capable LCFI regulator could have a salutary effect in improving the quality of LCFI corporate governance.

4. Other regulatory approaches, such as that proposed by the U.S. Treasury, involve the potential for cross-regulation and conflict among various regulatory bodies, as well as informational fault lines at the LCFI level that could be exploited. A dedicated LCFI regulator offers a solution to this problem.

5. Perhaps most important, the LCFI regulator, by gathering information within the LCFI, will be better able to price both the explicit and implicit TBTF guarantees prevalent today in the financial system. As discussed, an LCFI regulator offers the best hope for accurate risk pricing of TBTF guarantees.

Determining Which Firms Are LCFIs

This approach to regulation would require identifying LCFIs, beginning with an agreed cohort of such firms. At the initial stage, this might be measured by both on- and off-balance-sheet size. Later a regulator could set standards also taking into account balance sheet trading exposures and other factors that could cause an intermediary to be considered TBTF. LCFIs would certainly include the largest commercial banks, investment banks, and insurance companies plus large financial units of industrial conglomerates such as Berkshire Hathaway and General Electric, as well as any asset managers or hedge funds that could generate concentrated size and exposures constituting a systemic danger to the financial system if the institution should fail. Once an institution is designated TBTF in one country, other countries in which it operates would be advised and encouraged to regulate it accordingly.[4] At the same time, firms may opt out of LCFI regulatory overview by breaking themselves up into smaller businesses or reducing risky areas of activity exposure that cause them to be classified as such.

A key initial issue will be determining the size break-point that defines an institution as TBTF. Discriminators between systemic and nonsystemic financial intermediaries will be critical in view of the additional regulatory costs associated with a dedicated LCFI regulator and the incremental costs imposed on them in return for the TBTF guarantees from which they benefit. Firms will naturally try to position themselves to be perceived by the market as TBTF without having to bear the cost of any guarantees. Consequently, discriminators that place a financial intermediary in the TBTF category must be straightforward, transparent, and verifiable using available data, and robust with respect to multiple reasons why a firm is TBTF—in the current crisis the creditors of a relatively small firm like Bear Stearns that might have escaped TBTF classification were nevertheless bailed out in view of the firm's interconnectedness, a guarantee after the fact that may have hardened following the market impact of the Lehman Brothers bankruptcy.

We propose four criteria for defining firms engaged in some combination of commercial banking, securities, insurance, and asset management that generate systemic risk:

1. *Asset size.* The metric in this case is straightforward and available in databases maintained by regulators and central banks. It would involve setting an asset-size cutoff, with all firms exceeding that level automatically considered TBTF.
2. *Rate of asset growth.* The date of expansion of total firm assets may also be a reason for concern about systemic risk. Such firms may fall below the total asset cutoff, but their rate of expansion through organic growth or M&A transactions or high growth just below that level may nevertheless have a systemic effect in case of failure. The firm would then have a choice of moderating its growth or becoming subject to LCFI regulation. Absent a growth criterion, LCFI regulation runs the risk of falling behind the curve at critical times in market or firm development.
3. *Complexity.* Firms may avoid LCFI designation on the basis of the first two criteria, but nevertheless pose systemic risk due to complexity. Since risk, like capital, is fungible within financial firms, functional bank regulators may not be able to capture a holistic view of risk. Credit risk, market risk, and liquidity risk may be interrelated in complex financial firms in ways that conventional risk models cannot capture. A metric for complexity may be devised from risk exposures of different business units, which are then aggregated and weighted according to an industry scale.
4. *Interconnectedness.* In addition to complexity, interconnectedness should be capable of qualifying a financial firm as a generator of systemic risk even if it may not qualify under the other three criteria. A firm may be a central node in financial flows across the system so that its failure causes systemic damage. Firms that are counterparties to traded

products or that are major players in other networked activities such as clearance and settlement or custody may qualify on these grounds. Although it is beyond the scope of this discussion, network economics and the role of network externalities in other sectors of the economy such as telecommunications can probably be adapted to the financial services sector and built into a workable discriminator that would define a break point for "too interconnected to fail" (TITF). The key difference between TITF and aforementioned measures of systemic risk exposure is that TITF cannot be defined for one firm at a time, so it fundamentally changes the way regulators operate. It is not enough to embed regulators in each firm. There must be a working group that aggregates all of the pertinent information. Network analysis can be used to define firms that are TITF—the basic idea being that a firm is TITF if and only if it is significantly connected to other firms that are themselves TITF. *Significantly connected* means that default by one materially raises the likelihood of default by the others. This definition makes it clear that TITF requires computation of a fixed point.

Figure 5.6 lists a number of U.S. and foreign-based financial services firms that might be included among the LCFI cohort based on the first two of these criteria, although some of them could well qualify under the last two as well.

5.7 GLOBAL DIMENSIONS

It is clear that the proposed approach cannot be confined to the United States alone or to U.S.-based LCFIs.[5]

For example, U.S. regulators must have oversight powers extended to American LCFI activities overseas since size (both on and off balance sheet) has global dimensions. A large number of LCFIs are based in Europe and elsewhere, and their failure could have systemic effects locally and on globalized financial markets. LCFIs, such as HSBC and UBS, have large-scale operations in the United States and would have to be regulated in the United States as LCFIs.

To make this work effectively, there would have to be alignment of national LCFI regulators on joint approaches to key issues, perhaps organized under a Basel Accord type structure.[6] National LCFI regulators would participate in a special unit of a supranational organization, with a mandate to coordinate LCFI regulation and impede regulatory arbitrage on the part of systemically sensitive institutions. The advantage of this "regulatory college" approach is that it allows considerable international diversity in

U.S. Bank-Based LCFIs
- Bank of America (incl. Merrill & Countrywide)
- Citigroup
- JPMorgan Chase (incl. Bear Stearns & Washington Mutual)
- Wells Fargo (incl. Wachovia)
- Goldman Sachs Group
- Morgan Stanley

U.S. Insurance-Based LCFIs
- American International Group
- Berkshire Hathaway
- Prudential Financial

Other U.S. LCFIs
- American Express (now a BHC)
- Bank of New York Mellon
- CIT Financial (now a BHC)
- General Electric Capital
- Fidelity Investments
- State Street Global

Foreign Bank-Based LCFIs with Major U.S. Businesses
- Barclays PLC
- Deutsche Bank AG
- HSBC Holdings
- ING Group
- UBS AG
- Credit Suisse

Foreign Insurance-Based LCFIs with Major U.S. Businesses
- Allianz SE
- Groupe AXA
- Munich Re
- Swiss Re

FIGURE 5.6   Examples of LCFIs

regulating non-systemic institutions while maintaining safeguards against systemic collapse via a coordinated approach to LCFIs.

The proposed SSW model would involve a limited number of LCFIs in each country, all of which would be subject to focused regulation aimed at ensuring the safety and soundness of the financial intermediaries concerned, and by implication the financial system as a whole.

NOTES

1. See Chapter 15, "The Financial Sector Bailout: Sowing the Seeds of the Next Crisis?"

2. The placing of Fannie Mae and Freddie Mac under government conservatorship is not considered here, although both institutions were clearly TBTF. Whether they will be fully nationalized or restructured into LCFIs remains to be seen.
3. See Chapter 13, "Regulating Systemic Risk."
4. See Chapter 13, "Regulating Systemic Risk."
5. See Chapter 18, "International Alignment of Financial Sector Regulation."
6. The broad outlines, falling short of a new Bretton Woods Agreement, can be found in the text of the November 2008 G20 summit at www.nytimes.com/2008/11/16/washington/summit-text.html?pagewanted=2&_r=1&sq=g-20&st=cse&scp=1.

REFERENCES

Ahn, S., D. J. Denis, and D. K. Denis. 2006. Leverage and investment in diversified firms. *Journal of Financial Economics* 79:317–337.

Berger, A. N., and D. B. Humphrey. 1992. Measurement and efficiency issues in commercial banking. In *Output measurement in the service sector*, ed. Z. Griliches. Chicago: University of Chicago Press.

Boyd, J., S. Graham, and R. S. Hewitt. 1993. Bank holding company mergers with non-bank financial firms: Effects on the risk of failure. *Journal of Financial Economics* 17:43–63.

Campa, J. M., and S. Kedia. 2002. Explaining the diversification discount. *Journal of Finance* 57:1731–1762.

DeLong, G. 2001. Stockholder gains from focusing versus diversifying bank mergers. *Journal of Financial Economics* 59:221–252.

Denis, D. J., D. K. Denis, and A. Sarin. 1997. Agency problems, equity ownership, and corporate diversification. *Journal of Finance* 52:135–160.

Laeven, L., and R. Levine. 2007. Is there a diversification discount in financial conglomerates? *Journal of Financial Economics*.

Saunders, A., and I. Walter. 1994. *Universal banking in the United States*. New York: Oxford University Press.

Schmid, Markus M., and I. Walter. Forthcoming. Do financial conglomerates create or destroy economic value? *Journal of Financial Intermediation*.

Servaes, H. 1996. The value of diversification during the conglomerate merger wave. *Journal of Finance* 51:1201–1225.

Stiroh, K. J., and A. Rumble. 2006. The dark side of diversification: The case of US financial holding companies. *Journal of Banking and Finance* 30:2131–2161.

Walter, I. 2004. *Mergers and acquisitions in banking and finance*. New York: Oxford University Press.

CHAPTER 6

Hedge Funds in the Aftermath of the Financial Crisis

Stephen J. Brown, Marcin Kacperczyk, Alexander Ljungqvist, Anthony W. Lynch, Lasse H. Pedersen, and Matthew Richardson

6.1   WHAT ARE HEDGE FUNDS?

There is no such thing as a well-defined hedge fund strategy or approach to investing. Rather, a hedge fund is a limited investment partnership otherwise exempt from registering with the Securities and Exchange Commission (SEC) under Sections 3C1 and 3C7 of the Investment Company Act of 1940. The available data show a remarkable diversity of styles of management under the "hedge fund" banner.

The long-short strategy often associated with hedge funds captures about 30 to 40 percent of the business. The style mix has been fairly stable (in terms of percentage of funds), but there have been shifts in market share as a fraction of assets under management. Based on data from the Lipper TASS database, Figure 6.1 plots the total number of U.S. dollar mutual funds by style and the fraction of these funds by style from January 2000 to September 2008. While the total number of funds steadily rose until the end of 2006 before declining modestly in 2007 and 2008, the first graph of Figure 6.1 shows that the percentages of funds in the various styles have remained relatively stable.

Using the same database, Figure 6.2 plots the total value of U.S. dollar mutual funds by style and the fraction of the total value by style from January 2000 to September 2008. Comparing Figures 6.1 and 6.2, there is much more temporal variation in the fractions of assets under management by the various styles than in the fractions of funds following the various styles. For example, funds of funds have risen in market share from 15 percent

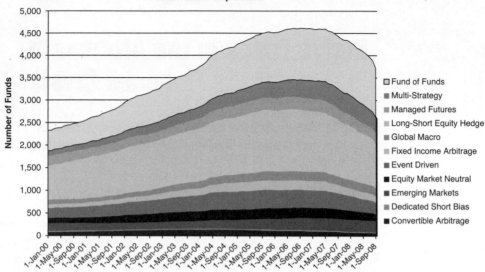

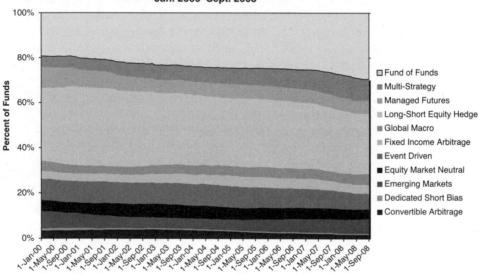

FIGURE 6.1   Number and Percentage of \$US Hedge Funds by Style, January 2000 to September 2008

Source: Lipper TASS database.

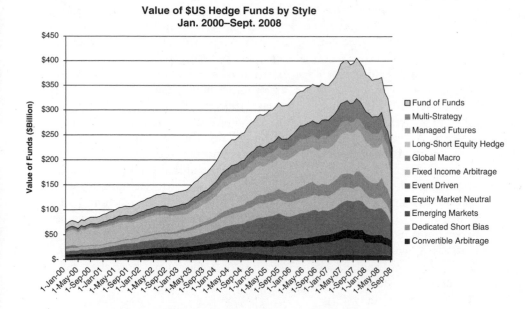

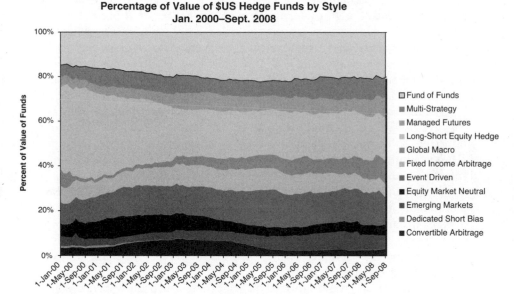

FIGURE 6.2 Asset Values of $US Hedge Funds by Style, January 2000 to September 2008

Source: Lipper TASS database.

to 20 percent over the past decade, while long-short equity hedge funds have actually fallen from 35 percent to 20 percent. According to Brown and Goetzmann (2003), accounting for style differences alone explains about 20 percent of the cross-sectional dispersion of hedge fund returns.

The hedge fund industry has experienced rapid growth since 1992. According to the Hennessee Group, assets under management by hedge funds have grown from $35 billion in January 1992 to $1.535 trillion in January 2007. However, the financial crisis has certainly affected the hedge fund industry. According to data compiled by Hedge Fund Research, more than 75 hedge funds have liquidated or restricted investor redemptions since the start of 2008 as they cope with fallout from the global financial crisis. Investors pulled $40 billion from hedge funds during a recent month, while market losses cut industry assets by $115 billion. The average fund had a return of −10.11 percent for the year through September 2008, while equity hedge funds had a return of −15.45 percent. Based on these numbers, hedge funds are down less than the equity market for the year through September 2008. However, hedge funds could actually be down by more than these numbers suggest, due to self-reporting biases contaminating the reported performance numbers.

Turning to fund manager incentives, aggressive incentive fee structures (often 20 percent of any profits, plus a management fee of about 2 percent of assets under management) encourage risk taking, while career concerns provide the opposite incentive. According to Brown, Goetzmann, and Park (2001), managers can be quite risk averse because of career concerns; the typical hedge fund has a half-life of five years or less, and it is hard to restart a hedge fund career after a failure.

Operational controls in hedge funds are often weak, which can lead to excessive risk taking by fund managers. According to Brown, Goetzmann, and Liang (forthcoming), operational risk is a more significant explanation of fund failure than is financial risk. They find that financial risk events typically occur within the context of poor operational controls.

Hedge funds are reluctant to reveal their trading strategies for fear of imitation. According to Glode and Green (forthcoming), private equity partnerships are widely reported to be secretive about their strategies and return histories. However, there is a market for information about hedge fund positions; for example, private investigator reports exist for a large number of hedge funds.

Hedge funds have the ability to short sell assets, which allows them to use leverage. And leverage means their equity value, absent limited liability, can go negative. Leverage is more important for some strategies than others and is most concentrated in funds conducting fixed income arbitrage, which is a very small proportion of all hedge funds. Quantitative funds, implementing long-short equity positions, also use leverage, and there is evidence that these funds have been using more and more leverage over time.

It is important to understand the current regulatory environment in which hedge funds operate. Hedge funds typically issue securities in private offerings that are not registered with the SEC under the Securities Act of 1933. In addition, hedge funds are not required to make periodic reports under the Securities Exchange Act of 1934. But hedge funds are subject to the same prohibitions against fraud as are other market participants, and their managers have the same fiduciary duties as other investment advisers.

6.2 HOW DO HEDGE FUNDS ADD VALUE?

Hedge funds are major participants in the so-called shadow banking system, which runs parallel to the more standard banking system. Along with hedge funds, this shadow financial system includes insurance companies, broker-dealers, money market funds, mutual and pension funds, structured investment vehicles (SIVs), conduits, and so forth. Within this system, it is quite possible for participants, such as hedge funds, to provide functions more typically associated with banking. While some criticize this system because of the ability of its participants to conduct regulatory arbitrage, it should be noted that many parties, including hedge funds, are provided no explicit government guarantees.

Hedge funds add value to the financial system in a number of ways. First, hedge funds are primary providers of liquidity to the market. Many securities probably could not be issued in the first place without hedge funds being willing to hold them in the secondary market. It may be too costly, both internally and from a systemic point of view, for the banking sector to hold certain illiquid securities. Because the investors in hedge funds tend to be well-capitalized institutions or individuals, their price for liquidity may be much lower. Moreover, hedge funds help firms raise capital by extending the investor pool, especially with respect to difficult-to-value securities like convertible bonds and asset-backed securities, among others.

Second, hedge funds help correct mispricings in the market, to the extent that there are mispricings. So, for example, their actions may reduce the likelihood of speculative bubbles or, more important, excess volatility. To the extent it is better for market participants to be allocating capital under conditions in which asset prices reflect their fundamental economic value, hedge funds are therefore an important part of the financial system. In addition, to the extent hedge funds are willing to trade opaque securities, their investment decisions help incorporate information into the market. And, alternatively, their unwillingness to purchase certain securities (e.g., subprime-backed assets) also reveals valuable information. Last, hedge funds often play important corporate governance roles in those firms in which they hold significant stakes.

When thinking about whether to regulate hedge funds because they might impose externalities on the financial system, it is important to understand how hedge funds add value to their investors. First, they provide investment strategies that either outperform other comparable investment vehicles or generate returns with low correlation to traditional investments and asset classes. Second, they give investors access to leverage. The rapid growth of the hedge fund industry suggests that investors are firmly of the belief that hedge funds are adding value for them.

6.3 PROBLEMS ASSOCIATED WITH HEDGE FUNDS

While hedge funds can add value, they also create problems for the financial system as a whole and for their investors in particular. We discuss each in turn.

Systemic Risk within the Financial System

Funds that follow certain styles (e.g., quantitative funds implementing long-short equity positions) often follow similar strategies and therefore have interrelated and correlated positions. (Note that this is certainly not true for all fund styles.) Indeed, it is not surprising that funds with similar objectives have correlated positions. But funds following different styles have also become more interconnected over time. That probably isn't too surprising, either. Hedge funds provide liquidity to the aggregate of those who demand liquidity, so it is quite natural that hedge funds are similar; that is, they all take the other side of the liquidity demand and so end up with returns and positions that are correlated. That said, even if this commonality is a by-product of hedge funds providing a valuable function, it may create systemic risk.

Figure 6.3 describes 13 different hedge fund indexes and how they have grown more interconnected from the period 1994–2000 to 2001–2007.[1] In particular, the figure portrays three possible types of pairwise connections between any two hedge fund indexes: correlated returns over 50 percent (thick line), correlated returns between 25 and 50 percent (thin line), and correlations less than 25 percent (no connecting line). Two primary observations from Figure 6.3 are in order. First, the more recent period shows

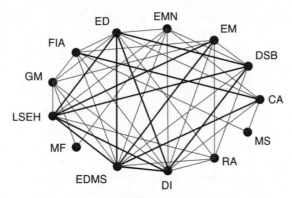

Return correlations across different hedge funds from 1994 to 2000

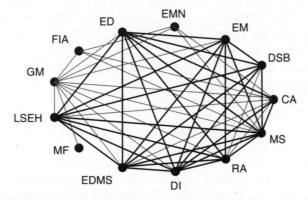

Return correlations across different hedge funds from 2001 to 2007

FIGURE 6.3 Hedge Fund Interconnectedness

Diagram of return correlations between 13 different hedge fund classes from the CS/Tremont hedge fund indexes. The thin lines represent correlations between 25 and 50 percent, while the thick lines respresent correlations above 50 percent. The hedge fund classes include CA—convertible arbitrage, DSB—dedicated short bias, EM—emerging markets, EMN—equity market neutral, ED—event driven, FIA—fixed income arbitrage, GM—Global macro, LSEH—long-short equity hedge, MF—managed futures, EDMS—event driven multi-strategy, DI—distressed index, RA—risk arbitrage, and MS—multi-strategy.

Source: Khandani and Lo (2007).

a much more correlated structure. That is, many more hedge fund classes are now connected, and, more important, their return correlations exceed 50 percent. The lines in the figure look much thicker for the more recent period. Second, and perhaps more alarming, the multistrategy class was barely connected to the hedge fund system in the earlier period, but now is highly correlated to most strategies. Thus, this figure suggests that the holdings of hedge funds overlap much more today than they did before 2000.[2]

How does this increase in connectedness lead to systemic risk? There are three main ways, all driven by the fact that capital erosion occurs at the same time for these funds because of price moves in the same or similar securities. First, hedge funds can enter into a "liquidity spiral" as described by Brunnermeier and Pedersen (forthcoming): Coordinated margin calls can lead to coordinated trading to satisfy those calls, which can cause liquidity in those stocks to dry up. When this happens, their trades can move prices away from fundamentals, which can create systemic risk in the financial system, especially if banks and other financial institutions have similar positions and so are also moving prices in the same directions with their trades as they tighten risk management (Garleanu and Pedersen 2007). This is a potential externality that hedge funds might impose on the financial system.

Second, hedge funds provide liquidity, and the simultaneous failure of a number of hedge funds (whose combined net asset value is large) because they are following similar strategies imposes costs on the financial system because of the loss of the liquidity services provided by these funds. It could be a few large funds with correlated positions or a large number of small funds with correlated positions. The individual funds may be small, but if a large number of funds follow similar strategies and so have highly correlated positions, these funds may still create systemic risk for the financial system, even though no one fund is particularly large.

What determines if the created risk is systemic? One important question is whether the total size of the hedge funds in question is sufficiently large that their collapse creates a vacuum in liquidity provision that imposes costs on the financial system. Another important question is whether the hedge funds in question are failing or losing large amounts of capital at the same time that other liquidity providers to the financial system are also experiencing severe capital erosion. In either case, new capital will likely flow back into the financial system eventually, but capital can be slow moving (Mitchell, Pedersen, and Pulvino 2007), and the question is the extent of the disruption to the financial system in the meantime.

Third, hedge funds impose counterparty credit risk on other participants in the financial system. The externality that this imposes on the financial system increases as hedge fund positions become more interrelated and correlated, especially if hedge funds impose high counterparty credit risk exactly when banks and other financial institutions also impose high counterparty credit risk. The externality is also greater when there is greater uncertainty about the exact magnitude of the counterpart risk imposed by hedge funds. So many hedge funds having interrelated and correlated positions exacerbates the systemic risk that hedge funds can generate because of the severe and uncertain counterparty credit risk they impose.

Note that the systemic risk we are discussing here has nothing to do with the argument that hedge funds manipulate markets to make profits at the expense of other market participants. Rather, this systemic risk stems from the risk of large coordinated losses or coordinated failures all at the same time of a large number of hedge funds following similar strategies.

There are two reasons why the systemic risk for the financial system created by the hedge fund industry can be larger and more significant than the systemic risk created by other asset management counterparties in the shadow banking system. First, hedge funds are able to use leverage, which can have a number of unfortunate consequences for the financial system. Leverage forces hedge funds to unwind their positions when confronted with margin calls, which can disrupt their ability to provide liquidity to the financial system. It also leaves hedge funds exposed to the possibility of negative equity positions if prices move against them, which can cause them to generate counterparty risk. Since leverage causes any given position to suffer larger losses as a percentage of capital (and to earn larger profits as a percentage of capital), it causes some hedge funds (the ones that often have interrelated and highly correlated positions) to have, all at the same time, even more depleted capital reserves than they otherwise would.

Second, a lack of transparency of hedge fund positions can make it difficult to assess how levered and exposed hedge funds are. It can also make it difficult to assess the magnitude of the counterparty risk being generated by hedge funds. Since systemic crises are characterized by investor panic and extreme flights to quality, this lack of transparency will most likely lead to more extreme reactions on the part of investors and ensuing liquidity runs on the system. As an example from the current crisis, consider another class of institutions from the shadow banking system, namely money market funds. After Lehman Brothers declared bankruptcy over the weekend of September 13 and 14, 2008, one of the largest money market funds, the Reserve Primary Fund, announced that it had "broken the buck" (i.e., its net asset value had fallen below par value) because of its ownership of a significant portion of Lehman Brothers' short-term debt. The possibility that money market funds were exposed in such a way to the financial crisis led to a run on money market funds, resulting in the government temporarily guaranteeing all losses in these funds. It is a small leap of faith to recognize that if lack of transparency in safe assets like money market funds can cause a liquidity spiral, then funds that are even less transparent and much riskier pose an even greater systemic risk.

The preceding example of the Reserve Primary Fund also shows that redemptions (i.e., runs on asset management funds) are an additional concern for hedge funds. Investors typically redeem shares after poor performance, and since hedge funds that follow certain styles often have interrelated and correlated positions, redemptions tend to occur all at the same time for funds following these styles. This, in turn, causes liquidations of the same positions by these funds at the same time, which can create systemic risk for the financial system. Finally, it is worth noting that weak operational controls can lead to excessive risk taking by fund managers, which in turn can cause some funds (the subsets that have interrelated and highly correlated positions) to generate even more systemic risk than they otherwise could.

Examples of Hedge Funds Generating Systemic Risk   We briefly describe two examples that show how hedge funds are capable of generating systemic risk in the financial system, the first being the Long-Term Capital Management (LTCM) collapse in September 1998, and the second, which occurred in the lead-up to the current crisis, being the quant meltdown of August 2007. Both provide warning signs as to the types of problems that can occur when hedge funds are allowed to impose systemic risk on the financial system.

Long-Term Capital Management   LTCM was founded in 1994 to take advantage of perceived mispricings in the fixed income market by investing in convergence trades—that is, between securities that are similar enough that they will eventually have similar values.[3] Because the fund would be subject to the aforementioned redemption risk, LTCM was structured to have a three-year lockup in order to allow the trades to converge. For its first four years, LTCM was enormously successful, becoming one of the largest hedge funds, if not the largest, at the time with $7 billion under management. By 1998, as more funds entered the fixed income arbitrage market and opportunities began to dry up, LTCM returned some funds to investors, but continued to manage the remaining money in the fund. To try to extract returns, the remaining $5 billion was levered up to $125 billion worth of assets, most of it funded short-term via the repurchase agreement (repo) market. Moreover, LTCM's off-balance-sheet positions included approximately $1.25 trillion notional values of swaps, options, and futures positions. While many of these positions netted out, only six banks worldwide had $1 trillion plus of derivatives positions.

One of the primary markets of convergence trades for LTCM was that of mortgage-backed securities (MBSs). In May and June 1998, a widening of spreads in the mortgage-backed securities market caused LTCM, with its degree of leverage, to lose an astonishing 16 percent of its value. Around the same time, Salomon Brothers decided to close its fixed income arbitrage group and liquidated its holdings very quickly. As one of the largest fixed income arbitrage groups, and the precursor to LTCM (i.e., most of the partners came from Salomon), there was a similarity among the trades of the two firms. This immediate price pressure in fixed income markets is generally considered to be a major cause of the mortgage-backed security price drop. Then, on August 17, 1998, Russia defaulted on its debt, causing a massive flight to quality. While LTCM had only limited exposure to Russia, other funds had to liquidate their positions, causing even greater losses in illiquid fixed income arbitrage positions. As a result, LTCM's positions worsened, and by the end of the month, it had lost 52 percent of its value, leaving it with over a 50:1 leverage ratio.

The following month, as risk appetite disappeared in the marketplace, almost all of LTCM's trades went in the wrong direction, leaving the fund with additional losses of 83 percent in September. Firms began to pull funding and to demand liquid collateral, which caused LTCM to go into a death spiral. Out of fear of the systemic consequences of an LTCM bankruptcy, both for its counterparty implications as one of the largest players in over-the-counter (OTC) derivatives and because of the effect of fire sales on other financial institutions, the Federal Reserve organized a bailout of LTCM by a consortium of investment banks on September 23, 1998.

Quant Meltdown   While hedge funds have certainly been in the middle of the current financial crisis, hedge funds didn't cause the growth in the subprime mortgage market, or make housing prices collapse so that subprime loans would default, or force financial institutions (GSEs, commercial banks, and broker-dealers) to hold $785 billion worth of collateralized debt obligations (CDOs) on their books. Nevertheless, it was the collapse of two highly levered Bear Stearns hedge funds on June 20, 2007, that started the ball rolling with respect to the collapse of the market for subprime-backed CDOs. In particular, as the prices of the CDOs began to fall with the defaults of subprime mortgages, lenders to the funds demanded more collateral. In fact, a creditor of the funds, Merrill Lynch, seized $800 million of fund assets and tried to auction them off. When only a small fraction could be sold, and even with Bear Stearns providing a loan to keep the funds afloat, a complete repricing of CDOs occurred, and by the end of the next month the funds had lost over 90 percent of their values.

Although it is difficult to link the collapse of these two hedge funds directly to other markets, on July 25, 2007, the largest and best-known speculative trade, the "carry trade" (in which investors go long the high-yielding currency and short the low-yielding one) had its largest move in many years. Specifically, being long 50 percent each in the Australian dollar and New Zealand kiwi and short 100 percent Japanese yen lost 3.5 percent in a single day. To give the magnitude of this move some context, the daily standard deviation over the previous three years for this trade was 0.6 percent. It is now widely believed that hedge fund losses in various strategies such as the carry trade, or perhaps a shift in risk aversion, led to the next major event, the meltdown of quantitative, long-short hedge fund strategies (value, momentum, and statistical arbitrage) over the week of August 6, 2007.

Specifically, from Monday, August 6 through Thursday, August 9, many successful quantitatively managed equity market neutral or statistical arbitrage hedge funds suffered enormous losses. By Friday, August 10, the equity prices causing the losses had rebounded significantly but not completely. However, faced with mounting losses on August 7, 8, and 9, many of the affected funds had cut their risk exposures along the way, causing them to miss out on a portion of the reversals on August 10. The financial press reported month-to-date losses ranging from –5 to –30 percent for some of the largest quantitatively managed funds.

One possible explanation is what's called the "unwind hypothesis."[4] This hypothesis suggests that the initial losses from August 6 through August 9 were due to the forced liquidation of one or more large equity market neutral portfolios, primarily to raise cash or reduce leverage, and the subsequent price impact of this unwinding caused other similarly constructed equity funds (long-short, 130/30, and long-only) to experience losses. These losses, in turn, caused these other funds to deleverage their portfolios, yielding additional price impact that led to further losses, more deleveraging, and so on. The precipitating factor for the initial liquidation was most likely the shutdown in late July of the securitization market for nonguaranteed credit securities such as subprime and Alt-A mortgages, corporate bonds, and leverage loans, leading to an immediate drop in their valuations. Risk spiked, with the carry trade in currencies suffering its largest move in several years, and this led to redemptions from certain hedge funds.

What Do These Examples Tell Us about Systemic Risk?   Both these examples have similar features. First, the trading strategies had become crowded with more and more capital chasing fewer and fewer opportunities.[5] As a result, the firms (i.e., LTCM and the quant funds) relied on more and more leverage. Any losses, therefore, would be amplified. Second, there was a general lack of transparency in the marketplace in that few participants realized how interconnected LTCM or the quant funds had become with the rest of the market. Third, a sudden event, either the Russian default or the collapse of the CDO market, created a climate of fear and panic, heightening the risk sensitivities of managers and investors across all markets and style categories. Fourth, a large liquidation by a participant in the market most likely started the downward spiral that rippled across firms.

Both these events underscore the apparent commonality among hedge funds. The coordinated losses in these two very different cases do imply a common component in the hedge fund sector. LTCM aside, the big question is whether any group of hedge funds with interrelated and correlated positions is large enough, as a group, that their simultaneous failure or collapse would create an externality for the financial system because of (1) the resulting loss of the liquidity services they provide, (2) the accompanying fire sales of illiquid securities that move prices far away from fundamentals and so affect the capital allocation decisions of other institutions, or (3) the associated counterparty risk.

Problems Faced by Hedge Fund Investors

When thinking about whether to regulate hedge funds because they might impose externalities on the financial system, it is important to be aware of any problems being faced by hedge fund investors, because the regulations may affect the severity of those problems. There are a number of problems that the hedge fund industry inflicts upon its investors. First, a lack of transparency of hedge fund positions can allow hedge funds not to disclose their leverage levels to their investors. To deal with this, investors can require leverage limits in contracts (and violating these limits is fraud). Even so, funds with bargaining power because of high demand can insist on no leverage limits.

Second, hedge funds earn liquidity premiums most of the time. But interrelated and highly correlated positions across certain groups of hedge funds can lead to periods when these hedge funds are forced to unwind similar positions at the same time to meet margin calls or satisfy redemptions. At these times, these funds are forced to *pay* liquidity premiums to obtain the immediacy they need, which adversely affects their performance.

Third, lockup periods force investors to keep their capital in hedge funds for prespecified periods, and the reduction in flexibility is not likely to be good for investors. However, it may sometimes be in the investors' best interests that they're all locked up, as it might prevent a run of redemptions that would otherwise force the hedge fund to sell at fire sale prices. Fund size affects the likelihood of the hedge fund getting only fire sale prices; small funds are less likely to be subject to fire sale prices than large funds. Moreover, investors can always wait and redeem later when the fire sale is over, though if others redeem early, those who redeem late may end up with the fire sale price as part of their fund performance. Faced with this choice, it may be that investors would redeem gradually. The fact that investors can redeem later (and their shares of the assets will still be there) may distinguish this situation from the typical bank run situation. Last, operational risks adversely affect the returns earned by investors from investing in hedge funds.

6.4 PRINCIPLES

There is considerable discussion about the unregulated nature of hedge funds both in the public policy arena and in the academic arena. At first glance, hedge funds being unregulated would seem to be patently unfair as it allows them to take advantage of regulatory arbitrage, namely the ability to offer intermediation services in direct competition against regulated institutions like banks. However, this ignores the substantive advantage banks have through either the explicit guarantee of deposit insurance or the implicit guarantee of being considered too big to fail, which gives them a lower financing cost. In fact, one could argue that one of hedge funds' primary functions, that of proprietary trading, could be a quite dangerous systemic function as part of a large, complex financial institution (LCFI) because of LCFIs' cheap access to financing. For example, in the current crisis, many of the major write-downs were tied to explicit bets on subprime-backed assets—Morgan Stanley losing $15 billion on a proprietary trade, UBS writing down $20 billion on its mortgage book, Merrill Lynch losing $30 billion plus on its nonprime mortgage portfolio, and so on.

This stated, however, the analysis in the preceding section does suggest that either a large hedge fund or a collection of smaller ones within this shadow financial system could be systemically important. Thus, regarding the impact of hedge funds on the financial system as a whole, all the following are undesirable because they impose externalities on the financial system: (1) counterparty credit risk due to the possibility of coordinated fund failure, (2) correlated trades by hedge funds that move prices away from fundamentals, and (3) loss of liquidity services provided by hedge funds due to synchronized capital erosion. Regulation that limits the ability of hedge funds to impose these externalities on the financial system often adversely affects the ability of hedge funds to add value by providing liquidity, correcting mispricing, and generating good performance for their investors. Balancing these considerations is important.

Determining the amount of transparency in the hedge fund industry involves balancing these considerations as well. Fund investor transparency allows investors to better monitor the hedge fund managers and to better assess the operational risks of funds. But it is costly since transparency of positions allows imitation, which adversely affects fund performance. Nondisclosure agreements between funds and their investors may be able to limit these imitation costs. In addition, transparency to regulators is desirable, as it can help the regulator measure and manage potential systemic risk.

Hedge funds need to have in place well-functioning operational controls, because these controls can limit the adverse impact of hedge funds on the financial system by reducing the possibility that the failure of one institution brings the system down. Last, it must be remembered that many hedge funds can easily leave the United States and will do so if regulation becomes too burdensome.[6] This consideration limits the amount of regulation that can be imposed on the mutual fund industry.

6.5 REGULATION OF HEDGE FUNDS IN THE AFTERMATH OF THE CRISIS

It is worth noting that there is very little evidence to suggest that hedge funds caused the current financial crisis or that they contributed to its severity in any significant way. That being said, it is possible that hedge funds, or subsets of hedge funds, may still impose externalities on the financial system. If so, the question is how to manage those externalities. With respect to any measure designed to limit the externalities for the financial system created by an entity, hedge funds should not receive any special treatment, either preferential or discriminatory. The exception, of course, is that financial institutions that receive explicit guarantees from the government (e.g., deposit institutions) necessarily require additional oversight relative to hedge funds.

Transparency

Most important is the idea that transparency to regulators is desirable, as it can help the regulator measure and manage potential systemic risk. Consequently, hedge funds should be required to provide regulators with regular and timely information about both their asset positions and their leverage levels. The required information would include the hedge fund's asset size, both on and off balance sheet, its leverage, its proportion of illiquid positions, its risk concentration, and its contribution to aggregate systemic risk.[7]

Public disclosure of hedge fund positions and leverage levels also reduces the externalities that hedge funds impose on the financial system, because such disclosure can reduce the counterparty credit risk that hedge funds impose. But there is a secondary issue regarding public transparency. While transparency is important to regulators, it may also be important to financial participants at large. Public transparency allows fund investors to make better-informed decisions and to better allocate capital across funds, which benefits both of them. However, requiring public disclosure of positions imposes costs on hedge funds since position disclosure by a hedge fund facilitates imitation by others, which likely leads to deterioration in the hedge fund's performance. Determining whether there is a need for special regulation of hedge funds with respect to public transparency involves balancing these benefits and costs. If the benefits outweigh the costs, it might make sense to impose regulation on hedge funds with respect to public transparency that is designed to help fund investors better monitor their funds. For example, hedge funds could be required to periodically disclose summary leverage measures.

One of the major ways hedge funds currently disclose their positions is through Form 13F. Specifically, 13F requires hedge funds with more than $100 million under management to disclose their long positions as of the end of each calendar quarter to the SEC and the public within 45 days of the end of the quarter. It is difficult to understand why long positions are required to be disclosed but short positions are not. Either long and short positions should both be required to be disclosed or neither should be required to be disclosed.[8]

Hedge funds need regulation that encourages them to implement well-functioning operational controls. The reason is the considerable benefits for fund investors of well-functioning operational controls. Penalties for violating operational controls in place should be sufficiently harsh to act as a deterrent.

Systemic Risk

Since hedge funds do not receive guarantees from the government and so are not subject to the moral hazard problems associated with such guarantees, any additional regulation of hedge funds is in general not warranted. As mentioned earlier, however, the exception is when a hedge fund imposes externalities on the financial system. If a hedge fund falls into the class of large, complex financial institutions (LCFIs), like the LTCM example in Section 6.3, then it is fairly clear it needs to be treated as a systemic institution and regulated (and taxed) as such.[9] If a hedge fund falls into the class of firms considered to be systemic, then it would be subject to an externality tax; in other words, it would be required to purchase insurance against systemic states.[10] More generally, any fees levied on a financial institution for using the financial system in a manner that generates systemic risk should also be levied on a hedge fund if it uses financial markets in this manner. The regulatory difficulty is ascertaining when (if ever) a hedge fund is using the financial system in this manner.

A further regulatory difficulty arises if a subset of funds together imposes externalities on the financial system because those funds are capable of generating considerable and uncertain counterparty credit risk in the financial system, because they are capable of large trades that move prices far away from fundamentals, or because of the capacity of those funds for severe and synchronized capital erosion. Each fund alone, though, would not qualify for the LCFI category.

Figure 6.3 suggests a high degree of interconnectedness across styles. Nevertheless, one way to distinguish funds may be to look at them style by style (or by groups of styles that we expect to be related) to see if any fund style contains a group of funds that might constitute a systemic subset. For a subset to be regarded as imposing such externalities on the financial system, one would need all the following to be satisfied: (1) the total net asset value of funds in the subset must be above a given cutoff, (2) the subset must contribute a certain amount to aggregate systemic risk, (3) the leverage level of the subset taken as a group must exceed a given cutoff, and (4) the extent of the correlation across the fund returns in the subset must exceed some threshold.[11] When considering a style as a possible subset, any fund following that style whose return does not exceed the specified correlation threshold should be excluded from the subset. This recognizes that even within a style, there can be considerable variation in the strategies actually being implemented by funds.

Each hedge fund in such a subset may be too small in terms of its positions or trade volume to be subject to any fees that might be levied on financial institutions for using financial markets in a manner that generates systemic risk (and the associated externalities). However, if the subset taken together as a single entity qualifies to pay such fees, then each fund in the subset should pay a fraction of the fees, depending on its contribution to the subset along whatever dimension (most likely positions or trade volume) is being used to determine the fees to be paid.

Runs

A final concern lies with the shadow banking system in general. Institutions in the shadow banking system world borrow short-term in rollover debt markets, leverage themselves significantly, and then lend and invest in longer-term and illiquid assets. However, unlike commercial banks, they do not have access to the safety nets—deposit insurance and lender of last resort of the central bank—that have been designed to prevent runs on banks. This is why, in the current financial crisis, we observed runs on seemingly safe managed funds, such as SIVs, asset-backed commercial paper (ABCP) conduits, and money market funds. On the one hand, hedge funds would appear to be even more susceptible to these runs; for example, they invest in less liquid yet riskier assets and they are less transparent. On the other hand, compared to money market funds, they are more diverse and face quarterly (as opposed to daily) redemptions. It may in fact be the lack of diversity across conduits and money market funds that caused their runs once one fund reported poor performance.

Nevertheless, it is worth thinking about whether hedge funds that belong to one of the subsets imposing externalities on the financial system may need regulation that discourages investors from withdrawing funds after bad performance. Since bad performance by a fund may lead to a run on the fund's assets under management, correlated performances lead to correlated runs, which may contribute to the externalities that the subset is imposing on the financial system. Here are some possible channels that could be used to limit runs.

- Lockup periods could be lengthened, though this imposes a cost on investors who otherwise would like to withdraw their money. There is a trade-off and it is not clear exactly what restrictions would best balance the competing considerations.
- Redemptions could be regulated. Right now, most funds that allow redemptions allow them at the end of calendar quarters. The externality to the financial system that hedge fund redemptions cause could be reduced if hedge funds stagger redemptions across the year. There could be three cycles (more if midmonth redemptions are encouraged): (1) December, March, June, and September; (2) January, April, July, and October; and (3) February, May, August, and November. Again, there is a cost to investors since this staggering either reduces investment options available to investors after redemptions (if hedge funds accept new funds only at the times when they allow redemptions) or increases the trading costs incurred by hedge funds (if hedge funds accept new funds at the end of each month or even more frequently).
- The length of notice that investors must give hedge funds before they can withdraw their money could also be regulated.

On first reflection, it would seem that lockup restrictions would be difficult to either enforce or regulate, but that is not the case. Lockups help stabilize the system. If funds within a systemic subset do not impose lockups, then they would be charged a fee (i.e., taxed). In equilibrium, whether a fund imposes a lockup restriction or not depends on the fees it pays the regulator if it doesn't versus its increase in funds under management if it doesn't (since investors prefer funds not to be restricted). The most likely system would have unlocked funds charging higher management fees, which would be used to help pay the regulator. In general, the costs of the tax would be shared between the hedge fund principals and investors.

Capital Markets Safety Board

In their research paper, Getmansky, Lo, and Mei (2004) proposed the following idea for hedge fund regulation.[12] Because hedge funds are so diverse and complex, it is currently impractical to regulate and impose rules that are appropriate for every hedge fund. As an alternative, they suggest a Capital Markets Safety Board (CMSB) modeled on the National Transportation Safety Board (NTSB). Similar to the NTSB, the CMSB would investigate and report on financial industry disasters. The CMSB would bring together an experienced team of professionals—accountants, finance professionals, and lawyers. Because these professionals would investigate all disasters together, then, through experience, a set of systemic risk measures, important principles, and possible regulatory rules would emerge. Most important, the CMSB could learn about the cracks in the system. The cost of such an exercise would be quite low, with the potential to be quite informative. In contrast, poor regulation based on conjectures (as opposed to underlying factual information) can have many unintended consequences.

6.6 CONCLUSION

The hedge fund industry has grown rapidly over the past 15 years. As of January 2007, hedge funds had upwards of $1.5 trillion of assets under management. However, there is very little evidence to suggest that hedge funds caused the current financial crisis or that they contributed to its severity in any significant way. That being said, it is possible that a particularly large hedge fund of the LTCM type (or some subsets of the hedge fund industry) may still be imposing externalities on the financial system if capable of (1) generating considerable, uncertain counterparty credit risk in the financial system, (2) large synchronized trades that move prices far away from fundamentals, or (3) severe and synchronized capital erosion that compromises its ability to provide liquidity services. We argue that the LCFI hedge fund (or subset of smaller hedge funds) imposing externalities on the financial system may require additional regulation to manage these externalities. Just as important, the rest of the hedge fund industry, which is not imposing such externalities, should not be subject to the same regulation. It is essential to always remember that hedge funds are an organizational form, not an investment strategy.

NOTES

1. The diagram is taken from Khandani and Lo (2007).
2. One important caveat to this conclusion follows from the fact that stock returns tend to move together and the betas of hedge funds with respect to the market tend to be positive, most likely because hedge funds typically are net long stock. In Andrew Lo's textbook (Lo 2008a), Table 1.9 on page 23 lists the betas (with respect to the S&P 500) of the same 13 hedge fund indexes computed for 1994–2007. Eight of the 13 betas are significantly positive and one is significantly negative. Thus, since many of the betas are clearly nonzero, the increase in the return correlations across the hedge fund indexes may be due to an increase in the betas of the indexes going from the first period to the second period rather than an increase in the overlap in their positions.
3. See Jorion (2000) for details regarding LTCM.
4. This mechanism is modeled by Brunnermeier and Pedersen (forthcoming), and Khandani and Lo (2007) provide empirical evidence from the quant event.
5. See Jorion (2000) and Khandani and Lo (2007) for descriptions of the environments for LTCM and the quant fund meltdown, respectively.
6. See Chapter 18, "International Alignment of Financial Sector Regulation."
7. See Chapter 13, "Regulating Systemic Risk."
8. The only possible reason to require disclosure of long positions but not short positions is that long positions have voting rights, which can have implications for corporate control. But Schedule 13D already addresses this concern. When a person or group of persons acquires beneficial ownership of more than 5 percent of a voting class of a company's equity securities registered under Section 12 of the Securities Exchange Act of 1934, they are required to report the acquisition and other information by filing Schedule 13D with the SEC within 10 days after the purchase. The schedule is provided to the company that issued the securities and each exchange where the security is traded.
9. See Chapter 5, "Enhanced Regulation of Large, Complex Financial Institutions."
10. See Chapter 13, "Regulating Systemic Risk."
11. The threshold could be applied to the minimum of the pairwise return correlations for the funds in the subset or to the minimum of the percentage return variation explained by the first principal component for the returns of the subset.
12. See also Andrew Lo's written testimony for the House Oversight Committee Hearing on Hedge Funds (Lo 2008b).

REFERENCES

Brown, Stephen, and William Goetzmann. 2003. Hedge funds with style. *Journal of Portfolio Management* 29:101–112.

Brown, Stephen, William Goetzmann, and Bing Liang. Forthcoming. Estimating operational risk for hedge funds: The ω-score. *Financial Analysts Journal*.

Brown, Stephen, William Goetzmann, and James Park. 2001. Careers and survival: Competition and risk in the hedge fund and CTA industry. *Journal of Finance* 61:1869–1886.

Brunnermeier, Markus, and Lasse Heje Pedersen. Forthcoming. Market liquidity and funding liquidity. *Review of Financial Studies*.

Garleanu, Nicolae, and Lasse Heje Pedersen. 2007. Liquidity and risk management. *American Economic Review, P&P* 97 (2):193–197.

Getmansky, Mila, Andrew Lo, and Shauna Mei. 2004. Sifting through the wreckage: Lessons from recent hedge-fund liquidations. *Journal of Investment Management* 2:6–38.

Glode, Vincent, and Richard C. Green. Forthcoming. Information spillovers and performance persistence in private equity partnerships. *Journal of Financial Economics*.

Jorion, Philippe. 2000. Risk management lessons from Long-Term Capital Management. *European Financial Management* 6:277–300.

Khandani, A., and A. Lo. 2007. What happened to the quants in August 2007? *Journal of Investment Management* 5:5–54.

Lo, Andrew. 2008a. *Hedge funds: An analytic perspective.* Princeton, NJ: Princeton University Press.

Lo, Andrew. 2008b. Hedge funds, systemic risk, and the financial crisis of 2007–2008. Written Testimony for the House Oversight Committee Hearing on Hedge Funds.

Mitchell, Mark, Lasse Heje Pedersen, and Todd Pulvino. 2007. Slow moving capital. *American Economic Review, P&P* 97 (2):215–220.

Three

Governance, Incentives, and Fair Value Accounting Overview

Viral V. Acharya and Rangarajan K. Sundaram

How did we end up in such a mess? The view we saw in the preceding chapters focused on mortgage brokers' incentives, government-sponsored enterprises (GSEs), and the shadow banking system, and placed the blame—at least partially—on mispriced guarantees and flawed regulation of the financial sector. In this view, banks were put in an arena where regulators laid down the rules of the game; subject to the rules, banks competed as well as they could; but the rules were so defective to begin with that mayhem inevitably resulted. But there is another view, one less charitable to bankers, that makes it harder to rationalize the generous bailout packages they have received: that the origins of the crisis lie in the financial institutions themselves, in a collapse of corporate and regulatory governance and the provision of ill-designed incentives.

It is this second view that is discussed in the two chapters that follow ("Corporate Governance in the Modern Financial Sector" and "Rethinking Compensation in Financial Firms"). The overarching theme is that it has become increasingly unlikely that regulatory governance (based on supervision and pricing of guarantees) and external corporate governance (based on vigilance of board members) will succeed by themselves in disciplining the risk-taking incentives in large, complex financial institutions (LCFIs). The reasons are simple. While regulators can and should price guarantees fairly, they have little direct influence over the day-to-day operational risks that LCFIs take on. Ditto for board members; while they might succeed in meeting audit requirements and thereby ensure regulatory compliance, it is unlikely they can expect to understand in detail exactly how or why the star trader who took home a $30 million bonus last year blew up the floor in the time since.

Herein lies the real issue. Financial firms can alter their risk profiles swiftly, almost instantly, unlike industrial firms. As financial products become ever more complex and opaque, financial firms need to be disciplined through the provision of appropriate incentives rather than through direct control over the products. In order to understand how incentives in financial firms could be improved, it is useful first to understand what the problems are with the current incentive structures.

Let us take a hypothetical situation, a caricature but one not too far removed from what went on in the years leading up to the crisis. Suppose there is demand in the economy for insurance against certain bad, but infrequent, outcomes, say outcomes that occur on average once every seven years. A profit center inside an insurance firm identifies this demand and designs a product that will provide a payout to investors if these outcomes arise. The product is akin to the insurance company writing an out-of-the-money put option to investors. Investors are willing to pay a fee for this product as long as the insurance firm has a sufficiently healthy balance sheet (at least from the outside!). Now, the bad outcomes occur infrequently, so how is the profit center to be compensated in the meanwhile? The wrong rule, and unfortunately the one that has been the most prevalent in financial firms, is to reward the profit center based simply on the net fees it generated from selling the insurance in the past year. Under this rule, the profit center has an incentive to sell large quantities of the insurance to the market, thereby generating so-called "fake alpha" and resulting in generous bonuses at the end of each year. In the process, firm risk gets built up to a point where, when the put option is exercised, the firm is unlikely to have enough cash to pay off all the investors, and will probably be close to default. But by this time, the profit center and the firm have grown so large that they are too big to fail (TBTF) and very likely will be rescued by the government. Top management may get fired in the process, but the profit center is quite central to the firm's franchise. In anticipation of these events, the puts are worth selling (and indeed buying, too) in the first place.

Why are such short-term incentives in place in financial firms? Does the top management of these firms not have sufficient skin in the game to put in place long-term compensation plans for their subordinates? The reasons are somewhat subtle. Top management does certainly have a fair amount of shareholdings in many of these firms, and many at the top did lose sizable personal fortunes as their firms collapsed over the past year. But this does not in itself enable them to provide long-term incentives to the high-performance (risk-taking) profit centers, because the problem is one of *industry-wide* coordination. Traders and analysts at these profit centers are highly fungible across firms (yet another important difference between financial and industrial firms), so no one financial firm can subject its employees to tough longer-term evaluation and compensation contracts for fear of losing them to competitors that do not use a similar tough standard. A "prisoner's dilemma" type of outcome results, with every bank choosing the socially inferior short-term compensation structure. The real governance problem is thus one of externality; it is *internal to the entire financial sector*, and can be solved only if firms coordinate to implement significant changes—or are led to do so by regulators.

Thus, we make the following three recommendations for the design of compensation packages of senior management and trading desks/high-performance profit centers:

1. Greater disclosure and transparency of compensation packages and assessment criteria.
2. Longer stock holding periods and stricter forfeiture rules—for example, failed senior executives and traders who are ejected might confront a minimum 36-month holding period for the shares they take with them.
3. A bonus/malus approach to compensation that represents a multiyear structure where good performances accumulate in a bonus pool used to subtract bad performances in the future, not to be cashed out as and when the pool is augmented, but only in a staggered manner over time.

In order to implement these changes, regulators should take two steps:

1. Regulators should adopt a convoy approach wherein they employ suasion to get the most important LCFIs to agree on a basic code of best practice for compensation based on the preceding principles. Indeed, the current leverage that regulators have gained over the financial sector because of the bailout packages should be used to effect such an arrangement.
2. In addition to improving the compensation practices, regulators should limit regulatory arbitrage by ensuring that guarantees provided to the financial sector are priced fairly (as explained in chapters to follow), and perhaps as a cautionary step, also provide—or help provide—basic

education to board members of LCFIs on capital budgeting principles that rely on long-term return on assets (ROA) rather than on risk-inducing short-term return on equity (ROE).

An important issue not touched in this discussion but one that has come up repeatedly during the crisis is the role of fair value or mark-to-market accounting. In particular, if fair value accounting is abandoned during stress times when assets become illiquid, mark-to-market values cause markdowns on portfolios of healthier institutions too, even though they might not need to sell these assets right away, and these markdowns in turn raise concerns about their solvency when the issue may just be one of illiquidity. This theme is at the center of discussion in the third chapter to follow in this part ("Fair Value Accounting: Policy Issues Raised by the Credit Crunch").

In our view, the argument against fair value accounting, even in stress times, is unconvincing. Marking his book to the market is perhaps the most important function a trader performs for the financial firm. Without such marking, the firm would not be able to aggregate its various positions or understand its risk exposures. This is, of course, the rationale for fair value accounting in the first place. Critics of fair value accounting miss the crucial point that the willingness of market participants to trade with a firm or provide it with credit or finance would be *even lower* if it suspended fair value accounting in times of stress. How are arm's-length financiers to know what the firm's balance sheet looks like or is worth in liquidation if the firm were to simply stop reporting any reasonable value for it? A salient case in point is the announcement by BNP Paribas on August 9, 2007, that it was suspending net asset value (NAV) calculations for three of its money market funds since the market for asset-backed securities (ABSs), especially in subprime mortgages, had become rather illiquid. The consequence was a market freeze wherein money market investors abstained from rolling over asset-backed commercial paper (ABCP) altogether. Financing of this form has not returned to asset-backed securities since that day.

Worse yet, the practice of suppressing fair value accounting *only* in bad times will also induce excessive risk taking at financial firms. Consider the earlier example of the insurance firm selling put options and booking fees as profits each year. If outcomes insured by the firm became less likely in some years, the fair values of put options sold in the past would fall. This would result in a mark-to-market gain for the profit center, which managers would eagerly want to cash out as bonuses that year-end. However, when the law of averages catches up and the bad outcomes do become imminent, fair values of put options would rise, resulting in a mark-to-market loss for the profit center. It should come as no surprise that the profit center cries out for a suspension of fair value accounting at this point.

We believe thus that:

- Regulators such as the Financial Accounting Standards Board (FASB) and the Securities and Exchange Commission (SEC) should continue to support existing fair value accounting requirements and their extension to all financial instruments.
- But regulators may wish to consider providing additional guidance on how firms might be allowed to use internal models for fair value calculations of illiquid assets, but only with additional mandatory disclosures of the basis of such calculations and transparency about gains or losses not recognized due to illiquidity of certain assets.

CHAPTER 7

Corporate Governance in the Modern Financial Sector

Viral V. Acharya, Jennifer N. Carpenter, Xavier Gabaix, Kose John,
Matthew Richardson, Marti G. Subrahmanyam,
Rangarajan K. Sundaram, and Eitan Zemel

7.1 INTRODUCTION

Large, complex financial institutions (LCFIs) are highly levered entities with over 90 percent leverage, many with access to explicit deposit insurance protection and most with implicit too big to fail (TBTF) guarantees.[1] Together, these features of LCFIs have created several important problems. First, they have induced excessive leverage- and risk-taking tendencies. Second, the presence of implicit or explicit government guarantees—often unpriced and at best mispriced—has blunted the instrument of debt monitoring that would otherwise impose market discipline on risk taking by these firms. Third, the size of these institutions has shielded them from the disciplinary forces of the otherwise vibrant market for takeovers and shareholder activism. Finally, their ever-increasing complexity has diminished the power of governance from existing shareholders and non–executive board members. Unlike in industrial firms, it has become increasingly difficult for infrequently meeting boards to fully grasp the swiftness and forms by which risk profiles of these institutions can be altered by traders and securities desks. Figure 7.1 depicts the current governance structure of LCFIs and serves as a framework for the discussion and regulatory proposals provided in this chapter.

Although there is mounting evidence that points to weaknesses in equity governance of these firms in the months leading up to the financial crisis, the extreme leverage undertaken by these firms and the failure of their

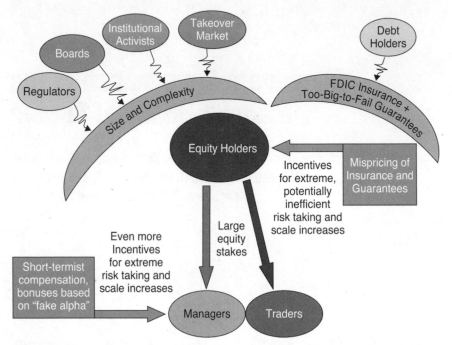

FIGURE 7.1 Current Corporate Governance of Large, Complex Financial Institutions

This graph presents the corporate governance structure of large, complex financial institutions (LCFIs). The figure in particular shows two impediments to governance, namely the mispriced government guarantees afforded LCFIs and the size and complexity of the LCFIs. Both of these components are shown here to create barriers to the market discipline that typically takes place under standard governance practices. As a consequence, equity holders have an incentive to take excessive risk, and possibly pass on the costs of short-termist compensation practices to other stakeholders down the line.

internal risk management practices suggest failure of regulatory governance as well. Ironically, reports of risk management failures suggest that simply meeting regulatory constraints was often perceived by bankers as a sufficient and prudent risk management objective. Given that guarantees take away the discipline that creditor runs bring to financial firms and any attempts to undo the excessive risk-taking incentives suffer from the possibility of regulatory arbitrage, can the regulatory governance of LCFIs be altered in some robust way to bring this risk taking down to efficient levels?

On this regulatory front, our most important policy recommendation is that the guarantees be priced correctly (i.e., to the extent feasible, commensurately with the level of risk of these institutions), and this pricing should be updated on a continuing basis. In addition, a potential mechanism for strengthening regulatory governance may be to require that the board of directors of these LCFIs include a regulator and prominent subordinated debt holders. Since there could be several impediments, political as well as practical, to implementing this uniformly at all banks, an alternative proposal is that all independent board members be educated in the operational details and complex products of the LCFIs, as well as on capital budgeting practices and performance assessment standards suitable for such highly levered, multidivisional firms.

Perhaps even more important, we recommend that given the increasing complexity of these institutions, the policy discussions also pay close attention to *internal* governance. Can boards and regulators that do not interact on a daily basis with the relevant profit centers of LCFIs ever be expected to achieve desirable outcomes based purely on monitoring and questioning? We believe not. They may, however, be able to ensure that internal governance practices are set up to achieve this.

On this front, we have several concrete proposals, all implemented through judicious design of incentives and compensation for top management (and potentially also for important lower-level employees such as traders). First, the compensation structure should induce management to maximize the total value of the enterprise, or return on assets (ROA), and not just maximize the equity value or return on equity (ROE), as is common practice. Maximizing the latter when debt is not fairly and continually priced creates excessive leverage- and risk-taking incentives. Second, the value created at the enterprise should be benchmarked against a cost of capital that reflects not just the cost in good times, when guarantees render the cost of debt essentially flat and invariant to risk, but also in bad times, when these firms are forced to make capital issuances that dilute shareholder value. These first two aspects aim to achieve better capital budgeting decisions.

Third, existing compensation structures seem too short-term, which also induces excessive risk taking. We propose that LCFIs should use more long-term contracts that include deferred compensation features. Restricted stock, clawbacks, incentive accounts (see, for example, Edmans, Gabaix, and Sadzik 2008), and bonus pools tied to long-term profits would all improve top-management compensation structures. We do not propose that the regulators mandate compensation structures at micro levels, but seek relatively unintrusive ways of shifting the industry equilibrium away from short-term performance assessment and toward long-term perspectives. Helping the industry coordinate this effort may perhaps be the best service regulators can provide here, given that financial firms seem to be caught in an inefficient equilibrium where a firm that implements compensation structures that are overall more efficient (for example, based on long-term performance) fears losing its employees to firms that retain existing short-termist compensation structures.

7.2   CORPORATE GOVERNANCE AT LCFIs

In general, corporate governance mechanisms attempt to align the managerial objectives with the interests of investors. Managers generally hold only a small fraction of the claims in the firm and enjoy a high degree of discretion because of the incompleteness of the contracts that dictate their decisions. Corporate governance usually consists of two types of mechanisms: mechanisms that monitor the managers (corporate boards, monitored debt, large block holders) and mechanisms that align the managers with the claim holders (high-powered incentives in compensation structures, performance-related dismissals of CEOs, hostile takeovers with replacement of incumbent management). How is corporate governance different in LCFIs?

To understand this, we need to examine how the claim structure of the LCFIs is different from that of a regular nonfinancial firm. On the liability side, LCFIs are highly levered entities. At least 90 percent of the claim holders of an LCFI are debt holders (including depositors). Another claimant is the Federal Deposit Insurance Corporation (FDIC), which has written a put option to the LCFI as deposit guarantor. Given this structure of claims, corporate governance mechanisms that align the manager with equity holders may deviate significantly from those that maximize firm value. Put differently, corporate governance mechanisms in LCFIs have to be designed so as to align the manager with the interests of the debt holders and the FDIC as well as the shareholders.

Monitoring by debt holders and the regulator would also be important components of corporate governance in LCFIs (see John and John 1993 for details). What kind of monitoring can one expect from debt holders? This depends on whether the LCFI is a depository institution. In a depository institution, the prominent debt holders are the depositors. For the most part, depositors are small claimants, possess little incentive to monitor, and are subject to the conventional free-rider problem. More problematic is deposit insurance, which further reduces incentives to monitor. It is not practical, then, to assume that the depositors would do any significant amount of monitoring. This means that the regulator, as a social planner, must play the monitoring role on behalf of the depositors. Of course, the regulator already has an incentive to monitor depository institutions, given that such institutions are insured by the regulator. Thus, for depository institutions, the role of the regulator is crucial.

If the LCFI has subordinated debt, the subordinated debt holders can play a role in monitoring as well. Concrete mechanisms by which the subordinated debt holders are able to monitor the LCFI include the enforcement of debt covenants and the proper pricing of the subordinated debt, which can be undermined by the presence of implicit too big to fail (TBTF) guarantees. Indeed, in the case of a nondepository financial company with high leverage levels, appropriate governance would rely in an important way on monitoring by prominent debt holders.

In order to assess the role of possible governance failures in LCFIs, it is useful to characterize conceptually the optimal governance system that the LCFI should have. Let us take the example of FDIC insurance. (The same reasoning holds for other types of insurance provided by the government—for instance, implicit insurance provided to TBTF institutions.) Assuming that the debt and the FDIC insurance are correctly priced, the correct governance system for the LCFI is one that provides managers with incentives to maximize the total value of the LCFI (the sum total of the value of all the claims outstanding against the LCFI) and not just the value of the equity of the LCFI. In other words, the equity holder governance that is conventionally thought of as corporate governance is only a part of the optimal governance that an LCFI should have. Moreover, even if the equity governance had worked well in a particular time period, it is possible that the total value of the LCFI was not maximized during this period.

If the FDIC insurance is properly priced, maximizing the with-guarantee value of the LCFI would be equivalent to maximizing the without-guarantee value of the LCFI. In contrast, if the FDIC insurance is not properly priced, then the appropriate objective in structuring corporate governance and managerial incentives would be to maximize the without-guarantee value of the LCFI. Otherwise, the LCFI management might make value-destroying choices to game the discrepancy in the pricing of the FDIC insurance. By recently changing its formula for how it charges institutions for deposit insurance, the FDIC has moved in the right direction since it imposes a fee on financial institutions that recognizes the risk-taking incentives of deposit institutions. The new pricing scheme for deposit insurance premiums attempts to capture risk by combining examination ratings, financial ratios, and, for large banks, long-term debt issuer ratings. It is important, however, that during normal periods, the premiums that go unused by the FDIC not be returned to the banking system (a current practice), or else the insurance is effectively mispriced.

In the preceding discussion, we assumed that the positive and negative externalities imposed by the LCFI on the financial system (and the society as a whole) are not significant. In reality, these externalities may be large. If that is the case, the design of the optimal governance for the LCFI and the corresponding managerial incentives should take into account the positive and negative externalities caused by the LCFI. For example, if the risk-shifting activities by an LCFI impose negative externalities on the financial system and the society at large, the governance of the LCFI should be structured to induce more conservative choices by the management compared to those that maximize the total value of the LCFI. For example, a natural solution would be to charge deposit institutions not just an insurance fee, but also a risk fee for their contribution to systemic risk. This might amount to a multiplier on the individual financial ratios under current FDIC rules or to the addition of a systemic risk factor to the FDIC pricing formula.[2] Since the majority of financial firms contribute only marginally to systemic risk, the LCFIs would bear the brunt of the tax.

In the following discussion, we examine whether corporate governance in LCFIs has failed and whether managerial compensation design has been optimal. We make a distinction between equity governance and debt governance in LCFIs. In addition, we discuss the accounting principles that go into the design of top-management compensation and capital budgeting. We also examine the incentive effects of the contracts of managers and traders that have become increasingly short-term. We close by providing some solutions for strengthening debt or regulator governance of the LCFIs and improving the compensation structures of managers and traders of the LCFIs.

7.3 DID GOVERNANCE FAIL?

In the introductory section, we argued that an optimal governance structure for LCFIs should balance equity governance with appropriately strong debt or regulator governance. In this section, we evaluate whether there was a failure to achieve this balance. We first examine whether the outcomes were consistent with a failure in equity governance. Subsequently, we consider whether the same factors that might have weakened equity governance might have damaged debt governance even more.

Equity Governance

On the one hand, equity governance may have been strong, though perhaps misguided. In particular, some aspects of top management compensation may have aligned managers strongly with shareholders. The managers of most of these financial institutions received a great deal of their compensation in the form of the equity of the firm with multiyear vesting restrictions. In fact, substantial portions of the equity of both the commercial and investment banks were held by employees. Indeed, the risk-shifting strategies, involving high leverage and high scale of operations, and the curbing or silencing of risk management may have been entirely consistent with a management being strongly aligned with equity holders (i.e., with a high level of equity governance).[3] This is one possible interpretation of then Citigroup CEO Chuck Prince's statement that "As long as the music is playing, you've got to get up and dance" (*Financial Times*, July 9, 2007). Furthermore, although some view the high level of compensation paid to bankers as a symptom of weak equity governance, others can explain the high pay level as appropriate for executive talent in a competitive labor market. Gabaix and Landier (2008), for example, show how such a mechanism can explain pay scales in corporate America.

It is hard to say how many of the large losses we have seen were the result of inefficient risk choices and how many were simply bets gone awry. But there are several reasons why even a strong equity governance system could have given rise to risky strategies with the outcomes that we have observed. Gaming of TBTF guarantees, priced deposit insurance, and coarse capital requirements would all have led to similar strategies even if equity governance was effective.

On the other hand, there are several reasons why equity governance may have been weak. The distinguishing features of LCFIs may have obstructed the conventional mechanisms of equity governance. First, given the enormous size of the LCFIs, the stake of equity ownership needed for effective monitoring and intervention was simply too great for even large institutions and hedge funds. While typical hedge fund activists consider an ownership of 5 to 15 percent of equity appropriate for launching activism, they found it difficult to hold even 1 percent of the equity of some of the LCFIs. An additional factor that discouraged institutional activism and hostile takeovers was the complexity of these financial institutions. The intricate nature of the financial products and the complexity of the positions that they maintained in derivatives, credit swaps, and other complex instruments made it difficult for these institutions and raiders to exercise external market discipline.

In the absence of external market discipline, the corporate boards could have become more active. However, the same factors of size and complexity hindered boards as well. The board members' ownership in these large LCFIs was minuscule. The activities of the LCFIs became increasingly complex and technical. Board members may have found it difficult to ask the hard questions, leading to asymmetric information between the corporate board and the management.

Finally, the disciplining effect of market competition was also unable to compensate for the weakening of other governance mechanisms. Entry in the banking sector is difficult due to the initial capital requirements in this regulated industry. Moreover, it is not easy for new, small banks to compete with an incumbent LCFI, because of the fixed costs in setting up large trading desks, trade settlement and clearing, enterprise-wide risk management, and so on.

Debt and Regulatory Governance

While there may be some symptoms of a failure in equity governance, the failure in regulatory and debt governance, for many of the same reasons, may have been the more important governance problem that led to the risky strategies implemented by the LCFIs. The size and complexity of the LCFIs, and the intricacies of their financial products and transactions, may have made it impossible for many regulators to ask the relevant hard questions, leading to ineffective regulation.

The solutions, therefore, involve strengthening regulatory monitoring. Similar in spirit to the Sarbanes-Oxley requirement of an independent audit committee, one possibility is that the board of directors of the LCFI should include a prominent debt holder or a regulator. Given the hordes of information from bank examiners, this regulator would at least ask the difficult, probing questions during board meetings. In nondepository finance companies that also have very high leverage levels, monitoring by debt holders would be important, and prominent debt holders could similarly serve on the board.

Including a regulator or debt holders on the board of directors uniformly at all large banks could have several impediments—political as well as practical. Some may argue that the current system of regulatory monitoring through a large number of bank examiners assigned to the LCFIs already does a good job of protecting the interests of the regulator. There may be political opposition to implementing an untried alternative scheme if the banking community believes that the current systems work well enough. Moreover, the regulator's only interest would be serving the depositors and could therefore steer management away from innovative and risky, albeit positive, net present value (NPV) projects. Finally, the regulator may be more prone to political pressure, which may not serve the best interests of the financial institution.

An alternative idea is to improve the monitoring ability of the board by strengthening its information and competence in the area of the operational details and products of the LCFIs. All board members, including the regulator, should be provided with information and training in the important operational details of the LCFI and its complex financial products. Such information may include aspects of capital budgeting in multidivisional firms, capital budgeting that accounts for hurdle rates for business and financial risk, and capital budgeting that appreciates the difference between costs of capital in good times and bad times; pros and cons of different accounting principles such as ROA or return on invested capital (ROIC) versus ROE; valuation metrics; different leverage and funding ratios such as ratios of loans to assets, deposits to assets, and tangible equity to tangible assets; and general risk management principles, terms, and measures.

7.4 COMPENSATION AT FINANCIAL FIRMS

In this section, we discuss several features of compensation in financial firms. In particular, we address two important areas: (1) the relationship between the firm's investment decisions and a CEO's compensation package, and (2) the relationship between the incentives of employees within these firms to take risky bets and their compensation.[4] We conclude with a discussion of possible remedies.

CEO Compensation and Optimal Investment Policy

Like optimal corporate governance, optimal CEO compensation should be designed to induce the CEO to make investment choices that maximize the total value of the LCFI, and this value should account for externalities that the LCFI imposes on the financial system and society. Such an optimal compensation system would not simply align the CEO incentives with those of equity holders.

There have been several flaws in the structure of top-management compensation in LCFIs. Given weak debt holder governance, management compensation has directed the manager toward equity value maximization based on accounting measures that reward excessive risk taking, such as ROE instead of ROA or ROIC. Indeed, almost all LCFIs rely on ROE, and most employ thresholds that are independent of business risk and financial leverage (see Acharya and Franks 2008). Such a compensation structure induces high leverage choices and risk taking on the part of the managers and traders.

To provide incentives for value maximization and appropriate risk taking, top-management compensation structures for financial firms should include debtlike securities, such as deferred compensation, in addition to stock-based pay (see John, Saunders, and Senbet 2000). Managerial compensation should also include mechanisms for giving the CEO a longer-term perspective. For example, LCFIs should use more long-term contracts, such as restricted stock, clawbacks, incentive accounts (see Edmans, Gabaix, and Sadzik 2008), and bonus pools tied to long-term profits. CEOs should also be made to hold on to the LCFI stock for a period of time after they leave the firm. See, for example, details of recent UBS revamping of pay structure and bonuses (*Financial Times*, November 18, 2008), or the pay structure for Goldman Sachs. A well-designed compensation structure that has such long-term components will induce value-maximizing strategies on the part of the CEO.

This principle of total value maximization in designing compensation also provides the correct benchmark to gauge performance. The value created at enterprises should be benchmarked against a cost of capital that reflects not just the cost in good times, when guarantees render the cost of debt essentially flat and invariant to risk, but also in bad times, when these firms are forced to make shareholder-value-diluting equity or subordinated debt issuances. This will lead to better capital budgeting decisions.

Compensation of Traders and Perverse Incentives

Arguably, the most important issue facing the governance of financial institutions is the existence of perverse incentives for bankers and traders within the organization. Because traders get little or no nonpecuniary benefits from the firm and their actions have mostly marginal effects on the firm's overall prospects, there is a large moral hazard problem that encourages excessive risk taking. Since most of the compensation is in the form of bonuses tied to short-term profits with little or no risk adjustment, and because such bonuses are one-sided (i.e., positive in good times and at worst zero when returns are poor), traders may have an incentive to take much bigger risks than justified by shareholder value maximization, let alone firm value maximization.

In the current crisis, this led to collateralized debt obligation (CDO) desks accumulating extraordinarily large portfolios of so-called AAA-rated tranches of subprime pools. These portfolios are essentially equivalent to writing put options on rare events such as a large accumulation of defaults of subprime mortgages. In most periods, the CDO desks will earn huge fees from the option premiums, book them as profits, and then pay out a fraction as huge bonuses. In fact, some of the biggest bonuses paid on Wall Street from 2004 to 2006 were associated with structured products like these. Of course, when the rare event occurs, the entire firm is put at risk. Most of the costs, however, are borne by the other employees and shareholders. This is precisely what happened in 2007 and 2008.

This fake alpha in the industry—that is, compensation based on short-term excess returns in the current bonus pool—does not take into account lower returns or losses in subsequent periods for which current activities are responsible. This creates a perverse system in which traders are encouraged to maximize current compensation to themselves, possibly at the expense of shareholders. They are encouraged to maximize the use of leverage without regard to its impact on bankruptcy risk of the firm. They are encouraged to report to risk managers, senior management, and regulators that all is well when in fact it is not. These issues are discussed in detail in Chapter 8, "Rethinking Compensation in Financial Firms."

Proposals

We do not propose that regulators mandate specific contracts for LCFIs or micromanage compensation structures. Rather, we seek relatively unintrusive ways of shifting the industry equilibrium away from short-term performance assessment toward rewarding long-term perspectives. We believe that an infrastructure of light regulation can encourage firms to upgrade the design of their CEO compensation, while still leaving room for firms to tailor pay structure to specific settings. Helping the industry coordinate this effort may in fact be the best service regulators can provide here, given that financial firms seem to be stuck in an inefficient equilibrium in which no firm wants to be the first to innovate for fear of losing its employees.

We provide two specific regulatory directives that may help the economy move to a better equilibrium: (1) correct pricing of FDIC premiums, and (2) preferential tax treatment for deferred compensation. For example, John, Saunders, and Senbet (2000) make the following proposal. If FDIC insurance is rationally priced, anticipating the investment policy that would be implemented, such pricing would naturally be a function of the incentive features included in the compensation structure. A high-powered incentive structure would have a higher premium because such compensation structure would induce riskier investment choices compared to one that includes deferred compensation by the manager. In other words, rational pricing of the FDIC premium would by itself give LCFIs incentives to design for their top management compensation structures that would induce them to implement investment choices that maximize total firm value.

In addition to the put option that has been written by the regulator through deposit insurance, the regulator has additional claims in the LCFI in the form of implicit guarantees to bail out the firm in some future states of the world. One possibility is for the regulator to impose some constraints on the compensation structures of the LCFIs. In the current FDIC Improvement Act of 1991, there are restrictions imposed on the levels of compensation and the option component in the top-management compensation of severely undercapitalized banks. Our view is that there should be only minimal regulation of compensation structures of individual LCFIs. For the LCFIs in good standing, we propose preferential tax treatment for certain features such as deferred compensation and long-term compensation. Under this tax treatment, LCFIs would still be able to design their compensation structures optimally. Since all LCFIs face similar tax environments, they can compete for talent on a level playing field. There is precedent for such preferential tax treatment of specific compensation features (see, for example, Section 162(m) of the Internal Revenue Code, a tax law enacted in 1994 that gives preferential treatment for incentive compensation). A similar preferential treatment for deferred compensation would be desirable.

Even with an optimally designed compensation structure that induces the best actions, the ability of the regulator to monitor the LCFI and directly limit risk taking through fully enforced leverage constraints, capital requirements, or position limits may still be an essential ingredient of a sound financial system.

NOTES

1. See Chapter 5, "Enhanced Regulation of Large, Complex Financial Institutions."
2. See Chapter 13, "Regulating Systemic Risk."
3. Of course, if the equity held by management is a significant fraction of their wealth, then risk aversion on their part may mitigate their risk-taking incentives.
4. See Chapter 8, "Rethinking Compensation in Financial Firms."

REFERENCES

Acharya, Viral, and Julian Franks. 2008. Capital budgeting at banks: The role of government guarantees. Report prepared for Knight Vinke Asset Management.

Edmans, Alex, Xavier Gabaix, and Tomasz Sadzik. 2008. Dynamic incentive accounts. Working paper, New York University.

Gabaix, Xavier, and Augustin Landier. 2008. Why has CEO pay increased so much? *Quarterly Journal of Economics* 123:49–100.

John, Kose, and Teresa A. John. 1993. Top-management compensation and capital structure. *Journal of Finance* 48:949–974.

John, Kose, Anthony Saunders, and Lemma Senbet. 2000. A theory of bank regulation and management compensation. *Review of Financial Studies* 13:95–125.

CHAPTER 8

Rethinking Compensation in Financial Firms

Gian Luca Clementi, Thomas F. Cooley,
Matthew Richardson, and Ingo Walter

8.1 INTRODUCTION

Conventional wisdom in market economies is that employee compensation is ultimately driven by the marginal product of labor. Those who contribute more to whatever market value business firms produce will see that reflected in their compensation levels. This relationship is supposed to set the basis for compensation practices in public and private companies. Since the shareholder reaps the residual benefit of employee effort and therefore has a vital stake in pay for performance, this ought to be carefully reflected in the firm's governance process.

There are, of course, plenty of broad-gauge exceptions to the link between pay and performance as concerns about social justice (minimum wage legislation) or bargaining power (labor unions) in the real world override pure economic outcomes in the market for human resources. Still, overall compensation levels are basically the result of a complex interplay of supply and demand in the market for labor—with highly diverse skills, motivation, and personal attributes. In public companies, boards of directors set compensation levels for senior management, and senior management sets compensation levels and remuneration policies for all other employees.

The same broad relationships should apply in the financial services industry. There is no particular reason why this sector of the economy ought to be considered special, and therefore require external intervention in the compensation process. Yet public debate regarding allegedly dysfunctional approaches to employee compensation has reached a crescendo in the current financial crisis. With some $7 trillion in taxpayer guarantees of all kinds of financial contracts so far—including underwriting direct obligations of premier institutions like JPMorgan Chase, Fannie Mae, Freddie Mac, and AIG—and $350 billion in government equity holdings in a broad range of financial firms, the public naturally wants to know who was responsible for the train wreck and how highly paid financial talent ended up burdening society as a whole with unprecedented exposure to financial risk.

Inevitably, therefore, the unprecedented public bailout has forced the executive compensation issue into the open. The cat's out of the bag, and won't be recaptured anytime soon. The public demands a policy response that will help prevent yet another financial disaster down the road. Having been forced into taking equity stakes in most of the largest financial firms, taxpayers, through their elected representatives, now feel empowered to have a say in how this is going to happen—for better or worse.

8.2 EXAMPLES OF MISALIGNED APPROACHES TO COMPENSATION

Whereas the issue of appropriate management compensation aligned as closely as possible to the interests of shareholders is a generic one, in institutions that are deemed too big to fail (TBTF) the compensation alignment issue takes on even greater importance. Compensation systems must be aligned to the avoidance of systemic risk. Several examples from the global financial crisis may be instructive.

In the summer of 2005, one of the major players in subprime mortgage collateralized debt obligations (CDOs), UBS, ramped up its CDO warehouse business.[1] In this business, UBS would purchase residential mortgage-backed securities (RMBSs) primarily made up of subprime mortgages, house them in its CDO warehouse, prepare them for securitization, and then sell the multi-tranche CDOs in the marketplace. UBS's CDO desk received structuring fees on the notional value of the deal ranging from 30 to 150 basis points, depending on the credit quality of the tranche. Because this process from start to finish took two to four months, the CDO warehouse was an important component of UBS's value at risk and UBS recognized this as such. In 2005, the CDO business, albeit a risky one, worked as intended. UBS faced short-term holding risk during the securitization process but was compensated by being paid considerable fees. The credit risk that would normally be held by banks or mortgage lenders was transferred to the capital market.[2]

Starting in 2006, however, UBS began to hold the so-called AAA-rated, super-senior tranches of the CDOs rather than sell them. These tranches have the highest priority within the CDO and thus are somewhat protected by the junior tranches. The senior tranches are hit only if there are substantial defaults and low recoveries. That said, the super-senior tranches were structured to hold as much of the pool of subprime loans as possible and still maintain the AAA rating given by rating agencies.[3] From holding almost none of these securities in February 2006, the UBS CDO desk was holding over $50 billion worth in September 2007. The main reason for retaining these tranches on their books was that these securities offered a yield above UBS's internal funding rate, which hovered around the London Interbank Offered Rate (LIBOR), yielding an immediate ongoing profit. Moreover,

- Because these securities were rated AAA, they barely registered on UBS's value at risk or stress tests even when totally unhedged.[4] Thus, the excess yield was treated as pure alpha.[5]
- As a result of this pure alpha, there were no aggregate notional limits placed on the CDO warehouse. Thus, every extra dollar of CDOs retained increased the desk's profit.
- Moreover, because the UBS compensation structure did not differentiate between profits derived from a low cost of funding versus the generation of true excess return (i.e., alpha), the desk's compensation was directly linked to the size of the CDO's mortgage book.
- There was no liquidity premium charged to the group. That is, there was little or no differentiation between liquid and illiquid assets even though there are many examples of almost identical securities offering different yields in the markets (e.g., off-the-run versus on-the-run Treasuries).

These facts meant that the CDO desk had the incentive to grow the balance sheet as large as possible because, by construction, their bonuses were tied to instant profits with no recognition of any risk. This growth continued even during the first half of 2007 as subprime lenders were going bankrupt and hedge funds were reporting losses. In fact, UBS shut down one of its own operations, Dillon Read Capital Management, in May 2007 for losses in its subprime investment portfolio. In March 2007, the Treasury group within UBS, alarmed at the tremendous growth of the balance sheet, especially in relatively illiquid asset-backed securities (ABSs), argued for a limit on illiquid assets, a haircut funding model (in which illiquid assets would no longer get short-term funding), and an overall freeze on the balance sheet. This call went unanswered.

Putting aside the issue of whether these securities were truly AAA in quality, there is no doubt that their underlying risk was very asymmetric. That is, the securities would pay a premium above LIBOR in most states of nature, but in the rare event that there were substantial defaults and low recoveries, they would get hit. Historically, this rare event would arise only if the underlying collateral (i.e., house prices) fell dramatically or there was a sharp economic downturn (i.e., as in previous recessions). In finance terms, due to the priority structure of the claims, the holders of the senior tranche were essentially invested in a risk-free asset, like LIBOR, while simultaneously writing a way out-of-the-money put option on the market.[6]

If the aforementioned description of the governance (or lack thereof) of the CDO desk at UBS was an aberration, then there would not be a potential issue for regulation. Unfortunately, it seemed to be the norm during this period and endemic to many firms.[7] Some further examples:

First, over the period 2005–2007, Citigroup was one of the largest CDO issuers (ranked first in 2005 with $28 billion, third in 2006 with $33 billion, and first again in 2007 with $40 billion). There are remarkable similarities to UBS: (1) by the third quarter, Citigroup had accumulated over $55 billion of AAA-rated higher-tranche mortgages; (2) there was no clear separation between risk management and trading in the fixed income group, leading to misaligned incentives; (3) according to the *New York Times*, despite their size, yet using the rating agencies as justification, these securities did not show up on the firm's value at risk analysis;[8] and (4) the CDO group was one of the highest paid in the firm.

During this same period, Merrill Lynch also poured into this sector, ranking second in CDO issuance in 2005 with $27 billion, first in 2006 with $54 billion, and second in 2007 with $38 billion. Before 2005, like UBS and Citigroup, Merrill would hold on to the AAA-rated tranches and get them insured via a credit default swap (CDS) with the insurance giant AIG. In 2005, after AIG decided not to insure subprime-backed CDOs any longer, Merrill continued to issue CDOs and hold them, essentially unhedged. With risk management taking a backseat to the carry profit of the AAA tranches (i.e., the premium minus Merrill's short-term funding), Merrill held over $70 billion of these securities by the time the financial crisis started.[9]

A second example involves AIG. One of the more profitable groups within the AIG financial empire was AIG Financial Products (representing 17 percent of AIG's operating income in 2005).[10] As one of its many investments, the group ended up writing a staggering $500 billion worth of CDSs on mostly the AAA-rated tranches of CDO-like structured products on mortgages, corporate bonds, and loans. Like the banks discussed earlier, at AIG risk management was not a separate function. The model was essentially identical to that of UBS, Citigroup, and Merrill—that is, one of writing out-of-the-money puts on the underlying assets, in this case, many defaults. In fact, in August 2007, Joseph Cassano (the former head of the group) stated, "It is hard for us, without being flippant, to even see a scenario within any kind of realm of reason that would see us losing one dollar in any of those transactions." Because these CDSs were claims on the upper priority of portfolios of loans that could get hit only upon a large systematic shock, it essentially meant that AIG would receive fees most of the time. These fees were booked as income, resulting in huge compensation packages for the group (e.g., compensation hovered around $500 million for a staff of 300 or so). Of course, there was no accountability to this group for the rare event that would result in essentially all CDSs being hit and a significant fraction of $500 billion having to be paid out, bringing down the firm.

While AIG is arguably the most extreme example of the governance and compensation problems within the financial sector, the same problems also show up during this crisis for the aforementioned UBS, Citigroup, and Merrill Lynch; for Bear Stearns, Fannie Mae, Freddie Mac, and Lehman Brothers; and most likely for other undocumented cases. What is it about corporate governance and particularly compensation issues that so pervades this sector to put the system at risk? Is there a role for regulation, or can we rely on market discipline and possibly industry alignment to best practices in a highly competitive sector of the economy? Two issues appear to stand out—compensation of senior management and compensation of key cohorts of high-performance employees.

8.3 SENIOR MANAGEMENT COMPENSATION

Much attention has been focused in recent years on compensation of senior management of financial firms—usually comprising the chairman and/or chief executive officer, the chief financial officer, the chief risk officer, and perhaps the heads of major operating units, often conjoined in the firm's executive committee. Senior management remuneration packages are usually the responsibility of the compensation committee of the board of directors in the United States (or the supervisory board in many other countries). To the extent that compensation packages deviate materially from sustainable competitive performance of the firm and the long-term financial interests of shareholders, the overcompensation problem is an apparent result of governance failures. The severance packages of most senior managers fired as a result of the financial crisis—those triggering the most public outrage—suggest the extreme level of agency costs imposed on shareholders in this industry. A common question in polite company: "Would you rather manage a Wall Street firm or own shares in one?"

So far, senior management and boards of shipwrecked U.S. financial firms have not publicly accepted responsibility for the disasters on their watch, almost uniformly holding "unpredictable market turmoil" responsible. Perhaps it's the American tendency to blame the other guy when something bad happens. Perhaps it's the fear of accountability in a highly litigious society. Who knows? Contrition is not part of the vocabulary. In contrast, Swiss former senior managers of UBS recently acknowledged that they were in fact on the bridge of the ship and have repaid or forgone some $35 million in compensation accrued during the time the bank struck the iceberg. Perhaps in contrast to small countries like Switzerland, with powerful social mores and long memories, disgraced U.S. senior managers and board members can count on the camouflage of an impersonal society and short memories.

Remedying problems of senior management compensation in banking and finance is arguably no different than it is in nonfinancial firms. The central issue is framed in terms of in the classic agency problem reflected in sometimes dramatic divergences between management compensation and shareholder returns. In the case of the major financial firms, the big exception is that government now has an equity stake in most of them (and debt stakes in all of them), and therefore has the ability to call the shots.

The United States has now imposed fixed compensation caps—as in the German case of €500,000 in any bank that accepts government equity, or the UK case of strong government inputs into compensation schemes. Efforts to preempt government intervention have undoubtedly encouraged a certain amount of firm-level rethinking, along with cuts or elimination of some senior management bonuses for 2008. AIG froze the compensation of its seven top executives after two government bailouts. The seven members of Goldman Sachs' top management announced that they would forgo 2008 bonuses. There are undoubtedly others, and more to come. Merrill Lynch's top management agreed to forgo bonuses for 2008 (including a proposed $10 million bonus for its CEO), as did Morgan Stanley (including a 75 percent cut in bonuses for the firm's 14-person operating committee). Few advocated direct or indirect government intervention in senior management compensation, especially given the law of unintended consequences. Some proposed rules about compensation restrictions for banks are silly—enforcement through limiting tax deductibility, for example, is a nonstarter if past losses generate long-duration loss carryforwards. But with the taxpayer as shareholder and risk underwriter of many financial institutions, the politics of executive pay are for the moment a reality. Now pay restrictions have come to the United States as well.

It is also important to note that most top executives of banking and financial firms are largely paid in shares, with at least some minimum retention period required, and that some of the top executives in the banks that melted down have lost fortunes. In this sense, at least, the system has shown itself to work pretty well. In Section 8.5 we show how that the financial sector tends to have a higher portion of compensation in the form of stock grants than do other sectors of the economy. This is consistent with research (Clementi, Cooley, and Wang 2006) that shows that restricted stock grants are the best way to align the incentives of managers with those of shareholders in a dynamic setting. It may be that the financial industry has a better senior management pay-for-performance track record than many other sectors, but there are some significant caveats, as we describe later. When the system fails, it often seems to involve an executive liquidating shares that turn out, after the fact, to have been overvalued at the time of sale. In such cases, current stock performance determines a liquidation value well above what comes later, after the chickens have come home to roost. So the real issue may not be the design of top management compensation, but rather the difficulties of investors in perceiving risks and accurately valuing the equity of financial firms. Consequently, an appropriate remedy would involve more disclosure and transparency, not necessarily major retargeting of top management compensation.

We thus prefer efforts to harness market discipline and investor activism, working through an approach to governing special businesses by competent boards that are acutely aware of their twin duties of care and loyalty. Whether modifying the rules of governance or other remedies make sense is discussed in another chapter of this book.[11] We do think that longer stock holding periods and stricter forfeiture rules for top management would probably make sense; for example, failed senior executives who get ejected could have a minimum 36-month holding period for the shares they take with them.

8.4 COMPENSATING HIGH-PERFORMANCE EMPLOYEES IN BANKING AND FINANCE

Bonus season among the major financial firms usually begins in December of each year and lasts through the first quarter of the following year. The public has become used to eye-popping numbers and the predictable media commentary. High-performance employees regularly make more than their CEOs or members of senior management—and usually far more than professionals responsible for risk management, internal audit, or other control functions. Compensation is only part of the story. Power within the firm's bureaucracy is another—"Those who put up the biggest numbers get to call the shots"—potentially leading to a dangerous misalignment in the delicate balance between risks and returns.

During the past quarter century, financial sector profits grew from 10 percent to 40 percent of U.S. corporate profits, and the market capitalization of financial firms increased from 6 percent to 22 percent of U.S. listed corporations. This remarkable ascendancy of finance was amply reflected in compensation levels, notably in trading and investment banking and other risk-taking functions. Between 2002 and 2007 compensation expense of U.S. investment banks and investment banking divisions of financial conglomerates rose from about 31 percent to about 60 percent of gross revenues.

The market for human capital in finance has a number of unusual attributes.

- It attracts some of "the best and the brightest" worldwide, people who are very bright, highly trained, and highly committed and motivated by performance-based compensation.
- Performance is relatively transparent, with the attribution of revenues and earnings to teams and individuals fairly tractable and built into overall compensation practices. People who do well by whatever metrics used can expect outsized formula-based compensation. People who do not can expect to be let go.
- Performance-based compensation can lead to epic battles over revenue attribution among business units as well as an unusual degree of mobility between firms thanks to highly portable skill sets. Firms often show little loyalty to their people (especially in tough times) and can expect equally limited loyalty in return. And in some of the businesses, clients have a tendency to follow their bankers.
- The half-life of many high-performance bankers—especially in financial engineering, trading, and other key functions—is relatively short. As a "young person's game," the premium on current compared to future earnings is very high, not unlike professional athletics, promoting both free agency and extreme preference for immediate rewards.
- Given short-termism in compensation preferences among high-performance bankers, they in turn transmit pressure for high levels of capital deployment to their businesses and tend to have little tolerance for intrusive risk or compliance controls. Like pit bulls pursuing a juicy cut of meat, they can be intolerant of a short leash, and can argue forcefully that short leashes tend to kill performance.

It has been suggested that the dynamics of the market for high-performance talent in wholesale finance, together with the established bonus-pool reward system, had led to an epidemic of fake alpha—that is, short-term excess returns as the basis for the current bonus pool.[12] The bonus pool is normally divided among entitled employees according to an assessment of contribution that is as fair as possible and is intended to motivate their performance in the next period. Since alpha is calculated over the current accounting period, it does not take into account reduced returns or losses in subsequent periods that the current year's activities eventually create. Since it is impossible to determine true alpha until some time has passed, compensation based on current reported earnings represents fake alpha. True alpha, assuming it can be determined with some precision, may be higher or lower. It all depends.

The fake alpha problem has been blamed for perverse incentives among key employees in the financial services sector, particularly where there is strong alignment between current performance and current compensation through bonus pool allocations. In some cases compensation is set by a straight formula; in others there is substantial discretion. Examples of areas subject to current performance-based compensation include trading in financial instruments, commodities, and derivatives; development and marketing of structured financial products; management of in-house hedge funds and other alternative investment vehicles; some areas of corporate finance; and probably others.

As described earlier, to understand how this point is relevant for the current financial crisis, note that financial firms (i.e., the government-sponsored enterprises [GSEs], banks, and broker-dealers) held 48 percent of the $1.65 trillion of AAA-rated collateralized debt obligations (CDOs) of nonprime mortgages. This is puzzling because the whole purpose of securitization is to transfer the credit risk away from financial institutions to capital market investors. By holding on to such large amounts of the AAA-rated, non-agency-backed CDOs, the CDO desks of firms were for all economic purposes writing deep out-of-the-money put options on the housing market. In other words, these desks were taking huge asymmetric bets that would pay out in most periods, albeit with large exposure to a significant economy-wide shock. Because the risk management systems of the firms treated these AAA CDOs as essentially riskless, the CDO desks booked the premiums as instant profit (which had a spread roughly double that of other AAA-rated securities) and thereby receiving big bonuses with the incentive to load up on them—hence, the financial crisis of 2007–2009.

The potential for perverse incentives is clear. Employees are encouraged to maximize current compensation to themselves, possibly at the expense of shareholders. They are encouraged to maximize the use of leverage without regard to its impact on bankruptcy risk of the firm. They are encouraged to report to senior management and regulators that all is well when in fact it is not. Robert Rubin, the former highly compensated Citigroup board member and counselor, recently noted, "The board can't run the risk book of a company. The board is not going to have the granular knowledge."[13] If Rubin's defense holds up, then alpha-chasing employees have had plenty of opportunities to bamboozle the elected representatives of shareholders in the financial industry. To that end, they would have had plenty of motivation to steamroller the pesky squad of pedestrian risk managers and compliance officers and cheer sloppy internal audit practices.

There is another issue. Incentive systems and short-term alpha can easily compound the problem of effective regulation and monitoring in the financial industry. In their constant search for market imperfections, it is unsurprising that some alpha seekers have pushed the envelope in terms of what is legal, ethical, or professionally acceptable. Front-running client trades, misuse of private information, and exploiting conflicts of interest are some examples. If employees can figure out how to get paid before the fat hits the fire, they may well yield to temptation.

Meanwhile, high-performance employees are encouraged to take as much of the money off the table as possible and leave the shareholders holding the bag if things later turn out badly. There are no clawbacks. What's off the table stays off the table. And people defect—either individually or in teams—if there is a better offer on the table from a competitor, compounding the challenges facing senior management in creating sensible checks and balances.

8.5 HOW DOES THE FINANCIAL SERVICES SECTOR COMPARE TO OTHERS?

A discussion of executive compensation has to begin with a definition of what one measures. Clementi and Cooley (2009) use a total compensation concept, which comes as close as possible to capturing the alignment of incentives of managers and shareholders in the long run. The managers' economic interest in the firm is dictated not just by current compensation but also by the portion of their wealth that is tied up in the firm. To examine the structure of compensation in the financial services sector—finance, insurance, and real estate (FIRE)—and compare it to other sectors, we use this concept.[14]

Two definitions are used. The first is CEO wealth, which is defined as the sum of:

- Salary.
- Bonus.
- Expected discounted value of future salaries.
- Market value of all stock in CEO's portfolio.
- Market value of all options in CEO's portfolio.
- Amounts paid to the executive under the company's long-term incentive plan.
- Other items such as: severance payments, debt forgiveness, tax reimbursement, signing bonuses, 401(k) contributions.

The second, CEO total yearly compensation, is defined as the sum of:

- Salary.
- Bonus.
- Year-on-year change in market value of stock in portfolio.
- Market value of stock awarded during the year.
- Year-on-year change in market value of options in portfolio.
- Black-Scholes value of options awarded during the year.
- Amounts paid to the executive under the company's long-term incentive plan.
- Other items such as: severance payments, debt forgiveness, tax reimbursement, signing bonuses, 401(k) contributions.

Based on this definition—essentially the change in CEO wealth associated with the firm—it is clear that total compensation could be negative in a year in which the firm's stock performs poorly.

Figure 8.1 shows the composition of median total CEO wealth in 2006 for six sectors of the economy.

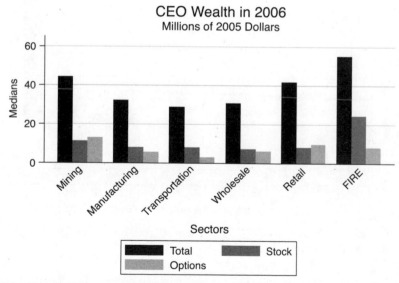

FIGURE 8.1 CEO Wealth across Sectors

This graph presents the wealth of CEOs in 2006 across the mining, manufacturing, transportation, wholesale, retail, and financial/insurance/real estate (FIRE) sectors.

Sources: Standard & Poor's ExecuComp, Clementi and Cooley (2009).

There are two features that stand out. Median CEO wealth in the FIRE sector is considerably higher than in the other sectors, a fact that confirms the impression that most people have that the rewards are highest in financial sector jobs. Second, stock holdings represent a higher percentage of total wealth for the FIRE sector, which is potentially consistent with the better alignment of incentives.

Note that the data presented are for median CEO wealth. The reason for this is that the distribution of compensation (and wealth) for CEOs is highly skewed. The reporting of averages of CEO compensation, as is common in both the press and in empirical research, is highly misleading. Figure 8.2 shows the distribution of total yearly compensation in 2006 for the FIRE sector, reported as means by decile. The exact same pattern holds true in other sectors.

The top decile consists mostly of CEOs with large equity stakes in their companies. It looks like CEOs' compensation—correctly conceived—is very

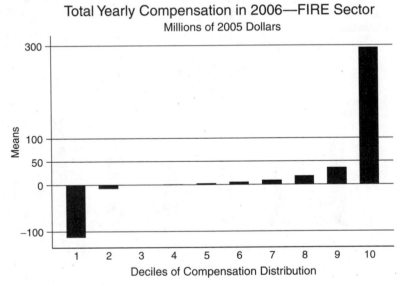

FIGURE 8.2 Distribution of CEO Compensation in the Financial, Insurance, and Real Estate Sector

This graph shows the distribution of 2006 compensation in the financial/insurance/real estate (FIRE) sector across 10 deciles. Note that this compensation includes salary, bonus, and year-on-year changes in the market value of stock and options in the CEO's portfolio, among other items, so the value can go negative.

Source: Standard & Poor's ExecuComp, Clementi and Cooley (2009).

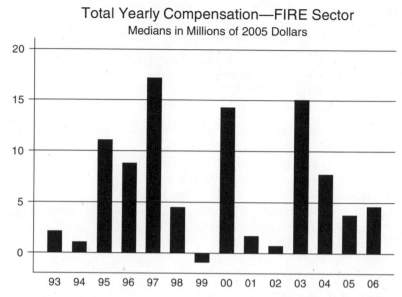

FIGURE 8.3 Yearly Compensation in the Financial, Insurance, and Real Estate Sector, 1993–2006

Source: Standard & Poor's ExecuComp, Clementi and Cooley (2009).

sensitive to changes in the value of the shares and options that they hold. It is rather striking that the lowest deciles actually show significant negative compensation. Clearly, when we read about excessive CEO compensation, the focus is on the upper decile of the distribution. The cases that make the news are mostly drawn from there.

One implication of the skewness and the sensitivity to stock holdings is that compensation, properly measured, will be very volatile over time. Figure 8.3 shows median total yearly compensation in the FIRE sector from 1993 to 2006 (the latest year for which we have complete data).

The volatility of compensation is quite remarkable, but entirely in keeping with the volatility in market values in the FIRE sector. Similar patterns hold true in other sectors.

The data presented so far are consistent with the notion that top managers' annual compensation and wealth are sensitive to the values of the firms they lead. But that does not reflect the whole story about the alignment of shareholders' and managers' interests. The question we want to ask is: How correlated are shareholders' and managers' fortunes? Table 8.1 shows the elasticity of CEO wealth with respect to shareholder value for six

TABLE 8.1 Elasticity of CEO Wealth with Respect to Shareholder Value

Mining	Manufacturing	Transportation	Wholesale	Retail	FIRE
0.681	0.528	0.580	0.800	0.594	0.441

Source: Clementi and Cooley (2009).

sectors—that is, the percentage change in CEO wealth following a 1 percent increase in shareholder wealth (market cap).[15]

These results are quite striking. They show that in the FIRE sector CEO wealth is far less sensitive to changes in shareholder value than in any other sector—this in spite of the fact that equity holdings are a more important component of compensation. This explains the widespread perception that top managers of financial firms do not suffer as much when their firms perform poorly.

8.6 SEEKING CHANGE

Various attempts have been made over the years to address the perverse aspects of wholesale banking's compensation structures, with limited success. The objective is always the same—to align the financial interests of the management and high-performance employees with those of the shareholders, all within the regulatory constraints that characterize this "special" industry—special because it creates systemic risk and because it deals with other people's money. Ownership by dispersed shareholders interacting with the too-big-to-fail characteristics of these firms is at the root of the compensation issue—to the extent an issue exists.[16]

Arguably, this is a relatively recent situation. Historically, many such firms were relatively small partnerships, which were both nonsystemic and managed by their owners, thereby avoiding both agency problems and systemic risk. But today things are what they are, so new approaches to compensation are in the interests of both shareholders and taxpayers.

One obvious approach is to compensate both senior managers and other employees in shares or share options, together with lockups designed to align their interests with those of shareholders, and in the process help to reduce systemic risk. There are a range of well-known problems with this approach, with plenty of historical examples of manipulation by management and side effects that are hard to predict. And it is not easy to fine-tune and apply incentive-compatible approaches in the financial sector.

A second problem resides in the open market for banking talent. Probably the best-known example goes back to Salomon, Inc., which in the early

1990s got close to a criminal indictment for manipulating the Treasury auction market and stayed alive mainly by wholesale change in management and throwing itself on the mercy of the government. Warren Buffett was the hero of that story (motivated by a large equity stake in the firm), and was horrified by the perverse incentives he saw in the firm's compensation structure. His subsequent effort to realign compensation practices led to wholesale defections of top bankers and traders to competitors, followed inevitably by a reversal of many of the reforms. Recent history is not much different. High-performance employees—with finite professional life spans and personal franchises with clients or trading counterparties—have been able to jump ship, quickly and at low cost to themselves, either to competitors or to other financial players like hedge funds and private equity firms.

The current period, when much of the financial industry is in the doldrums and has become dependent on government support, may offer a unique opportunity to experiment with new ways of compensating senior management and high-performance employees without potentially destructive meddling by government.

Examples are already at hand, with wholesale and investment banking groups beginning to execute clawbacks of bonuses that turn out to have been unwarranted—emulating a practice that has been common among hedge funds and private equity firms for some time. Morgan Stanley announced that a significant part of 2008 year-end bonuses vesting over the next three years and covering some 7,000 employees would be "subject to a clawback provision that could be triggered if the individual engages in conduct detrimental" to the firm, including a subsequent loss revelation, the need for an earnings restatement, or reputational damage.[17] According to a Morgan Stanley spokesperson, "So if you're a trader and you've had a huge year and you get paid a lot of money and then the following year it turns out you were taking outsize risk, we can go back and ding your pay from the year before."[18] Goldman Sachs, in contrast, suggested that no clawbacks were needed since bonuses are heavily stock-based and vest over a period of time during which they can be reduced at the discretion of management.

Another example is the bonus/malus approach of UBS. The underlying notion is that the term *bonus* has become corrupted, and operates only in one direction—including the widespread use of guaranteed bonuses, signing bonuses, "bonuses for being around," and "bonuses for going away." Along with bonuses for succeeding, the UBS approach introduces "maluses" for failing, with an extended time horizon for deciding whether something has succeeded or failed.

Having been rescued by a CHF6 billion injection of government funds that made possible offloading most of its toxic assets at book value into a "bad bank" workout vehicle—also involving a major equity stake by the Swiss Confederation in the surviving "good bank," UBS is the first to publicly announce a new set of management compensation policies. The main features are as follows:[19]

- The chairman of the bank's supervisory board is no longer bound to the same incentive system as the group executive board (management board) and will no longer receive variable compensation components. Variable cash compensation for the group executive board is based on an innovative bonus/malus system. The malus component involves significant give-backs if the bank does badly.
- An approach similar to the bonus/malus system will be implemented for variable equity compensation as well.

According to the new approach,

The Chairman of the Supervisory Board and the members of the Group Executive Board will receive no variable compensation for 2008. The size, composition, and allocation of 2008 variable compensation for other employees will be determined by the Board of Directors once 2008 Group results are known and after consultation with the Swiss Federal Banking Commission (SFBC). The new compensation system was discussed with the SFBC in accordance with the requirements listed in the action plan of the Swiss authorities and the standards for the financial sector which are currently being established. These discussions will be continued and the salary system will be regularly assessed with respect to these standards.[20]

Starting in 2009 UBS's compensation model is to comprise both fixed and variable components, with the latter clearly linked to risk-adjusted value creation over a longer period of time and designed to reflect sustainable profitability. The intent is to be competitive in the market for human capital and at the same time strike a balance between creation of durable alpha, awareness of the associated risks, and preservation of the firm's reputational capital—the latter being critical in view of the UBS's most valuable business, its global private banking franchise.

Naturally, the devil is in the details. The new approach for top management includes (1) a fixed base salary; (2) variable cash compensation, up to one-third paid out immediately and the balance held in escrow in a bonus account, which will decline and possibly be wiped out (the "malus") if UBS results are poor, if there are regulatory violations, or if "unnecessarily high" risks are taken; and (3) variable equity compensation, whereby awarded shares vest only after three years and depend on long-term value creation (senior managers are locked in beyond the standard three years). The same formula, with some variations, applies to key managers and so-called risk-taking employees throughout the organization, while all other employees remain under the previous variable compensation system.

Critics of clawbacks and other approaches to link risk-taking employee compensation to performance over longer time periods have argued that there could be significant unintended consequences. These include incentives for traders to hide losses and inducing a reduction of risk-taking willingness on the part of the best traders.

This approach is nevertheless consistent with sensible compensation of traders though the cycle. In good times, with a rising tide lifting all boats, the combination of the rising tide and leverage makes it impossible to tell good traders from bad ones, since most people generate decent to spectacular returns. It is in bad times that the wheat separates from the chaff. This is precisely why compensation should have a multiyear structure, with bad performances subtracting from the bonus pool in the same way that good performances add to it.

It would be surprising if other firms in the wholesale banking industry—besides widespread cutting of conventional bonuses as a result of collapsed business conditions—have not thought through similar bonus/malus approaches. Unless they do, and the industry moves in tandem toward a new and more rational way of compensating its key performers, individual experiments will surely fail as business picks up, competition intensifies, and happy days are here again.

NOTES

1. This account is taken from UBS's "Shareholder Report on UBS's Write Downs," prepared for the Swiss Federal Banking Commission.
2. See Chapter 1, "Mortgage Origination and Securitization in the Financial Crisis," for a description of the securitization process.
3. See Chapter 3, "The Rating Agencies: Is Regulation the Answer?" for a description of the rating agency process.
4. A majority of the super-senior tranche holdings were partially hedged and treated as having zero effect on the firm's value at risk.
5. See Chapter 2, "How Banks Played the Leverage Game."
6. Coval and Jurek (Forthcoming).
7. The following description is based on a series of articles in the *New York Times* called "The Reckoning," which covered, among other firms, Citigroup, Merrill Lynch, AIG, Fannie Mae, and Freddie Mac.
8. Eric Dash and Julie Creswell, "A Blind Eye," *New York Times*, November 22, 2008.
9. Gretchen Morgenson, "Double Down," *New York Times*, November 8, 2008.

10. The facts are taken from the article by Gretchen Morgenson, "A Spreading Virus," *New York Times*, September 27, 2008.
11. See Chapter 7, "Corporate Governance in the Modern Financial Sector."
12. See Raghuram Rajan, "Bankers' Pay Is Deeply Flawed," *Financial Times*, January 8, 2008.
13. Ken Brown and David Enrich, "Rubin, under Fire, Defends His Role at Citi," *Wall Street Journal*, November 29, 2008.
14. The data source is the ExecuComp data set, assembled and distributed by Standard & Poor's. The executive compensation data is drawn from documents filed by companies with the SEC. In the starting sample, we have the population of CEOs of firms whose stock is traded on public exchanges in the United States. See also Yermack (1995), Yermack and Ofek (2000), and Frydman and Saks (2007).
15. It is obtained by running a median regression (not OLS, because of the skewness in the data) of log(CEO wealth) on log(shareholder wealth), including year fixed effects. We use all data in the panel (1992 to 2006).
16. See Chapter 5, "Enhanced Regulation of Large, Complex Financial Institutions."
17. Scott Patterson, "Securities Firms Claw Back Failed Bets," *New York Times*, December 9, 2008.
18. Louise Story, "Bonus Season Afoot, Wall Street Tries for a Little Restraint," *New York Times*, December 8, 2008.
19. See www.ubs.com/1/e/investors/releases?newsId=158103.
20. Ibid.

REFERENCES

Clementi, Gian Luca, and Thomas F. Cooley. 2009. Executive compensation: Facts. Working paper, New York University Stern School of Business.

Clementi, Gian Luca, Thomas F. Cooley, and Cheng Wang. 2006. Stock grants as a commitment device. *Journal of Economic Dynamics and Control* 30 (11): 2191–2216.

Coval, Josh, and Jakub Jurek. Forthcoming. Economic catastrophe bonds. *American Economic Review*.

Frydman, C., and R. E. Saks. 2007. Executive compensation: A new view from a long-run perspective, 1936–2005. Unpublished manuscript, MIT Sloan School.

Rajan, R. 2008. Bankers' pay is deeply flawed. *Financial Times*, January 9.

Yermack, D. L. 1995. Do corporations award CEO stock options effectively? *Journal of Financial Economics* 39.

Yermack, D. L., and E. Ofek. 2000. Taking stock: Equity-based compensation and the evolution of managerial ownership. *Journal of Finance* 55.

CHAPTER 9

Fair Value Accounting

Policy Issues Raised by the Credit Crunch

Stephen G. Ryan

9.1 INTRODUCTION

Fair value accounting is a financial reporting approach in which firms are required or permitted to measure and report on an ongoing basis certain assets and liabilities (generally financial instruments) at estimates of the prices they would receive if they were to sell the assets or would pay if they were to be relieved of the liabilities. Under this approach, firms report unrealized losses when the fair values of their assets decrease or liabilities increase, thereby reducing their owners' equity and (in most cases) net income. Firms report unrealized gains when the fair values of their assets increase or liabilities decrease, thereby increasing their owners' equity and (in most cases) net income.

Although fair values have played a role in U.S. generally accepted accounting principles (GAAP) for more than 50 years, accounting standards that require or permit fair value accounting have increased considerably in number and significance in recent years. In September 2006, the Financial Accounting Standards Board (FASB) issued an important new accounting standard, Statement of Financial Accounting Standards No. 157, *Fair Value Measurements* (FAS 157), which provides significantly more comprehensive guidance to assist firms in estimating fair values. The practical applicability of this guidance has been tested by the severely illiquid and otherwise

---

This chapter is based on my (longer) paper commissioned by the Council of Institutional Investors, "Fair Value Accounting: Understanding the Issues Raised by the Credit Crunch," available at www.cii.org.

disorderly markets for subprime and some other asset and liability positions during the ongoing credit crunch.[1] This fact has led various parties to raise three main potential criticisms of fair value accounting. First, unrealized losses recognized under fair value accounting may reverse over time. Second, market illiquidity may render fair values difficult to measure, yielding overstated or unreliable reported losses. Third, firms reporting unrealized losses under fair value accounting may yield adverse feedback effects that cause further deterioration of market prices and increase the overall risk of the financial system (systemic risk). These parties typically advocate either abandoning fair value accounting and returning to some form of amortized cost accounting or, less extremely, altering fair value accounting requirements to reduce the amount of firms' reported losses.

In this chapter, I address these criticisms of fair value accounting from an accounting and economic policy perspective. Like any other accounting system, fair value accounting has its limitations, both conceptual and practical. The relevant questions for policy makers to ask are: Does fair value accounting provide more useful information to market participants than the alternatives, generally some form of amortized cost accounting? If so, can the FASB improve FAS 157's guidance regarding fair value measurement to better cope with illiquid or otherwise disorderly markets? I conclude that, while the FASB can and should provide additional guidance regarding the measurement of fair values in illiquid markets, even fair value accounting as currently specified and practiced is decidedly preferable to the alternatives advocated by parties critical of fair value accounting. This is because those alternatives would suppress the reporting of losses and reduce the incentives for voluntary disclosure, and thereby would prolong the price and resource allocation adjustment processes that are necessary to put this crisis behind us.

The thrift (savings and loan) crisis provides a telling historical analogy. This crisis began when interest rates rose during the first oil crisis/recession in 1973–1975, causing thrifts' fixed rate mortgage assets to experience large economic losses that were not recognized under amortized cost accounting. This nonrecognition of economic losses led bank regulators and other economic policy makers to allow the crisis to fester for a decade and a half—effectively encouraging thrifts to invest in risky assets, exploit deposit insurance, and in some cases even commit fraud in the meantime, activities that significantly worsened the ultimate cost of the crisis—until the crisis was effectively addressed through the Financial Institutions Reform, Recovery, and Enforcement Act of 1989 and the Federal Deposit Insurance Corporation Improvement Act of 1991. These acts required troubled thrifts to be shut down and their assets sold through the Resolution Trust Corporation, prohibited regulatory forbearance, and took various other direct actions. Similarly direct actions are needed now, and we should not deter such actions by throwing an accounting cloak over very real and sizable problems.

The following section is an overview of the differences between fair value accounting and the alternative accounting measurement attributes, abstracting from the issue of market illiquidity raised by the ongoing credit crunch. The next section describes FAS 157's measurement guidance and how it does and does not address the issue of market illiquidity. The final section evaluates the three potential criticisms of fair value accounting when markets are illiquid that were mentioned earlier.

9.2 OVERVIEW OF FAIR VALUE ACCOUNTING VERSUS THE ALTERNATIVES ABSTRACTING FROM THE CREDIT CRUNCH

Fair Value Accounting

The goal of fair value measurement is for firms to estimate to the degree possible the prices at which the positions they currently hold would change hands in orderly transactions based on current information and conditions. To meet this goal, firms must fully incorporate current information about future cash flows and current risk-adjusted discount rates into their fair value measurements. When market prices for the same or similar positions are available, FAS 157 generally requires firms to use these prices in estimating fair values. The rationale for this requirement is that market prices should reflect all publicly available information about future cash flows, including investors' private information that is revealed through their trading, as well as current risk-adjusted discount rates. When fair values are estimated using unadjusted or adjusted market prices, they are referred to as mark-to-market values. If market prices for the same or similar positions are not available, then firms must estimate fair values using valuation models. FAS 157 generally requires these models to be applied using observable market inputs when they are available and unobservable firm-supplied inputs otherwise. When fair values are estimated using valuation models, they are referred to as mark-to-model values.

The main issue with fair value accounting is whether firms can and do estimate fair values accurately and without discretion. When identical positions trade in liquid markets that provide unadjusted marked-to-market values, fair value generally is the most accurate and least discretionary possible measurement attribute, although even liquid markets get values wrong on occasion. Fair values typically are less accurate and more discretionary when they are either adjusted mark-to-market values or mark-to-model values. In adjusting mark-to-market values, firms may have to make adjustments for market illiquidity or for the dissimilarity of the position being fair valued from the position for which the market price is observed. These adjustments can be large and judgmental in some circumstances. In estimating mark-to-model values, firms typically have choices about which valuation models to use and about which inputs to use in applying the chosen models. All valuation models are limited, and different models capture the value-relevant aspects of positions differently. Firms often must apply valuation models using inputs derived from historical data that predict future cash flows or correspond to risk-adjusted discount rates imperfectly. The periods firms choose to analyze historical data to determine these inputs can have very significant effects on their mark-to-model values.

This issue with fair value accounting is mitigated in practice in two significant ways. First, FAS 157 and the accounting standards governing certain specific positions require firms to disclose qualitative information about how they estimate fair values as well as quantitative information about their valuation inputs, the sensitivities of their reported fair values to those inputs, and unrealized gains and losses and other changes in the fair value of their positions. These disclosures allow investors to assess the reliability of reported fair values and to adjust or ignore them as desired. Second, most fair value accounting standards require fair values to be reestimated each quarter, and so past valuation errors can and should be corrected on an ongoing and timely basis.

Fair value accounting is the best possible measurement attribute for inducing firms' managements to make voluntary disclosures and for making investors aware of the critical questions to ask managements. When firms report unrealized gains and losses, their managements are motivated to explain in the management discussion and analysis sections of financial reports and elsewhere what went right or wrong during the period and the nature of any fair value measurement issues. If a firm's management does not adequately explain its unrealized gains and losses, then investors at least are aware that value-relevant events occurred during the period and can prod management to explain further.

Amortized Cost Accounting

The alternative to fair value accounting generally is some form of amortized cost accounting (often referred to overbroadly as accrual accounting). In its pure form, amortized cost accounting uses *historical* information about future cash flows and risk-adjusted discount rates from the inception of positions to account for them throughout their lives on firms' balance sheets and income statements. Unlike under fair value accounting, unrealized gains and losses are ignored until they are realized through the disposal or impairment of positions or the passage of time. When firms dispose of positions, they record on their income statements the *cumulative* unrealized gains and losses that have developed since the inception or prior impairment of positions.

Amortized cost accounting raises three main issues, all of which arise from its use of untimely historical information about future cash flows and risk-adjusted discount rates.

1. Income typically is persistent for as long as firms hold positions, but becomes transitory when positions mature or are disposed of, and firms replace them with new positions at current market terms. This can lull investors into believing that income is more persistent than it really is.
2. Positions originated at different times are accounted for using different historical information and discount rates, yielding inconsistent and untimely accounting for the constituent elements of firms' portfolios. This obscures the net value and risks of firms' portfolios.
3. Firms can manage their income through the selective realization of cumulative unrealized gains and losses on positions, an activity referred to as gains trading.

In practice, financial report disclosures mitigate these issues with amortized cost accounting in very limited ways. This is because amortized cost accounting does not incorporate most value- or risk-relevant events that occur after the inception of positions, and so it does not prompt either mandatory or voluntary disclosure. In particular, management is not motivated to explain the consequences of any such events that occurred during the period. Market participants that read financial reports carefully may not even be generally aware when such events occur.

Mixed-Attribute Accounting Model for Financial Instruments

Generally accepted accounting principles (GAAP) require various measurement attributes to be used in accounting for financial instruments. This is referred to as the mixed-attribute accounting model. The mixed-attribute model often allows firms to choose the measurement attribute they desire for a position through how they classify the position. Reflecting some firms' exploitation of this discretion, in 2005 the Securities and Exchange Commission (SEC) concluded that "the mixed-attribute model has prompted a significant amount of accounting-motivated transaction structures."

Similar to (and in some respects worse than) amortized cost accounting, the mixed-attribute model poorly describes the net value and risks of financial institutions' portfolios of financial instruments. In particular, this model can make effective risk management by these institutions appear to be speculation, and speculation appear to be risk management.

Because of these severe limitations, consistent fair value accounting for all of financial institutions' financial instruments is clearly preferable to either the current mixed-attribute accounting model or a pure amortized cost model.[2]

9.3 FAS 157's MEASUREMENT GUIDANCE

FAS 157 contains essentially all of the current GAAP guidance regarding how to measure fair values. FAS 157 does not require fair value accounting for any position; its guidance is relevant only when other accounting standards require or permit positions to be accounted for at fair value. This section describes the critical aspects of FAS 157's definition of fair value and hierarchy of fair value measurement inputs. It also indicates where this guidance does not deal with the issues raised by the credit crunch with sufficient specificity.

Definition of Fair Value

FAS 157 defines fair value as "the price that would be received to sell an asset or paid to transfer a liability in an orderly transaction between market participants at the measurement date." This definition of fair value reflects an ideal "exit value" notion in which firms exit the positions they currently hold through orderly transactions with market participants at the measurement date, not through fire sales.

"At the measurement date" means that fair value should reflect the conditions that exist at the balance sheet date. For example, if markets are illiquid and credit risk premiums are at unusually high levels at that date, then fair values should reflect those conditions. In particular, firms should not incorporate their expectations of market liquidity and credit risk premiums returning to normal over some horizon, regardless of what historical experience, statistical models, and/or expert opinion indicate.

"An orderly transaction" is one that is unforced and unhurried. The firm is expected to conduct usual and customary marketing activities to identify potential purchasers of assets and assumers of liabilities, and these parties are expected to conduct usual and customary due diligence. During the credit crunch, these activities could take considerable amounts of time because of the few and noisy signals about the values of positions being generated by market transactions and because of parties' natural skepticism regarding those values. As a result, a temporal slippage arises between the "at the measurement date" and "orderly transaction" aspects of FAS 157's fair value definition that raises practical problems for preparers of financial reports.

"Market participants" are knowledgeable, unrelated, and willing and able to transact. Knowledgeable parties are not just generally sophisticated and aware of market conditions; they have conducted the aforementioned due diligence and ascertained to the extent possible the fair values of the positions under consideration. FAS 157 presumes that, after conducting these activities, either market participants are as knowledgeable as the firms currently holding the positions or they can price any remaining information asymmetry. The standard does not contemplate the idea that information asymmetry between the current holders of positions and potential purchasers or assumers of positions is so severe that markets break down altogether, as appears to have effectively occurred for some positions during the credit crunch.

Hierarchy of Fair Value Measurement Inputs

FAS 157 creates a hierarchy of inputs into fair value measurements, from most to least reliable. Figure 9.1 summarizes these inputs.

Level 1 inputs are unadjusted quoted market prices in active markets for identical items. With a few narrow exceptions, FAS 157 explicitly requires firms to measure fair values using level 1 inputs whenever they are available.

Level 2 inputs are other directly or indirectly observable market data. There are two broad subclasses of these inputs. The first and generally preferable subclass is quoted market prices in active markets for similar items or

Level 1: Quoted market prices (unadjusted) in active markets for identical items.

Level 2: Other directly or indirectly observable market inputs:
 ■ Some inputs yield mark-to-market valuations with adjustments:
    ❑ Quoted market prices in active markets for similar items or in inactive markets for identical items.
 ■ Other inputs yield mark-to-model valuations:
    ❑ Yield curves, correlations, and so forth.

Level 3: Unobservable inputs: ■ Yield mark-to-model valuations.   ■ Should reflect assumptions that market participants would use.

FIGURE 9.1 FAS 157 Hierarchy of Fair Valuation Inputs from Most to Least Reliable

in inactive markets for identical items. These inputs yield adjusted mark-to-market measurements that are less than ideal but usually still pretty reliable, depending on the nature and magnitude of the required valuation adjustments. The second subclass is other observable market inputs such as yield curves, exchange rates, empirical correlations, and so on. These inputs yield mark-to-model measurements that are disciplined by market information, but that can only be as reliable as the models and inputs employed. This second subclass usually has less in common with the first subclass than with better-quality level 3 measurements described next.

Level 3 inputs are unobservable, firm-supplied estimates, such as forecasts of home price depreciation and the resulting credit loss severity on mortgage-related positions. These inputs should reflect the assumptions that market participants would use, but they yield mark-to-model valuations that are largely undisciplined by market information. Due to the declining price transparency during the credit crunch, many subprime positions that firms previously fair valued using level 2 inputs inevitably had to be fair valued using level 3 inputs.

While level 2 inputs generally are preferred to level 3 inputs, FAS 157 does not necessarily require firms to use level 2 inputs over level 3 inputs. Firms should use "the assumptions that market participants would use in pricing the asset or liability." When markets are illiquid, firms can make the argument that available level 2 inputs are of such low quality that market participants would use level 3 inputs instead.

If a fair value measurement includes even one significant level 3 input, then it is viewed as a level 3 measurement. FAS 157 sensibly requires considerably expanded disclosures for level 3 fair value measurements.

9.4 POTENTIAL CRITICISMS OF FAIR VALUE ACCOUNTING DURING THE CREDIT CRUNCH

This section discusses the main potential criticisms of fair value accounting during the credit crunch. It also indicates the guidance in FAS 157 that is most relevant to these criticisms and provides some factual observations as well as the author's views about these criticisms and guidance.

Unrealized Gains and Losses Reverse

There are two distinct reasons why unrealized gains and losses may reverse with greater than 50 percent probability. First, the market prices of positions may be bubble prices that deviate from fundamental values, with this deviation possibly being partly or wholly caused by market illiquidity. Second, these market prices may not correspond to the future cash flows most likely to be received or paid because the distribution of future cash flows is skewed. For example, the distribution of future cash flows on an asset may include some very low-probability but very high-loss-severity future outcomes that reduce the fair value of the asset.

Bubble Prices

The financial economics literature now contains considerable theory and empirical evidence that markets sometimes exhibit bubble prices that either are inflated by market optimism and excess liquidity or are depressed by market pessimism and illiquidity compared to fundamental values. Bubble prices can result from rational short-horizon decisions by investors in dynamically efficient markets, not just from investor irrationality or market imperfections.[3] Whether bubble prices have existed for specific types of positions during the credit crunch is debatable, but it certainly is possible.[4]

In FAS 157's hierarchy of fair value measurement inputs, market prices for the same or similar positions are the preferred type of input. If the market prices of positions currently are depressed below their fundamental values as a result of the credit crunch, then firms' unrealized losses on positions would be expected to reverse in part or whole in future periods. Concerned with this possibility, some parties have argued that it would be preferable to allow or even require firms to report amortized costs or level 3 mark-to-model fair values for positions rather than level 2 adjusted mark-to-market fair values that yield larger unrealized losses.[5]

If level 1 inputs are available, then with a few narrow exceptions FAS 157 requires firms to measure fair values as these active market prices for identical positions without any adjustments for bubble pricing. However, if only level 2 inputs are available and firms can demonstrate that these inputs reflect forced sales, then FAS 157 (implicitly) allows firms to make the argument that level 3 mark-to-model based fair values are more faithful to FAS 157's fair value definition.

The FASB's decision in FAS 157 that the possible existence of bubble prices in liquid markets should not affect the measurement of fair value is correct. It is very difficult to know when bubble prices exist and, if so, when the bubbles will burst. Different firms would undoubtedly have very different views about these matters, and they likely would act in inconsistent and perhaps discretionary fashions. To be useful, accounting standards must impose a reasonably high degree of consistency in application.

It should also be noted that amortized costs reflect any bubble prices that existed when positions were originated. In this regard, the amortized costs of subprime-mortgage-related positions originated during the euphoria preceding the subprime crisis are far more likely to reflect bubble prices than are the current fair values of those positions.

Skewed Distributions of Future Cash Flows

Fair values should reflect the expected future cash flows based on current information as well as current risk-adjusted discount rates for positions. When a position is more likely to experience very unfavorable future cash flows than very favorable future cash flows, or vice versa—statistically speaking, when it exhibits a skewed distribution of future cash flows—then the expected future cash flows differ from the most likely future cash flows. This implies that over time the fair value of the position will be revised in the direction of the most likely future cash flows with greater than 50 percent probability, possibly considerably greater. While some parties appear to equate this phenomenon with expected reversals of unrealized gains and losses such as result from bubble prices, it is not the same thing. When distributions of future cash flows are skewed, fair values will tend to be revised by relatively small amounts when they are revised in the direction of the most likely future cash flows, but by relatively large amounts when they are revised in the opposite direction. Taking into account the sizes and probabilities of the possible future cash flows, the unexpected change in fair value will be zero on average.

It is far more informative to investors for accounting to be right on average and to incorporate the probability and significance of all possible future cash flows, as fair value accounting does, than for it to be right most of the time but to ignore relatively low-probability but highly unfavorable or favorable future cash flows. Relatedly, by updating the distribution of future cash flows each period, fair value accounting provides investors with more timely information about changes in the probabilities of large unfavorable or favorable future cash flows. Such updating is particularly important in periods of high and rapidly evolving uncertainty and information asymmetry, such as the credit crunch.

Market Illiquidity

Together, the "orderly transaction" and "at the measurement date" elements of FAS 157's fair value definition reflect the semantics behind the *fair* in "fair value." Fair values are not necessarily the currently realizable values of positions; they are hypothetical values that reflect fair transaction prices even if current conditions do not support such transactions.

When markets are severely illiquid, as they have been during the credit crunch, this notion yields significant practical difficulties for preparers of firms' financial statements. Preparers must imagine hypothetical orderly exit transactions even though actual orderly transactions might not occur until quite distant future dates. Preparers will often want to solicit actual market participants for bids to help determine the fair values of positions, but they cannot do so when the time required exceeds that between the balance sheet and financial report filing dates. Moreover, any bids that market participants might provide would reflect market conditions at the expected transaction date, not the balance sheet date.

When level 2 inputs are driven by forced sales in illiquid markets, FAS 157 allows firms to use level 3 model-based fair values.[6] For firms to be able to do this, however, their auditors and the SEC generally require them to provide convincing evidence that market prices or other market information is driven by forced sales in illiquid markets. It may be difficult for firms to do this, and if they cannot, they can expect to be required to use level 2 fair values that likely will yield larger unrealized losses.

The FASB can and should provide additional guidance to help firms, their auditors, and the SEC individually understand and collectively agree what constitutes convincing evidence that level 2 inputs are driven by forced sales in illiquid markets. The FASB could do this by developing indicators of market illiquidity, including sufficiently large bid-ask spreads or sufficiently low trading volumes or depths. These variables could be measured either in absolute terms or relative to normal levels for the markets involved. When firms are able to show that such indicators are present, the FASB should explicitly allow firms to report level 3 model-based fair values rather than level 2 valuations as long as they can support their level 3 model-based fair values as appropriate in theory and with adequate statistical evidence. Requiring firms to compile indicators of market illiquidity and to provide support for level 3 mark-to-model valuations provides important discipline on the accounting process and cannot be avoided.

The FASB can and should also provide some guidance regarding the measurement of illiquidity risk premiums. These premiums are more difficult to measure than are other risk premiums, since market prices inherently provide less information about illiquidity risk premiums. In addition, these premiums are difficult to distinguish from credit risk premiums, since credit riskier assets are more likely to be illiquid.

Finally, the FASB should require firms to disclose their significant level 3 inputs and the sensitivities of the fair values to these inputs for all of their material level 3 model-based fair values. If such disclosures were required, then level 3 model-based fair values likely would be informationally richer than poor-quality level 2 fair values.

Adverse Feedback Effects and Systemic Risk

By recognizing unrealized gains and losses, fair value accounting moves the recognition of income and loss forward in time compared to amortized cost accounting. In addition, unrealized gains and losses may be overstated and thus subsequently reverse if bubble prices exist. If firms make economically suboptimal decisions or investors overreact because of reported unrealized gains and losses, then fair value accounting may yield adverse feedback effects that would not occur if amortized cost accounting were used instead. For example, some parties have argued that financial institutions' write-downs of subprime and other assets have caused further reductions of the market values of those assets and possibly even systemic risk. These parties argue that financial institutions' reporting unrealized losses has caused them to sell the affected assets either to raise capital, to remove the taint from their balance sheets, or to comply with internal or regulatory investment policies.[7] These parties also argue that financial institutions' issuance of equity securities to raise capital have crowded out direct investment in the affected assets.

It is possible that feedback effects related to fair value accounting have contributed slightly to market illiquidity, although I am unaware of any convincing empirical evidence that this has been the case. However, it is absolutely clear that the subprime crisis that gave rise to the credit crunch was primarily caused by firms, investors, and households making bad operating, investing, and financing decisions, managing risks poorly, and in some instances committing fraud—not by accounting. The severity and persistence of market illiquidity during the credit crunch and any observed adverse feedback effects are much more plausibly explained by financial institutions' considerable risk overhang[8] of subprime and other positions and their need to raise economic capital, as well as by the continuing high uncertainty and information asymmetry regarding those positions. Financial institutions actually selling affected assets and issuing capital almost certainly have mitigated the overall severity of the credit crunch by allowing these institutions to continue to make loans. Because of its timeliness and informational richness, fair value accounting (and associated mandatory and voluntary disclosures) should reduce uncertainty and information asymmetry faster over time than amortized cost accounting would, thereby mitigating the duration of the credit crunch.

Moreover, even amortized cost accounting is subject to impairment write-downs of assets under various accounting standards and accrual of loss contingencies under FAS 5. Hence, any accounting-related feedback effects likely would have been similar in the absence of FAS 157 and other fair value accounting standards.

NOTES

1. Ryan (2008) provides a detailed description of the causes and evolution of the subprime crisis, which began in February 2007, and the credit crunch it engendered, which began in July 2007.
2. Whether fair value accounting is desirable for nonfinancial (e.g., manufacturing and retailing) firms that primarily hold tangible and intangible assets with very different risk characteristics than their primarily financial liabilities is a more complicated question that is beyond the scope of this chapter. Nissim and Penman (2008) argue that amortized cost accounting has a transaction/outcome-oriented focus that better reveals how these firms deliver on their business plans and thereby earn income over time.
3. Barlevy (2007) is a very readable discussion of asset price bubbles and the related financial economics literature.
4. There is little or no reason to believe that relatively junior subprime positions have exhibited bubble pricing during the credit crunch. For example, Markit's indexes for relatively junior subprime MBS positions generally have declined toward zero with no significant reversals over time, even after market liquidity improved somewhat beginning in March 2008. Moreover, Bank of England (2008, 7, 18–20) finds these indexes to be fairly close to the model-based values, given reasonable loss scenarios. In contrast, there is at least some reason to believe that relatively senior subprime positions may have exhibited bubble pricing during this period. For example, Markit's indexes for these positions exhibited sizable reversals of prior losses during November–December 2007 and again in March–May 2008, although both these reversals can be explained by interventions by policy makers (the first by the Treasury Department's rescue plan for SIVs and the second by various aggressive actions taken by the Federal Reserve in March 2008). Moreover, Bank of England concludes that these indexes are considerably below modeled values even in extremely adverse loss scenarios. This could be explained by the fact that the credit derivatives on which Markit's indexes are based are themselves subject to illiquidity and counterparty risk.
5. See Johnson (2008a,b) and Rummell (2008) for discussion of parties holding such views.
6. That FAS 157 allows firms to use level 3 model-based fair values when level 2 inputs are driven by forced sales in illiquid markets is implicit in FAS 157 as originally written and explicit in FSP FAS 157-3, *Determining the Fair Value of a Financial Asset When the Market for That Asset Is Not Active*, issued in October 2008.
7. For example, the International Monetary Fund (2008) states, "Accounting standard setters will increasingly need to take into account the financial stability implications of their accounting practices and guidance." (p. xiv) Also, while "fair value accounting gives the most comprehensive picture of a firm's financial health ... investment decision rules based on fair value accounting outcomes could lead to self-fulfilling forced sales and falling prices when valuations fell

below important thresholds (either self-imposed by financial institutions or by regulation)." (p. 127)

8. Gron and Winton (2001) show that financial institutions' risk overhang (i.e., risk remaining from past business decisions that cannot be eliminated due to market illiquidity) can cause them to reduce or eliminate their trading activity in positions whose risks are correlated with their risk overhang.

REFERENCES

Bank of England. 2008. *Financial stability report*. Issue no. 23 (April).

Barlevy, G. 2007. Economic theory and asset bubbles. *Economic perspectives* (3rd quarter): 44–59.

Financial Accounting Standards Board (FASB). 2006. *Fair value measurements*. Statement of Financial Accounting Standards No. 157. Norwalk, CT: FASB.

Gron, A., and A. Winton. 2001. Risk overhang and market behavior. *Journal of Business* 74:591–612.

International Monetary Fund. 2008. Containing systemic risks and restoring financial soundness. April.

Johnson, S. 2008a. The fair-value blame game. www.cfo.com, March 19.

Johnson, S. 2008b. How far can fair value go? www.cfo.com, May 6.

Nissim, D., and S. Penman. 2008. Principles for the application of fair value accounting. White Paper No. 2, Center for Excellence in Accounting and Security Analysis, April.

Rummell, N. 2008. Fair-value rules get more blame for crunch. www.financialweek .com, March 24.

Ryan, S. 2008. Accounting in and for the subprime crisis. *Accounting Review* (November).

United States Securities and Exchange Commission. 2005. *Report and recommendations pursuant to Section 401(c) of the Sarbanes-Oxley Act of 2002 on arrangements with off-balance sheet implications, special purpose entities, and transparency of filings by issuers*. June 15.

Four

Derivatives, Short Selling, and Transparency

Viral V. Acharya

The pressure on regulators to regulate even more increases substantially during and immediately after financial crises. This crisis has been no different on this front. Unfortunately, quite often market participants, commentators, politicians, and (even!) some academics mistake symptoms for causes and advocate regulation that fixes symptoms rather than getting at the root causes.

In two of the chapters that follow (Chapter 10, "Derivatives: The Ultimate Financial Innovation," and Chapter 12, "Short Selling"), we discuss the case for and against regulation of financial derivatives and short selling. We argue that financial derivatives such as options and futures allow risk sharing in the economy; for example, pension fund managers buy index puts from financial intermediaries as insurance against a severe market decline. Derivatives also allow market participants to take focused bets, thereby revealing the information underlying these bets and performing a valuable information-generation role for the economy. For example, the credit default swap (CDS) spreads on financials had been rising gradually since the beginning of 2007—that is, even before the crisis truly took hold in the third quarter of 2007. There is little merit in simply killing this "canary in the coal mine."

A similar argument applies to the practice of short selling, which allows bearish investors who do not currently hold a company's stock to trade on the stock—and thereby convey—their negative views about the stock. Reflection of such bad news in market prices is as important as reflection of good news. Short selling is often blamed for causing some firms' stocks to crash—beyond what is commensurate with their true health. Most often, however, it is found in such cases that the company's health has indeed deteriorated and it is the selling by investors holding the stock that causes prices to crash rather than short selling itself. It has also been alleged by some that around the failures of Bear Stearns and Lehman Brothers, investors holding short positions in these stocks might have engaged in market manipulation—for instance, by spreading rumors. It seems best for regulators to deal with these cases through investigation and tough enforcement of penalties so as to discourage such foul play in the first place, rather than simply closing the arena by banning short sales.

However, we do believe that the current crisis has highlighted some shortcomings in the trading infrastructure of relatively newer derivative products, especially credit derivatives. These shortcomings call for prompt regulatory attention, and possibly intervention. In particular, in Chapter 11, "Centralized Clearing for Credit Derivatives," we suggest that the over-the-counter (OTC) nature of trading in credit derivatives, and the resulting opacity, contributed significantly to counterparty risk concerns surrounding the failure or near failure of significant players such as Bear Stearns, Lehman Brothers, and AIG. Again, we attribute the problem to the nature of trading in these instruments rather than to the instruments per se. Hence, we recommend that instead of regulating the instruments directly, the focus should be on the root cause of counterparty risk concerns—which is the lack of centralized counterparty clearing.

The rationale for regulatory intervention in getting credit derivatives to trade through a centralized clearinghouse is twofold. First, when one party trades with another, the two parties currently do not internalize the counterparty risk externality they impose on others: That is, they do not recognize that by requiring both sides/parties to post sufficiently high margins, they reduce the uncertainty that their defaults create losses to other parties connected to them. Second, large players benefit substantially from the relatively opaque nature of OTC contracts—both in terms of low trade execution costs and access to privileged information contained in order flow. Hence, large players are unlikely to coordinate, if left to private incentives, to eliminate the risk externality by moving to alternative platforms that feature centralized trading and greater transparency.

To us, the case for a centralized clearinghouse—a single counterparty for all trades—is thus clear. A centralized clearinghouse internalizes the risk externality and would thus impose efficient collateral and margin requirements on market participants. Such a clearinghouse structure has worked well historically, for instance for exchange-traded derivatives, since clearing members are required to be well capitalized. This ensures minimal, near-zero counterparty risk on all trades. Equally important, clearing members monitor each other, given their co-insurance arrangement.

Since the nature of default events underlying credit derivatives is inherently binary, the clearinghouse we propose would require higher initial margins from participants holding larger positions, potentially also enforce position limits and employ intraday margin calls. These features should rein in risk taking in credit derivative markets. While this may seem costly in normal times, it is essential to ensure minimal counterparty risk during a crisis, an outcome that would benefit even the large players. A clearinghouse would also provide a central registry through which regulators can obtain information on bilateral exposures to assess the consequences of the failure of an institution. Finally, such platforms could also disseminate publicly aggregated information on prices, volumes, and open interest, for example, to attract retail participation in some products.

Our overall policy recommendations are thus as follows:

- Large, standardized markets such as credit default swaps and related indices should be traded on centralized counterparty-cum-clearinghouses or exchanges.
- Smaller, less standardized markets such as those in collateralized debt and loan obligations (CDOs and CLOs), which also pose significant counterparty risk concerns, should have at the very least a centralized clearing mechanism so that the clearing registry is available to regulators to assess contagion effects of a large institution's failure.
- Finally, OTC markets can continue to remain the platform through which financial products are innovated; but, to give these markets an incentive to move to centralized registry and eventually to a clearinghouse, there should be an explicit regulator in charge of (1) enforcing higher transparency in OTC markets—possibly in the form of bilateral information on net exposures, with some time delay, and (2) providing infrastructure for enforcement relating to insider trading and market manipulation practices.

How should these recommendations be implemented? The regulator may simply have to play the coordinating role—possibly requiring some firmness with large players—to get market participants to set up centralized trading infrastructures. Also, the global nature of these markets may require a certain degree of international coordination among regulators, especially to provide timely counterparty information to each other when required.

CHAPTER 10

Derivatives: The Ultimate Financial Innovation

Viral V. Acharya, Menachem Brenner, Robert F. Engle,
Anthony W. Lynch, and Matthew Richardson

10.1 GENERAL BACKGROUND AND COST-BENEFIT ANALYSIS OF DERIVATIVES

Derivatives are financial contracts whose value is derived from some underlying asset. These assets can include equities and equity indexes, bonds, loans, interest rates, exchange rates, commodities, residential and commercial mortgages, and even catastrophes like earthquakes and hurricanes. The contracts come in many forms, but the more common ones include options, forwards/futures, and swaps. It is not an exaggeration to say that a considerable portion of financial innovation over the past 30 years has come from the emergence of derivatives markets. Exchange-traded derivatives are dominated by equity derivatives and commodity derivatives. Over-the-counter (OTC) derivatives are mainly in fixed income and currencies. According to the Bank for International Settlements (BIS), in OTC markets as of the middle of 2008, interest rate derivatives had a notional amount outstanding of $460 trillion, currency derivatives a notional amount outstanding of $60 trillion, and the total credit default swaps (CDS) notional amount outstanding was around $55 trillion. The benefits of derivatives are threefold: (1) risk management, (2) price discovery, and (3) enhancement of liquidity. We briefly describe each of these in turn.

Benefits

This risk management (hedging) benefit of derivatives to a wide spectrum of economic agents has been recognized centuries ago. Two well-known examples are the Dojima rice futures market in eighteenth-century Japan and the establishment of the Chicago Board of Trade (CBOT) in 1848 to trade forwards on agriculture commodities. Of course, the primary use of derivatives is to hedge one's positions (i.e., to reduce or eliminate the risk inherent in commodities, foreign currencies, and financial assets). Farmers who want to guarantee the prices of their future crops can sell them at any time in the futures or forwards market. Exporters, exposed to foreign exchange risk, can reduce their risk using derivatives (forwards, futures, and options). Pension funds that invest in securities can avoid disastrous consequences by buying insurance in the form of put options. The risk management benefits of derivatives are not limited to hedging one's exposure to risk but to a whole spectrum of risk-return combinations that can be achieved using options. For example, these features allow one to protect oneself in extremely volatile times like what we are witnessing now.

Another important benefit is the information that can be extracted from various derivatives. Price discovery is one aspect of it. Some examples include the ABX indexes (portfolios of collateralized debt obligations [CDOs] of subprime mortgages), which were one of the first instruments to provide information to the marketplace on the deteriorating subprime securitization market;[1] exchange-traded funds (ETFs), which provide information on the prices of securities ahead of the stale indexes (e.g., SPY vs. SPX); and option prices on individual equities, which reveal private information more quickly into the market.[2] Derivatives also allow market participants to extract forward-looking, as opposed to historical, information. For example, it is commonplace now to back out volatility, skewness (e.g., crash risk), and kurtosis (e.g., fat tails) of an underlying asset from option prices on that asset. Such information is used, among others, by central banks in making policy decisions, investors for risk and return decisions on their portfolios, and corporations for managing financial risk. Another example is the expected Federal Reserve rate decision obtained from federal funds futures.

An additional advantage is the enhancement of liquidity. Adding derivatives to an underlying market has two effects; (1) it brings to the market additional players who use the derivatives as a leveraged substitute to trading the underlying asset, and (2) derivatives provide a hedge to market makers, allowing a reduction in transaction costs through a lower bid-ask spread. By and large, spot markets with derivatives have more liquidity and thus lower transaction costs than markets without derivatives.

Given these seemingly important benefits, why are derivatives, and especially credit derivatives, viewed so negatively in the current financial crisis? We feel this opinion on derivatives is misguided. The problem is not with the derivatives as an instrument, but with (1) the way they were traded and cleared, and (2) how they were used by some financial institutions to increase their exposure to certain asset classes. Before addressing specific examples of the credit derivatives market and the current crisis in Section 10.2, we discuss some concerns about derivatives that arise quite generally.

Costs

In terms of the trading and clearing of derivatives, exchange-traded derivatives are standardized (or quasi-standardized) instruments that are marked to market where clearing and settlement are done by a clearing corporation. Though over the years there were some hiccups, mainly due to attempts to corner the market, the exchanges managed to deal with them and improve the system. By and large, this arrangement has operated smoothly. Since the inception of derivatives trading (1848), no clearing corporation has ever gone bankrupt. Nowadays, clearing corporations are large, and some clear for several exchanges—for example, the Options Clearing Corporation (OCC) and the Chicago Mercantile Exchange (CME).

The main problems that have now surfaced, in force, are associated with OTC derivatives where the focus is on CDSs, but not limited to this derivative.[3] While the CDS market is large, the OTC derivatives market has many other large markets (e.g., the foreign exchange derivatives market and the interest rate swaps market, among others). In general, the contracts are bilateral, typically with collateral depending on the type of contracts and the rating of the counterparty. Marking-to-market arrangements vary. In cases where one party has a big position and a highly correlated product trades on an exchange, that party may hedge its position with the exchange-traded product (e.g., the well-known Metallgesellschaft case in which the company hedged a forward contract with futures, exposing it to basis risk). The advantage of OTC contracts is that they are tailor made, which is important to entities that want to be perfectly hedged. That is, they can trade a big size without having a market impact, and they can have full anonymity. Unfortunately, this feature also describes the main problems, namely that these parties face (1) a potential lack of liquidity if they wish to liquidate their position and (2) counterparty risk.

Moreover, an issue that supersedes these two problems is the lack of transparency within the system. Unlike in the case of a central clearinghouse, no one knows precisely what the total exposure is, where it is concentrated, what the values of such contracts are, and so on. These issues always exist but rarely surface as long as the sizes of positions are small. However, when the sizes become large, and combined commitments are many times larger than the underlying assets, the lack of transparency makes the system prone to a systemic failure. Perhaps the best-known example from the recent past was Long Term Capital Management (LTCM). At the time of its collapse, LTCM had derivatives positions with a notional outstanding value of over $1.25 trillion, including swaps, futures, and options. In contrast, only six banks had derivatives positions greater than $1 trillion. And, in the current crisis, who could have known that AIG had written $400 billion worth of CDSs on AAA-tranched CDOs of mortgages, loans, and bonds?

Regulatory oversight and jurisdiction are another important issue. Currently we have the Commodity Futures Trading Commission (CFTC), the Securities and Exchange Commission (SEC), and the Federal Reserve regulating exchange-traded derivatives, resulting in inefficiencies and the waste of valuable resources. In contrast, OTC derivatives are mostly unregulated, leading to regulatory arbitrage. This lack of regulation of OTC derivatives received a seal of approval by the passage of the Commodity Futures Modernization Act of 2000 (CFMA). In fact, a number of policy makers have argued that CFMA led to a number of serious deficiencies in the system, including Enron taking advantage of this legislation in some of its fraudulent accounting practices, and, perhaps more important, the unchecked growth of the CDS market.

A final comment on potential costs is that the complexity of some derivatives makes them open to abuses such as biased reporting by corporations and financial institutions, and misrepresentation of their risks to unsophisticated investors (e.g., some structured products). Complexity, like a lack of transparency, may also impose a negative externality on the financial system. When the financial system is hit by a significant shock and there is a general flight to quality, complexity and lack of transparency in the system together amplify and speed up this flight, leading to a greater probability of systemic collapse (i.e., liquidity runs, death spirals, and so forth). From a societal point of view, all else held equal, complexity is a negative.

10.2 THE CREDIT DERIVATIVES MARKET AND THE FINANCIAL CRISIS

An important example of a credit derivative is a credit default swap (CDS). A credit default swap is an exchange of a fee in return for a payment if a credit default event occurs. In other words, it represents insurance against default. The buyer of protection pays a fee (credit swap premium) each period (e.g., 75 basis points) until the maturity of the CDS or an occurrence of the credit event. If a credit event (e.g., bankruptcy, failure to pay, restructuring, etc.) occurs, then the buyer receives the difference between par value of a reference asset and its market value. Much like its predecessors, the interest rate swap and the currency swap, CDSs were designed to allow market participants to hedge their credit risk. The growth in the market has been extraordinary. Based on data obtained from the International Swaps and Derivatives Association (ISDA), Figure 10.1 graphs the notional amount of outstanding CDSs in billions of dollars semiannually over the period from 2001 to 2008. Ignoring the netting across contracts, the size of the CDS market grew from $631 billion outstanding in the first half of 2001 to $54.6 trillion in the first half of 2008.

While much has been made of the size of the market, and therefore by induction its contribution to the existing crisis, most of the outstanding CDSs derive from the investment grade and high yield corporate bond markets. As defaults in the corporate bond market occur, exposure to these CDSs may become an issue. But to this date, the CDSs that have contributed to the write-downs in the current financial crisis have been those referencing residential mortgage-backed securities (RMBSs), commercial mortgage-backed securities (CMBSs), and collateralized debt obligations (CDOs). These CDSs represent only a small fraction of outstanding notional amounts. In contrast to corporate CDSs, the motivation for the CDSs referenced against asset-backed securities is one of guaranteeing the defaults on these securities or slices of these securities (i.e., tranches).

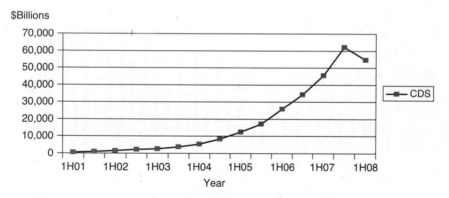

FIGURE 10.1 Notional Amount of Outstanding Credit Default Swaps (CDSs) ($ Amounts in Billions)

This graph presents the growth in notional amount of CDS contracts outstanding in billions of dollars over the period from 2001 to 2008.

Source: International Swaps and Derivatives Association (ISDA).

In particular, RMBSs, CMBSs, and CDOs are securities backed by pools of debt, usually mortgages, bonds, or loans. These securities are often tranched. For example, a typical structure might have four tranches, the first of which (the so-called equity tranche) would absorb the initial losses, the next tranche absorbing the losses after the equity tranche fully defaults, and so on, until the final AAA tranche, which defaults only after all the previous tranches are fully depleted. Figure 10.2 shows the issuance in the CDO market from 2001 to 2008. For example, mortgage-backed CDO issuance went from $28 billion in the first quarter of 2005 to $94 billion in the second quarter of 2007 until the market collapsed thereafter as the subprime crisis developed. A common CDS on these CDOs was one that covered any losses of the AAA tranche. It was these securities that were at the epicenter of the current financial crisis.

Benefits

Without access to credit derivatives, lenders would not be able to hedge their risk and expand the market for credit. That is, without hedging, lenders

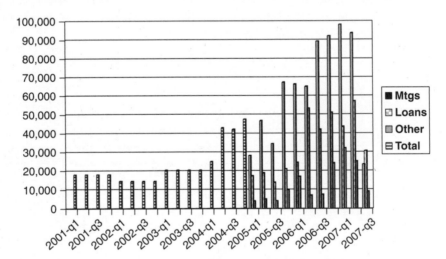

FIGURE 10.2 Collateralized Debt Obligation Issuance ($ Amounts in Millions)

This graph presents the various types of CDO issuance starting in 2005, namely mortgages, leveraged loans, and other asset classes. Prior to 2005, and starting in 2001, the graph provides the total CDO issuance.

Source: Securities Industry and Financial Markets Association (SIFMA).

would not be willing to supply a large number of loans at their fundamental prices and instead would demand an extra premium as the supply of loans increased. It can be argued that banks fared quite well during the 2001 recession with the economy's high rate of defaults because of the banks' ability to lay off the credit risk of their loans to capital markets. Even in the current crisis, there are a number of examples of benefits of CDSs. For instance, JPMorgan Chase is a major participant in the leveraged loan market. One of the ways JPMorgan expands the loan market is to take the loans, pool them to form CDOs, and then sell off these CDOs to a clientele of investors willing to purchase them. When the CDO market shut down in July 2007, it meant that JPMorgan was left holding a large number of leveraged loans on its books that were intended for the securitization market. This dramatically increased the bank's exposure to credit in what was becoming a high-risk environment. JPMorgan, however, was able to employ CDSs to reduce its exposure. Ex post, this was a good strategy, as credit market conditions deteriorated rapidly over the next year, putting other nonhedged financial institutions at risk.

CDOs have been greatly criticized as "derivatives gone wild." But the truth is that these securities allowed an expansion of credit markets by spreading the credit risk across a wide variety of global investors and away from capital-constrained financial institutions. This helps credit to reflect its true economic value (and not demand/supply imbalances), namely the probability of default, recovery in default, and any aggregate risk premiums associated with default. This expansion of credit enabled individuals to access the subprime or Alt-A mortgage market, and allowed companies to issue high yield bonds or leveraged loans for efficient recapitalizations or capital investments. The mere fact that a shock to the fundamentals of the economy (i.e., the burst of the housing bubble and a more general economic downturn) led to credit losses should not have caused a financial crisis. The problem was that this credit was not sufficiently sold to investors, but instead was held on the bank's balance sheets. In other words, the issue was not with the derivatives, but how they were misused in practice.

In addition, during the current crisis, CDSs and other credit derivatives have played a very important role in disseminating information both to the public and to regulators. Due to the complexity of financial firms' capital structures, it is difficult to infer general credit quality from the secondary market in underlying bonds, especially given that some of the bonds rarely trade. In contrast, from very early on during the financial crisis, the CDS market has judged the quality of financial firms' bankruptcy prospects in a remarkably prescient way. As an example, consider seven financial institutions from the onset of the crisis in July 2007 to November 2008, namely

Bear Stearns, Lehman Brothers, Merrill Lynch, AIG, Citigroup, Morgan Stanley, and Goldman Sachs. Figure 10.3 graphs their CDS premiums on a monthly basis in comparison to the other evaluator of credit, the rating agencies. As can be seen from the figure, the market very early on figured out that the financial institutions had become much riskier due to the onset of systemic risk.

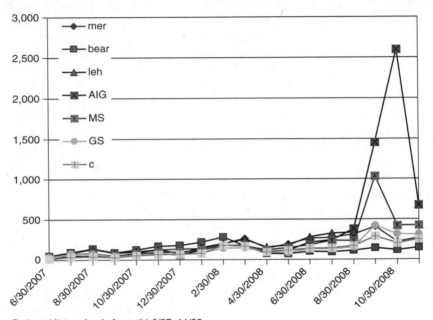

Ratings History (end of month) 6/07–11/08

Bear Stearns A+ 6/07, A 11/07, BBB 3/08, AA– 4/08
Lehman A+ 6/07, A 6/08, neg watch 9/08
Merrill Lynch AA– 6/07, A+ 10/07, A 6/08
AIG AA 6/07, AA– 5/08, A– 10/08
Citi AA 6/07, AA– 11/07, neg watch 4/08 and 9/08
Morgan Stanley AA– 6/07, A+ 6/08
Goldman Sachs AA– 6/07

FIGURE 10.3 Credit Default Swap Premiums (Basis Points) and Ratings of Financial Institutions, July 2007–November 2008

This figure provides a time series of CDS premiums on a month-end basis from June 30, 2007, to November 30, 2008. The premiums are given for the major financial institutions—Bear Stearns (bear), Lehman Brothers (leh), Merrill Lynch (mer), AIG (AIG), Citigroup (C), Morgan Stanley (MS), and Goldman Sachs (GS). Provided immediately below is the time series of rating changes for these same institutions.

Source: Bloomberg.

Costs

As illustrated by Figures 10.1 and 10.2, the CDS and CDO markets had grown to well over $50 trillion in notional amounts by the middle of 2008. Yet there was a complete lack of transparency about the underlying exposures of financial institutions to these markets. For example, the central idea of securitization is to pool relatively illiquid loans—mortgages, corporate bonds, and bank loans—that banks have trouble keeping on their balance sheets into more liquid CDOs that would then be passed on to a wide variety of investors willing to assume the risks. The surprising part of this crisis, however, is that these securities were held in large amounts by commercial and investment banks. As housing prices started falling and subprime mortgages began to default, CDOs began to lose value, and financial institutions began to suffer large write-downs. As it became clear that many highly levered financial institutions, some at unprecedented ratios, were highly exposed to these derivatives, counterparty uncertainty in the OTC market spread through the system, causing systemic risk to spread as well.

For example, on March 14, as Bear Stearns was on the brink of bankruptcy, Figure 10.3 shows that CDS spreads of financial institutions jumped. As a result of this contagion, the government engineered a bailout of Bear Stearns by guaranteeing $29 billion worth of subprime-backed securities and its sale to JPMorgan Chase. Some months later, however, as credit markets deteriorated further and the deterioration moved beyond subprime-backed securities, Lehman Brothers declared bankruptcy on September 15, leading to systemic pressure on AIG, the Reserve Primary Fund, and then Morgan Stanley and Goldman Sachs, resulting in the government bailing out the entire financial system. Transparency (or lack thereof) was the common characteristic of these entities—the market, and certainly regulators, were unaware of AIG's $400 billion one-sided exposure to CDSs on CDOs, of the Reserve Primary Fund's massive exposure to Lehman short-term debt, and ultimately the credit exposures of Morgan Stanley and Goldman Sachs.

While transparency of the derivatives market is a major issue, its effect is amplified by the complexity of credit derivatives.[4] In stating their complexity, however, it is useful to separate out CDSs on corporate bonds from CDSs on CDOs, the latter being much more complicated. As the market for credit derivatives took off rapidly after 2001, its growth closely mirrored a related market, the collateralized mortgage obligations (CMO) market, in the mid-1990s. Both these markets got away from their initial purpose, creating more and more complex structures (e.g., the interest-only [IO] Z tranche of a 50-tranche structure for CMOs versus the synthetic CDO-squareds of the current crisis). Both markets went through a significant shock (e.g., the 200-basis-point interest rate move in 1994 versus the 20 percent housing price drop in 2006–2007), and both markets collapsed shortly thereafter. Eventually, the CMO market came back completely, albeit in a much simpler form and with a well-developed investor base. One might expect the CDO market to come back similarly if allowed the opportunity.

Even for the simplest form of CDOs, there are still three outstanding issues, all of which were severely missed by the rating agencies and, apparently, by some of the leading financial institutions in the securitization business.[5] First, on an ex ante basis, the assumptions used to value the CDOs seemed very poor. Some examples include: little or no modeling of the effect of a housing decline on defaults even though local evidence showed such a relationship and ample discussion of a housing bubble had occurred, and no modeling of lower recovery rates on loans even though loans were no longer at the very highest priority of the capital structure. Second, the assumptions did not take account of the adverse selection and moral hazard created by securitization, namely that securitization reduces the incentive to provide high-quality loans and then monitor them. Third, the correlation and recovery structures of the loans, the key ingredients to CDOs, were simple inputs to the modeling structures. All of these need to be improved moving forward.

Even if the issues of transparency and complexity, however, were solved, it is still not clear that the problem of systemic risk would be solved. Financial institutions and market participants will all act in their own interest to manage their risk/return trade-off. These actions may not take into account the spillover risk throughout the system. Therefore, there is a role for the regulation of OTC derivatives. At a minimum, this would mean the regulator could use the information on the firm's exposure to derivatives and then employ the tools discussed elsewhere in these chapters to tax or reduce the systemic risk in the system. At a maximum, this might involve regulation along the lines seen either with exchange-traded derivatives (à la the CFTC) or traded securities more generally like stocks and bonds (à la the SEC). At face value, other than one-off, customer-specific OTC derivatives, which may be too unwieldy and costly to monitor, there appears to be no reason for the lack of regulation of more standardized OTC derivatives.[6]

10.3 PRINCIPLES OF REGULATING DERIVATIVES

The most important principle underlying the regulation of derivatives must encircle three primary issues: (1) uncertain counterparty credit risk exposure, which can generate illiquidity and can cause markets to break down; (2) capital erosion, which can cause the financial system to break down if the erosion is large and concentrated in institutions that provide liquidity to the financial system; and (3) prices that are away from fundamentals due to illiquidity in the market, which can cause distortions in capital allocation.

Since the most important component for understanding counterparty credit risk is the level of transparency, any regulatory action should explicitly be organized around increasing the level of transparency to, at the very least, the regulator. In fact, real-time availability of prices, volumes, and positions at the trade level to regulators is unambiguously beneficial so long as the costs associated with gathering and processing the information are not prohibitive. This information would allow regulators to manage systemic risk in the financial system. For example, AIG's $400 billion worth of exposure to credit defaults across markets presumably would have alerted regulators.

There are, of course, also strong benefits to providing transparency to the public as well. Regulators may not always be able to monitor or understand the exposures. The market may discipline the counterparties in question. For example, would Goldman Sachs, Merrill Lynch, and others have entered into agreements with AIG knowing the degree to which AIG was exposed similarly to all its counterparties? Unlike with regulators, unfettered transparency of prices, volumes, and positions to the public at large involves a trade-off. On the positive side, greater transparency helps limit the risk externality created by counterparty credit risk. On the negative side, transparency may be onerous for institutions since (1) it may reveal their trading strategies, and (2) it may reduce their inclination to trade, and thereby also affect liquidity in an adverse manner. Moreover, there are costs to collecting and processing information, which are likely higher in more diffuse markets such as the swaps market and lower in more concentrated markets such as the CDS market, where there are only around 25 key players.

10.4 REGULATION OF DERIVATIVES— SOME SUGGESTIONS

As stated earlier, the primary regulatory issue is that lack of transparency in the market for OTC derivatives can result in (1) uncertain counterparty credit risk, which may cause markets to shut down, (2) capital erosion of a major financial institution that leads to a ripple effect across the financial system and a loss of liquidity services, and (3) prices that are away from fundamentals due to illiquidity in the market, which can cause distortions in capital allocation. The following suggestions are designed to address these issues and also some secondary concerns.

A Central Clearinghouse

The main reason for systemic risk in OTC markets is that bilaterally set collateral and margin requirements in OTC trading do not take account of the counterparty risk externality that each trade imposes on the rest of the system, allowing systemically important exposures to be built up without sufficient capital to mitigate associated risks. The top part of Figure 10.4 shows the interaction of six financial institutions in an OTC market. There are 15 possible bilateral transactions taking place in the market. Without additional information, it is not possible for a counterparty to know the overall credit risk of the other counterparty it is trading with. This is not just because of its other four transactions, but also because of the transactions between other counterparties that might put the system at risk. As a solution to this problem, therefore, OTC markets that grow sufficiently large should be migrated to clearinghouse and exchange market structures. With appropriate collateral and margin requirements, these structures have little or no counterparty credit risk. The lower part of Figure 10.4 illustrates this mechanism where now there are just six transactions, one for each counterparty, with a common intermediary, the central clearinghouse.

In general, new instruments will almost always start off being traded in an OTC market before moving to a registry structure as the market for these instruments grows larger. As this growth occurs and standardization becomes easier to implement, the instruments will move to either a clearinghouse structure or an exchange structure. Chapter 11, "Centralized Clearing for Credit Derivatives," explains these arguments in more detail. The chapter makes several suggestions with respect to market structures. First, standardized products such as credit default swaps (CDSs) on corporate or credit indexes should be considered for migration to exchange-based trading where well-capitalized market makers provide liquidity. The clearinghouse of the exchange acts as a counterparty to all trades and provides transparency in terms of aggregated or trade-level price and volume information. Second, OTC markets that may be important for counterparty risk but that are small in nature should be subject to a centralized registry. Third, regardless of the market structure (OTC without a registry, centralized registry, centralized counterparty, or exchange), regulators should have access to information on bilateral positions. Fourth, given the binary nature of default events, collateral and margining arrangements based on daily marking to market should be carefully designed to ensure minimal counterparty risk of centralized counterparties in credit derivatives, recognizing that some counterparty risk may be unavoidable.

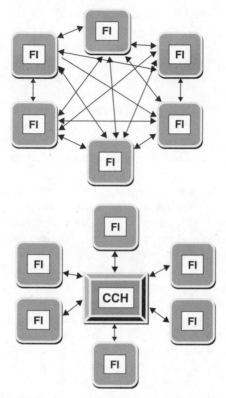

FIGURE 10.4 Over-the-Counter Market versus Central Clearinghouse

This figure provides a comparison of an over-the-counter market versus a central clearinghouse. Here, in the OTC market, each financial institution (FI) has bilateral trading with each of the others. Each counterparty knows only its trades with the other party and not that party's trades with the other four FIs. In contrast, with the central clearinghouse (CCH), each FI trades with the central party, so there is full transparency.

Transparency

Transparency of all information for regulators is necessary. In the event of systemic stress, regulators ought to have this information to assess the damage to the financial system of letting a counterparty fail. For the clearinghouse and exchange market structures mentioned earlier, the regulators (and the public) can obtain this information in real time. For the registry market structure, this information can easily be made available to regulators by the registry at the end of each trading day. For OTC markets, counterparties to any trade must report asset terms, price, and volume information in a timely manner to the regulatory body charged with managing systemic risk in the financial system.

Transparency of all information for registries, clearinghouses, and exchanges is also necessary. Registries, clearinghouses, and exchanges need this information to proactively limit counterparty credit risk through the setting of margin and collateral requirements. For the clearinghouse and exchange market structures, this information is available to the relevant clearinghouse or exchange in real time. For the registry market structure, this information is obtained by the registry at the end of each trading day as a matter of course. But it may be better to require that the parties to any trade report asset terms, price, and volume information in a more timely manner to the registry.

Transparency for the public of trade-level information on volume and prices in real time without revealing who is trading also seems reasonable. This is a feature of most markets and is now a feature of the corporate bond market, which was hitherto entirely OTC but now has trade-level disclosure to TRACE. For example, the CDS market for corporate bonds is a natural OTC market for which a TRACE-like system seems appropriate. Real-time public transparency of prices and volumes at the trade level is unambiguously beneficial for small trades (since it ensures smoother revelation of information into prices and more orderly liquidation of positions, which both lower volatility) but involves trade-offs for large trades (since revealing the volume may reveal who is trading). As a solution for large trades, the TRACE system reports the trade price, but does not reveal the volume. The cost of revealing the volume of a large trade, which makes it easier for market participants to determine the parties to the trade, needs to be traded off against the benefit of revealing the volume of a large trade, which aids the dissemination of information into prices.

Finally, does the market need public transparency of positions? The exact level of transparency that is desirable is a function of the exact nature of margining/collateralization associated with the market structure in place. In particular, less transparency is needed as better margining/collateralization drives counterparty credit toward zero. In particular, if the margining and collateralization requirements that are put in place are able to reduce counterparty credit risk to zero, there is little need for public transparency of positions since such transparency does not help manage systemic risk in the financial system. For clearinghouse and exchange market structures, where there is little or no counterparty credit risk, there is little or no need for public revelation of positions held by market participants. For the OTC and registry market structures, where there is substantial counterparty credit risk, however, there is a need for transparency of positions for the public.

The timing and frequency of the public revelation of positions can be used to manage and reduce the costs of public revelation of positions. In terms of timing, if a participant has a large position and needs to unwind the position, and other parties were to know about this position, then these parties could take advantage if the position is revealed in real time. Therefore, a lag between the date of the position snapshot and its public revelation may limit the ability of other parties to take advantage of participants with large position exposures. The analogous mechanism would be the delayed 13-F filings by institutions of their long positions in equities and bonds. In terms of frequency, frequent public snapshots of a participant's positions, even with a lag, allow other market participants to infer that participant's trading strategy. Reducing the frequency of the snapshots makes it more difficult to use those snapshots to infer a player's trading strategy.

Last, what form would this transparency of positions take? Would transparency of positions be trade by trade, or would there be some aggregation, and if so would this aggregation be bilateral (i.e., knowing all of a party's positions in a security and the counterparty for each position) or institutional (i.e., knowing only a party's net position in a security)? While bilateral aggregation would allow counterparty credit risk to be more accurately assessed, it might reveal how various participants are providing liquidity to the market.

Oversight of Derivatives

As a backdrop, consider the past and current regulatory environment. The Commodity Exchange Act (CEA) of 1936 was enacted to deal with manipulation and cornering attempts in agricultural futures. The act did not cover forward contracts that were considered cash sales. This was changed in 1974 with the act that created the Commodity Futures Trading Commission (CFTC). This act has actually expanded the range of derivatives that CEA applies to. The definition of *commodity* now includes "all other goods and articles . . . in which contracts for future delivery are presently or in the future dealt in." Moreover, all derivatives contracts had to be traded on futures exchanges. As stated earlier, this requirement excluded forward contracts where actual delivery was taking place. The other exclusion, provided by the Treasury Amendment (to the same act), were OTC derivatives based on foreign exchange or U.S. Treasury securities. In the 1980s, interest rate and currency swaps were created with an unclear regulatory status. As a result, in 1989, the CFTC issued a swaps exemption, and, in 1993, it issued an exemption for OTC derivatives on energy products. In 1998, the CFTC was considering modifying the regulation of the OTC market but, in November

1999, the President's Working Group on Financial Markets recommended that essentially financial OTC derivatives should be excluded from the CEA and from the CFTC's jurisdiction. Based on this, the Commodity Futures Modernization Act of 2000 (CFMA) stated that OTC financial derivatives were not subject to the CEA as long as they were not marketed to small investors. Thus, as long as credit derivatives, for example, are not marketed to small investors, they are exempt from regulation. If an exchange were formed to trade such derivatives, however, they would fall under the jurisdiction of the CFTC.

This latter distinction is not particularly logical, especially in the context of whether derivatives are a possible contributor toward systemic risk for the reasons described earlier. Therefore, it seems perfectly reasonable that there should be consistent regulation across derivatives. This would require an agreed-upon set of rules for all derivatives. A natural place to start would be to apply similar requirements to the exchange-traded market. For example, alerting potential participants to the risks and complexity of derivatives products would fall into this category. Of course, one of the attractive features of the OTC derivatives market is its flexibility and customer-specific derivatives contracts. It may well be the case that the OTC derivatives market might have to reach a particular threshold, either in volume or in transaction size, to fall into the class of regulated securities.

An even deeper issue is whether derivatives should be treated differently than any other securities. Because derivatives are usually claims on underlying securities, such as equities, bonds, and loans, there is not a big difference economically between the underlying asset and the derivative. In fact, the fundamental basis behind the valuation of many derivatives is dynamic trading of the underlying and a riskless security. It is not clear, therefore, why the regulatory treatment of derivatives should be different than other securities. This would suggest a single regulatory agency that would cover all securities, in other words, a combination of the SEC and the CFTC. One ancillary benefit is that this by construction would end the infamous turf battles of these two commissions.

NOTES

1. A specific analysis of the price discovery function of the ABX index is provided in Gorton (2008).
2. See, for example, Chakravarty, Gulen, and Mayhew (2005) and Pan and Poteshman (2006).
3. A recent example is the exotic foreign exchange options scandal in Korea, which was an OTC bilateral deal.

4. See Chapter 1, "Mortgage Origination and Securitization in the Financial Crisis."
5. See Chapter 3, "The Rating Agencies: Is Regulation the Answer?"
6. One argument against regulation might be the regulatory arbitrage that can take place internationally. As mentioned throughout these chapters, international coordination is an important element of any reform.

REFERENCES

Chakravarty, Sugato, Huseyin Gulen, and Stewart Mayhew. 2005. Informed trading in stock and option markets. *Journal of Finance* 59:1235–1258.

Gorton, Gary. 2008. The panic of 2007. Yale working paper.

Pan, Jun, and Allen Poteshman. 2006. The information in option volume for future stock prices. *Review of Financial Studies* 19:871–908.

CHAPTER 11

Centralized Clearing for Credit Derivatives

Viral V. Acharya, Robert F. Engle, Stephen Figlewski,
Anthony W. Lynch, and Marti G. Subrahmanyam

The subprime crisis has highlighted several shortcomings of over-the-counter (OTC) trading in credit derivatives, most notably counterparty and operational risk concerns and the lack of transparency. The primary issue is that collateral and margin requirements are set bilaterally in OTC trading and do not take account of the externality that each trade's counterparty risk imposes on the rest of the system. This allows systemically important exposures to grow without sufficient capital backing. We propose the following comprehensive solution to address this and other shortcomings:

- OTC markets that grow sufficiently large should trade through a centralized clearinghouse that also acts as a counterparty to *all* trades, ensuring minimal, near-zero counterparty risk.
- Well-standardized products such as credit default swaps (CDSs) or credit indexes should ideally move to exchange-based trading where well-capitalized market makers provide liquidity, the exchange clearinghouse acts as the counterparty to *all* trades, and there is significant transparency in terms of aggregate and trade-level price and volume information.
- OTC markets that are not large enough to require a centralized clearinghouse but where deals are deemed to have important counterparty risk should be subject to a centralized registry.
- Given the binary nature of default events, collateral and margining arrangements should be marked to market daily and should be carefully designed to ensure that centralized counterparties in credit derivatives

face minimal counterparty risk, recognizing that higher counterparty risk than that in other products may be unavoidable. Requiring an appropriate level of transparency regarding bilateral exposures can mitigate the adverse consequences arising from residual counterparty risk.

- Regardless of market structure (centralized registry, centralized counterparty, or exchange), regulators should have expedient access to information on bilateral positions in significant OTC markets.

- Finally, since counterparty risks in OTC and registry structures would remain significant, a higher level of disclosure could be required of market participants—for example, disclosure, with a delay, of all net positions of each institution. This would provide an incentive to move away from these structures to centralized counterparty ones. However, where such disclosure is costly (for participants and regulators), there should at least be an effort to require bilateral collateral arrangements already in place in OTC markets to be sufficiently responsive to credit and market risks.

11.1 OTC CREDIT DERIVATIVES— A SNAPSHOT

Credit derivatives, mainly credit default swaps (CDSs) and collateralized debt obligations (CDOs), have been under great stress since the inception of the subprime financial crisis, and in turn, they have contributed to the severity of the market disruption.[1] It has been argued that this is in large part because these relatively new products are traded over the counter in bilateral transactions between banks and other institutions, unlike other financial derivatives such as equity options and futures contracts, which are mainly traded on exchanges.

Although OTC contracts can be more flexible than standardized exchange-traded derivatives, they also suffer from greater *counterparty and operational risks*, as well as less *transparency*. Each party in an OTC contract bears the risk that the counterparty will fail to fulfill its obligation in the future. Operational risk creates uncertainty about whether OTC trades will be cleared and settled in an orderly manner; for example, a market participant that takes a large hedging position in a credit derivative risks that settlement may be delayed if the trading and settlement infrastructure is poor. Counterparty and operational risks may also interact, whereby there is greater uncertainty about clearing and settlement when an important counterparty experiences distress. Finally, since there is no centralized trading platform in OTC markets, information about prices and trading volume is very limited. OTC trading is much less transparent than on an exchange, which, as we explain later, is detrimental to financial stability in a stressed environment. Even the most basic information desirable to manage risks in such times—the total amount of outstanding credit derivatives—is misleading because of a lack of a centralized database. The Depository Trust and Clearing Corporation (DTCC) recently began publishing some disaggregated information on volumes of one credit derivative, credit default swaps, but it is only a small step toward the level of transparency desirable for market resilience during stress.

Consider first the CDS market. This market has grown by leaps and bounds since its inception in the mid-1990s, with reported total notional amounts outstanding rising from around $180 billion in 1998 to a peak of over $60 *trillion* by mid-2008. Many commentators express concern that this is much more than the total value of the underlying corporate bonds and loans that these contracts are designed to insure. But in this OTC market, the outstanding notional principal is estimated from surveys of dealers. To see how this distorts the picture, consider an investor who owns $100 million in XYZ corporation debt and buys protection by entering into a $100 million credit default swap with Bank A. Since both counterparties are surveyed, this would be reported as two new $100 million CDS contracts. Bank A then hedges its exposure by buying a CDS from Bank B. This raises the increase in outstanding CDSs to $400 million. Bank B buys a CDS from Bank C—another $200 million in CDSs—and finally, to cut the example short, Bank C hedges by buying protection on XYZ from an end investor, that is, an investor that wants to bear XYZ's credit risk rather than hedge it, in return for receiving the swap spread as a premium. Due to the bilateral nature of OTC trading, this chain, which involves one buyer of $100 million of protection, one ultimate protection seller, and three market-making intermediaries, would be reported as an increase of $800 million in outstanding CDS notional principal.

The settlement of CDS contracts written on Lehman Brothers, following its bankruptcy in September 2008, provides a striking example of this phenomenon. About $400 billion of CDSs were presented for settlement, but once all the offsetting trades, like those between Banks A, B, and C in the preceding example, were netted out, the DTCC estimated that only about $6 billion ultimately changed hands. The key issue is that investors do not know how to translate the $400 billion of gross notional amount outstanding to the $6 billion net. The substantial uncertainty about the net figure that would have to change hands in Lehman Brothers' bankruptcy, and whether this would lead to counterparty losses for other banks, contributed to the paralysis in interbank lending markets.

Although both CDSs and CDOs have contributed to the credit crisis, they have done so in quite different ways because the instruments themselves have quite different risk characteristics. Most CDOs represent claims on an underlying pool of risky debt instruments, such as corporate bonds or mortgage loans. In the securitization process, exposure to the default risk that is inherent in the securities placed in the pool is split up among the different CDO tranches that are created, with buyers of the riskiest equity and mezzanine tranches bearing most of it.[2] These investors may end up losing most or even all of their principal value. But this risk is comparable to the risk on a bond: the investor cannot lose more than was invested initially. By contrast, a credit default swap is like an insurance contract. The protection buyer pays a regular premium, maybe a few hundred basis points a year, while the protection seller is exposed to the risk that the reference entity (the firm or sovereign borrower the CDS is written on) will default. If that happens, the seller is immediately liable for the default loss on the obligor's debt, which can be as much as the entire principal amount of the CDS. In the Lehman case, the protection sellers had to pay out about 92 cents on the dollar, several times the initial cost of the protection.

We therefore feel that the need to bring credit derivatives out of the purely OTC market in which they are currently traded is most pressing for the CDS market. We concentrate on them in this chapter, discussing briefly at the end the relevance of our proposal for other credit derivatives such as CDOs.

Note also that outside of the current crisis, the CDS market has experienced some problems when the number of contracts to be settled is large relative to the physical supply of the underlying reference securities. This raises the question whether these contracts should be settled by physical delivery of the underlying assets or in cash based on the price of the underlying. We relegate discussion of this issue to Box 11.1, focusing here on issues related to counterparty risk in CDSs and its mitigation.

11.2 WEAKNESSES IN THE CDS TRADING INFRASTRUCTURE: SOME EXAMPLES

A firm's CDS spread—the fee a buyer pays for default protection—is widely believed to be one of the best market indicators of credit risk. The spread tends to widen dramatically during a period of general financial stress, such as we are experiencing now. Is this widening entirely due to an increase in the credit risk of the underlying obligors? Higher default risk for obligors is clearly the most important factor, but an increase in perceived counterparty risk—the risk that the writer of the CDS contract will fail to fulfill its obligations or that the buyer of the contract will default, leaving the seller with the risk of replacing the contract at new prices and terms—is also an

BOX 11.1 CASH SETTLEMENT OR PHYSICAL SETTLEMENT?

An important aspect of all derivative contracts is how they are settled upon exercise. Two alternative methods, physical delivery and cash settlement, are prevalent in both exchange-traded and over-the-counter derivatives. For example, physical delivery is used for options on individual stocks. Upon exercise, shares of the stock in question are delivered in exchange for cash. By contrast, settlement of most index options and derivatives based on interest rates, such as Eurodollar futures, is done only in cash. The settlement amount is determined by the observed value of the underlying in the market. Both procedures are in use for settlement of credit default swaps (CDSs).

With physical delivery it is possible that the available supply of the deliverable security may be insufficient to meet the requirements of the net short positions on the maturity or exercise date. The problem is aggravated if the aggregate positions requiring delivery are not visible to the market. The market may experience a classic short squeeze in which participants with short positions suddenly have to scramble to buy the security, thus pushing the price up sharply over a brief period of time.

A prominent example of this phenomenon was the settlement of CDSs on Delphi in 2005, when the net outstanding position in CDS contracts to be settled far outstripped the floating supply of bonds that were deliverable into this contract. A more recent example occurred in the equity market when a short squeeze developed in shares of Volkswagen, in the presence of a large position in call options held long by Porsche and sold by many prominent hedge funds.

Another problem with physical delivery is that there is often a potentially large set of related things that can be delivered, such as multiple securities issued by the reference entity for a CDS, or different grades of a commodity that can all be delivered against a futures contract, and these trade at different prices in the market. This leads to the well-known cheapest-to-deliver issue, which introduces ambiguity into exactly what the long will receive upon delivery and how a hedge of the not-cheapest-to-deliver instrument will perform.

Cash settlement has its own problems, the most important of which is that the settlement price must be determined in the market. Anything that makes the market price differ from the full equilibrium value of

(Continued)

BOX 11.1 *(Continued)*

the underlying, such as a badly designed auction process or, again, an imbalance between the size of short positions and the outstanding amount of the underlying covered by the contract. If the auction becomes lopsided, a variant of the short squeeze can occur even with cash settlement.

What is the solution? If the floating stock of deliverable securities is small in relation to the outstanding position, the problem cannot be avoided by either cash or physical delivery. It may be mitigated by allowing the short position a broader range of settlement options, to include a choice of either physical delivery or settlement in cash. This may also work well in the case of nonstorable agricultural commodities.

In any case, increased transparency about the aggregate net position to be settled would warn market participants when there is an imbalance between the outstanding derivatives positions and the amount of the underlying available to be delivered. This is particularly relevant to the CDS market, where the market currently does not have a good idea of the net outstanding position in individual contracts.

important culprit. In fact, when the underlying obligor is a financial institution, credit correlation can have a substantial effect on the counterparty risk, as the intermediaries in the CDS market are also other financial institutions. In particular, large global financial firms fluctuate in value together due to their interconnectedness in the global markets, so that an increase in the credit risk of one is generally adverse news about the credit risk of others. This effect, along with the fact that such institutions are tied to each other through chains of OTC derivatives contracts as described earlier, means that the failure of one institution can substantially raise CDS spreads on other institutions, making it difficult for investors to separate the credit risk of the obligor from CDS counterparty risk.

Such systemic concerns arising from counterparty risk in CDS contracts have grown dramatically over the past year. For example, Bear Stearns was a leading clearer of the CDS contracts between financial institutions, like Bank B in our example. Its imminent failure in the first half of March 2008 sparked fear among them over the settlement and clearing of many trades—that its failure would have resulted in market disruption and mark-to-market losses for other institutions. The lack of transparency in the exposures of different institutions to each other aggravated such fears immensely, causing

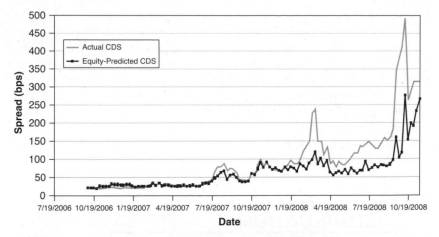

FIGURE 11.1   The Relative Behavior of CDS Spread and Equity-Implied CDS Spread for Goldman Sachs during the Subprime Crisis

Source: Leland (2008).

CDS spreads on financials to rise well beyond what would be based *only* on their credit risk. Deciding that Bear Stearns was too interconnected to be allowed to fail, the Federal Reserve and the Treasury orchestrated a bailout. The consequences of allowing a large OTC derivatives intermediary to fail rather than bailing it out became painfully visible when Lehman Brothers filed for bankruptcy shortly thereafter, once again causing CDS spreads to rise sharply and precipitating a freeze in interbank markets as well. Many observers now feel, with the benefit of hindsight, that Lehman was a systemically important counterparty and it was a serious mistake to let it fail.

Empirical evidence that widening of CDS spreads around these bank failures is partly attributable to concerns about counterparty risk can be seen in Figure 11.1, which compares the behavior of the market-quoted CDS spread on Goldman Sachs to its equity-implied CDS spread.[3] The two series grow increasingly out of sync as the Bear Stearns default approaches; the dislocation diminishes after the resolution of Bear, retaining nevertheless a higher level than during the pre-March period; dislocation skyrockets again around the Lehman Brothers and AIG episode of mid-September, again falling to an extent in October 2008 following the announcement of the rescue package for banks. While there may be other liquidity factors delinking the CDS and equity markets, counterparty risk and clearing concerns stand out as primary candidates.

The specific problems experienced by AIG during September 2008 highlight yet another shortcoming of OTC credit default swaps. AIG was in the position of the ultimate protection seller in our example, taking on the default risk of XYZ and not hedging. AIG regarded default protection as just another kind of insurance, like insuring automobiles. Because of its AAA credit rating, AIG's counterparties did not require it to post collateral when it sold protection, but they did impose the condition that collateral would be required if AIG's credit rating fell. On September 17, 2008, AIG was downgraded to A– by Standard & Poor's and to A2 by Moody's, which touched off an immediate collateral call for over $13 billion. AIG could not raise that amount quickly and had to be saved from insolvency by a hasty bailout by the Federal Reserve and the Treasury.

11.3 THE BENEFITS OF CENTRALIZED CLEARING

The preceding examples show that OTC markets have some undesirable features, especially during a financial crisis. Yet the huge OTC market for interest rate swaps has thrived for the past 25 years. Why can't participants in the CDS market privately achieve outcomes that efficiently address these undesirable features? Put another way, why might a regulatory solution in the form of a centralized clearinghouse or exchange be desirable for credit default swaps?

First, all OTC contracts, including CDSs, feature collateral or margin requirements, wherein counterparties post a deposit whose aim is to minimize counterparty risk. The deposit is marked to market daily, based on fluctuations in the value of the underlying contract and the creditworthiness of the counterparties (as we discussed in the case of AIG). The difficulty, however, is that such collateral arrangements are negotiated on a bilateral basis. Parties in each contract do not take full account of the fact that counterparty risk they are prepared to undertake in a contract also affects other players; indeed, they often *cannot* take account of this counterparty risk externality in an OTC setting, due to inadequate transparency about the counterparty's other positions and its interconnectedness with the rest of the market. While bilateral collateral arrangements do respond to worsening credit risk of a counterparty, such response is often tied to agency ratings, which are sluggish in capturing credit risk information and potentially inaccurate.[4]

Futures and options exchanges frequently set maximum position limits for participants. A position limit is not unlike an infinite margin requirement. In a clearinghouse or exchange setting, even without position limits, it would be natural to impose higher collateral requirements on counterparties with unusually large exposures. Otherwise there will be concerns that severe price pressure may be exerted on markets if these large exposures are unwound under duress, as could well have happened with Lehman or

AIG. Since OTC markets prevent aggregating information about institution-specific positions, they also preclude a ready identification of large exposures. AIG was an extreme case, but it also showed clearly that each of its individual counterparties did not fully internalize the benefit of its margining on other counterparties, resulting in low overall margins, which allowed AIG to underwrite a systemically large amount of CDS protection. Had the counterparties been aware of AIG's total exposure, they might well have insisted on larger margins, which would have restricted AIG's ability to accumulate such large positions.

Finally, the same forces outlined earlier create resistance from large players to move trading from OTC markets to centralized clearing or exchanges. Large players benefit from the lack of transparency in OTC markets since they see more orders and contracts than other players do. They can also unwind or take on large positions in an OTC setting with less market impact (that is, without moving the market much) as they can trade with multiple counterparties, and thereby ensure that their overall trade remains disguised. Not only would large players lose these benefits in a clearinghouse or exchange setting, but they would also be required to post higher collateral. However, we will argue that during a systemic crisis, no player enjoys a significant relative advantage of trading on its own credit. Hence, in a situation such as the one we are in right now, the public goods aspect of reducing systemic risk in the context of a clearinghouse or an exchange likely far outweighs any specific benefits that even the best-rated and largest players may enjoy from bilateral contracting in an OTC market.

11.4 POSSIBLE SOLUTIONS AND THEIR RELATIVE MERITS

In what specific form should OTC trading move to centralized clearing? Let us first distinguish three forms a clearing facility might take (see Table 11.1).

Solution I: Registry. The most basic form would just be a central registry of deals that are set up privately in bilateral negotiations between counterparties. This kind of clearing facility could perform such functions as holding collateral for the counterparties, marking deals and collateral to market daily, and facilitating the associated transfers of funds, with appropriate netting of amounts, among all of the institutions it deals with. Centralizing information about outstanding CDS deals would allow a major improvement in market transparency, and netting of margin flows among the counterparties would increase efficiency. But counterparty credit risk would

TABLE 11.1 Three Possible Solutions to Centralized Clearing and Their Relative Merits

Market Characteristic	OTC	Market Organization Registry (Solution I)	Clearinghouse (Solution II)	Exchange (Solution III)
Trading style	Bilateral negotiation	Bilateral negotiation	Bilateral negotiation	Continuous auction
Market participants	Large, well-capitalized firms	Large, well-capitalized firms	Well-capitalized counterparties only	Retail trade possible; largest trades arranged in upstairs market
Flexibility/ standardization of contracts	Maximum flexibility	Maximum flexibility	Flexible terms; standardized credit enhancement	Largely standardized contracts
Counterparty credit risk	Substantial	Substantial	Little to none	Little to none
Collateral/margin requirements	Bilateral negotiation and management	Consistent mark-to-market valuation of positions and collateral; required amounts set bilaterally by counterparties	Consistent mark-to-market valuation of positions and collateral; required amounts standardized and set by clearinghouse	Consistent mark-to-market valuation of positions and collateral; required amounts standardized and set by clearinghouse
Currently enforced levels of price information	Largely opaque; daily quotes available	Currently largely opaque; daily quotes available	More transparent; daily settlement prices publicly available	Transparent to all
Current levels of volume and open interest information	Opaque	Largely opaque	More transparent	Transparent to all
Current level of information on large trader positions	Opaque	Available only to regulators	Available only to regulators	Available only to regulators
Netting of cash flows	Bilateral only	Yes	Yes	Yes
Netting of offsetting positions	Bilateral only	Bilateral only	Yes	Yes
Secondary market	Only by mutual agreement between counterparties	Only by mutual agreement between counterparties	Yes	Yes

remain a problem to be dealt with privately by the participants. At this time, the DTCC performs some of these functions for a large fraction of the OTC-traded CDSs.

An important limitation of this level of centralization is that the risk of counterparty failure prevents two offsetting contracts from being netted out; thus, the gross principal amounts outstanding would be much larger for a registry than for the next two approaches. Another limitation is that even though in principle regulators can access information on positions from the DTCC, strictly speaking there is no requirement on the part of the DTCC to provide that data; such a requirement should be put in place. But, even if regulators could obtain the information, they would still have to mark these positions to market and translate the network of gross positions into net ones, a step that requires additional regulatory infrastructure that would have to be standardized to cover new products as and when they arise. In essence, under a pure registry solution, information on exposures that would be desirable for efficient response in a stressed environment is unlikely to be available to regulators with expediency.

Solution II: Clearinghouse. The next level of centralization would be for the clearing facility to become the counterparty and guarantor to each of the original counterparties in a deal. Each trade would be set up bilaterally, but then the CDS would be broken into two separate contracts with the clearinghouse in the middle, as is done by the clearinghouse of a futures exchange or by the Options Clearing Corporation for exchange-traded options.[5] This kind of clearinghouse would greatly reduce counterparty risk in the market, as long as it was adequately protected against default. An important element of that protection is that the clearinghouse would set uniform margin requirements on all deals. In contrast to a pure registry arrangement (Solution I), a centralized counterparty-cum-clearinghouse would enable netting of identical offsetting contracts, an attractive feature given the problems witnessed in CDS markets during the current crisis. However, by designating a single entity as the centralized counterparty, this arrangement puts the onus of maintaining near-zero counterparty risk *entirely* on that one entity.

Solution III: Exchange. The most centralized form of market organization would be for CDS trading to move to a formal exchange. An exchange eliminates the bilateral nature of OTC trading and opens it up to a much broader range of market participants, at highly visible prices. As with a centralized clearinghouse, two offsetting contracts are netted out: in other words, a counterparty can completely exit a position by putting through an offsetting trade on the exchange. In effect, the clearing corporation of the exchange still absorbs the counterparty risk. However, instead of there being just one centralized counterparty, trading on an exchange would be supported by licensed market makers who would be required to meet standard collateral requirements, and who would serve as the first line of defense if a customer defaults. If a market maker defaults, the exchange clearinghouse would use its resources to honor all affected contracts, and if necessary, could draw upon the capital of its member firms. One important benefit of this structure would be that the CDS market-making function—which currently sits under the universal banking structure that is subsidized by government guarantees—would be spun off and separately capitalized, reducing significantly the likelihood of systemic spillovers from the failure of a CDS intermediary to the banking sector.

Exchanges also set margin requirements for individual buyers and sellers. Whenever the amount on deposit becomes too low, the exchange sends a margin call, and failure to restore the margin to the required level leads to immediate liquidation of the position. This system mitigates counterparty risk between a trader and the brokerage firm and between the broker and the clearinghouse, thus effectively eliminating it entirely for contracts traded on the exchange. Futures exchanges proudly point to the fact that no trader of an exchange-traded futures contract has ever lost money due to a default by the clearinghouse.

Finally, exchanges also aggregate trade-level information and provide transparent dissemination of information about prices, volumes, and open interest to market participants and the general public. This information makes it possible for regulators, both at exchanges and at government agencies, to monitor the outstanding positions of a particular institution, and also of a particular contract. Going beyond issues of counterparty risk, exchange-based trading would also facilitate introduction and enforcement of other rules, such as prohibitions on insider trading and market manipulation.

One significant inconvenience of exchange trading of derivatives is that the contracts need to be quite standardized to permit a large number of traders to be trading the same instrument. Standardization would be a challenge for many OTC products, like CDO tranches. However, OTC credit default swaps are already highly standardized with regard to maturities and other terms that are mostly specified by selecting standard options in an International Swaps and Derivatives Association (ISDA) agreement. A bigger issue is resistance from large players to move trading from OTC markets to centralized exchanges, because they benefit from lack of transparency of OTC markets and would likely be required to post higher collateral to clearinghouses and exchanges.

Of course, such higher collateral requirements would reduce the willingness of some players to take large positions, and standardized contracts would limit customization and innovation. However, in the current context, reining in risk taking by financial institutions and limiting the possibility of trading toxic securities in opaque markets may be seen as desirable objectives. With exchange-based trading, the most creditworthy institutions would not enjoy much comparative advantage, given uniform collateral requirements and anonymous trading. Also, greater transparency would reduce the profits of institutions with large market-making shares. For example, it would be harder to disguise their activities in putting on or unwinding large trades. However, exchanges, such as the New York Stock Exchange, have successfully dealt with such concerns by creating an upstairs market for negotiation and execution of large trades.

In considering the three levels of centralized clearing, we feel that the lowest level—a basic registry of deals—is not enough. While transparency is substantially improved and some efficiency is gained in dealing with cash flows, the critical problem of counterparty risk is not dealt with. However, while we see significant value in moving to a fully public exchange, the need to standardize products sufficiently to allow a liquid market would be a problem for credit derivatives other than the CDS, and of course the overhead cost of setting up and running an exchange could be substantial. The major gains from establishing a centralized clearing facility are obtained once there is a clearinghouse that assumes the role of counterparty and guarantees every trade.

The key issue in ensuring minimal, near-zero counterparty risk is how to set margin requirements such that the creditworthiness of the clearinghouse is never called into question. A trader must have confidence that there is no counterparty risk in a contract with the clearinghouse on the other side. This is where credit default swaps present a different type of risk exposure than other derivatives that are traded on or off exchanges. Established exchanges set the initial and maintenance margin requirements for derivatives contracts based on the estimated size of daily price changes. The amount on deposit should be more than adequate to cover the loss that would occur on a day when the price moves by an unusually large amount. When there is a deficiency, the margin call must be satisfied by the next day. By marking the position to market daily and requiring that at least the maintenance margin amount be on deposit each day, the clearinghouse is almost completely protected against default by a market participant.

Similar to a futures contract, the daily fluctuations in a CDS market spread are quite visible, and the clearinghouse would have no trouble establishing settlement prices for mark-to-market calculations. But, unlike futures contracts, when there is a credit event, the liability of the protection seller in a CDS immediately jumps to a much higher level, possibly up to the entire amount of the protected principal in case recoveries in default are low (as was the case with the Lehman CDSs). No margin requirement less than 100 percent of the notional principal can provide *full* protection against the counterparty risk borne by the clearinghouse. This presents an important problem. If 100 percent margin were required to sell protection on an obligor whose probability of defaulting may be only a few percent or less, the market would disappear. But if the clearinghouse is exposed to a significant default risk whenever a CDS protection seller has to pay off, its guarantee loses effectiveness.[6] One possibility might be to require that participants (or market makers in case of an exchange) post significant *initial* margins to the clearinghouse. While this would limit entry, it would ensure that CDS market-making activity is always well-capitalized.

A better alternative is to set 100 percent margin for a protection seller's largest position across different reference entities (perhaps even setting limits on maximum exposures, as many futures exchanges do), with substantially lower amounts for additional positions. This would cover the clearinghouse fully in case of a single default, and provide time to issue a margin call for additional collateral on the remaining positions. The assumption that no more than one credit event would occur on the same day is less problematic if intraday margin calls could be made, which would be more important in CDS margining compared to non-credit-related products. Nevertheless, the clearinghouse would have to accept the risk of collateral shortfalls when credit events occur in rapid succession, and manage its liquidity accordingly. The clearinghouse can, for example, prearrange a line of credit to be drawn down in the event of such a contingency.

However it is handled, the issue of how to protect the clearinghouse from counterparty default when a credit event occurs must be dealt with carefully. Some experimentation in setting margin requirements to address this issue will be natural and should help convergence to feasible solutions. In cases where counterparty risk cannot be fully eliminated, then *transparency* levels could play a substitute role, as we explain next.

11.5 DESIRABLE LEVELS OF TRANSPARENCY

As discussed earlier, systemic risk arises naturally from the exposure to counterparty risk that is inherent in OTC markets. We argued so far that a centralized clearing and counterparty system would essentially eliminate counterparty risk. In markets where this solution is not adopted, counterparty risk should be priced in terms of exchange or bilateral margin and collateral arrangements, and for this case it must be visible and easy to evaluate. This creates an important role for transparency in OTC markets.

In order to determine the appropriate risk premium for an OTC contract with a counterparty, an investor needs to be able to calculate not only the counterparty's probability of default but also its exposure to various other risks. For example, if the investor is buying protection on a particular reference entity, the protection is less valuable if the counterparty also has a big exposure to default of the same entity. In just the state of nature when the protection is most important, the counterparty is more likely to default. A good example of this so-called wrong-way counterparty exposure occurred when the monoline insurers sold a large amount of protection on highly correlated risks. A similar problem arises if the first counterparty is exposed to a second counterparty that in turn is exposed to the reference entity. While it is not possible to know the full risk exposure of any counterparty, it would clearly be useful to know the exposure of every counterparty to major risks. Prices for bilateral OTC contracts should take into account the relevant counterparty exposure, which would provide an incentive for the counterparties to reduce risk.

Of course, in regulations to promote derivatives markets transparency it is essential not to eliminate the incentive to invest in research and information gathering. If transparency requires trading strategies to be made public, so that their price impacts become large, then the survival of the market will be jeopardized. The following proposal on required transparency for credit derivatives is designed to balance these considerations by adjusting the detail and timeliness of public disclosure.

In all three solutions described in Table 11.1, both price and contract information and counterparty positions should be visible to the relevant regulatory authorities. In the registry solution, aggregate exposure of each counterparty to a particular contract should be made public on a delayed basis such as monthly or biweekly. That is, the public should be able to find out the net notional value of CDSs written by one company on a particular reference entity. This means that a bank or hedge fund would periodically report its net exposures to a list of reference names. At this time the DTCC reports on roughly 1,000 underlying names; hence, under our proposal, this report would give the net notional position of each bank to each of these 1,000 names one month ago, for example.

In the clearinghouse and exchange solutions, the counterparty reports would not need to be made public, because counterparty risk is not priced for these contracts. The information would still need to be visible to regulators and to the clearinghouse for use in margin requirements, but the centralized trading arrangement facilitates such information gathering. Importantly, lack of public disclosure with centralized trading would be an incentive for OTC market players to migrate the market to a clearinghouse or an exchange.

We acknowledge that the level of transparency for the registry solution we propose is not as great as could be desired. It does not reveal counterparties of counterparties nor a counterparty's noncredit derivatives exposures, both of which would be needed to assess overall counterparty risk accurately. A more detailed report would include the entire matrix of net exposure of counterparty A to counterparty B with respect to reference entity C. But, even such bilateral transparency is deficient when similar products are traded simultaneously on exchanges and over the counter. The OTC contracts would be revealed, but the exchange positions would not. Regulators could therefore see these relationships but investors could not. Further, the reports we propose would only be released with a lag, which would make them outdated measures of counterparty exposures in some cases. Finally, if the level of transparency just described is deemed to be too costly, regulators should at least investigate how the current bilateral margining procedures in OTC deals could be improved to reduce counterparty risk further.

Nevertheless, the improvement in risk assessment from even a crude level of transparency would be enormous. An investor would be able to price contracts to take account of a counterparty's exposures much better than in the currently opaque OTC environment. If the counterparty subsequently takes on even more risk, because this is public information, the investor will have a capital loss on his or her position. As a consequence, counterparties would have incentives to manage their risk exposures in order to continue business.

To summarize, transparency and margining or collateral arrangements act as partial substitutes. Where the latter are sufficiently rich to ensure near-zero counterparty risk, public transparency of bilateral exposures is redundant. Absent such collateral arrangements, transparency can provide incentives to market participants to manage their risks prudently.

11.6 RECENT PROPOSALS AND WILL THEY SUCCEED?

In response to concerns regarding the OTC nature of credit derivatives markets, the Federal Reserve is supporting a move toward central clearing of credit default swap contracts. One platform is being developed jointly by the Chicago Mercantile Exchange and the hedge fund Citadel. The Intercontinental Exchange (ICE) has a competing proposal, and others are being developed in Europe.

The DTTC (New York) and LCH.Clearnet Group (London) have announced a merger to create the world's largest derivatives clearinghouse, also providing services for OTC products such as interest rate swaps and credit default swaps. These developments augur well for the credit derivatives market and overall financial stability. The AAA credit rating and risk-management expertise of centralized clearinghouses will help assuage fears over counterparty and operational risks. Centralized clearing will also enable aggregation of trade-level information so that prices, volumes, and open interest can be disseminated to market participants beyond the direct participants. This information will also make it possible for regulators to monitor the outstanding positions of a particular institution and of a particular contract. And prices of credit default swaps would reflect what they are supposed to—the credit risk of the underlying obligor—rather than that of the counterparty providing the insurance.

Will these initiatives succeed? Some institutions, especially large players, will likely resist calls to move away from the OTC markets. Hence, the regulatory resolve must be strong. The resisting players must realize (or be informed) that OTC markets can continue to arise whenever the financial sector needs to innovate and customize new products, but once these markets grow beyond a critical size, the standardized versions of the products should move to a centralized clearing counterparty structure or to exchanges (Solutions II or III).

11.7 IMPLICATIONS FOR OTHER MARKETS

Although we have focused on CDS markets as the proximate example, many other markets that have figured prominently in the current crisis—most notably those trading mortgage-backed securities (MBSs), collateralized debt obligations (CDOs), and asset-backed commercial paper (ABCP)—have also experienced severe stress. Fundamentally, there is no reason why these products cannot be traded and cleared more centrally. The key difference between them and CDSs is in the relatively standardized nature of CDS contracts. But this simply suggests that some of these other derivatives should be provided the centralized counterparty-cum-clearing structure (Solution II), unlike the CDS, which can potentially even trade on an exchange (Solution III). In principle, centralized counterparty and exchange-trading solutions can be applied also to traditional OTC markets such as those in foreign exchange derivatives, commodity derivatives, and equity- and credit-linked structured products.[7] Migration of some of these products away from the OTC markets will help reduce counterparty and operational risk concerns, and also allow for an explicit assignment of jurisdiction applicable to these products—Federal Reserve, Commodity Futures Trading Commission (CFTC), or Securities and Exchange Commission (SEC)—something that is unclear at best in the status quo trading infrastructure for these products.

In summary, we believe it is high time to lift the veil of opacity of bank balance sheets and interbank linkages, starting with more transparent trading infrastructure for credit derivatives.

NOTES

1. See Chapter 10, "Derivatives: The Ultimate Financial Innovation."
2. See Chapter 1, "Mortgage Origination and Securitization in the Financial Crisis."
3. This graph by Hayne Leland employs a structural model of credit risk to find the asset volatility and asset value level that matches the model equity volatility with the options market's implied volatility, and the model equity value with actual equity value. It assumes a constant (and relatively low 9 basis points) liquidity premium on CDS contracts. The model builds on Leland's 2006 Princeton University lectures, which include jump risk and liquidity premiums on debt (www.princeton.edu/bcf/newsevents/events/links/lectures-in-finance/index.xml). We are grateful to Hayne Leland for sharing the figure with us.
4. See Chapter 3, "The Rating Agencies: Is Regulation the Answer?"
5. This kind of hybrid trading arrangement, which essentially blends private negotiation of specific deal terms with a full clearinghouse guarantee of the final deal and substitution of itself as counterparty to each of the original transactors, resembles the procedure used in the Chicago Board Options Exchange's long-maturity FLexible EXchange (FLEX) options.
6. Note that this issue of margining for the "binary" or "digital" nature of an obligor's default applies also to bilateral contracts in OTC credit derivatives markets. To our knowledge, margining in bilateral contracts does not explicitly deal with the issue, perhaps explaining the significant counterparty risk concerns that arose with regard to the CDS contracts during the subprime crisis.
7. Indeed, over time existing exchanges have innovated their products to compete with OTC markets even on nonstandardized contracts, like FLEX options.

REFERENCE

Leland, Hayne. 2008. Structural models and the credit crisis. Presentation at the Financial Intermediation Research Society, Anchorage, Alaska.

CHAPTER 12

Short Selling

Menachem Brenner and Marti G. Subrahmanyam

12.1 BACKGROUND

Until the current global financial crisis, the practice of selling shares that one did not own, known as short selling, was generally permitted in most countries. Of course, some restrictions were placed on such transactions, such as the need to borrow the stock prior to the sale (no naked shorts), the requirement to sell at a higher price than the previous trade (the uptick rule), and disallowing short selling to capture gains and postpone tax payments (no shorting against the box).

In a dramatic decision in the early weeks of the current crisis, the Securities and Exchange Commission (SEC) banned short sales of shares of 799 companies on September 18, 2008, and lifted the ban on October 8. However, most countries around the globe, and in particular the United Kingdom and Japan (which are homes to the two other major financial centers, London and Tokyo), have declared a ban on short selling for "as long as it takes" to stabilize the markets. Even in the United States, there is continuing pressure on the regulators to reinstate the ban, at least in selected securities.

12.2 THE ISSUES

The immediate policy issues are as follows:

- Should there be any restrictions on short selling equity shares of individual companies, if not a total ban on such transactions?
- If so, what specific restrictions should be instituted, and under what circumstances should they be enforced by the regulators?

- What is the appropriate framework for timely reporting of short interest and/or short sales to ensure transparency of these transactions to the market?

12.3 FINANCIAL MARKETS: FAIRNESS AND EFFICIENCY

A highly desirable feature of financial markets is that they be fair to all participants who wish to trade. An aspect of this fairness is that these markets operate in a transparent manner, making available information to all participants at the same time, so that the markets can be efficient. In efficient financial markets, the prices of financial assets reflect all available information—favorable and unfavorable—that may affect the magnitude and the risk of future cash flows from these assets. For markets to be efficient, we need to allow for the unimpeded flow of such information and the unfettered actions of all participants in the markets. Along the same lines, an important tenet of adequate regulation and taxation of financial markets is the symmetrical treatment of buyers and sellers of financial assets. This symmetrical approach should always prevail, as an Occam's razor, in normal times and during a crisis, so that neither party has an unfair advantage. Exceptions to this principle ought to be few and far between.

The combined actions of buyers and sellers reacting to new information, both public and private, as well as their own liquidity needs, cause the information to be reflected in market prices. This process, often referred to as price discovery, occurs not just as a result of purchases and sales of *current* owners of the equity of a company, but also by those of *potential* buyers and sellers. Thus, any restrictions on short selling not only constrain the supply of shares from short sellers, but also inhibit the demand from potential buyers. This reduction in transactions, in turn, curtails liquidity and causes prices to fall further. It also increases liquidity risk, if the volume of these future transactions is uncertain. Thus, a ban on short sales would generally have adverse consequences for liquidity, and hence, for the prices of such securities.

12.4 WHO BENEFITS FROM SHORT SALES?

For the most part, short sellers are market makers (in the stocks and in equity derivatives like options and futures), hedgers of various sorts (such as buyers of convertible bonds), risk arbitrageurs (profiting from the relative mispricing of the stocks of acquirers and targets in acquisitions), and hedge funds that use long-short strategies (where they buy undervalued stocks and sell short overvalued stocks). Of course, pessimistic speculators who deem a stock to be overvalued may also take a risk by selling it short, hoping to be rewarded with an appropriate return. By the same token, if their guess proves to be wrong, they will pay a heavy price, since their losses would be potentially unlimited if the stock rallies contrary to their expectation (see the recent example of Porsche and Volkswagen in Germany). Of course, optimistic speculators would take the other side, with concomitant risks and rewards, ensuring a nice symmetry in the actions of speculators. The collective action of all these participants provides the following benefits: Information about the company is disseminated faster than in a market with restrictions on short selling, volatility is reduced, the risk premium is diminished, and, most important, liquidity is enhanced.

In fact, speculators who are considered the culprits in the recent decline of financial stock prices actually provide benefits to investors. By supplying important liquidity to the market, they lower the transaction costs that investors pay to execute their trades. Ultimately, investors are willing to pay for this improvement in liquidity, raising the prices of liquid stocks in relation to their less liquid counterparts.

When market prices decline due to adverse information, many market participants, such as mutual fund managers, want to avoid booking a loss. Thus, they are reluctant to sell losing stocks even if they consider them to be overvalued. Their withdrawal from the market in such times causes their pessimistic views not to be reflected in the stock price. This irrational behavior is remedied, to some degree, by the rational activity of short sellers who step in and incorporate their negative views into the market by their sales. The pessimistic information is then reflected in market prices. If not for these short sellers, potential buyers would not be able to consummate their purchases in the market as easily, since there would be fewer potential sellers.

12.5 MARKET MANIPULATION AND REGULATORY RESPONSE

Regulators as well as the exchanges may be required to intervene in the event a stock is manipulated by the spreading of unfounded rumors about a company, especially in the case of small companies or where the floating stock in the market is a small proportion of the outstanding shares. Spreading false information is equally harmful whether the information is positive or negative. Thus, the Securities and Exchange Commission (SEC), the Financial Industry Regulatory Authority (FINRA), and the exchanges, as well as their counterparts in other countries, should take steps in such cases, even going to the extent of halting trading in extreme cases, and enforce strict penalties on the perpetrators of the manipulation, if possible. A so-called bear raid (selling a stock short with the intention of forcing the price down in order to buy it back later at a lower price) falls under the heading of manipulation and should be treated as such. However, even in clear-cut cases of market manipulation, a ban in one direction is not the answer. It goes without saying that this discretion should be used very sparingly, since the test of whether the information is indeed false may be difficult to implement in general.

It has been argued that short sales in a particular stock can affect the stock price adversely by triggering stop-loss orders and margin calls for leveraged investors who are then forced to sell. This presumes that other investors ignore this deviation from fundamental value and stay on the sidelines. A related argument is often made in the context of highly leveraged firms such as those in the financial services industry; in this case, it is argued that a decline in the stock price triggers demands for collateral or additional capital to meet capital adequacy requirements, in the case of banks. This may indeed happen, but it should be emphasized that it is caused by *selling*, rather than by *short selling* in particular. In this case, too, if the regulators believe that selling should be restrained because it is based on incorrect or misleading information, the appropriate regulatory prescription is to halt all trading, rather than banning short sales.

What about the argument that short selling, in certain industries, such as banking or financial services, may have systemic consequences and thus should be treated differently? As with the argument that a particular firm is too big to fail (TBTF), what are the boundaries of this argument? Which firms and industries should be covered? Is systemic risk confined to the banking industry, or can similar arguments be made for other industries, such as automobiles and health care? As the current debate on the bailout for the automobile industry well illustrates, it is difficult for legislators and regulators to agree where the "systemic risk" and "too big to fail" arguments end. The steady stream of appeals for bailouts from several industries, in the United States and in other countries, illustrates how difficult it is to circumscribe the extent of public support for particular firms and industries.

A particular issue that arises in the context of short selling is whether naked short selling, which involves selling shares without having to borrow and deliver them in the first place, should be permitted. Naked short sales lead to the possibility of creating an unusually large supply of stocks, larger than the number of shares outstanding, since the same stock could be offered and sold at any particular instant several times over. Consequently, it may sometimes create a temporary pressure on prices away from fundamental values. To prevent such abuse, the regulator should strictly enforce the current requirement that one must borrow the stock *prior* to a short sale.

If naked short selling is disallowed, then the maximum number of shares that could be offered simultaneously for short sales is the number of shares outstanding. This should alleviate the pressure on the stock price in one direction. It will also reduce the possibility of manipulating stocks that are difficult to borrow: small stocks or those that have a small float. That said, we should continue the current practice of exempting market makers in stocks, futures, and options from borrowing the stocks as long as they turn around their positions in a rather limited time period. (In the current electronic age, it may be prudent to reduce the current six-day settlement period to a day or two.)

What about the uptick rule, another frequent issue that crops up in the context of short sales? Although short selling has been permitted for a long time in the United States, there was a restriction on the timing of the sale in the form of an uptick rule whereby a short sale could not be undertaken following a downtick or decline in the stock price. The traditional argument was that this restriction brings a pause to the momentum caused by a wave of selling. However, there is no clear evidence of its efficacy. Indeed, in the spirit of improving market liquidity, the uptick rule was lifted in July 2008 based on a pilot study of 1,000 stocks commissioned by the SEC. Reinstating the uptick rule, as has been advocated by many market participants during the current crisis, is again a violation of the symmetry principle and is a futile and costly exercise. Forcing sellers to sell only when prices tick up prevents the rapid dissemination of negative information. If indeed there is adverse information about a company, there is no reason to impede the flow of this information into the market and its reflection in market prices by adding frictions to the normal process of price discovery. Existing owners of the stock, as well as participants in the derivatives markets, who are not bound by the uptick rule, will be able to sell the stock or its equivalent using replicating strategies, creating an inconsistency between different investors and markets for the same stock. The most telling problem with the uptick rule is its sheer unenforceability. There are many trading strategies that allow market participants to get around the rule. It is sufficient to cite just one common strategy, which is akin to "shorting against the box": During an up or flat market, traders can buy stocks in one account and sell short the same stocks in another account, effectively having a neutral position that enables them to sell the stocks they own without being bound by the uptick rule.

At a broader level, the wealth of available evidence suggests that restrictions on short sales are largely ineffective in halting declines of stock prices. All they do is throw some sand in the gears and delay the inevitable incorporation of bad news into stock prices. Academic research suggests that stocks with greater short-sales constraints exhibit greater momentum return[1] (i.e., they will eventually experience greater volatility). Similarly, stocks were shown to be overpriced when there were short-selling constraints, especially during the Internet bubble. These stocks had significantly more negative returns when the constraints were eventually relaxed.[2] It has also been shown that in countries with fewer short-selling constraints, there is more efficient price discovery, less co-movement of stocks, and lower volatility than in those where short selling is more restricted.[3] Most important, no study has shown that short-selling constraints reduce the likelihood of crashes.

12.6 TRANSPARENCY AND REPORTING

As argued earlier, a strong case can be made in favor of allowing short selling and against the imposition of various restrictions on this activity. These arguments presume that information is available to market participants in a timely manner. Thus, transparency in the form of *timely* reporting is a precondition for efficient financial markets. In most markets, such information is not always available to prevent potential, albeit rare, abuses that some believe are prevalent in the market. We propose that daily short selling trading activity, and not just short interest reported with a lag, on all listed stocks be transmitted online to the exchange/clearing corporation. Every short sale that appears on the sales and trade ticker should be marked as such. (Of course, the identity of the seller would not be public information.) This change in reporting requirements will also provide us with timely short selling trading activity and short interest information. It will also make it easier for the exchange/clearing corporation to check if the stock was borrowed and is being delivered. This should not be burdensome, as the FINRA has put in place a system for collecting similar information from the over-the-counter corporate bond market, known as the Trade Reporting and Compliance Engine (TRACE). TRACE has contributed to the efficiency and liquidity of the corporate bond market, and a similar effort in the stock market with regard to short selling should have a salutary effect on market liquidity and efficiency.

12.7 CONCLUSION

Short selling is an important activity in a well-functioning financial market. Its contribution to price discovery, lower volatility, and liquidity improves the fairness and efficiency of markets. A short sale should be considered on a par with a sale by existing shareholders and hence should be treated the same as buying activity, its symmetrical counterpart. It goes without saying that regulators should be extremely concerned with market manipulation that may be perpetrated by buyers or sellers, including short sellers, and take appropriate and timely action to curb such practice. Regulators should also strictly enforce the requirement that stocks should be borrowed *prior* to a short sale by any investor who is not a market maker. In the interest of transparency and consistency, the regulators at the SEC, FINRA, and the exchanges, as well as their counterparts in other countries, should require timely reports on short selling activity in line with the existing reporting requirements placed on buyers and sellers.

NOTES

1. See Ali and Trombley (2006).
2. See Ofek, Richardson, and Whitelaw (2004), Ofek and Richardson (2003), and Jones and Lamont (2002).
3. See Bris, Goetzmann, and Zhu (2007).

REFERENCES

Ali, A., and M. Trombley. 2006. Short sales constraints and momentum in stock returns. *Journal of Business Finance and Accounting* 33:587–615.

Bris, A., W. Goetzmann, and N. Zhu. 2007. Efficiency and the bear: Short sales and markets around the world. *Journal of Finance* 62:1029–1079.

Jones, C., and O. Lamont. 2002. Short-sale constraints and stock returns. *Journal of Financial Economics* 66:207–239.

Ofek, E., and M. Richardson. 2003. Dotcom mania: The rise and fall of Internet stock prices. *Journal of Finance* 58:1113–1138.

Ofek, E., M. Richardson, and R. F. Whitelaw. 2004. Limited arbitrage and short-sales restrictions: Evidence from the options markets. *Journal of Financial Economics* 74:305–342.

Five

The Role of the Federal Reserve

Thomas F. Cooley and Thomas Philippon

The current financial crisis has been a watershed moment for the U.S. Federal Reserve and for central banks around the world. The Federal Reserve has been criticized for having created the conditions for the massive expansion of credit that was a forerunner of the crisis. It has also been attacked for being slow to recognize the extent and implications of the problems in credit markets and for being excessively improvisational or inconsistent in its responses to faltering financial firms. At the same time, the Fed has been credited with being creative and forceful in extending its normal mandate to address the crisis. It has created a dozen new vehicles to provide liquidity to the financial sector and to foreign banks, and has been actively involved in brokering rescues of systemically important financial institutions.

The textbook description of the Federal Reserve is that it has always had three tools at its disposal: (1) control of the federal funds rate, which is currently the principal instrument for monetary policy; (2) the ability to set reserve requirements, a tool that has become largely meaningless because of financial innovations; and (3) access to the discount window, which could provide liquidity to solvent but illiquid institutions. The Fed has also always had a broad responsibility and broad latitude to do what is necessary to ensure the stability of the financial system. In the current crisis, the Fed took its role as lender of last resort (LOLR) and expanded it into a systemic-risk lending facility. Hence, the balance sheet of the Fed has become a powerful and critical tool; it has expanded from $900 billion to more than $2 trillion at the end of 2008.

The Federal Reserve has been forced to innovate in the past year because the financial system faced and continues to face a severe liquidity crisis, and because the institutions at risk posed severe systemic risks, endangering many other parts of the system by their fragility. The current chairman of the Fed has bemoaned the fact that there are too many institutions that are too big to fail (TBTF). These are the large, complex financial institutions (LCFIs) we have discussed in great depth elsewhere in this report.* Our goal in this part of the book is to propose methods for assessing and dealing with systemic risk to the financial system and to propose some design principles for lending facilities to deal with financial crises. These two issues are clearly linked as a matter of long-term policy, because systemically important institutions require access to the lender of last resort facilities of the Fed. We summarize these two issues next before turning to a discussion of monetary policy.

SYSTEMIC RISK

Chapter 13, "Regulating Systemic Risk," deals with the question of how best to regulate systemic risk. Current financial regulations seek to limit the risk of individual institutions in isolation, but do nothing to address the risk more broadly. Systemic risks arise because of externalities between institutions: the risks of a given firm increase because of decisions made by other players. As these risks cumulate, they can pose a threat to the whole system. We have seen many examples in recent months of liquidity crises that lead to downward pressure on asset prices, which impact the entire market. In addition, the very fact that some institutions are too big to fail creates a bias toward firms that are too large and too highly leveraged, and have too much counterparty risk.

The novel idea in this chapter is to tax firms based on their contribution to systemic risk in order to give them an incentive to internalize the cost of this systemic risk and induce them to create less of it. The first step in regulating systemic risk is to measure it, and we propose several measures that are based on tools that are already in widespread use in financial institutions. Having presented a methodology for measuring systemic risk, we next address the question of how to regulate it. We describe several alternative methods for regulating systemic risk: (1) a systemic capital charge (or

---

*See Chapter 5, "Enhanced Regulation of Large, Complex Financial Institutions."

capital requirement) based on the contribution of an institution to systemic risk, (2) a Federal Deposit Insurance Corporation (FDIC)-style tax based on the contribution to systemic risk, and (3) a market-based insurance system.

One of the critical lessons we have learned from the current crisis is that systemic risk can be very large and very dangerous. An essential part of prudential regulation is to measure this risk and try to mitigate it. The proposals offered here suggest how this can be done.

LENDER OF LAST RESORT FACILITIES

We noted earlier that the balance sheet of the Federal Reserve has arguably become its most important tool in the current crisis. The Fed has expanded its lending facilities, dramatically providing funds to financial institutions in exchange for illiquid and risky collateral. Although the lender of last resort facilities of the Fed have been used many times in the past to provide needed liquidity, the massive scale of the recent expansion suggests a rethinking of how the Fed uses these powers.

Just as the notion that some institutions are too big to fail may lead to firms that are indeed too big and excessively levered, so too the notion that the central bank, in its role as the lender of last resort, will lend against risky and illiquid assets may lead to firms choosing illiquid portfolios and failing to address issues of capital adequacy in times of falling asset prices and economic contraction. Moreover, in a rapidly evolving economic crisis the notion that the central bank should lend to illiquid but solvent institutions can become moot because it is very difficult to tell who is solvent. There have been multiple examples of this over the past year.

The essence of the proposal in Chapter 14, "Private Lessons for Public Banking: The Case for Conditionality in LOLR Facilities," is that central banks could address the adverse incentive effects of the LOLR facility and induce more prudent behavior by firms if central bank lending operated more like private sector lines of credit. Private lines of credit are designed to address liquidity issues for firms. In this view, the LOLR facilities should be conditional on borrowers meeting minimum capital and maximum leverage standards, and have a "material adverse change" clause that can allow central banks to deny lending to institutions that have become excessively risky.

The proposed changes to LOLR facilities would encourage troubled institutions to restructure (by reducing leverage and risk or converting debt to equity) or recapitalize (by issuing preferred or equity capital in markets). The possibility that liquidity provisions could be denied based on bank health and characteristics will improve the incentives for banks to behave prudently.

MONETARY POLICY

As we noted earlier, some observers attribute the credit bubble and the subsequent financial meltdown to the Fed's excessively easy monetary policy under Chairmen Alan Greenspan and Ben Bernanke.* There was indeed a vast expansion of credit and widespread mispricing of credit risks. One view is that this occurred because monetary policy was too myopic—focused largely on inflation in the intermediate term, and not sufficiently concerned with other developments in asset markets.

Certainly monetary policy and financial stability are linked, and any discussion of financial crises has to address that linkage. If conditions in financial markets lead to dramatic changes in the balance sheets of households or firms, this may be a legitimate concern for monetary policy.

The old argument that the Fed can't or shouldn't do anything about asset bubbles or excessive expansion can't be completely right. As an academic matter bubbles are hard to define, yet it is sometimes quite clear that asset price increases are not supported by fundamentals. More importantly, it needs to be said that not all bubbles are the same. A bubble in one particular asset class such as dot-com initial public offerings (IPOs) is not the same as a bubble-like aggregate credit expansion. The Greenspan Fed may have been right to restrain from using interest rates to address a sectoral bubble. However, economy-wide credit expansions or rapid price appreciations in pivotal sectors, such as housing, are different from simple sectoral bubbles and should concern the monetary authority long before they turn into full-blown bubbles.

In this regard we have two concrete proposals:

1. The Monetary Policy Report to Congress should be transformed into a Monetary Policy and Financial Stability Report.
2. The Fed should build the staff expertise to analyze and report on overall financial stability indicators and begin research programs on early warning indicators and related topics. In particular, the trends and norms for credit growth should be the subject of research, so there is an improved ability to distinguish between growth-oriented credit deepening and financial fragility resulting from credit booms.

Finally, as we mentioned earlier, the balance sheet of the Fed has become its most important tool during the crisis. (See Tables V.1 and V.2.) The new

---

*Although we do not include a separate chapter on monetary policy, it is a critical piece of the Fed's role. This section was also contributed to by Nouriel Roubini and Paul Wachtel.

TABLE V.1 Consolidated Balance Sheet of the Federal Reserve System, August 1, 2007 ($ Amounts in Billions)

Total Assets	$874.1	Currency	$777.0
Gold, Special Drawing		Reverse Repurchase	
Rights, Coin	14.3	Agreements	31.5
Treasury and Agency		Deposits of DIs	17.1
Securities Held	790.8	Deposits—Treasury,	
Repurchase Agreements	24.8	Foreign, Other	5.2
Loans to DIs	0.2	Other Liabilities	9.7
Other Assets	44.0	Capital	33.6

Source: Federal Reserve Board Statistical Release H.4.1, August 2, 2007.

lending programs by the Federal Reserve and the Treasury have changed the face of U.S. monetary policy dramatically. In August 2007, the Fed had less than $900 billion in assets; as of year-end 2008, it has almost two and a half times as much. Deposit balances at the Fed held by depository institutions (DIs) are almost 50 times larger than they were in the summer of 2007. Loans to financial institutions have gone from $0.2 billion to over $150 billion.

When the Fed started its new lending programs in 2007, the effect of lending on reserves was offset by sales of Treasury securities. By the end of 2008, the portfolio of government bonds had dwindled, but the volume of lending continues to balloon. There has been an enormous expansion of aggregate liquidity in the financial system as the Fed attempts to mitigate the effects of deleveraging by financial institutions, the closing down of interbank lending, and the collapse of commercial paper markets.

TABLE V.2 Consolidated Balance Sheet of the Federal Reserve System, January 14, 2009 ($ Amounts in Billions)

Total Assets	$2,058.4	Currency	844.1
Gold, Special Drawing		Reverse Repurchase	
Rights, Coin	14.9	Agreements	78.8
Treasury, Agency, and Other		Deposits of DIs	827.5
Securities Held	505.3	Deposits—Treasury,	
Repurchase Agreements	40.0	Foreign, Other	248.5
Term Auction Credit	371.3	Other Liabilities	17.2
Other Loans	155.2	Capital	42.4
Net Portfolio Holdings	408.6		
Other Assets	563.0		

Source: Federal Reserve Board Statistical Release H.4.1, January 15, 2009.

This vastly expanded balance sheet will pose new challenges when the Fed decides to delever its balance sheet. It will not be a simple matter of increasing the federal funds rate when the economy recovers. The challenge will be to restructure the balance sheet in a timely fashion so that it doesn't impair monetary policy objectives.

Finally, a crucial policy question will need to be addressed: Which of the new facilities should be phased out and over what time table? Provision of lender of last resort support to systemically important nonbank financial institutions may make sense if these institutions become part of the regulatory and supervisory umbrella of the Fed. Provision of market making of last support (repos and/or purchases of illiquid assets in periods of market stress) may also make sense, as long as the moral hazard effects of such support are constrained by proper regulation and supervision of financial institutions in good times.

CHAPTER 13

Regulating Systemic Risk

Viral V. Acharya, Lasse H. Pedersen, Thomas Philippon,
and Matthew Richardson

13.1 INTRODUCTION

We advocate that financial regulation be focused on limiting systemic risk—that is, the risk of a crisis in the financial sector and its spillover to the economy at large. To this end, we provide a simple and intuitive way to measure systemic risk in the financial sector and suggest novel regulations to limit it.

Current financial regulations seek to limit each institution's risk (for example, market and credit risk) seen in isolation; they are not sufficiently focused on systemic risk. As a result, while individual risks are properly dealt with in normal times, the system itself remains, or is induced to be, fragile and vulnerable to large macroeconomic shocks.

There are two separate challenges in the regulation of systemic risk. First, systemic risk must be measured. Second, sound economic theory suggests that the tightness of regulation should be based on the extent to which a given firm is likely to contribute to a general crisis, so that the correct price can be charged to each firm for its contributions to systemic risk. We propose a framework to achieve this goal.

We argue that such regulation of systemic risk of financial firms can be accomplished by: (1) a set of risk management tools applied at the macro level to the regulation of all financial institutions, and (2) a market-based system to charge each firm according to its contribution to systemic risk.

Regarding (1): The regulator would assess the contribution of each firm to the downside aggregate risk of the economy, using standard risk management tools routinely used within financial firms to manage firm-level risk. Hence, the regulator in charge of systemic risk would act like the headquarters of the economy, and each regulated firm would be considered as a component of the system, just like a trading desk or a division is considered a component of a financial institution. The individual contribution to aggregate risk would then determine the extent of regulatory constraints, which can be implemented as ex ante capital requirements and required contributions to capital insurance.

Regarding (2): Each firm would be required to buy insurance against its own losses in a scenario in which the whole financial sector is doing poorly. In the event of a payoff on the insurance, the payment should not go to the firm itself, but to the regulator in charge of stabilizing the financial sector. This would provide incentives for a company to limit systemic risk (to lower its insurance premium), provide a market-based estimate of the risk (the cost of insurance), and avoid moral hazard (because the firm does not get the insurance payoff).

The main four advantages of our approach are that:

1. It forces regulators and financial firms to deal explicitly with systemic risk.
2. It reduces moral hazard in that it provides incentives for regulated firms not to take on excessive systemic risk.
3. It reduces the pro-cyclicality of risk taking.
4. It is based on tools tested and well understood by the private sector.

13.2 WHY SYSTEMIC FINANCIAL RISK MUST BE REGULATED

Systemic risk can be broadly thought of as the failure of a significant part of the financial sector—one large institution or many smaller ones—leading to a reduction in credit availability that has the potential to adversely affect the real economy.

The scope of our proposed regulation is the financial industry, rather than any cyclical sector in the economy, because of the financial industry's intermediation role. Financial institutions are a unique part of the economy in that they act as intermediaries between parties that need to borrow and parties willing to lend. Indeed, poor performance of the financial industry will impose *additional* losses to the rest of the economy, from entrepreneurs to retirees.

Given the interconnectedness of the modern financial sector, and for the purposes of systemic regulation, one should think of a "financial firm" as not just the commercial bank taking deposits and making loans, but also include the shadow banking sector consisting of investment banks, money market funds, insurance firms, and potentially even hedge funds and private equity funds.

We first use some examples from the current crisis to illustrate these ideas. We then discuss more formally the need for systemic regulations.

Systemic Risk in the Current Crisis

To conceptualize systemic risk in more detail, consider the current crisis and the government's intervention (or lack thereof) with respect to the failure of Bear Stearns and Lehman Brothers. More details on these and other cases are in the appendix later in this chapter.

On the weekend following Friday, March 14, the government helped engineer JPMorgan Chase's purchase of Bear Stearns by guaranteeing $29 billion of subprime-backed securities. Without this involvement, it is highly likely Bear Stearns would have declared bankruptcy, as there had been a classic run on its assets. Though Bear Stearns was the smallest of the major investment banks, it had a high degree of interconnectedness to other parts of the financial system. It was a major counterparty risk for three reasons: (1) it was an important player in the repo market, (2) it was the leading prime broker to hedge funds, and (3) it was a major counterparty in the credit default swap (CDS) market.

Over the weekend following Friday, September 12, the government attempted to engineer a purchase of Lehman Brothers by other financial institutions, but attempts failed without any direct government support and Lehman went bankrupt. In hindsight, Lehman Brothers contained considerable systemic risk and led to the near collapse of the financial system (though that may have occurred regardless).

Why did the government let Lehman fail? Ex post, it is not clear whether (1) the government thought Lehman was no longer systemic because of the Fed's opening of lending facilities to financial institutions, or (2) as the government now argues, Lehman could not be rescued because Lehman did not have adequate collateral to post to access these facilities. In any event, like Bear Stearns, Lehman was a major player in various parts of the capital market. Its bankruptcy opened up the possibility that similar firms could also go bankrupt, causing a potential run on their assets. This led to Merrill Lynch selling itself to Bank of America. The other two investment banks, Morgan Stanley and Goldman Sachs, saw the cost of their five-year CDS protection rise from 250 basis points (bps) to 500 bps and from 200 bps to 350 bps (respectively), and their stock prices fell by 13.54 percent and 12.13 percent (respectively) from Friday, September 12, to Monday, September 15. (See

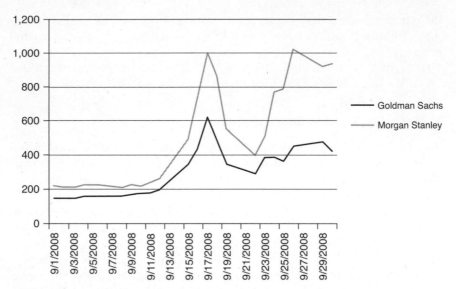

FIGURE 13.1   Five-Year Senior Unsecured CDS Spread (in basis points) for
Goldman Sachs and Morgan Stanley in September 2008
Source: Datastream.

Figures 13.1 and 13.2.) Both these investment banks adopted the status of
bank holding companies.

The irony of the situation is that letting Lehman fail was supposed to
draw a line in the sand and limit moral hazard, but it had precisely the opposite effect. Having been to the brink of collapse, it is now clearer than ever
that the government will not let any other large complex financial institution
fail. Moral hazard has therefore been strengthened, not weakened.

These examples make it clear that there are two distinct reasons for
regulating systemic risk: externalities and implicit guarantees.

We emphasize that systemic risk is not driven just by the size of the
failed institutions. While it is possible that the failure of a large individual
institution could cause interbank markets to dry up, such contagion risk
becomes a systemic concern only when other institutions are not healthy to
start with (e.g., the failure of Lehman Brothers in 2008 compared to the
failure of Barings in 1995).

Externalities

The first reason to regulate systemic risk is the presence of externalities
between institutions. By its very nature, systemic risk is a negative externality

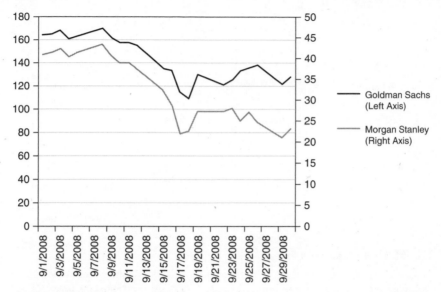

FIGURE 13.2 Share Price Behavior of Goldman Sachs and Morgan Stanley in September 2008

Source: Datastream.

imposed by each financial firm on the system. Each individual firm is clearly motivated to prevent its own collapse but not necessarily the collapse of the system as a whole. So when a firm considers holding large amounts of illiquid securities, or concentrates its risk into particular ones (e.g., subprime-based assets), or puts high amounts of leverage on its books (as a way to drive up excess returns), its incentive is to manage its own risk/return trade-off and not take into account the spillover risk it imposes on other financial institutions. The spillover risk arises as one institution's trouble triggers liquidity spirals (see Figure 13.3), leading to depressed asset prices and a hostile funding environment, pulling others down and thus leading to further price drops, funding illiquidity, and so on.[1]

Another externality comes from the rescue of failed institutions. When banks fail individually, other healthy banks can readily buy them or otherwise take up most of their lending and related activities. Thus, real losses primarily arise when banks fail together and this collective failure cannot be readily resolved.[2]

Our suggestion then is to give financial institutions an incentive to internalize this negative externality. Doing so will give them an incentive to limit their contribution to systemic risk.

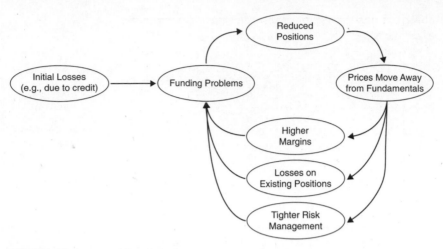

FIGURE 13.3 Liquidity Spirals

A shock to bank funding leads to reduced positions, depressing prices, with the financial sector spiraling into liquidity crisis as (1) increased margins force deleveraging, (2) losses continue, and (3) risk management is tightened, all exacerbating the need for more funding.

Source: Brunnermeier and Pedersen (forthcoming), Garleanu and Pedersen (2007).

Implicit Guarantees

In addition to direct externalities, implicit government guarantees[3] also create the need for regulating systemic risk. Implicit guarantees create moral hazard in three ways:

1. "Too big to fail" creates a bias toward firms that are too large and excessively levered.
2. "Too interconnected to fail" leads firms toward excessive counterparty risk.
3. "Too many to fail" leads firms to take on too much systemic risk.[4]

Moral hazard in all these cases is particularly severe. Even if the regulator would like to commit ex ante to not bail out failed institutions, this is not credible ex post. The costs of such bailouts tend to be significant, often a nontrivial fraction of the gross domestic product (GDP) of economies involved.[5] All these reasons warrant prudential regulation of systemic risk rather than of individual institutions' risk of failure.

Firms are often regulated to limit their pollution or are taxed based on the externality they cause. Similarly, we propose to regulate or tax firms' contributions to systemic risk. But first we must measure the extent of the externality.

13.3 MEASURING A FIRM'S CONTRIBUTION TO SYSTEMIC RISK

To understand our proposed measurement of systemic risk, consider a large negative aggregate shock, say the 1 percent worst-case scenario of the shock's distribution at the monthly or quarterly frequency. Then ask the question: During that month (or week, or quarter), how much does any financial firm contribute to the aggregate economic collapse? Aggregate economic collapse could be proxied by a severe fall in the aggregate economy's output (for example, negative GDP growth rates) or stock market crashes (assuming that these precede real sector losses) or the banking sector's loss of profitability. A financial firm that contributes a lot to such aggregate economic risk poses systemic risk.

Acharya (2001) and Lester, Pedersen, and Philippon (2008) argue that there is an analogy between the allocation of economic capital within a firm and the allocation of capital requirements within an economy. Indeed, the problem faced by a regulator is similar to that facing senior management when trying to avoid financial distress and fire sales. The senior management will look at the contributions of various trading desks and divisions to the total risk of the firm. All units are backed by the same pool of firm equity, and firm equity is a public good for the firm. Each unit must therefore be charged according to how much it uses (implicitly) of the firm's equity to support its operations. Similarly, we propose to measure how much of the economy's capital is being put at risk by each firm and charge each accordingly so as to create incentives to allocate risk efficiently. As we discuss next, we can use simple ways to estimate this using standard risk management tools already applied in the private sector, namely statistical measures (relying on historical distributions) and stress tests (relying on specific crisis scenarios).

Measures of Systemic Risk Based on Value at Risk and Expected Shortfall

The common risk management tools value at risk (VaR) and expected short-fall (ES) seek to measure the potential loss incurred by a firm in an extreme event. Further, the aggregate loss can be broken down into its components using so-called marginal VaR and marginal ES (also called component VaR and component ES). We recommend estimating each bank's marginal ES for an aggregate shock, that is, its contribution to the aggregate risk.[6]

To estimate this, one collects historical data on losses experienced by each firm (or each division within each firm) for several years and identifies the quarters where the aggregate losses are large. In these quarters, one computes the contribution of each firm (or each division, each line of business) to the aggregate losses. This contribution is what we are looking for: the marginal expected shortfall. It is a measure of the systemic risk posed by the firm.

If one has data on the current positions of each firm, this method can be implemented in a more forward-looking way: Rather than computing the loss a firm experienced in past contractions, one can compute the losses it would have experienced with its current positions—this captures increased risk for firms that recently increased their positions. Calculations like this are performed on a daily basis in financial institutions. They are used to allocate capital across divisions, to integrate firmwide capital management activities, and to measure and compare performance across lines of business.

Let us briefly illustrate how one could implement the calculations for the aggregate economy. We stress that the numbers in this section are used only to illustrate the argument.

The appropriate measure to use in the calculations depends on what the systemic externalities are. Economic theory suggests two sources of externalities. First, some externalities depend on the scale and scope of the firm's activities. Liquidity externalities depend on the scale of liquidations undertaken in times of distress. A simple place to start would be to use firm value (equity, or, better, asset value), or the firm-level daily mark-to-market profit-and-loss statements (P&Ls). The second major source of externality is directly linked to the occurrence of default. In this case, the measures based on overall assets should be supplemented with credit risk measures, such as CDS spreads.[7]

For the purpose of illustrating our argument, let us use equity market value. We condition on aggregate shocks as measured by the 5 percent worst drops in the market value of all publicly traded stocks. Based on these aggregate shocks, we estimate each financial firm's systemic risk as its average loss during these crises (i.e., its marginal ES), where we proxy its loss by its drop in the equity market values. We then rank the companies by their marginal-ES contribution, and report the result in Figure 13.4.[8]

These numbers illustrate the contributions of each firm to systemic risk over the period 2006–2007. The contributions take into account the size of the firm and its extreme downside correlation with the overall market.[9]

While this calculation is done using equity returns, similar downside risk decompositions can be done for credit losses and, further, decompositions

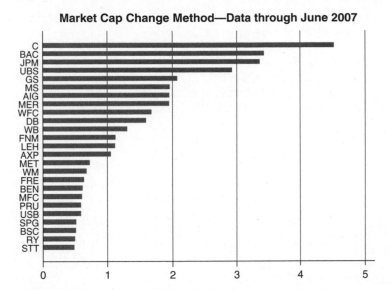

Market Cap Change Method—Data through June 2007

FIGURE 13.4 Expected Shortfall (\$ Amounts in Billions)

Source: Lester, Pedersen, and Philippon (2008).

can be done for divisions within a firm, asset classes, and geographical regions, given appropriate data (which regulators typically obtain).[10]

Stress Tests and Aggregate Risk Scenarios

Statistical risk models have limitations and must always be complemented with stress tests and scenario analysis.[11] For the measurement of systemic risk, we would emphasize:

- Concentration risk.
- Cyclical risk taking.
- Forward-looking scenarios.

Stress tests can be used to assess risk concentration and interconnected counterparty risks. The regulator could estimate the consequences of the failure of a large institution. These tests could also help refine the concept of large, complex financial institution (LCFI).[12]

In addition, scenario analysis can limit excessive risk taking in good times. After prolonged periods of low volatility, statistical measures of risk go down. As a result, risk taking becomes procyclical, and this increases the likelihood and severity of a financial crisis. In his letter to shareholders, Jamie Dimon, CEO of JPMorgan Chase, writes:

> *I would argue that fair value accounting rules, margining require-*
> *ments, rating agencies and regulatory rules add to procyclical behav-*
> *ior. Thoughtful policy changes could provide a substantial cushion*
> *to the procyclical forces that make a financial crisis worse.*[13]

An important advantage of scenario analysis is that it does not induce procyclical risk taking.[14] The "September–October 2008" scenario will remain in effect with the same parameter values in 2010 and in 2015, even if the economy is quiet between 2010 and 2015. It will become part of standard scenarios, like "Russia–LTCM 1998" or "9/11." Scenarios can be subjective and can become outdated, but this can be mitigated if regulators and firms engage in a constructive dialogue to figure out how downside risks to the economy evolve over time.

Pricing Systemic Risk

Having identified each firm's contribution to systemic risk, we additionally want to know the market price of this risk. For this, one can look to existing financial markets for the price of economic catastrophes that usually follow from systemic risk. For example, out-of-the-money put options on the stock market or AAA tranches of portfolios of corporate bonds (i.e., the CDX contracts) give an idea of the cost of insuring against such events. Next, we discuss a system in which financial institutions would pay a fee depending on the amount of systemic risk, implemented as a fraction of the total price of its contribution to systemic risk. Of course, there can be economic catastrophes that have nothing to do with the financial sector, so the total fees would be only a fraction of the total price of systemic shocks. The price of a firm's systemic risk can alternatively be measured using a market-based insurance program as discussed next.

13.4   REGULATING SYSTEMIC RISK

In the preceding section, we discussed one way to measure systemic risk. Our next task it to define the correct regulatory response. We present three regulations, in ascending order of complexity and novelty.

Capital Requirements: Our Suggested "Basel III"

Under this scheme, a systemic risk regulator would first measure each firm's systemic risk contribution as discussed previously. Then the regulator should impose requirements and/or costs depending on each firm's contribution. One natural way to do this that is consistent with current regulation is to impose capital requirements. That is, the regulator should impose a capital requirement that depends explicitly on systemic risk contributions. This gives the right incentives to firms to limit their loading on aggregate risk since keeping capital reserves is costly and, additionally, it gives the firm an appropriate safety buffer in systemic crises.[15]

For instance, the systemic capital charge (SCC) would be:

$$SCC = s \times MES\% \times A$$

where s would be the systemic factor chosen by the regulator to achieve a given degree of aggregate safety and soundness; $MES\%$, the marginal expected shortfall expressed in percent of assets, would measure the aggregate tail risk on the firm; and A would be the assets of the firm.

This is, in effect, Basel II with systemic risk, or, in other words, "Basel III." The focus on systemic risk would be a clear improvement over existing regulations, but it must be enforced efficiently. We would insist on two key points. First, there must be a limit on the ability to decrease apparent leverage by moving of assets off the balance sheet but with recourse[16] or by relying too much on book values.[17] Second, the measurement of systemic risk must be either acyclical or even countercyclical, so as to avoid fire sales induced by violations during crises (see the preceding section).

Taxing the Externality—An FDIC-Style Methodology

A second possibility is to "tax" the activity that imposes a negative externality on the system, that is, to tax activity leading to systemic risk. The tax has two benefits: (1) it discourages behavior that leads to systemic risk, and (2) the generated levies would go towards a general "systemic crisis fund" to be used in the future by the regulators to inject capital into the system (at their discretion). Of course, in equilibrium, some institutions will find it optimal to still engage in these behaviors and therefore pay the higher taxes, while others will lessen their use.

The discussion in Section 13.2 showed that the financial institutions that pose systemic threats have three characteristics: excessive leverage, highly illiquid securities, and concentration of aggregate risk. Given these characteristics, what form should the tax take?

Fortunately, the government has had some experience with this issue via deposit insurance.[18] Institutions that take deposits are governed by sequential servicing rules in terms of deposit withdrawals (i.e., first come, first served). This increases the probability of a run on the financial institution's assets. The probability of a run imposes discipline on the financial institution, but, in a world of balance-sheet opacity, runs on poorly per-forming institutions can lead to runs on good institutions and to systemic risk. As a result, the government offers guaranty programs by insuring the deposits of participating institutions up to a certain amount.

In recognition that insurance is not free, the FDIC imposes a fee on financial institutions. Until 1993, this fee was based only on the size of the institution's deposits and not on its risk. This created a severe moral hazard problem, because these institutions could borrow at artificially low rates and undertake risky investments. As FDIC losses mounted up during the 1980s, the government redesigned the FDIC contracts.[19] It is important to note, however, that while the new contracts do lead to premiums increasing in relation to the risk characteristics of financial institutions, no systemic measure is incorporated into the assessment rate formula.[20]

We propose to charge an additional *systemic risk fee* to all financial institutions based not only on the amount of assets they hold, but also on their contribution to systemic risk (as described in the preceding section); on individual risk characteristics, including the ones just described under current FDIC rules; and on measures of complexity and interconnectedness. The majority of financial firms contribute only marginally to systemic risk, so presumably their fees would be close to zero. The large, complex financial institutions (LCFIs), however, would bear the brunt of the tax.

A Market-Based System

Our first two proposals rely on the regulator measuring the systemic risk of various institutions. A complementary system would be to let the market estimate the systemic risk. Each regulated firm would be required to buy insurance against future losses, but only losses during a future general crisis. The insurance provider would then have to estimate the systemic risk of a firm, and it could use the method outlined ealier, or any other it sees fit to use (we present some alternatives in the next subection). The insurance payment during the crisis would go to a financial stability regulator (e.g., the Fed), not the firm, to prevent moral hazard and help finance the actions taken to mitigate the crisis.

This insurance scheme gives an incentive to limit systemic risk or to be well capitalized against systemic risk in order to reduce the cost of insurance. Thus, institutions will internalize their externality, and the market price helps measure it.

The insurance contract would need to be clearly specified. At a high level, we suggest the following: Each financial institution would have a target capital of, say, 8 percent of current assets in the event of a crisis.[21]

For every dollar that the institution's capital falls below the target capital in the crisis, the insurance company would have to pay one cent to the regulator (the systemic fund).

To fully insure against the capital falling below the target, the institution would need to buy insurance for the remaining 99 cents of losses. To limit the need for private insurance, we suggest that this part is bought from the government at a price that is related to the private-market price.[22]

This joint private-public insurance scheme addresses the problem that the size of the insurance market for systemic risk may be too large for the private sector to handle. This is because, by definition, systemic insurance requires large amounts of capital that is rarely touched. If the system is not capitalized against worst-case scenarios (i.e., poor systemic states), then who will insure the insurers? One possible solution is to require that the competing insurance companies have to insure only a small percentage (e.g., 1 percent) of the losses, as mentioned previously. If the losses occur, the insurance company would transfer the small fraction to the financial stability regulator. Then, the financial institution could be required to buy additional insurance from the government, where the premium would be related to the market-based premium.[23] The key feature is that the private sector would be pricing the insurance, as opposed to the formulaic procedure described in the preceding section on FDIC-style methodology.

We note that the main point here is not that the insurance payments would necessarily be enough to fully cover the capital needed to stabilize the system during a crisis. The Federal Reserve would still be the lender of last resort. The main points are that this system would give the insurance provider an incentive to carefully scrutinize the systemic risk of each firm (in a way that is less subject to gaming than fixed regulatory fees or capital requirements), the firm would have an incentive to limit its systemic risk and provide transparency in order to reduce its insurance premium, and the regulator and the public would be able to assess the risk by looking at the insurance cost.

The firms would need to keep acquiring insurance on a continuing basis to ensure continued monitoring and price discovery, and to prevent sudden high insurance premiums from causing funding problems because the purchases of premiums are spread out. For example, each month, each firm would need to buy some small amount of insurance to cover the next future five years. Hence, the coverage of the next month would be provided by the insurance purchased over the previous five years.

This market-based system could be used in combination with the system of direct regulation—indeed, the market price of insurance could be one of the several inputs into the regulator's estimate of systemic risk.

Alternative Proposals

Of course, we are not the first to discuss systemic risk—it is a general rationale for regulating the banking industry. Note, however, that even though systemic risk provides the rationale for regulation, the regulatory measures used in practice actually do not focus on systemic risk. Systemic risk is often acknowledged, but the solutions proposed make capital requirements just as sensitive to specific risks as to systemic risks.

An interesting idea, and one that has been around for some time, is to create recapitalization requirements, in addition to capital requirements. One way to do so is to force levered financial institutions to issue securities that provide automatic recapitalization if the firm's value decreases. The important insight is that equity capital on the balance sheet of financial institutions is expensive. Contingent capital is therefore a more efficient form of regulation. Wall (1989) proposed subordinated debentures with an embedded put option. Doherty and Harrington (1997) and Flannery (2005) proposed reverse convertible debentures. These securities limit financial distress costs ex post without distorting bank managers' ex ante incentives.

Kashyap, Rajan, and Stein (2008, henceforth KRS) argue that the idea of automatic recapitalization can be applied to systemic risk. They propose a capital insurance scheme based on systemic risk. Each bank would issue capital insurance policies that would pay off when the overall banking sector is in bad shape, *regardless of the health of a given bank at that point*. The insurer would be a pension fund or a sovereign wealth fund that would essentially provide fully funded "banking catastrophe" insurance.

There are two issues with this proposal. First, KRS do not provide a link between a firm's *own contribution* to the aggregate losses and the insurance fees it must pay. The financial institution still has the incentive to lever up, take concentrated bets, and build illiquid positions that may improve the risk/return profile of the firm but nevertheless increase the systemic risk in the system. In other words, the negative externality still exists and is not priced. In fact, capital insurance policies could encourage institutions to load on aggregate risk.[24] In contrast, our third implementation proposal requires the insurance payment to go to the regulator, which then has discretion over whether the insured institution deserves the capital injection. The recent crisis has shown that moral hazard linked to aggregate risk taking is just as pervasive as moral hazard linked to specific risk. It is therefore crucial to reward firms that do not take too much aggregate risk, and to punish those that do. Our proposal is meant to deal with precisely this issue.

Another limitation of this sort of proposal is that if the crisis is large enough, no amount of private money will ever be enough, and the Fed is always going to be the lender of last resort. But the mere existence of LOLR creates moral hazard unless LOLR services are properly priced ex ante. Once again, the measurements in Section 13.3 can be used to obtain the correct incentives.

A final comment is that, in the KRS proposal, the market would have to find institutions willing to lock up and provide capital when the rare event occurs, all for just a Treasury return plus insurance premium. In terms of its potential for success, the catastrophe insurance market is a good place to look for answers. One finds that, in general, this market is not particularly liquid or well-functioning (e.g., excessively high risk premiums). As mentioned earlier, private markets do not do a good job of insuring systemic risk. Of course, the solution of part-public/part-private insurance could also be applied here.

APPENDIX: EXAMPLES OF SYSTEMIC RISK IN THE CURRENT CRISIS

In this appendix, we describe some of the ways in which major financial institutions posed systemic risk.

Bear Stearns

On the weekend following Friday, March 14, the government helped engineer JPMorgan Chase's purchase of Bear Stearns by guaranteeing $29 billion of subprime-backed securities. Without this involvement, it is highly likely Bear Stearns would have declared bankruptcy, as there had been a classic run on its assets. Bear Stearns had substantive systemic risk. Though Bear Stearns was the smallest of the major investment banks, it had a high degree of interconnectedness to other parts of the financial system. In other words, it was a major counterparty risk. For example, as a major player in the $2.5 trillion repo market (which is the primary source of short-term funding of security purchases), bankruptcy would have meant that the typical lenders in these markets—money market mutual funds and municipalities—would have received collateral rather than cash on the following Monday. Since some of this collateral was illiquid, it is quite possible that these lenders would have had to pull their funds from other institutions, sparking a run on the financial system. In fact, in the week leading up to that Friday, Lehman Brothers' five-year CDS spread rose from 285 basis points to 450 basis points in anticipation of a run.

Also, Bear Stearns was the leading prime broker on Wall Street to hedge funds. Failure of Bear Stearns would have put at risk any hedge fund securities hypothecated at the firm. Depending on the outcome of the failure, hedge funds might pull assets from other financial institutions that faced even slight bankruptcy risk, again leading to a run on the financial system and failures of other financial institutions. Further, Bear Stearns was a major participant in the credit default swap (CDS) market. Bankruptcy of Bear Stearns would have meant the closing out of all outstanding CDS contracts. Again, depending on how these contracts were netted out within the system, a number of these CDSs would have to be liquidated. Given the nature of the illiquidity of CDS contracts, the fire sales of these CDSs could have had a ripple effect across the financial system.

Lehman Brothers

Over the weekend following Friday, September 12, the government failed in its attempt to engineer a purchase of Lehman Brothers by other financial institutions without any direct government support. In hindsight, Lehman Brothers contained considerable systemic risk and led to the near collapse of the financial system (though that may have occurred regardless). Ex post, it is not clear whether (1) the government thought Lehman was no longer systemic because of the Fed's opening of lending facilities to financial institutions, or (2), as the government now argues, Lehman could not be rescued because Lehman did not have adequate collateral to post to access these facilities. In any event, similar to Bear Stearns, Lehman was a major player in various parts of the capital market. Its bankruptcy opened up the possibility that similar firms could also go bankrupt, causing a potential run on their assets. This led to Merrill Lynch selling itself to Bank of America. The other two institutions, Morgan Stanley and Goldman Sachs, saw the cost of their five-year CDS protection rise from 250 basis points (bps) to 500 bps and 200 bps to 350 bps (respectively), and their stock prices fall by 13.54 percent and 12.13 percent (respectively) from Friday, September 12, to Monday, September 15. Both these institutions filed for bank holding company status soon after.

Fannie and Freddie

Under the Housing and Economic Recovery Act of 2008, the government placed Fannie Mae and Freddie Mac, the government-sponsored enterprises (GSEs), into conservatorship on September 7, 2008, thus preventing their possible bankruptcy. At the time, it became clear to the markets that the GSEs were quite likely insolvent due to their mortgage portfolios' investments in subprime and Alt-A loans and the firms' degree of leverage. The GSEs imposed large systemic risk. Due to their owning over $1.5 trillion of relatively illiquid MBSs, failure of the GSEs would have led to a fire sale of these assets that would infect the rest of the financial system holding similar assets. To the extent that the MBS market is one of the largest debt markets, the fire sale could have caused other financial institutions to fail, similar to what actually happened with the subprime CDOs. Furthermore, as one of the largest investors in capital markets, the GSEs presented considerable counterparty risk to the system, holding, in 2007, $1.38 trillion and $523 billion total notional amount of swaps and OTC derivatives, respectively. Failure of GSEs would have led to winding down of large quantities of OTC derivatives with systemic consequences. Finally, the failure of the GSEs would have shut down MBS issuance with guarantees. Since the GSEs represent over 60 percent of the entire $5.7 trillion securitization market, and with no substitute available (in the short term), the result would likely have been a systemic failure of the U.S. mortgage system with obvious dire consequences for the real economy.

Another source of the meltdown, however, had little to do with Lehman's interconnectedness, and more to do with the systemic risk of a large money market mutual fund. On September 16, one of the larger money market funds, the Reserve Primary Fund, suspended redemptions because of its unusually large exposure to short-term bonds of Lehman, causing its net asset value to fall below par, the dreaded "breaking the buck." This failure of the money market fund to protect its investors against losses led to a freeze in money markets, causing the government to guarantee all money market fund losses. It would likely have been unthinkable prior to this crisis that a money market fund could induce systemic risk.

American International Group (AIG)

As yet another example of possible systemic risk, consider the government's injection of funds into AIG on September 15. AIG received an $85 billion loan secured against all its assets, including its insurance subsidiaries, as a way to meet the collateral obligations of its $400 billion portfolio of CDSs against a variety of higher tranches of CDOs and CLOs of mortgages, bonds, and loans. AIG posed two forms of systemic risk. The first was that its exposure to CDSs was all on one side—the firm was receiving small premiums to insure against large, yet highly unlikely, losses. Of course, the unlikely event that these losses would occur would be systemic in nature, causing the CDSs to be highly correlated in these states. AIG would then have to fork over large amounts of capital it would not have access to at the parent level. As this systemic event became even slightly likely, AIG's counterparties demanded collateral to protect themselves against further declines, which caused AIG to be strapped for funds. As it became clear AIG could no longer post collateral, AIG's forced bankruptcy would mean that $400 billion worth of securities on other financial institutions' balance sheets would no longer be safely insured, leading to substantial write-offs, which in turn would cause a fire sale of assets that could ripple across the financial system. At the very least, the insurance market for financial claims would freeze up.

Of course, as it turned out, with Morgan Stanley and Goldman Sachs on the brink of bankruptcy the week of September 15, the government announced a possible marketwide bailout on September 19. While the bailout changed forms a number of times over the next several weeks, the eventual plan resulted in, on an ex ante basis, a substantial transfer of wealth from taxpayers to financial institutions. The issue is whether a regulatory system could have been in place that would have made this crisis (or some future unknown crisis) and resulting losses to taxpayers less likely.

NOTES

1. Brunnermeier and Pedersen (forthcoming); Garleanu and Pedersen (2007); and Mitchell, Pedersen, and Pulvino (2007).
2. See Acharya (2001) for a discussion. Hoggarth, Reis, and Saporta (2002) find that the cumulative output losses ("gap" compared to normal-time GDP) have amounted to a whopping 15 to 20 percent annual GDP in the banking crises of the past 25 years. Recent evidence from the current crisis suggests that there has been a freezing up of lending from banks to corporations, except for drawdowns on banks' precommited lines of credit (Ivashina and Scharstein 2008), which would significantly affect growth in the real sector of the economy.
3. See Chapter 5, "Enhanced Regulation of Large, Complex Financial Institutions."
4. See Acharya (2001) and Acharya and Yorulmazer (2007) for a discussion.
5. Caprio and Klingebiel (1996) argue that the bailout of the thrift industry cost $180 billion (3.2 percent of GDP) in the United States in the late 1980s. They also document that the estimated costs of bailouts were 16.8 percent for Spain, 6.4 percent for Sweden, and 8 percent for Finland. Honohan and Klingebiel (2000) find that countries spent 12.8 percent of their GDP to clean up their banking systems, whereas Claessens, Djankov, and Klingebiel (1999) set the cost at 15 to 50 percent of GDP. The costs of the rescue package in the United States during the current crisis could easily mount to similar figures, if not more.
6. VaR can be gamed to the extent that asymmetric, yet very risky, bets may not produce a large VaR. The reason is that if the negative payoff is below the VaR 1 percent or 5 percent threshold, then VaR will not capture it. Indeed, one of the concerns about VaR in this current crisis has been the failure of VaR to pick up potential losses in the AAA tranches.
7. This is with the important caveat that TBTF guarantees will pollute CDS spreads. In addition, counterparty externalities depend on the connectedness of the firm and would require additional measures.

8. The data are from the Center for Research in Security Prices (CRSP)'s daily stock and index database for 2006 and 2007, where financial companies (banking, insurance, real estate, and trading) are identified as those listed on the New York Stock Exchange in the SIC code range of 6000 to 6999. The calculations are taken from Lester, Pedersen, and Philippon (2008).

9. One caveat is that VaR and ES measure statistical contributions. They do not measure directly the economic forces responsible for the crisis. To take an extreme example, suppose firm A creates a crisis all by itself. Because of externalities, other firms experience losses (part of this may be because they chose to be exposed to this risk). Our statistical approach would attribute only part of the crisis to firm A, even if it is in fact entirely responsible.

10. The approach is therefore fully flexible and consistent with continuing evolution of the finance industry. If the risk profile of a firm changes because of different capital allocations, spin-offs, or mergers, this will be reflected in the risk measure.

11. Stress tests simulate the consequence of large movements in a particular market. Scenarios analyze the consequences of a systemic crisis, inspired by historical episodes or based on relevant potentialities.

12. See Chapter 5, "Enhanced Regulation of Large, Complex Financial Institutions."

13. JPMorgan Chase & Company, 2007 Annual Report, published on March 10, 2008.

14. The Spanish system requires higher capital adequacy in good times and lower requirements during the crisis. This helps provide a capital buffer before the crisis hits, and it allows flexibility during it.

15. Purely idiosyncratic risk would require less capital, and firms might occasionally fail if they took significant risk; but an isolated failure can generally be resolved by the private sector and would not cause externalities (deposit insurance creates the need for additional regulations, but this is not our focus here).

16. See Chapter 2, "How Banks Played the Leverage Game."

17. The recent crisis has shown that firms such as Bear Stearns and Citigroup looked extremely well capitalized even at points when it became clear that due to erosion of their equity's market values, they had limited funding capacity (if any) to perform day-to-day operations and manage their liquidity in an orderly fashion.

18. Of course, the same analogy can be given to life insurance policy holders, mutual fund shareholders, limited partners of hedge funds, and so on.

19. The Federal Deposit Insurance Corporation (FDIC) was created in the depths of the Great Depression to address the massive number of bank runs that took place from 1930 to 1933. The contracts went through several iterations, ending with the Federal Deposit Reform Act of 2005 which instituted a pricing scheme for deposit premiums that attempted to capture risk by combining examination ratings, financial ratios, and, for large banks, long-term debt issuer ratings. All institutions are broken into four risk categories, I through IV. The lowest risk category contains institutions considered healthy by the examiners that are well capitalized, with total risk-based ratio of 10 percent, Tier 1 risk-based ratio of 6 percent, and Tier 1 leverage ratio of 5 percent. Within risk category I, a premium between 5 and 7 cents per $100 of deposits would be assessed, depending

on a formula that takes into account Tier 1 leverage ratios—loans past due 30 to 89 days/gross assets, nonperforming assets/gross assets, net loan charge-offs/gross assets, and net income before taxes/risk-weighted assets. As health and capitalization weaken for the firm, the risk category increases, eventually leading to premiums as high as 43 cents per $100 of deposits.

20. The historical mandate that the FDIC must return premiums to the sector if losses are low is a very poor idea. It is paramount to returning fire insurance if there has been no fire yet.

21. As mentioned in Section 13.3, a crisis would be defined by the regulator as a time when the aggregate losses in the financial industry (or the economy at large) exceed a specified amount.

22. To the extent the government's cost of capital is less than the insurance company's, the regulator could take a price discount on the insurance premium.

23. This type of co-insurance program is not without precedent. The Terrorism Risk Insurance Act (TRIA), first passed in November 2002, offers federal reinsurance for qualifying losses from a terrorist attack. TRIA is a good place to start and includes industry loss triggers and government excess of loss coverage. These features help minimize the insurance industry's losses yet also provide insurors with an incentive to monitor and reduce risks. It would work similarly here.

24. KRS acknowledge this issue (page 38).

REFERENCES

Acharya, Viral V. 2001. A theory of systemic risk and design of prudential bank regulation. Working paper, New York University Stern School of Business.

Acharya, Viral V., and Tanju Yorulmazer. 2007. Too many to fail—An analysis of time-inconsistency in bank closure policies. *Journal of Financial Intermediation* 16 (1): 1–31.

Brunnermeier, Markus, and Lasse Heje Pedersen. forthcoming. Market liquidity and funding liquidity. *Review of Financial Studies*.

Caprio, Gerard, and Daniela Klingebiel. 1996. Bank insolvencies: Cross country experience. Policy Research Working Paper No. 1620, World Bank.

Claessens, Stijn, Simeon Djankov, and Daniela Klingebiel. 1999. Financial restructuring in East Asia: Halfway there? Financial Sector Discussion Paper No. 3, World Bank.

Doherty, Neil A., and Harrington, Scott. 1997. Managing corporate risk with reverse convertible debt. Working paper, Wharton School, University of Pennsylvania.

Flannery, Mark J. 2005. No pain, no gain? Effecting market discipline via reverse convertible debentures. In *Capital adequacy beyond Basel: Banking, securities, and insurance*, ed. Hal S. Scott. New York: Oxford University Press.

Garleanu, Nicolae, and Lasse Heje Pedersen. 2007. Liquidity and risk management. *American Economic Review, P&P* 97 (2): 193–197.

Hoggarth, Glenn, Ricardo Reis, and Victoria Saporta. 2002. Costs of banking system instability: Some empirical evidence. *Journal of Banking and Finance* 26 (5): 825–855.

Honohan, Patrick, and Daniela Klingebiel. 2000. Controlling fiscal costs of bank crises. Working Paper No. 2441, World Bank.

Ivashina, Victoria, and David Scharstein. 2008. Bank lending during the financial crisis of 2008. Working paper, Harvard Business School.

Kashyap, Anil, Raghuram Rajan, and Jeremy Stein. 2008. Rethinking capital regulation. Kansas City Symposium on Financial Stability.

Lester, Ashley, Lasse H. Pedersen, and Thomas Philippon. 2008. Systemic risk and macroeconomic capital. Mimeo, New York University.

Mitchell, Mark, Lasse Heje Pedersen, and Todd Pulvino. 2007. Slow moving capital. *American Economic Review, P&P* 97 (2): 215–220.

Wall, Larry. 1989. A plan for reducing future deposit insurance losses: Puttable subordinated debt. *Federal Reserve Bank of Atlanta Economic Review* 74 (4).

CHAPTER 14

Private Lessons for Public Banking

The Case for Conditionality in LOLR Facilities

Viral V. Acharya and David K. Backus

14.1 INTRODUCTION

As we work our way through the current financial crisis, central banks have shifted their attention from managing short-term interest rates to providing liquidity to the financial system. In the United States, for example, the Federal Reserve's balance sheet has expanded rapidly, as it offered funds to banks and accepted securities in return. This lender of last resort (LOLR) role is neither new nor unusual, but its massive scale suggests that it is worth some thought to get the details right. In this chapter we make what may seem right now to be a perverse argument: that central banks can learn something from the private sector about how to manage their provision of liquidity.

Central banks have traditionally offered secured loans—cash for securities—to sound financial institutions that find themselves temporarily illiquid. In 1985, when a bug in the Bank of New York's clearing system for Treasury bills left it short of cash, the Fed stepped in immediately. Ditto the Bundesbank (1974) and the Bank of England (1995) when failures of major banks threatened to dry up liquidity for others. Situations like this occur periodically in all countries. Less frequently, the financial system as

We are grateful to Jon Gold and Irvind Gujral for excellent research assistance.

a whole finds itself short of cash: Securities that in normal times can easily be exchanged for cash become illiquid, putting stress on the entire system. In the past two decades, Japan, Norway, Sweden, and many developing economies have experienced widespread financial difficulties that demanded central bank action. These episodes are, however, somewhat regular events, and should be dealt with in predetermined ways.

Other chapters in the book address issues of prudential regulation designed to minimize the chances of financial crises[1] and reorganization and capitalization of insolvent institutions.[2] We focus here on the provision of liquidity. We argue that lines of credit made by banks to corporations (and small banks) are a private solution to a similar problem, and their terms might well be adopted by central banks.

We recommend that central banks' liquidity facilities, like private lines of credit, should be *conditional*. In particular, they should include a material adverse change (MAC) clause that allows the lender to refuse credit if the borrower's credit quality has deteriorated materially. MAC clauses are indeed invoked by banks in practice for firms that violate covenants.[3] Similarly, central banks should verify that they are indeed lending to sound institutions.

A straightforward way to achieve this objective is to include conditionality in the LOLR facilities: Banks should be eligible for central bank credit *only if* they meet prespecified requirements—for example, maximum leverage and minimum capital ratios. Such conditionality will reduce the moral hazard likely to be induced by central banks' provision of liquidity insurance to banks, and make it more likely that they are moderating temporary liquidity problems, rather than allowing insolvent banks to continue to operate. Put another way, conditionality in LOLR would give weak banks an incentive to recapitalize when their losses mount to retain access to the LOLR facilities. Without such conditionality, weak banks may access liquidity facilities and play the waiting game: avoid raising new capital, which would dilute current shareholders and perhaps keep current management in control. The cost is delay in recapitalizing the financial system and a risk of making the institution even more insolvent. As the Federal Reserve expands its liquidity operations to a wider set of institutions (often unregulated ones such as investment banks), the role for such conditionality in its liquidity facilities seems imperative.

14.2 BAGEHOT RECONSIDERED

Walter Bagehot codified the nineteenth century's collective wisdom on central bank provision of liquidity in Chapter VII of *Lombard Street* (1873).

In many respects, the same principles guide modern central banks. Our summary includes these four elements:

1. Central banks should hold large reserves. Until World War II, these reserves were gold—or paper backed explicitly by gold. In developed countries today, reserves are effectively limited only by the borrowing capacity of national governments. In developing countries, explicit foreign exchange reserves play an important role.
2. In times of panic, the central bank should freely advance these reserves to any private bank able to offer "what in ordinary times is reckoned a good security" as collateral. Bagehot seems to assume here that the difficulty is liquidity (good securities in a bad market) rather than solvency (bad securities). In that case, he argues that the solution is for the central bank to apply a liberal interpretation of good security and accept securities that it might not accept in ordinary times. Most central banks have done just that during the current crisis, expanding the set of securities they accept as collateral.
3. These advances should be charged a penalty rate to discourage applications from banks that do not need it. In modern terms, we would probably stress the incentives of such a policy, but Bagehot is concerned primarily with the practical goal of conserving limited reserves. We argue that a penalty rate may not be enough: there may be better ways to discourage or deny inappropriate borrowing.
4. This policy of using reserves to stem panics should be clearly communicated. Otherwise, uncertainty about central bank actions can themselves contribute to the panic. We suggest the same for more complex lending arrangements: that setting clear terms in advance is a powerful tool for stability and gets the incentives right.

These guidelines remain insightful, but we think they miss an important aspect of financial crises: It is not easy to tell the difference between an illiquid and an insolvent institution. In fact, that is usually what precipitates matters: No one is sure who is solvent. In those circumstances, a central bank can easily find itself lending to an insolvent institution, perhaps delaying its timely reorganization and recapitalization unnecessarily.

Consider an undercapitalized and possibly insolvent bank; call it Lehman Brothers if you like. If it can borrow from the central bank, it faces less pressure to raise more capital privately to address its lack of capital. Figure 14.1 shows the total capital raised (public and private) and total losses incurred by financial institutions worldwide (including banks, broker-dealers, insurers, and government-sponsored enterprises [GSEs]) from the third quarter of 2007 to date. The picture is striking. With the exception

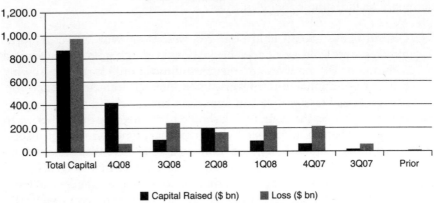

FIGURE 14.1 Capital Issuance and Losses Incurred by All Financial Firms (Including Banks, Broker-Dealers, Insurers, and Government-Sponsored Enterprises) Worldwide

Source: Bloomberg.

of 4Q 2008, which features large-scale capital infusions from governments into the financial sector, private firms did not raise enough capital to cover their announced losses. By this measure, they remained (as a whole) under-capitalized.

One interpretation is that investors believed that many of these institutions were insolvent and hence were reluctant to provide them with capital; under this view, insolvent institutions survived only because they had explicit or implicit government guarantees and access to liquidity facilities. Another interpretation is that these institutions could have raised new capital in private markets, but decided not to, perhaps to protect current shareholders and management. This decision (to refuse new capital) was enabled by access to guarantees and liquidity from central banks.

Could central banks provide liquidity to these institutions without undercutting their incentive to restructure or raise new capital? We believe the answer is yes, provided the liquidity facilities created by central banks include provisions to deny credit to unhealthy institutions. Private lenders have exactly such provisions, as we show next.

14.3 PRIVATE LINES OF CREDIT

In the private sector, lines of credit (LCs) serve a similar purpose for firms as central banks' LOLR facilities do for banks: They provide liquidity to firms when they need it. Indeed, LCs often constitute a firm's last line of defense against an economy-wide shortage of credit, as in the current crisis.[4] The trade-offs involved are also the same: Providing liquidity allows firms to avoid the costs of financial distress to a sound enterprise but reduces the discipline on the enterprise to avoid being in such a situation in the first place. How does the structure of private insurance deal with this trade-off?

Table 14.1 lists the terms of some lines of credit arranged by Boeing, which we think are typical. The LC is effectively an option to borrow money in the future. Boeing (in this case) pays a commitment fee up front. The amount and maturity are fixed from the start. The interest rate, if the loan is drawn, is tied to the credit rating. The use of the funds is specified in the arrangement. Finally, and most importantly from the standpoint of this chapter, the contract includes both covenants and a material adverse change (MAC) clause that give the lender the ability to refuse the loan if the conditions of the borrower have deteriorated.

The terms suggest that lines of credit are private solutions to liquidity issues, *not solvency issues*. For example, the commitment fee and interest rate are both tied to the firm's credit rating, which allows the lender to respond to changes in credit quality. More important are the covenants and the material adverse change condition. For Boeing, the conditions include reporting requirements, limits on debt, and restrictions on the sale or lease of assets. The clear intent, we think, is to rule out loans to firms whose credit quality has changed markedly for the worse.

14.4 CENTRAL BANK LENDING FACILITIES

Does such conditionality feature in central banks' LOLR facilities? We do not find this to be so for the large number of liquidity facilities created by central banks around the world to deal with the subprime crisis. In Table 14.2, we list the major actions of the Federal Reserve (Fed), the European Central Bank (ECB), and the Bank of England (BOE) over the past 15 months. These actions, mostly taken in the form of liquidity facilities, have various restrictions with respect to eligible institutions, collateral, maturity, lending rates, and lending limits.

The eligible institutions for credit facilities were largely unchanged before and after the emergence of the current financial crisis. The ECB has permitted all established credit institutions that had been engaged in prior refinancing operations to continue to take advantage of the expanded suite of facilities. The BOE has two subsets of eligible institutions—those that participate in standing facilities and those that participate in open market operations; like the ECB, these are established credit institutions. Eligible institutions vary the most under the Fed's plans—each facility has specific

TABLE 14.1 Private Lines of Credit for Boeing Corporation

Date	Description of Facility	Size of Facility	Interest Rate	Maturity	Lender	Permitted Uses	Covenants	Other Fees
11/14/08	364-Day Credit Agreement	$1.0 billion	Base rate (higher of published Citigroup rate and fed funds rate plus 50 basis points) + applicable margin (higher of credit default swap rate minus 100 bps and 0). (If credit rating better than A/A2, swap rate range from .350% to 1.500%, else its range is 0.50% to 2.00%.)	1 year	Citigroup and JPMorgan	General Purposes	Timeliness of reporting and payments. Debt cannot exceed 60% of total capital. Cannot sell, transfer, or lease substantially all of its assets. No material adverse change has occurred since last accounting period.	Commitment fee (based on rating): A+/A1: 0.060% A/A2: 0.080% Else: 0.125%
11/16/07	5-Year Credit Agreement	$2.0 billion	Base rate (higher of published Citigroup rate and fed funds rate plus 50 basis points) + applicable margin. Applicable margin based on credit rating: AA−/Aa3 or better: 0.060% A+/A1: 0.100% A/A2: 0.140% A−/A3: 0.180% BBB+/Baa1: 0.270% Else: 0.425%	5 years	Citigroup and JPMorgan	General Purposes	Timeliness of reporting and payments. Debt cannot exceed 60% of total capital. Cannot sell, transfer, or lease substantially all of its assets. No material adverse change has occurred since last accounting period.	Facility fee based on credit rating: AA−/Aa3: 0.040% A+/A1: 0.050% A/A2: 0.060% A−/A3: 0.070% BBB+/Baa1: 0.080% Else: 0.125% Letter of credit commissions: AA−/Aa3: 0.150% A+/A1: 0.200% A/A2: 0.250% A−/A3: 0.300% BBB+/Baa1: 0.400% Else: 0.650%

| 2/6/03 | 2013 Notes | $600 million | 5.13% | 2013 | Public Offering | General Purposes | Timeliness of reporting and payments. No material adverse change has occurred since last accounting period. | Underwriter discounts and commissions of 0.450% |
| 2/6/03 | 2033 Notes | $400 million | 6.13% | 2033 | Public Offering | General Purposes | Timeliness of reporting and payments. No MAC has occurred since last accounting period. | Underwriter discounts and commissions of 0.875% |

Source: EDGAR Online, company filings at Securities and Exchange Commission.

TABLE 14.2 Liquidity Facilities of the Federal Reserve, European Central Bank, and Bank of England

(a) Federal Reserve (*Source:* New York Federal Reserve)

Date Announced	Description	Eligible Institutions	Eligible Collateral	Maturity of Lending	Lending (Penalty) Rate	Ending Date of Facility	Collateral Requirements	Lending Limits
12/12/07	Term Auction Facility	Depository institutions	U.S. and other high-rated government debt; corporate market instruments; investment-quality commercial paper; sound bank-issued assets; high-quality customer obligations.	28–84 days	Rate determined by auction. Minimum bid rate determined based on expected fed funds rate.	Indefinite	The same collateral values and margins applicable for other Federal Reserve lending programs will also apply for the TAF.	Limit of $150 billion per auction. Each institution can bid at most 10% of offered amount.
3/11/08	Term Securities Lending Facility	Primary dealers	Includes federal agency debt, federal agency residential mortgage-backed securities (MBS), and nonagency AAA/Aaa-rated private-label residential MBS.	28 days	Stop-fee determined by auction with minimum bids set at 10 or 25 basis points.	1/30/09	Collateral will be valued daily and adjustments to collateral levels may be required.	Up to $200 billion. Institutions can borrow at most 20% of auction value.
3/16/08	Primary Dealer Credit Facility	Primary dealers	U.S. Treasury obligations, U.S. government/agency obligations, investment grade debt securities, municipal securities, mortgage-backed and asset-backed securities.	Overnight	Primary credit rate.	1/30/09	Recourse beyond the pledged collateral to the primary dealer entity itself.	No designated limit. As of 11/12/08, ~$65 billion outstanding.

7/13/08	Permission granted to lend to Fannie Mae and Freddie Mac if necessary	Fannie Mae/Freddie Mac	U.S. government and federal agency securities.	Indefinite	Primary credit rate.	Indefinite		
9/16/08	Federal Reserve Bank of New York lends $85 billion to AIG (reduced to $60 billion on 11/10/08)	AIG	All the assets of AIG and of its primary nonregulated subsidiaries.	24 months	3-month LIBOR + 850 basis points (reduced to L + 300 on 11/10/08).		The U.S. government will receive a 79.9% equity interest and has the right to veto dividends.	
9/19/08	ABCP MMMF Liquidity Facility	U.S. depository institutions, bank holding companies, or U.S. branches and agencies of foreign banks	Asset-backed commercial paper, rated not lower than A1, F1, or P1. Must have been issued on or after 9/19/08. Has a stated maturity that does not exceed 120 days if the borrower is a bank or 270 days for nonbank borrowers.	Remaining term of ABCP used as collateral	Primary credit rate in effect at the Boston Fed offered to depository institutions.	1/30/09	The collateral valuation will be the amortized cost of the eligible ABCP pledged to secure an advance. This amount will not be margin adjusted.	As of 11/12/08, $80.2 billion outstanding.

(Continued)

TABLE 14.2 *(Continued)*

Date Announced	Description	Eligible Institutions	Eligible Collateral	Maturity of Lending	Lending (Penalty) Rate	Ending Date of Facility	Collateral Requirements	Lending Limits
9/19/08	Trading desk permitted to purchase debt issued by GSEs in secondary market							
10/6/08	Fed will pay interest on depository institutions' reserves	Depository institutions	None	Indefinite	On required reserves, 10 basis points under the average targeted fed funds rate. On excess reserves, 75 basis points under fed funds rate.	Indefinite		
10/7/08	Commercial Paper Funding Facility	U.S. issuers of Commercial Paper	U.S. dollar-denominated commercial paper (including asset-backed commercial paper) that is rated at least A-1/P-1/F-1.	Maturity of commercial paper	For unsecured, 3-month OIS + 100 basis points plus 100 basis point surcharge. For asset-backed, 3-month OIS + 300 basis points.	4/30/09		The issuer's outstanding paper cannot exceed its 2008 maximum. As of 11/12/08, $257.3 billion outstanding.

Date	Facility	Eligible	Description	Term	Rate	Expiration	Risk/Terms	Amount
10/21/08	Money Market Investor Funding Facility (MMIFF)	Money markets of financial institutions with a short-term rating > A-1/P-1/F-1	A private special purpose vehicle (PSPV) will purchase U.S. dollar-denominated certificates of deposit, bank notes, and commercial paper. The assets of the PSPV will act as collateral.	7–90 days	Primary credit rate.	4/30/09	If there is a substantial rating downgrade or default, all asset purchases are ceased until assets issued by that institution mature.	At most 15% for a single institution. Total limit will be $540 billion.
11/10/08	AIG's RMBS Facility	AIG	All the assets of a newly formed LLC containing AIG's residential mortgage-backed securities.				AIG will bear the risk for the first $1 billion of losses.	$22.5 billion
11/10/08	AIG's CDO Facility	AIG	All the assets of a newly formed LLC containing collateralized debt obligations on which AIG has written credit default swaps.				AIG will bear the risk for the first $5 billion of losses.	$30.0 billion
11/25/08	Term Asset-Backed Securities Loan Facility	All U.S. persons who own eligible collateral	AAA-rated U.S. dollar asset-backed securities (ABS). The underlying assets must be auto loans, student loans, credit card loans, or small business loans.	1 year	Determined by auction. Submitted bid must be greater than a minimum spread over the 1-year OIS.	12/31/09	Will not be subject to mark-to-market. TARP funds are subordinated to the Fed's loan.	Up to $200 billion

(Continued)

TABLE 14.2 *(Continued)*

(b) European Central Bank (*Source: Press Releases of European Central Bank*)

Date Announced	Description	Eligible Institutions	Eligible Collateral	Maturity of Lending	Lending (Penalty) Rate	Ending Date of Facility	Collateral Requirements	Lending Limits
12/12/07	U.S. Dollar Term Auction Facility	Credit institutions (including individual branches) established in member states that are fundamentally sound, and fulfill contractual obligations of specific national central bank	All debt issued by the ECB and by the national central banks of the Eurosystem. Marketable debt instruments denominated in the euro, U.S. dollar, British pound, and Japanese yen, and issued in the euro area. Euro-denominated syndicated credit claims. Debt instruments (including residential mortgage-backed) issued by credit institutions, which are traded on the accepted nonregulated markets. Subordinated debt instruments when they are protected by an acceptable guarantee as specified. Ratings threshold of BBB-.	7, 28, 84 days	Set to equal the resulting stop-out rate of the U.S. Federal Reserve's Term Auction.	Indefinite	While the collateral position will not be subject to any daily revaluations or margin calls due to movements in the exchange rate, it will be subject to the normal daily mark-to-market valuation and variation margins.	3 $20 billion 84-day and 1 $40 billion 28-day facilities. The maximum bid amount is 10%.
8/22/07	Supplementary long-term refinancing operation			3 months, 6 months	Main refinancing operations fixed rate.	Indefinite		3 EUR 50 billion 3-month facilities and 5 EUR 50 billion 6-month facilities.
9/18/08	USD overnight liquidity providing operation			Overnight	Variable-rate tender in the form of a multiple-rate auction.	Indefinite		$40–50 billion.
9/29/08	Special term refinancing operation			Reserve maintenance period	Set by ECB prior to auction.	Indefinite		Banks will be lent as much money as they ask for in the tender.

| 12/12/07 | U.S. Dollar Term Auction Facility | 7, 28, 84 days | Set to equal the resulting stop-out rate of the U.S. Federal Reserve's Term Auction. | Indefinite | | | 3 $20 billion 84-day and 1 $40 billion 28-day facilities. The maximum bid amount is 10%. |

(c) Bank of England (*Source: Press Releases of Bank of England*)

| 12/12/07 | Expanded long-term repo market | Institutions that are eligible to participate in open market operations | Gilts (including gilt strips). Sterling treasury bills. Bank of England securities. HM government nonsterling marketable debt. Sterling-denominated debt issued by European Economic Area central governments and major international institutions. Euro-denominated securities (including strips) issued by EEA central governments and central banks and major international institutions. | Initially 3, 6, 9, 12 months | Minimum bid rate equal to the equivalent maturity OIS rate. | Indefinite | Remargining will take place daily, subject to a threshold of £1 million. | Total reserves initially increased to £11.35 billion. On 9/26/08, added a new series of 3-month £40 billion facilities offered weekly. The maximum total size of a bid may not exceed 10% of the OMO. |

(Continued)

TABLE 14.2 *(Continued)*

Date Announced	Description	Eligible Institutions	Eligible Collateral	Maturity of Lending	Lending (Penalty) Rate	Ending Date of Facility	Collateral Requirements	Lending Limits
4/21/08	Special Liquidity Scheme	Institutions eligible to participate will be banks and building societies that are eligible to sign up for the Bank's standing facilities.	All domestic currency bonds issued by other sovereigns eligible for sale to the Bank. Bonds issued by sovereigns rated Aa3/AA– or above. Bonds issued by G10 government agencies guaranteed by national governments, rated AAA. Conventional debt security issues of the Federal Home Loan Mortgage Corporation, the Federal National Mortgage Corporation, and the Federal Home Loan Banking system, rated AAA. AAA-rated tranches of UK, U.S. and EEA asset-backed securities (ABS) backed by credit cards; and AAA-rated tranches of UK and EEA prime residential mortgage-backed securities (RMBS). Covered bonds rated AAA.	1 year (with option to renew for up to 3 years)	Spread between 3-month LIBOR and the 3-month interest rate for borrowing against the security of government bonds, subject to a floor of 20 basis points.	1/30/09	If the assets lose value or rating, they must be replaced, added to, or the treasury bills returned.	No limits, but estimated total ~£50 billion.
9/18/08	USD overnight facility	Institutions that currently participate in standing facilities, or that are OMO participants and part of a group in which there is an institution that participates in standing facilities.		Overnight	The minimum bid spread will be the spread of the Bank's standing lending facility rate to bank rate.	Indefinite	Remargining will take place daily, subject to a threshold of £1 million.	Initially $40 billion, but reduced to $10 billion. The maximum total size of a bid may not exceed 20%.
9/26/08	USD weekly facility			7, 28, and 84 days	Fixed rate determined before each auction.			Full allotment strategy at fixed rate. The maximum total size of a bid may not exceed 20%.

allowable institutions ranging from depository institutions and primary dealers to specific firms like AIG, Fannie Mae, and Freddie Mac.

The three central banks have, over time, chosen to allow similar sets of eligible collateral. They all accept government bonds, asset-backed debt instruments, and marketable debt instruments. The largest differences are in the required credit ratings. While the ECB allows ratings as low as BBB–, the BOE requires AA–. Also, while the ECB and BOE allow the same set of collateral across all facilities, the Fed specifies collateral for each facility. The latter seems desirable if the lending rate is set to be the same for all collateral in a given facility.

The specific maturities of lending vary across country and facility, but they all offer overnight, 7-day, 28-day, 84-day, and 6-month maturities. Interest rates on these facilities are either fixed or determined by auction with a minimum bid rate. The interest rates generally correspond to average expected interest rates over the length of the facility. For U.S. dollar facilities, the BOE and ECB rely on the Fed's term auction facility to set a fixed rate for their own offerings.

Generally, all three central banks have collateral requirements that in principle put the risk of deterioration of collateral on the borrower. Replacement of deteriorated assets is required by providing either higher-rated assets or additional lower-rated assets to fill the gap. The only exception to this has been with respect to the Fed's handling of AIG; for the initial $85 billion, the Federal Reserve Bank of New York received a 79.9 percent equity stake in the firm.

Finally, with respect to lending limits, two approaches are taken. First, auctions have been set with specific amounts outstanding, and potential borrowers bid up interest rates to obtain their desired proportion of the facility. The alternative is a full-allotment strategy where the central bank agrees to lend as much as any bank tenders at a specific fixed interest rate set by the bank. All three central banks employ both types of auctions with limits to specific borrowers at 10 to 20 percent of the total auction amount.

In some respects, these facilities resemble private lines of credit. Prices aren't tied to credit ratings, but central bank lending is secured against collateral, albeit illiquid. What's missing, however, is anything resembling the material adverse change clause. There's nothing, in other words, to keep an undercapitalized bank from using such a facility. We think this is a serious limitation.

Inability of firms to borrow against collateral because the collateral is illiquid may be undesirable when viewed in isolation. But, in a second-best view of the world, such illiquidity might in fact reduce banks' propensity to delay capital issuances. Central banks should not aim to fix the first problem—illiquidity—without paying attention to the second—insolvency.

Viewed in this light, it is theory of the second best at work, and by having a material adverse change clause, as in private lines of credit, central banks' LOLR facilities can prevent outcomes that are far worse than in their absence: Unhealthy institutions will be either denied central bank credit or be forced to reshape and redress for access to central bank funding.

14.5 CONCLUSIONS

Some reports suggest that the Federal Reserve tried its best to persuade Lehman Brothers to issue additional capital or find a suitor in the period between the failure of Bear Stearns (March 2008) and the failure of Lehman Brothers (September 2008). During this period, Lehman Brothers was borrowing heavily from the liquidity facilities of the European Central Bank, against illiquid collateral. While these two observations flag a coordination problem between different central banks, they also raise the issue that ready access to liquidity removed the pressure on Lehman to issue capital in time. As long as the lending rate against this collateral was moderate—in particular, lower than the dilution cost of issuing additional capital—this would have been an attractive strategy for Lehman. If such access had been denied, as with a private line of credit, Lehman would have been forced to issue capital or sell the firm. It's possible that the subsequent failure of Lehman could have been avoided.

We'll never know what might have happened if Lehman had not had access to inexpensive funds through the ECB, but it's worth thinking carefully about how central bank lending is structured. We believe that such lending should be conditional on characteristics of the borrower. We think borrowers must meet minimum capital and maximum leverage ratios, and perhaps also cash-flow-based conditions. All feature prominently in private lines of credit.

NOTES

1. Chapter 13, "Regulating Systemic Risk."
2. Chapter 15, "The Financial Sector Bailout: Sowing the Seeds of the Next Crisis?"
3. See Sufi (forthcoming) for empirical evidence. In a recent example of such revocation, Bank of America canceled its line of credit to Republic Windows and Doors, in Illinois, leading to a wave of protests against the bank for revocation in such troubled times ("Illinois Threatens Bank over Sit-In," *New York Times*, December 8, 2008). Such conditionality is of course the purpose of the material adverse change clause in the first place.

4. In particular, during the subprime crisis bank lending has largely frozen to corporations except the best-rated ones (and even for those since September 2008), except that firms are able to draw down on their lines of credit with banks unless their condition has deteriorated sufficiently for banks to be able to invoke the MAC clause. See Ivashina and Scharfstein (2008).

REFERENCES

Bagehot, Walter. 1873. *Lombard Street, a description of the money market.* Homewood, IL: Richard D. Irwin, Inc.

Ivashina, Victoria, and David Scharfstein. 2008. Bank lending during the financial crisis of 2008. Working paper, Harvard Business School.

Sufi, Amir. Forthcoming. Bank lines of credit in corporate finance: An empirical analysis. *Review of Financial Studies.*

Six

The Bailout

Thomas F. Cooley and Thomas Philippon

P art Five has laid out our proposals for the prudential regulation of systemic financial risk, for the conduct of monetary policy, and for the design of lending facilities to deal with liquidity crises. These proposals were aimed at reducing the likelihood of a systemic crisis.

Financial crises, however, are to some extent unavoidable. It is therefore important for contingency plans to be prepared, and, in that respect, we have much to learn from the current crisis. This is our focus in this part of the book.

Drastic interventions might be needed if and when a liquidity crisis threatens to turn into a systemic solvency crisis, as it did in September and October 2008. It is crucial, however, to minimize the costs to the taxpayer and to limit opportunistic behavior by the institutions that are bailed out. In addition, market participants need to have some idea of how the Federal Reserve and the Treasury will respond when banks and financial firms get into trouble. This financial crisis has been upon us for more than a year, but we still have only the vaguest notion of what considerations drove the decisions that have been made.

Our overall assessment is that the U.S. bailout was ill-conceived from the start, both technically and strategically. It gave away taxpayer money, it was confused and inefficient, and in some respects it worsened the crisis.

Chapter 15 ("The Financial Sector Bailout: Sowing the Seeds of the Next Crisis?") focuses on the financial side of the bailout. Since the intervention had to be quick, the tools to be used were loan guarantees and recapitalization. The critical issues are the pricing of the guarantees and the decision whether to make participation voluntary or compulsory. The U.S. financial bailout has been too generous to the financial industry and too costly for taxpayers, and it lacks a clear exit plan. The loan guarantee scheme has essentially transferred anywhere between $13 billion and $70 billion of taxpayer wealth to the banks. The compulsory nature of the loan guarantee and recapitalization schemes has furthermore made it more difficult to distinguish sound institutions from troubled ones. The U.S. scheme has therefore encouraged banks to become increasingly reliant on government guarantees until the crisis fully abates. All these features are in striking contrast to the UK scheme, which appears to have been fairly priced and is mostly voluntary.

We conclude that government financial guarantees should be priced fairly using market prices to the maximum extent possible. Our analysis also suggests that the default option in financial bailouts should be to make participation voluntary, unless one can show an overwhelming reason for compulsory participation.

The initial bailout plan also missed the elephant in the room: It ignored half of the economic crisis by not taking into account the issue of foreclosures. Chapter 16, "Mortgages and Households," assesses the existing proposals to stabilize the housing market, and presents a new, coherent solution.

Dealing with the housing crisis is critical for at least two reasons. The welfare losses from the housing crisis are large: On top of the distress of displaced families, the average cost of foreclosure is 30 to 35 percent of the value of a house, and foreclosed houses have negative externalities on their neighborhoods.

Moreover, mortgage default losses are at the heart of the financial crisis since default losses are concentrated in the "first loss" and mezzanine tranches of collateralized debt obligations (CDOs). The interconnections between mortgages and the balance sheets of financial firms are such that stabilizing the housing market would also help stabilize the economy as a whole.

Unfortunately, the plans put forward to address the mortgage crisis are not properly designed. We conclude that existing approaches to loan modification do not balance the incentives of the borrowers and the lenders. They give perverse incentives to borrowers to stop making payments, and/or they focus on restructuring mortgages, which is only a temporary solution.

We therefore advocate using shared appreciation mortgages, which are part of the Federal Housing Administration (FHA) plan. Shared appreciation restructurings offer a debt-for-equity swap whereby, in return for modifying the loan, the borrower must give up some of the future appreciation in the value of the property. Designed properly, this would discourage borrowers from seeking modifications if they can continue to pay their mortgages. In addition, Congress should address the legal barriers to modifying securitized loans.

Chapter 17 ("Where Should the Bailout Stop?") addresses the issue of whether the bailout should extend beyond the financial industry, and discusses in particular the case of the car manufacturers. We argue that government interventions should be based on a consistent set of four principles:

1. The market failure must be identified.
2. The intervention should use efficient tools.
3. The costs for the taxpayers should be minimized.
4. Government intervention should not create moral hazard.

Base on these principles, we conclude that there is indeed a case for government intervention in favor of General Motors (GM), but this intervention should not be a giveaway bailout. The market failure that we identify is the disappearance of the debtor-in-possession (DIP) market as a result of the financial crisis. This provides a rationale for government intervention (first principle). To be efficient, the reorganization should be thorough, and therefore may have to be lengthy. This is why it should take place under Chapter 11 of the Bankruptcy Code (second principle). To minimize the costs to the taxpayers, the government should provide DIP financing (directly or through private financial institutions), because DIP loans are well protected by the company's assets due to their seniority (third principle). Finally, reorganization in bankruptcy does not reward bad management, and therefore it minimizes moral hazard (fourth principle).

We advocate a massive DIP loan to GM in bankruptcy. The current bailout plan would offer less of a breathing space to GM and imply more job cuts in the short run than our proposed bankruptcy/DIP financing plan. The DIP loan would allow the restructuring to take place over 18 to 24 months, whereas the bailout would be barely sufficient to avoid liquidation in 2009. To further limit the ripple effects of GM's bankruptcy, the government should also consider backstopping warranties and spare parts availability, even if the reorganization fails.

CHAPTER 15

The Financial Sector Bailout

Sowing the Seeds of the Next Crisis?

Viral V. Acharya and Rangarajan K. Sundaram

The two-month period from September to November 2008 has been witness to the most extraordinary level of direct U.S. government involvement in financial markets in over seven decades.[1] In part, this intervention took on the form of ad hoc institution-specific rescue packages such as those applied to Bear Stearns, Fannie Mae, Freddie Mac, AIG, and Citigroup. But a substantial part of the effort and huge sums of money have also been committed to attempts to address the systemic problems that led to the freezing of credit markets. A multipronged approach has finally emerged with three key components:

1. A loan guarantee scheme administered by the Federal Deposit Insurance Corporation (FDIC) under which the FDIC guarantees newly issued senior unsecured debt of banks up to a maturity of three years.
2. A bank recapitalization scheme undertaken by the U.S. Treasury in which the Treasury purchases preferred equity stakes in banks.
3. A Commercial Paper Funding Facility (CPFF) operated by the Federal Reserve.

We discuss in this chapter the salient features of each of these programs, their pricing implications, and their possible economic consequences, and include—where relevant—comparisons with similar efforts undertaken in other countries, notably the United Kingdom.

Our overall conclusions are summarized in the following four points:

1. By adopting a one-size-fits-all pricing scheme that is set at too low a level relative to the market, the U.S. loan guarantee scheme represents a transfer of taxpayer wealth ranging between $13 billion and $70 billion to the banks. In contrast, the UK scheme, which uses a market-based fee structure, appears to price the guarantee scheme fairly.
2. By offering very little in terms of optionality in participation, the U.S. loan guarantee scheme is effectively forced on all banks, giving rise to a pooling outcome. In contrast, the UK scheme provides considerable optionality in participation which, combined with its pricing structure, has induced a separating equilibrium where healthy banks have not availed themselves of government guarantees but weaker banks have. Implicitly, the U.S. scheme encourages a system where banks are likely to remain (and to want to remain) on government guarantees until the crisis abates, whereas the UK scheme has paved the way for a smooth transition to market-based outcomes.
3. The U.S. recapitalization scheme has also provided little in terms of participation optionality for the large banks, and it is otherwise generous to the banks in that it imposes little direct discipline in the form of replacement of top management or curbs on executive pay, and secures no voting rights for the government. The UK scheme allows for optionality in accepting government funds, and is associated with government voting rights, replacement of management in some cases, and significant curbs on dividend and executive pay.
4. By requiring a threshold credit quality and using a wider spread, the U.S. Commercial Paper Funding Facility (CPFF) appears to be more fairly priced than the loan guarantee scheme, and does not appear to represent a net cost to taxpayers.

A possible justification for the overly generous nature of the U.S. schemes may be the need to take extreme measures given the depth of the current crisis, but this begs the question of what the regulators have planned in terms of exit from the guarantees and recapitalization. The egregious underpricing of the guarantees raises the possibility of the banks "asset substituting" inefficiently (for example, by undertaking acquisitions that are profitable *only* with the guarantee). The schemes further shield the unhealthy institutions and their management from market discipline, exacerbating moral hazard concerns. The typically sticky nature of regulatory responses during past crises raises the disturbing question: Are these efforts merely sowing the seeds of the next crisis?

15.1 THE RESCUE PACKAGE

Of the three rescue programs adopted in the United States, the most complete information is available about the loan guarantee scheme, so that is where we begin. Note that a fourth prong of the rescue effort, the Troubled Asset Relief Program (TARP), was abandoned in November 2008, and is therefore not discussed here, though it appears to have reappeared in the ad hoc bailout of Citigroup in the form of a government backstop guarantee against losses (beyond some threshold) on a large portfolio of assets, including some toxic housing-related assets.

The Loan Guarantee Scheme

The contours of the loan guarantee program were announced on October 14, 2008. Administered by the FDIC, it is in essence a simple scheme. It covers *all* financial institutions in the United States, guarantees *all* senior unsecured debt issued by these institutions, and charges *all* participants a flat fee of 75 basis points (bps) per annum for providing this coverage. More precisely:

- *Who may participate. All* banks, depository institutions, and savings and loan companies in the United States are eligible to participate in the program. In November 2008, the program was extended to include GE Capital, the financial services arm of General Electric (GE), making GE the first company with large industrial operations to participate in the loan guarantee program.
- *Optionalities in participation.* Eligible institutions were given a one-time option of *not* participating in the guarantee program, in which case they were required to communicate this to the FDIC before November 12, 2008. To our knowledge, no major institution opted out. For all participating institutions, *all* senior unsecured loans issued between October 14, 2008, and June 30, 2009, will be guaranteed by the FDIC for a maximum period of three years or until maturity of the debt, whichever comes first. The one exception to this blanket coverage is if a participating institution informed the FDIC (again prior to November 12, 2008) of its desire to also issue during this period *nonguaranteed* long-term debt maturing after June 30, 2012, in which case the guarantee applies to all new senior unsecured issues except these long-term issues.
- *Extent of coverage.* The maximum amount of liabilities issued by a single institution that will be guaranteed by the FDIC is 125 percent of the outstanding senior unsecured liabilities of the institution as of

September 30, 2008; no cap has so far been proposed on the overall liabilities that will be guaranteed under the plan.

- *Fee structure*. Each participating institution will pay a flat 75 basis points per annum on the entire amount of its new senior unsecured liabilities (subject to the 125 percent cap); if the institution has informed the FDIC of its intent to also issue nonguaranteed long-term debt, then the 75 basis points fee applies to the guaranteed portion of its new debt issues. But in the latter case, the institution must also pay a one-time fee of 37.5 basis points on that portion of its senior unsecured liabilities as of September 30, 2008, that will mature on or before June 30, 2009.

The UK Loan Guarantee Scheme

The loan guarantee program of the UK government offers, in every respect except for the maturity dimension, a sharp contrast to the U.S. program. Nine large financial institutions have been identified in the United Kingdom as initially eligible for the program (though more may be added later at the discretion of the UK Treasury). Senior unsecured borrowings of these institutions made on or prior to April 13, 2009, will be guaranteed by the UK government for a period of three years or until maturity of the issue, whichever comes first. Participation in the program is optional, not just at the institutional level, but at the *issue level*; that is, a prospective borrower wishing to issue a "guaranteed liability" applies to the UK government for a guarantee on that particular issue. Limits on the total volume of guarantees that may be sought by any one institution have not been laid out explicitly, but the UK Treasury has announced a cap of GBP 250 billion as the maximum amount of liabilities that will be guaranteed under the scheme. Of particular significance, pricing is institution-specific: An institution seeking a guarantee on an issue will be charged an annual fee of 50 basis points *plus* that institution's median five-year credit default swap spread observed in the 12 months preceding October 7, 2008.

15.2 THE IMPLICATIONS: QUESTIONS OF INTEREST

The contrasting structures of these programs raise at least two questions of policy and economic interest. First, what are the implications to the taxpayer of the vastly different pricing schemes? Second, what are the economic consequences of the very different participation optionalities and pricing methods?

Pricing Implications

Even a casual glance at the relevant numbers (see Table 15.1) indicates that the UK Treasury's fees for providing the guarantee, which vary between less than 109 basis points for HSBC Holdings at the low end to over 178 basis points for Nationwide, are a lot higher than the proposed U.S. flat fee of 75 basis points for all comers. Are the British banks that much riskier or is the American scheme underpricing the guarantee provided?

A natural benchmark "fair price" to use in this analysis is the three-year credit default swap (CDS) spread on the borrowing institution. This three-year spread represents the cost of insurance on that institution's senior unsecured credit, and is based on the market's perception of that risk. Which day's CDS spreads should we use? CDS spreads displayed considerable variability during the period October/November 2008. Spreads were exceptionally high in early October (Morgan Stanley's three-year CDS spread was, for example, over 1,600 bps on October 10, 2008), but came down considerably by early November. Taking a conservative approach, we use the average three-year CDS spreads during the month of November 2008. Tables 15.1 and 15.2 describe the average spreads over this period for selected U.S. and UK institutions.

For the UK institutions, the average spread was 109.6 bps; the averages were tightly bunched, ranging from a low of 71.2 bps for Abbey National to a high of 135.7 for Barclays. The cost of the UK loan guarantee is higher

TABLE 15.1 Credit Default Swap Fees and Loan Guarantee Fee for the UK Banks

Bank	Median 3-Year CDS Fee in Year Ending Oct. 7, 2008	Median 5-Year CDS Fee in Year Ending Oct. 7, 2008	UK Loan Guarantee Fee (Median 5-Year CDS + 50 bps)	"Fair Price" of Guarantee (Average 3-Year CDS Spread in Nov. 2008)
Abbey National	56.5	72.6	112.6	71.2
Barclays	66.0	81.4	131.4	135.7
HBOS	93.3	112.7	162.7	117.4
HSBC Holdings	48.5	58.8	108.8	102.1
Lloyds TSB	55.6	62.5	112.5	82.7
Nationwide	122.8	128.3	178.3	123.0
Royal Bank of Scotland	73.5	85.9	135.9	120.8
Std. Chartered	50.3	67.5	117.5	124.1
Average	**70.8**	**83.7**	**133.7**	**109.6**

Source: Datastream; CDS fees in bps.

TABLE 15.2 CDS Fees and Loan Guarantee Fee for Selected U.S. Banks

Bank	Median 3-Year CDS Fee in Year Ending Oct. 7, 2008	Median 5-Year CDS Fee in Year Ending Oct. 7, 2008	U.S. Loan Guarantee Fee	"Fair Price" of Guarantee (Average 3-Year CDS Spread in Nov. 2008)
Bank of America	71.0	85.0	75	126.0
Citigroup	100.0	115.2	75	238.3
Goldman Sachs	109.0	107.0	75	321.0
JPMorgan Chase	70.6	85.0	75	115.8
Morgan Stanley	174.1	159.4	75	475.7
Average	104.9	110.3	75	255.4

Source: Datastream; all fees in bps.

than these three-year CDS spreads in every single case, and is on average about 24 basis points higher. Thus, the program is fairly priced, and perhaps even slightly overpriced (which seems reasonable considering that the market price is for a private, not a sovereign, guarantee). On a principal amount of GBP 250 billion, the net tax on the borrowing institutions works out to be about GBP 1.8 billion over the three-year horizon.

The U.S. numbers present a very different picture. The average three-year CDS spread in November was 255.4 bps, and ranged between a low of 115.8 bps for JPMorgan Chase and a high of 475.7 bps for Morgan Stanley. In every single case, the CDS spread is far above the 75 bps cost of the U.S. loan guarantee, implying a huge subsidy from the government to the financial institutions. Averaged over the five institutions in the table, the subsidy amounts to a little over 180 bps per year, which on the program size of $1.4 trillion works out to over $70 billion over the three-year horizon. By any standards, this represents a very large giveaway, one that must be justified on the basis of the benefits expected from the program, but no such arguments have been forthcoming from the FDIC or the U.S. Treasury.

The one-size-fits-all pricing structure in the United States also means that the subsidies are unevenly distributed. A specific example will help highlight the nature of this subsidy. Consider General Electric, which through its financial services arm GE Capital was granted entry into the loan guarantee program on November 12, 2008. Roughly $139 billion of GE debt would be eligible for protection.[2] GE's average three-year CDS spread in the first three weeks of November was around 430 bps, so the 75 bps cost of protection represents a savings of over 350 basis points per annum. On a principal amount of $139 billion, the subsidy to GE alone amounts over a three-year period to over $13 billion.

The benchmark prices used in the preceding analysis are the actual market prices of protection, so the resulting estimates provide a ballpark true economic cost of providing the guarantee. A different question is how the pricing fares against three-year CDS spreads in more normal market times; that is, would the prices have been approximately fair in less turbulent times? For this purpose, we take the comparison point to be the median spread during the one year preceding the announcement of the guarantee program; more precisely, we use the median three-year CDS spread observed in the 12 months preceding October 7, 2008. This is the period used in the UK scheme. Table 15.1 also contains these numbers for the same list of select U.S. and UK financial institutions.

The numbers are not comforting to U.S. taxpayers. Even based on data from more normal times, a very large subsidy is provided to banks in the United States. The average three-year CDS spread for the chosen institutions works out to 104.9 basis points against the fee of 75 basis points. This means a subsidy of 30 basis points per guaranteed dollar per annum, or about $12 billion to $13 billion over three years on a guaranteed principal amount of $1.4 trillion.

The UK numbers are very different. The average CDS spread for UK banks is around 70.8 basis points, about 63 basis points *less* than the average fee of 133.7 basis points. The UK fee effectively represents a *tax* on participating banks that amounts, over the three years of the scheme, to over GBP 4.5 billion. Even if only the four weakest banks participate, then the tax figure still works out to GBP 3.3 billion.

In summary, the U.S. program involves a very substantial underpricing of the sovereign guarantee and results in a transfer ranging between $13 billion and $75 billion from taxpayers to the banks, with the higher figure likely to be a more accurate picture of the true cost. The UK scheme looks to be a breakeven scheme, and may even net a small profit to the taxpayers.

Optionalities, Pricing, and the Economic Implications

Within two weeks of the scheme's announcement, the importance of issue-level optionality in the UK scheme was highlighted by the contrasting actions of two British banks, Lloyds TSB and Barclays. On October 17, 2008, Lloyds TSB elected to issue a GBP 400 million debt issue *without* seeking a guarantee. Lloyds' median CDS spread during the 12 months preceding October 7, 2008, was only 62 basis points, among the lowest of any UK or U.S. financial institution. Four days later, on October 21, 2008, Barclays announced an issue of GBP 1 billion in three-year senior unsecured bonds backed by the UK government's guarantee. Since Barclays' median five-year CDS spread over the 12 months to October 7, 2008, was around 82 basis points, the cost to Barclays of this protection was 132 basis points—about GBP 13.2 million—per annum.

The UK scheme is likely to lead to what economists call a *separating equilibrium*. Banks (such as HSBC and perhaps Lloyds TSB) whose credit risk is low can opt out since the loan guarantee scheme provides them little subsidy relative to the fair price for guaranteeing their debt (and potentially imposes a cost). In contrast, banks with relatively poor creditworthiness will find it costly to opt out and thus will likely avail themselves of the scheme. Why is the signal to opt out credible? That is, why can unhealthy banks not mimic it? Banks whose balance sheets are healthy can credibly stay with the market and allow the market to generate relevant information about their health at the time they raise debt on their own without government guarantee. In contrast, banks whose balance sheets are weak will find it costly to let investors learn about their books at the time of issuing debt without the guarantee. Thus, separation induced by optionality in the guarantee scheme will reveal to the markets the banks that are healthy and the ones that are not, enabling banks and markets to provide credit at prices that more accurately reflect the credit risk of counterparties. Such pricing of credit risk and continued information generation (at least) about the healthier banks that opt out are important in ensuring that lending markets continue to function in an orderly manner once guarantees are removed. Quality signaling through separation also makes it costly for the unhealthy banks to raise debt and equity capital in future. In short, the UK scheme appears designed to achieve a market-style outcome, and an eventual withdrawal of the government, at little (and possibly even negative) cost to taxpayers.

In contrast, the U.S. program offers very little by way of optionality to the banks—a one-time option on participation and a limited option to issue nonguaranteed long-maturity debt. The scheme implicitly forces a *pooling* outcome in which *all* banks, regardless of their financial health, will elect to participate because it is not possible to reenter later should conditions worsen and capital become even harder to access. To this stick is attached the carrot of guarantee rates that seem to be heavily subsidized relative to their fair price.

The pooling outcome may keep the system reliant on government guarantees for a longer period since it does not facilitate a better pricing by banks and markets of individual banks' credit risk. It effectively gets healthy banks to subsidize the borrowing of unhealthy ones and does not impair capital-raising ability by the latter. The scheme is best characterized as a bailout that transfers taxpayer funds to the banking sector.

But might the UK scheme end up being too harsh under some scenarios? Perhaps so, and this one qualification goes in favor of the U.S. scheme of forced participation. The UK scheme implicitly relies on the assumption that following the capital injections, even the unhealthy players are now solvent to a point that they are simply unlikely to fail in the foreseeable future. If this assumption were proven false, say because of the financial crisis deepening for whatever reason, a bank that opted out believing itself to be healthy may fail, potentially precipitating a new systemic crisis. That is, the strength of the UK scheme—its attempting to achieve a market-style outcome—could also be its Achilles' heel in the case of further market stress. The U.S. scheme, by being a government bailout, has the one virtue in that it might smooth over such stress in the future.

Postscript

Despite the underpricing, the U.S. scheme has been slow to take off. In the first month after the scheme was announced, not a single U.S. financial institution used the guarantee to raise funds from the market. In contrast, by the second week of November, British banks had already issued over $21 billion in government-guaranteed bonds. The law firm of Sullivan and Cromwell, acting on behalf of nine leading U.S. institutions,[3] noted that the primary problem was that the FDIC guarantee was not "full, irrevocable, and unconditional" but rather dependent on the domestic bankruptcy process. This largely legal issue appears to have made the guarantee unattractive from the market's perspective. Perhaps more interestingly, Sullivan and Cromwell also requested, on behalf of the firm's clients, that issue-level optionality be introduced into the U.S. scheme along the lines of the UK scheme. At the time of writing, the FDIC has yet to make decisions regarding these suggestions, and only one bank (Goldman Sachs) has reported plans to raise money from the markets under the guarantee program.

15.3 THE CAPITAL INJECTION SCHEME

The second component of the financial system rescue package in the United States is injecting capital into the banking sector. A total of $250 billion has been set aside for this purpose, of which over two-thirds has already been used. A sum of $125 billion went toward recapitalizing nine leading financial institutions (JPMorgan Chase, Bank of America, Goldman Sachs, Morgan Stanley, Citigroup, Merrill Lynch, Wells Fargo, Bank of New York Mellon, and State Street), which were reportedly not given a choice concerning participation. The sums invested in these institutions range from

$2 billion in State Street to $25 billion each in Citigroup and JPMorgan Chase. All other U.S. banks are also eligible and may apply for participation in the program. In early November, the *Wall Street Journal* reported that around 1,800 banks were expected to apply, making it very likely that the funds required will far exceed the original earmark of $250 billion.

No precise information on the pricing of preferred shares was available at the time of writing, but the Treasury has announced that it will receive preferred stock "on the same terms" as other preferred shareholders. Banks can buy back the Treasury's stake after three years, if they have issued sufficient stock on their own by that point. The Treasury will also receive warrants for common stock equal to 15 percent of the preferred stock, convertible at the trailing 20-day average stock price when the preferred stock is issued. The preferred stock will pay a 5 percent dividend for the first five years, and 9 percent thereafter. We note that these dividend figures are lower than the 10 percent that Morgan Stanley and Goldman Sachs each committed to paying private preferred stock investors in September 2008.

It is furthermore noteworthy that this injection of public funds has not been accompanied by any real restrictions on the banks' operations. The U.S. government will have no voice in management, nor has there been any discussion of replacing current management; those who led their firms into the current debacle continue to remain at the helm in the new dispensation. There has been little discussion by the Treasury even on the issue of placing limits on managerial compensation as long as the firm remains on taxpayer money. Far less discussion has been focused on the incentive system for traders and others that some have argued encouraged an atmosphere of excessive risk taking.[4] Indeed, recent reports suggest that despite the financial system and many of the institutions remaining alive only on account of public funds, the vast majority of traders and investment bankers will continue to receive bonuses in 2008.

The British scheme offers a contrast of sorts here as well. GBP 50 billion has been set aside for recapitalizations. Participation is voluntary, and, in fact, the UK chancellor's statement of November 18, 2008, makes it clear that there is no automatic right of access to the scheme. At a minimum, participating institutions will be required to submit credible plans for raising further capital from the markets and reaching an adequate level of capitalization. For example, Barclays has agreed to raise GBP 10 billion by next spring, while HSBC announced an injection of GBP 750 million of capital into its UK banking operations.[5]

Only sketchy pricing information is available on the UK scheme, but the chancellor's statement of November 18, 2008, says that the price offered to the UK Treasury must be at a discount to the market price and must carry a competitive coupon rate. Further, recapitalized banks must maintain loans to the nonfinancial sector at 2007 levels, help people struggling with mortgages, and accept a governmental say on compensation, board membership, and dividends.

The UK recapitalization scheme is undoubtedly tougher on banks than its U.S. counterpart. But it may already be having the intended effect of pushing the banks toward the market. In November 2008, Barclays bypassed the government recapitalization offer and raised preferred capital directly from the markets at terms even more unfavorable than offered by the government; presumably, Barclays was motivated by the twin desire to ward off government interference in its operations as well as to avoid the stigma of appearing to survive on taxpayer funds.

15.4 THE COMMERCIAL PAPER FUNDING FACILITY

The Federal Reserve Bank of New York announced the creation of the Commercial Paper Funding Facility (CPFF) on October 27, 2008. The CPFF was created in response to the freezing up of the commercial paper (CP) market, which, in turn, resulted from the liquidity pressures facing money market mutual funds and other customary CP buyers. The CPFF aims to provide a liquidity backstop to U.S. issuers of commercial paper and will purchase as much as $2.4 trillion in unsecured and asset-backed commercial paper (ABCP) of selected issuers.

Participation in the CPFF is open to all U.S. issuers of commercial paper, which includes U.S. issuers with a foreign parent. The maximum amount of a single issuer's CP that will be purchased under the CPFF is the highest amount of U.S. dollar-denominated commercial paper that the issuer had outstanding between January 1, 2008, and August 31, 2008.

But while participation is open to all, the CPFF will buy only commercial paper rated at least A-1/P-1/F-1 by the rating agencies. (A-1 and A-1+ are the highest ratings afforded commercial paper by Standard & Poor's; P-1 is the highest rating awarded by Moody's; and F-1 and F-1+ are the highest ratings offered by Fitch). This represents an important point of difference between the FDIC's loan guarantee program and the CPFF; as we have seen, in the former case, all senior unsecured debt issues of all eligible participants are covered.

By contrast, the pricing scheme adopted by the Fed has the same one-size-fits-all flavor as the FDIC's loan guarantee program. All unsecured commercial paper purchased under the program will be priced at a 100 bps spread to the overnight index swap (OIS) rate, while all asset-backed commercial paper will be priced at a 300 bps spread to the OIS rate.

How does this 100 bps spread compare to the three-month CP-OIS spreads (for CP rated A-1/P-1/F-1)? If we take the average spread between

September 1, 2007, and August 1, 2008, we obtain a figure of roughly 55 bps. In September and October 2008, this spread widened sharply to an average level of over 150 bps and had been around 200 bps for about two weeks when the Fed announced the creation of the CPFF. (The volumes in the CP market had also fallen sharply during this period.) Taking all this into account, the Fed's rate of 100 bps over OIS rates appears fair, or at least not one that involves a huge taxpayer subsidy to the borrowing companies.

15.5 POLICY RECOMMENDATIONS

Let us start with the question: What might be the rationale for not relying on market indicators of bank credit quality in the U.S. loan guarantee schemes? One argument advanced has been that there are over 8,000 small banks in the United States, which too are suffering from house-price declines, and which also are eligible for the loan guarantees. For many of these banks, there are no readily available market indicators such as CDS spreads. This argument is weak. There is "tiering" in bank regulation at almost all levels, starting with which banks are required to hold reserves with the central bank and continuing to which banks are accorded the too-big-to-fail guarantees. A similar tiering would have sufficed here: For large banks above a threshold (or for all banks where CDS spreads were available), the pricing of the scheme could have relied on market prices and thus would reward banks that did better. For smaller banks (or banks without CDS spreads), a flat fee could have been applied based on average CDS spreads for other banks. At a minimum, the transfers of taxpayer funds to large banks such as Goldman Sachs and Morgan Stanley could have been avoided under this simple alternative.

Our overall conclusion is that properties of the UK bailout plan appear better grounded in sound economic principles. While bailouts are unavoidable under extreme economic stress, they ought to be designed and priced correctly even in such times. Some simple rules for regulators to follow are these:

- Do not employ a one-size-fits-all approach in charging for bailout packages.

And as corollaries to this overall principle:

- Rely on market prices wherever available.
- Reward those institutions that did well more relative to those that did not.

In addition, regulators should take advantage of the leverage offered to them by the bailout and review incentive systems within banks that led to the crisis in the first place.

By and large, adherence to these principles would reduce any unintended consequences (moral hazard) and ensure that the outcomes from the bailout represent a rescue of the system but still in a manner that accrues no undue advantage to a small set of institutions. When bailouts are organized in such orderly fashion, market participants are still disciplined ex ante by the prospect of relative gains and losses.

It is also important to ask what the regulators have planned in terms of exit from the guarantees and recapitalization programs. By not pricing the guarantees correctly and offering them for a period as long as three years, have the U.S. regulators raised the possibility of substitution by banks into inefficient assets (for example, by undertaking acquisitions that are profitable *only* with the guarantee)? The typically sticky nature of regulatory responses during past crises makes planned exit an important issue for regulators to ponder, lest we sow the seeds of the next crisis. When the economic outlook improves, we do not want abundant liquidity at artificially low prices (due to guarantees), as this may once again lead to the sequence of events just witnessed—excessive leverage, inefficient allocations of capital, asset price bubbles, and, alas, crashes.

NOTES

1. This article was written in early December 2008, and the information we have used was current at that point. Of course, in a fluid environment that has characterized the crisis right since its inception, things have been changing continuously, so readers should be aware that changes to the policies are being proposed on an ongoing basis.
2. Paul Glader, "Government Will Back Some GE Loans," *Wall Street Journal*, November 13, 2008.
3. JPMorgan Chase, Bank of America, Goldman Sachs, Morgan Stanley, Citigroup, Merrill Lynch, Wells Fargo, Bank of New York Mellon, and State Street.
4. See Chapter 7, "Corporate Governance in the Modern Financial Sector," and Chapter 8, "Rethinking Compensation in Financial Firms."
5. See the statement of the U.K. chancellor on October 13, 2008 (www.hm-treasury.gov.uk/statement_chx_131008.htm).

CHAPTER 16

Mortgages and Households

Andrew Caplin and Thomas F. Cooley

16.1 BACKGROUND

The damage caused by the collapse of the housing and housing finance sectors of the economy is spreading at an alarming rate. Foreclosure activity jumped 81 percent in 2008, with more than 3 million foreclosure filings on 2.3 million properties.[1] The increasing number of households who are upside down on their mortgages poses a growing threat to the financial system and the economy. There are large deadweight losses associated with default and foreclosure. The process is long, slow, and expensive. Moreover, there are externalities that are associated with properties that do foreclose in that they contaminate the value of neighboring properties, creating a further downward spiral in property prices. Absent some solution, many households may be better off defaulting on their mortgages.

This issue is also critical to restoring stability, because reducing losses to default and foreclosure will help stabilize the financial system by reducing the actual losses (and the uncertainty about them) that are passed through the financial system to the holders of the mortgages and mortgage-backed securities. Default losses are concentrated in the "first loss" and mezzanine tranches of CDOs, which has made them highly toxic to the financial institutions holding them. These have added to the instability in the financial system around the world.

Policy makers have paid lip service to the mortgage problem over the past year, but most of the solutions that have been offered so far have been astonishingly ineffective. Without a more thoughtful policy response than we have seen so far, we risk more unfocused programs that have little chance of success. Many of the proposals that have been on the table are potentially extremely costly and will saddle our children with massive tax obligations. Our generation will effectively be dimming the lights for the next generation.

There are many who believe that this is not an issue that merits government intervention. People made bad decisions, bought houses that were too big that they could not afford, and must now suffer the consequences, as should the investors who lent them the money. And, indeed, it is true that many loans were simply bad and there is no way homeowners could recover. At the other extreme are people who advocate brute-force intervention to try to eliminate much of the uncertainty associated with mortgages even if at great cost to the taxpayer.

We argue that there are grounds for government intervention because there is a market failure and there is an externality being created by the impending tsunami of foreclosures. But government intervention does not mean intervention on a huge scale as in the many proposals that would have the government assume, refinance, or guarantee mortgages.[2] Many of these plans imply huge costs to the taxpayer and have the potential to create additional moral hazard in the economy, something that is already abundant as a result of the many other government interventions that have occurred. In our view, an effective program would have the following attributes:

- It should align the interests of lenders and borrowers, which means they should share costs associated with the fall in house prices, as well as potential gains associated with their recovery.
- It should avoid *creating* incentives for default or delinquency.
- It should respect borrowers' ability to pay in the short run *and* the long run to avoid secondary default.
- It should provide a contractual form that is useful in the long run.
- It should bridge the contractual divide that separates borrowers from investors in securitized mortgages. This cannot be left to the household.

We present a plan of action that would greatly speed market normalization, reduce default and foreclosure, and increase asset values of holders of mortgage-backed securities, all the while costing taxpayers far less now than they will be due later if the policy is not implemented. Our plan has the virtue that it works simultaneously on the immediate problems and on the longer-term structural problems of mortgage markets. However, it is not a panacea: given that many who bought houses were unqualified to own them, there will need to be foreclosures.

16.2 INCOMPLETE CONTRACTS AND DEBT-FOR-EQUITY SWAPS

The centerpiece of our proposal is the renegotiation of underwater mortgages via debt-for-equity swaps. When a well-run business runs into an unforeseen problem, those who lent it money will commonly negotiate such a swap. The recent recapitalization of General Motors Acceptance Corporation (GMAC) and many other lending institutions is based on debt holders agreeing to replace debt with equity in the newly reorganized firm. It is a commonly used device in restructurings and recapitalizations.

A debt-for-equity swap replaces the fixed obligation of a debt contract with the more flexible obligation of an equity contract, in which the amount of the ultimate repayment depends on how well the business does. Such renegotiation is rationalized by the necessary incompleteness of the original contract. Both borrower and lender recognize at contract signing that there are circumstances that may make it impossible to make the previously scheduled debt payments, even though the business remains viable. Obvious examples are a massive unforeseen spike in the price of some material input due to a supply disruption; damage to transportation infrastructure (e.g., roads and railroads) necessary for efficient business; and a broad general turndown in the market. Rather than try to specify all such contingencies up front, it is taken for granted by both parties that the contract terms can be revisited in unusual contingencies and suitable adjustments can then be made. This is the essential economic rationalization of ex-post changes to the initial contract: it is simply not feasible to list all contingencies in the initial contract. Adjustable rate mortgages were seen as an improvement in the standard fixed rate contract because they built more contingency into the terms of the initial contract. We are proposing a contractual form that incorporates a contingency based on housing prices.

The standard fixed rate mortgage contract is a prime example of an incomplete contract. It commits a household to making fixed monetary payments for 30 years. Yet it is implicitly understood that such payments will not be possible in various states of the world. In some such contingencies, economic logic dictates enforcement of the contract. In others, it dictates large-scale renegotiation. This is the situation in which we find ourselves today. It is hard to see who benefits when masses of households default on their mortgages. Default and foreclosure are long, slow, and expensive processes, with the cost of foreclosure estimated to be at least $70,000 on a median home price of $200,000. Moreover, there are externalities that are associated with properties that are foreclosed in that they contaminate the value of neighboring properties.

We propose that some form of debt-for-equity swap be made available for households that find themselves thrust into problems by forces largely beyond their control. It was not foreseen in the initial mortgages that home values around the country would crash simultaneously with massive declines in income. Some may argue that it should have been foreseen, but that is beside the point now. Given that this negative outcome is largely out of the control of the individual homeowner and was the result of bad assumptions by both lenders and buyers, renegotiation is a viable solution that can balance the interests of both.

Shared Appreciation Example

Consider a homeowner who recently bought a house for $200,000 with a down payment of 10 percent and a standard mortgage for $180,000. Suppose now that the value of the house falls by 25 percent, leaving the homeowner upside down by $30,000. Given this negative equity, the household has an incentive to default. Recognizing that both the household and the lender lose heavily in the event, a debt-for-equity restructuring is in order. In such a restructuring the lender swaps part of the fixed mortgage obligation for a claim on home equity. For example, the lender might replace the existing loan with a standard mortgage of $135,000 (90 percent of house value) together with an equity claim giving the lender 50 percent of the value of the home above the initial debt of $135,000. The payoff to the lender on the equity portion at point of termination after, say, five years would depend on the value of the home.

- If the house stayed constant in value at $150,000, the borrower's obligation on the equity portion would be $7,500: 50 percent of the value above $135,000.
- If the house rose in value back to $200,000, the borrower's obligation on the equity portion would be $32,500: 50 percent of the value above $135,000.
- If the house fell in value to $100,000, the borrower would have no payment obligation on the equity portion, since the value was below $135,000.

Debt-for-equity swaps of this kind have many of the same virtues for households that they have for businesses. By reducing the fixed stream of payments, the renegotiation gives the borrower breathing room to recover. By lowering the fixed obligation, the renegotiation provides a strong incentive to manage the assets effectively.

16.3 \ AN ACTION PLAN

There are many proposals on the table and many programs in place that are intended to address the problems of households and their mortgages. Some of them include a debt-for-equity swap as part of the proposed solution. Unfortunately, these programs have not been sufficiently holistic to achieve success on a large scale.[3] One reason for this is that, while many servicing agreements give the servicers broad power to restructure mortgages, there is reluctance to do so because of the threat of lawsuits by investors.

Rather than list the many reasons for the current failure of large-scale renegotiation, our goal in this chapter is to show that they can all be overcome with appropriate actions on the part of regulators and legislators. We present here a five-part plan of action to overcome barriers to rational equity-based modifications of existing mortgage contracts.

Specify the Terms of Debt-for-Equity Swaps

Not all debt-for-equity swaps will be sensible or successful. For that reason it is important to specify a set of criteria that should apply. In practice, since such swaps currently fall afoul of various tax rules[4] (see Caplin, Cunningham, Engler, and Pollock [2008]), it will be necessary for legislators and regulators to carve out exceptions for renegotiations that satisfy key criteria. The following list is far from complete or comprehensive, yet indicates some of the desiderata.

- *Affordability.* It is essential that the fixed portion of the mortgage be affordable to the homeowners. Current restructurings peg payment streams to be between 31 and 38 percent of gross income, which is a reasonable standard for affordability. It may also be relevant to offer qualifying borrowers a Federal Housing Administration (FHA) guarantee on some part of the written-down mortgage. To reduce the cost to the FHA, one might limit the FHA guarantee for a first mortgage to a maximum of, say, 50 percent of the newly assessed value of the home. This would leave much of the residual risk with the original lender, ensuring that renegotiation would take place only in circumstances in which secondary default was unlikely.
- *Restoration of positive homeowner equity.* As in the preceding example, a key component of the debt-for-equity swap is to reduce the fixed debt sufficiently far to bring the homeowner to a position of positive equity. Hence a qualifying renegotiation would have to reset the fixed portion of the debt at least far enough to eliminate the homeowner's negative equity, and ideally somewhat further. A reasonable starting point would be 90 percent of (carefully reassessed) market value, but there should be other options open, provided the restructured loan passes standards that make secondary default unlikely.
- *Common interest in future appreciation.* It is crucial to provide homeowners with incentives to provide proper home maintenance. For this reason, it would be appropriate to insist on homeowners benefiting from

increases in house value, capturing a minimum of (say) 30 percent of future increases in value. Ultimately, this aligns the incentives of the homeowner and the lender, who both benefit when the equity in the house is restored.

- *Minimum term and assumability.* The term of the equity portion would have to be a minimum of (say) five years to provide time for the market and the homeowner to recover. The mortgage would also be assumable, so that any new buyer would inherit the borrower's obligation to pay future appreciation.

Create an Appropriate Fiscal and Accounting Framework

Shared appreciation mortgages were pioneered in the United States some 40 years ago, but have been allowed to languish due to an archaic IRS-imposed block. This institutional roadblock could be removed at the stroke of a pen. It is our hope and belief that the necessary steps will be taken expeditiously.

In addition to clarification of tax rules, changes in accounting rules are critical to the attractiveness of debt-for-equity renegotiations. One of the factors holding up renegotiation is the need for those writing down mortgages to acknowledge their losses in their accounts. Even when there are underlying losses, there is an incentive for the holders of mortgage assets to retain the assets at full value on their books, to avoid appearing insolvent, insolvent though they are.

Lenders that share in future equity may be due more than the original amount of the loan if the housing market recovers. With a little bit of creativity on the side of the banking regulators, it would be easy to restore the situation to sanity. There is much leeway in designing the valuation criteria for such hitherto unfamiliar assets as equity claims on residential homes. As has happened in past episodes (e.g., the Cottage Savings case during the savings and loan crisis), the federal banking authorities should use this leeway to prevent accounting rules from continuing to distort behavior.

As an essentially costless additional incentive for a write-down, it could be agreed that profits on the housing equity in this form of write-down be free of capital gains tax, as they would be now for the homeowner.

Demonstrate the Viability of Debt-for-Equity Swaps

Taxpayers are indirect owners of a growing proportion of the underwater mortgages. Hence there is the opportunity as well as the motivation for developing demonstration projects that clarify how appropriate debt-for-equity swaps can increase the economic return for holders of mortgage-backed securities. These projects would also enable market participants to gain understanding about which forms of debt-for-equity renegotiation recover most value.

In addition to aiding in the current episode, such learning would lay the foundations for a broader set of mortgage contracts. After a debt-for-equity renegotiation, the lender has a claim to housing equity that could be packaged, priced, and sold. By making visible how valuable these equity claims are, the demonstration projects would reveal how the market in equity strips should function, which would bring long-run as well as short-run benefits.

Address the Legal Obstacles Posed by Securitization

Currently, the contractual and legal issues that separate borrowers from investors in securitized mortgages are being allowed to destroy value for both homeowners and security owners. Even an economically rational restructuring of the underlying mortgages could be challenged legally even though it may be in the interest of the majority of investors to restructure. One problem in this regard is that those holding the lower tranches may wish to hold out for a more generous buyout scheme, either from other owners or from the federal government. Another problem is that existing commercial law allows loan servicers to make only changes that are in the holders' best interest—"not materially adverse to the Owner." The law also says that if a mortgage is in default or in the servicer's opinion close to it, then the servicer has no authority to make changes in interest rates, principal amount, or time of payments.

As with the original mortgage, the fundamental problem is one of contractual incompleteness. The owners of the various tranches of payments on a set of mortgages have different interests. For that reason, a contract is needed to guide them as to appropriate behavior in cases of disagreement. As ever, the initial contract among the owners of these divided interests in the mortgage-backed securities was incomplete. While giving minority-interest owners powerful blocking rights may be reasonable in the normal contingencies for which the contract was designed, it was very poorly designed for the highly unusual and largely unforeseen contingency in which we find ourselves. Hence renegotiation is rational. Yet there has been little practice in such renegotiations, resulting in the current impasse. Debt-for-equity swaps offer a way out of this impasse.

Congress can make clear through the proposed demonstration projects that more value is preserved for all the divided interests when the various owners agree to renegotiate the underlying mortgages using debt-for-equity swaps. With this known, servicers could engage in such renegotiations with the support of the majority of the security owners. Even in cases in which the divided interests were blocking renegotiations, new buyers could in principle step in, reconsolidate the interests in the underlying mortgages, and thereby recover more economic value. In case such rational renegotiation does not eventuate, Congress should make ready a law allowing servicers to modify loans by invoking a standard such as "a good-faith effort to advance the collective interests of holders." The precise measure would have to be carefully designed to avoid running into the Constitutional stipulation providing that "Congress shall make no law impairing the obligations of contract." Setting up hearings on just how to accomplish this while sharpening legislative pencils might bring home to all parties the seriousness with which future holdout behavior will be viewed.

Simplify Secondary Default

Currently, the process of foreclosing on a property is prolonged and costly, and results in continued wastage of the property and damage to the neighborhood. Any homeowners who benefit from a debt-for-equity swap should waive certain rights if they default on their written-down mortgage. This would reduce future costs to asset holders and the damage to the surrounding neighborhood. This measure would give lenders an incentive to offer more aggressive write-downs, and would make clear to homeowners that they must not accept a write-down if there is a high likelihood of further default.

One way to simplify secondary default would be for homeowners benefiting from a major write-down to agree to waive the right to a judicial foreclosure. More thoroughgoing would be placing title to the home into escrow, reverting to the owner only if payments are made on the written-down mortgage for, say, two years, and otherwise residing with the lender.

16.4 COMPARISON WITH ALTERNATIVE POLICIES

Our plan is but one of many that are either in place or under consideration for restructuring mortgages. To explain what we see as the advantages of our plan, we note some key respects in which it differs from various alternatives.

Perhaps not surprisingly, we view plans such as ours based on debt-for-equity swaps as having several positive features that are missing in other plans. While a plan such as ours is unlikely to be the whole solution, we are certain that it should be *part* of the solution.

■ **Restructuring based on debt-for-equity swaps reduces the incentives for default or delinquency now and in the future, greatly reducing the odds of secondary default.**

In this respect it compares favorably to many of the recent loan restructurings, including that introduced by the Federal Deposit Insurance Corporation (FDIC) and by such private-sector parties (whose toxic assets are now owned by the taxpayers) as JPMorgan Chase, Citigroup, and Countrywide. These generally involve temporary reductions in payments, but no reduction in the loan balance outstanding. Such restructurings achieve the worst of both worlds. They leave borrowers with either a hefty balloon payment if they sell or a very long time horizon for rebuilding equity in their home. With attenuated terms, homeowners effectively become renters with all of the adverse incentives that implies. Either secondary defaults will be massive, or there will be further renegotiations down the road, with the taxpayers getting stuck with the entire bill.

Mortgage loan cram-downs are ineffective because they force a household to get into bankruptcy before restructuring is forced on the lender. Even though private lenders and servicers like Citi have recently agreed to this form of loan restructuring, it seems completely wasteful. It forces the household into a bankruptcy proceeding and puts the renegotiation in the hands of the wrong people. Its only role is to give the renegotiation legal cover.

The FDIC plan is available only to families who are delinquent for two or more months. The Hope for Homeowners plan is targeted at homeowners who are three months delinquent. What kind of incentives does that create? Clearly if you want to restructure under those terms you would stop paying your mortgage.

■ **Due to the sharing of equity and the simplification of secondary default, homeowners are forced to give up something to restructure.**

This is an important deterrent to unnecessary renegotiation. Those who can manage to continue making their payments and who believe in the long-run value of their property will continue to fulfill their contract. We propose also that the scheme be made available on better terms to those who stay current on their mortgages through the renegotiation period. This will further discourage homeowners who can afford to stay current on their mortgages from suspending payments merely to attract a write-down.

- **By increasing the amount that owners of mortgages and mortgage-backed securities recover from write-downs, our plan encourages them to renegotiate at an earlier stage in the default cycle than they do at present.**

Also important here is the fact that the plan, properly implemented, will discourage investors in mortgage-backed securities from holding out for better bailout terms.

- **This proposal relies to the maximum extent possible on creative use of regulations to provide incentives for restructuring, greatly reducing costs to taxpayers.**

The extent of any required subsidies would be far lower than in many of the large-scale plans that have been proposed by Feldstein and Hubbard and Mayer[4] and others, which call for massive taxpayer subsidies.

- **It provides a contractual form that is useful in the long run.**

In this respect, it is the only plan we know of in which the current crisis can provide a positive legacy, as opposed to greatly diminishing the country and its future prospects.

In the end, there will be more than one solution to the mortgage problem, each of them suited for particular circumstances. This is particularly clear in the case of the Hope for Homeowners plan, which has many of the same features as our plan. Specifically, the current lender agrees to write down the mortgage to 90 percent of current market value of the home, and payments are reset to 38 percent of gross income. The standard mortgage itself is refinanced into a 30-year fixed rate FHA-insured mortgage on which mortgage insurance must be paid. Upon sale or refinancing, the borrower shares with the FHA the equity created as a result of the transaction: the FHA receives 100 percent during year 1, 90 percent during year 2, 80 percent during year 3, 70 percent during year 4, 60 percent during year 5, and 50 percent thereafter. In its current form, the plan is severely constrained in that it is available only to homeowners who are delinquent (creating bad incentives), it is not proactive, and it does not address the legal issues surrounding restructuring, requiring the homeowner to negotiate with lenders and investors. Yet, if suitably amended, we see this program as being of significant help to the market, providing a vehicle for any public subsidies that might be needed to jump-start debt-for-equity renegotiations. In this form, it is highly complementary to our proposed plan of action.

NOTES

1. Lynn Adler, Reuters, January 14, 2009.
2. R. Glenn Hubbard and Chris Mayer, The Original Hubbard Mayer Proposal, October 2, 2008: http://online.wsj.com/article/SB122291076983796813.html and www4.gsb.columbia.edu/realestate/research/mortgagemarket. Martin Feldstein: http://online.wsj.com/article/SB122697004441035727.html.
3. www.washingtonpost.com/wp-dyn/content/article/2008/12/08/AR2008120803425.html and www.bloomberg.com/apps/news?pid=20601213&sid=alLGOStji8c8&refer=home.
4. See note 2.

REFERENCE

Caplin, Andrew, Noel B. Cunningham, Mitchell L. Engler, and Frederick Pollock. 2008. Facilitating shared appreciation mortgages to prevent housing crashes and affordability crises. Hamilton Project Discussion Paper 2008-12, The Brookings Institution. www.brookings.edu/~/media/Files/rc/papers/2008/0923_mortgages_caplin/0923_mortgages_caplin.pdf.

CHAPTER 17

Where Should the Bailout Stop?

Edward I. Altman and Thomas Philippon

17.1 BACKGROUND

The massive U.S. government bailout originally intended for the financial industry has now spread to the nonfinancial sector. This is partly the fault of the financial bailout itself. Badly designed and too generous to the financial industry,[1] it has perhaps set a damaging precedent. If the government bails out AIG and Citigroup, among others, without holding their managers and directors accountable for their mistakes, is it then unfair for the government to let General Motors (GM) and Chrysler go bankrupt? Political considerations, the fear of job losses, and political ignorance about the bankruptcy process have overwhelmed sound economic policy.

We argue in this piece that the principles set forth in the various chapters in this volume can actually be applied to the design of interventions outside of the financial industry. These principles can help policy makers decide whether to intervene or to take a laissez-faire approach, and, in case they decide to step in, these principles can help design their intervention. We will also use the GM rescue as an example of where fundamental and objective bankruptcy prediction analysis can assist government planners in their bailout decisions.

Government interventions should be based on consistent principles—not because intellectual coherence is a virtue in and of itself, but because interventions without principles are almost guaranteed to be captured by interest groups, to become excessively politicized, and to be inefficient in the long run.

In what follows, we do not argue that the financial industry should be bailed out because it deserves more than any other industry. We argue that government interventions are needed to fix market failures and to control systemic risk. The various regulations proposed in the various chapters in this book focus on the financial industry because of the tendency of financial crisis to create systemic failures. In addition, we advocate regulations that would impose tighter regulations and taxes on systemic financial institutions. Thus, we do not propose a free lunch for the financial sector.

The principles discussed and applied in the various chapters are:[2]

- First, the market failure must be identified.
- Second, the intervention should use efficient tools.
- Third, the costs for the taxpayers should be minimized.
- And finally, government intervention should not create moral hazard.

We argue that, based on these criteria, there is indeed a case for government intervention in favor of GM, and perhaps Ford. But this intervention should not be a giveaway bailout and should not prevent reorganization under Chapter 11.

Our reasoning is the following. The market failure that we identify is the disappearance of the debtor-in-possession (DIP) market because of the financial crisis. This provides a rationale for government intervention (first principle). To be efficient, the reorganization should be thorough, and therefore may have to be lengthy. This is why it should take place under Chapter 11 of the Bankruptcy Code (second principle). To minimize the costs to the taxpayers, the government should provide DIP financing (directly or indirectly) because DIP financing is well protected (third principle). Finally, reorganization in bankruptcy does not reward bad management and therefore minimizes moral hazard (fourth principle).

17.2 ON THE PROPER USE OF CHAPTER 11

Reorganization under Chapter 11 is a fairly efficient process, especially for large firms. Indeed, all academic studies show that the direct, out-of-pocket costs of bankruptcy are between 1 and 5 percent of firm value. The indirect costs can be larger but, in the case of GM, these indirect costs, which include lost sales and profits due to the *prospect* of bankruptcy, have already taken place. So, an actual bankruptcy reorganization will not, in our opinion, result in significant additional bankruptcy costs beyond lawyer and other third-party out-of-pocket costs, such as the insertion of a professional turnaround management team to replace existing senior management.

This stands in sharp contrast with the costs of home foreclosures,[3] which destroy approximately 30 percent of home values. Thus, it is perfectly consistent to argue for government intervention to limit foreclosures, while simultaneously advocating that corporate bankruptcies run their course.

More than two-thirds of all large firms that attempt to reorganize under Chapter 11 of the Bankruptcy Code do emerge successfully either as an independent going concern or as a part of another, healthier entity.[4] Why then was Chapter 11 not widely used during the financial crisis?

The reason Chapter 11 was not used with financial firms (with the notable exception of Lehman Brothers) is that the speed at which the crisis unfolded made it impossible to use normal bankruptcy procedures.[5] The same argument does not apply outside the financial sector, however. Indeed, time is needed to work out a long-term plan for GM and the other car manufacturers. This makes reorganization under Chapter 11 an attractive option. The benefits afforded to firms whose assets are protected and whose fixed payments on most liabilities are suspended, while attempting to reorganize under Chapter 11 of the Bankruptcy Code, are clear. In addition, firms should be able to select the best time in their cash cycle to declare bankruptcy. This is usually possible for nonfinancial bankruptcies (e.g., in the case of Calpine in 2005), but it is often not possible for bankruptcies that take place during financial crises.

Finally, in the case of Lehman Brothers, it appears that the costs of bankruptcy were vastly underestimated. Standard Chapter 11 procedures appear too costly to be used effectively for large financial institutions caught in the midst of a financial crisis. We would therefore advocate the creation of specific bankruptcy procedures to deal with such cases in the future.[6] But it is important to understand that these arguments do not apply to nonfinancial firms.

17.3 DEBTOR-IN-POSSESSION FINANCING

We have argued that, in the case of GM, reorganization under Chapter 11 would be an efficient process. Does this mean the government should step back and let GM file for bankruptcy without intervening? Not quite.

Firms must be able to obtain financing while a reorganization takes place. An important, if sometimes overlooked, benefit for firms in bankruptcy is their ability to borrow substantial amounts of funds for continued operations under what is known as debtor-in-possession (DIP) financing. This unique aspect of our Bankruptcy Code gives the provider of funds a super-priority status over all existing unsecured claims and is almost always accompanied by specific collateral such that the chance of losing any of its investment is quite remote. Indeed, the number of DIP losses to lenders can be counted on one hand from the thousands of such financings in the past. GM (and probably Chrysler) still has some unencumbered assets that qualify as collateral, and even if it did not, the super-priority status would give the new lender a greater degree of confidence of being repaid.

DIP loans are crucial to provide the working capital to a bankrupt firm while it is shedding its unproductive assets and constructing its operational and capital structure plan so as to emerge as a viable going concern. No financial entity will lend money to a bankrupt firm unless the new financing is at least equal in priority to prebankruptcy claims. The Bankruptcy Code therefore provides a mechanism whereby the DIP lender has a super-priority status over all unsecured existing claimants and is typically secured as to all or most of the DIP facility with any remaining unencumbered assets of the debtor. In the case of GM, we have seen estimates of about $20 billion of unencumbered assets. The remainder of a $40 billion DIP loan would not have a priority over secured assets but would over prebankruptcy unsecured claims. As noted earlier, less than a handful of instances, out of thousands of DIP loans, have resulted in losses to the lender.

An excellent example of a successful DIP loan arrangement is the recent Delta Airlines DIP facility in 2005 of $2 billion, which was provided by GE Capital and others. Other recent large DIP loans include Kmart ($2 billion) and United Airlines ($1.3 billion). DIP loans must be paid back before a firm emerges from bankruptcy and are often financed by what is known as "exit financing." Of course, this presumes that the outlook when the firm emerges from bankruptcy is positive enough to assure the new (or old) lender that it will be repaid. So the economic climate when the firm emerges is important. In the case of a GM bankruptcy, a two-year restructuring period is more likely to coincide with a better economic climate than a restructuring that ends in mid-2009.

The financial crisis has induced a temporary market failure in what is normally an efficient bankruptcy process. DIP lending has essentially shut down, as financial institutions are in a massive deleveraging phase and DIP risk capital, even at spreads of 700 to 800 basis points (7 to 8 percent) over LIBOR, is currently unavailable. Circuit City's recent $1.1 billion DIP facility and Pilgrim's Pride's $0.5 billion facility did, however, show some life in the DIP market. Because of this and the enormous amount involved, the DIP lender of last resort must be the U.S. government, to permit a rational rightsizing of the bankrupt automaker, rather than resulting in our nation's vehicle production industry eventually being sold off in pieces.

17.4 OUR PROPOSED SOLUTION FOR AUTOMAKERS

We argue that a massive DIP loan to GM in bankruptcy will guarantee the firm's continued existence over an anticipated 18- to 24-month restructuring period, and the government should also consider backstopping warranties and spare parts availability, even if the reorganization fails. This is far more reassuring than a Band-Aid $10 billion to $12 billion bailout that will not materially reduce the public's uncertainty about a possible liquidation in 2009.

In addition to the DIP support, bankruptcy status enhances the ability of management to renegotiate existing and legacy pension and health care claims; it is much more difficult to do so outside the protective confines of the court system. Moreover, the savings alone on interest payments by GM/GMAC would be at least equal to the interest of about $3.5 billion to $5 billion a year to the government or its conduit on, say, a $40 billion to $50 billion DIP facility.

The government could work with one or more conduit organizations, like JPMorgan Chase, Citi, Wells Fargo, Bank of America, or GE, who are experienced in structuring and monitoring DIP loans. DIP loans can be increased over time, with appropriate fees, to sustain GM over the expected long and likely deep recession. We would also advise the U.S. Treasury to encourage institutions that have received Troubled Asset Relief Program (TARP) subsidies to participate in the DIP loan directly as investors.

Why This Plan Makes More Economic Sense than Alternatives

General Motors Corporation originally asked for a $12 billion loan and a $6 billion line of credit to provide the interim financing it said it needs to restructure the company. Under the revised bailout plan passed by Congress, GM's share was reduced to $10 billion. In addition, there is a plan to offer GM a distressed exchange arrangement with its creditors to reduce the amount of debt by as much as $30 billion.

Unfortunately, some form of traditional loan, for $10 billion or even more, is destined to fail in the current environment and will more than likely be followed by additional requests for more rescue funds or a bankruptcy petition once the initial loan has been exhausted. GM's cash-burn of over $2 billion a month will reduce its assets even further, and will have exhausted them within three months based on current conditions. The global automobile industry, not just GM, is facing the likely prospect of an extended and severe economic recession. Many economists and financial forecasters expect the recession to last at least another two years, with the likely prospect of the worst recession since World War II.

In these conditions, making a bridge loan and offering a credit line to GM are essentially a waste of taxpayer money. As we show, even with a more generous bailout package than the one GM is likely to get, it still will very likely go bankrupt in a year or so without a restructuring as described above.

In order to assess the financial viability of GM assuming that it would receive a loan of $10 billion to $12 billion from the government and perhaps even an additional line of credit of $6 billion, as well as exchange equity for debt and reduce existing debt by $30 billion, we can utilize a model called the Altman Z-Score model, shown here:

$$Z = 1.2 X_1 + 1.4 X_2 + 3.3 X_3 + 0.6 X_4 + 1.0 X_5$$

where: $X_1 = $ (Current Assets − Current Liabilities)/Total Assets
$X_2 = $ Retained Earnings/Total Assets
$X_3 = $ Earnings Before Interest and Taxes/Total Assets
$X_4 = $ Market Value of Equity/Total Liabilities
$X_5 = $ Sales/Total Assets

This model is extremely well known and respected by practitioners and academics and is taught in most corporate finance, investment, and accounting courses. Z-Scores can be converted into bond-rating equivalents (see Table 17.1), which can be used to estimate a firm's probability of default over various horizons.

General Motors' viability (including its 49 percent interest in GMAC) can be analyzed in the following way. We take its financial results as of the end of the third quarter of 2008 and estimate its fourth quarter's operating performance by assuming it was no better, or it was worse, than that of the third quarter (more likely its fourth quarter's results will actually be far worse). We also assume a $2 billion per month cash-burn for each month in the fourth quarter, as reported by the firm in many of its statements. We

TABLE 17.1 Average Z-Score by S&P Bond Rating (S&P 500 firms)

Rating	2004–2005	1996–2001	1992–1995
AAA	5.31	5.60	4.80
AA	4.99	4.73	4.15
A	4.22	3.74	3.87
BBB	3.37	2.81	2.75
BB	2.27	2.38	2.25
B	1.79	1.80	1.87
B−	1.34	1.31	1.38
CCC+	0.90	0.82	0.89
CCC	0.45	0.33	0.40
D	−0.19	−0.20	0.05

adjust its capital structure for the $30 billion reduction in debt and addition to equity based on its proposed massive equity-for-debt swap. Finally, we assume that GM will receive the $12 billion loan and then a $6 billion line of credit. Using the five-variable Z-Score model, as of the end of the third quarter of 2008, GM's Z-Score was −0.16, which places the firm clearly in the "D" (default) bond rating equivalent (BRE) category (see Table 17.2). Indeed, GM's Z-Score fell and became negative for the first time as of June 2008 and was in the "D" default zone.

The average Z-Score of a sample of hundreds of bankrupt firms in the recent past was −0.19. With the pro forma financial profile as of December 31, 2008, GM's Z-Score improves slightly to −0.09, assuming

TABLE 17.2 General Motors Corporation—Summary Analysis Assuming $12 Billion Government Loan

Date	Z-Score	BRE[a]	Z″ Score[b]	BRE[a]	S&P Rating	Moody's Rating
LTM[c] for year ended September 30, 2008	−0.16	D	−1.57	D	CCC+	WR[d]
LTM[c] for year ended December 31, 2008	−0.09	D	−0.46	D	NA	NA

Source: General Motors 10-K and 10-Q.
[a] Bond rating equivalent.
[b] Z-score model for manufacturers, nonmanufacturing industrials, and emerging market credits.
[c] Last 12 months.
[d] Withdrawn rating.

Assumptions:

EBIT calculation for LTM for year ended December 31, 2008: Q1 + Q2 + (Q3 × 2).

Revenues calculation for LTM for year ended December 31, 2008: Q1 + Q2 + (Q3 × 2).

Cash balance and working capital for LTM for year ended December 31, 2008: Balance in Q3 − $6bn + $12bn.

Outstanding debt calculation for LTM for year ended December 31, 2008: Assumed the write-off of the $30bn debt with a corresponding increase in book value of equity. Add $12bn to total liabilities.

Retained earnings calculations for LTM for year ended December 31, 2008: Q3 balance − $2.542bn.

Market value of company:
Q3 2008: Closing share price on September 30, 2008 × No. of shares outstanding.
Q4 2008: Closing share price on December 2, 2008 × No. of shares outstanding.

the receipt of $12 billion in loans and to −0.03 assuming an increase of $18 billion in cash from the government. These scores are still much closer to a D rating equivalent than to a CCC rating.

In conclusion, even with the generous assumptions as to fourth quarter operating results and carefully adhering to GM's own proposed restructuring, GM is still a highly distressed company and likely to go bankrupt, probably within one year.

Job Losses and Externalities

One argument for bailing out GM is simply that the alternative is worse. If GM fails, its employees will become unemployed in the midst of a crisis where the labor market outlook is dismal, and many of its suppliers and dealerships are likely to be liquidated, creating further job losses and economic disruptions.

There is indeed a strong case for helping GM's employees, but bailing out GM is simply not the solution. First, either with the bailout or in bankruptcy, job cuts and reductions in dealerships will be necessary if the firm is to survive. In fact, the current bailout plan would probably offer less of a breathing space to GM and imply more job cuts in the short run than our proposed bankruptcy/DIP financing plan. As we explained earlier, the DIP loan would allow the restructuring to take place over 18 to 24 months, whereas the bailout would be barely sufficient to avoid liquidation in 2009.

In addition, the bailout money does not offer a sustainable solution for GM's employees. What many employees of the car industry really need is to acquire new skills. Incidentally, a recession is not a bad time to invest in human capital. The money allocated to the proposed bailout would be better spent in vouchers for a massive training program for unemployed workers. This would not only alleviate their suffering in the short term, but it would also provide them with a better chance of landing a stable job once the economy recovers.

Our proposed solution would also limit the ripple effects of GM's bankruptcy. The government could backstop warranties and spare parts availability, even if the reorganization fails. This would limit the impact on suppliers and dealerships. Let us also note that concerns about the impact of a bankruptcy on pension benefits are not valid since the well-managed GM pension plan under General Motors Asset Management is overfunded (as of mid-December 2008).

In any case, it would be far better for the country and the economy to rightsize the auto business in the United States now and make it more competitive in the long run, rather than have it deteriorate further and be sold off at a later date with even more lost jobs and cuts in pension/health care benefits.

Moral Hazard

The management and boards of GM, Chrysler, and, to a lesser extent, Ford have until recently been in a state of denial. They should now face up to the reality of their dismal outlook, file for bankruptcy, and request the DIP loans. And, if the terms of the loans require changing senior management, so be it. The option to bring in a professional turnaround team is one of the advantages of Chapter 11.

Bailing out GM and Chrysler at the expense of taxpayers will only encourage bad management in the future. The plan proposed by the House of Representatives and the White House calls for the appointment of a "car czar" to oversee the restructuring. Unfortunately, since restructuring proposals will come from existing senior management, it will be difficult for the car czar, whoever he or she is, to obtain the timely information required to make decisions so critical in a difficult restructuring. Chapter 11 was created precisely to deal with these issues. It would be wise to use it.

17.5 CONCLUSION

The principles presented here offer a clear framework to organize government interventions, even outside the financial industry. It is only when existing remedies (such as the bankruptcy process) are not likely to avert a major systemic problem that the government should intercede with a direct bailout.

Applied to the case of the U.S. auto industry, the principles of government intervention suggest that U.S. car manufacturers should be allowed to reorganize under the protection of the Bankruptcy Code, and that the government should step in to provide DIP financing.

NOTES

1. See Chapter 15, "The Financial Sector Bailout: Sowing the Seeds of the Next Crisis?"
2. We propose prudential regulations to minimize systemic risk because systemic risk imposes negative externalities (Chapter 13, "Regulating Systemic Risk"). We advocate that large and complex institutions be subject to specific regulations, because being too big to fail or too interconnected to fail creates moral hazard (Chapter 5, "Enhanced Regulation of Large, Complex Financial Institutions").

We criticize the financial bailout because it is too generous to the industry and too costly for taxpayers (Chapter 15, "The Financial Sector Bailout: Sowing the Seeds of the Next Crisis?").

3. See Chapter 16, "Mortgages and Households."

4. There is no guarantee, however, that the firm might not encounter subsequent economic hardship and need to file for protection again under Chapter 11 (the so-called Chapter 22 phenomenon).

5. One anecdotal feature of the crisis suggests that decision makers were constantly running out of time: Bad news was often announced on Monday morning. This stands in sharp contrast with common wisdom and practice. Firms usually disclose negative information on Friday evening, after the markets have closed, so that investors can digest the bad news over the weekend. During the financial crisis, however, weekends were the only periods left to assess the situation and make decisions. As a result, major news, typically negative, was often announced on Sunday night or on Monday morning. In the case of AIG, officials did not even have the time to wait for the weekend, which only reinforces our point.

6. Specific procedures already exist to some extent for financial firms. For instance, derivative contracts are not subject to automatic stay.

CHAPTER 18

International Alignment of Financial Sector Regulation

Viral V. Acharya, Paul Wachtel, and Ingo Walter

18.1 THE CASE FOR INTERNATIONAL COORDINATION

Many of the policy recommendations we have put forward in the preceding chapters will prove to be ineffective—or at least their edge blunted—if there is a lack of international coordination among central banks and financial stability regulators in implementing them. This issue is important; although cross-border banking and financial flows are extensive, much of bank and financial supervision remains national. There is some consensus on prudential aspects of regulation such as capital requirements and their calculation, but there is hardly any consensus on how much forbearance regulators show toward their national banks and how they should share the burden of failures of global financial institutions.

Complications that could arise from lack of coordination between national regulators are many. These complications are largely due to regulatory arbitrage across national jurisdictions; that is, if institutions are more strictly regulated in one jurisdiction, they may move (their bases for) financial intermediation services to jurisdictions that are more lightly regulated. But given their interconnected nature, such institutions nevertheless expose all jurisdictions to their risk taking.

Here are six examples, mainly based on policy recommendations in this book, that illustrate the negative externalities that can arise due to lack of international coordination.

Treatment of Off-Balance-Sheet Leverage

Consider the off-balance-sheet credit risk transfers employed by banks to arbitrage capital requirements and thereby undertake a high degree of effective leverage.[1] The U.S. generally accepted accounting principles (GAAP) do not require structured investment vehicles (SIVs) and asset-backed commercial paper (ABCP) conduits to be treated as being on the balance sheet. In contrast, the European banks that follow the International Financial Reporting Standards (IFRS) are required to more or less treat their SIVs and conduits as being entirely on their balance sheets. The result is that U.S. banks' balance sheets have been somewhat more opaque, with as much as 40 percent of their assets often being off their balance sheets. Further, under the U.S. GAAP, banks have ways to bring onto their balance sheets profits from the SIVs and conduits even though they are not recognized as assets. Hence, even simple calculations such as return on assets are not straightforward or comparable between banks in the United States and Europe. While better and more consistent standards adopted in Europe have helped their banks somewhat during the crisis, the relatively greater opacity of U.S. bank balance sheets has hurt these banks, too. When the U.S. banks have failed, counterparty risk concerns have affected all global players likely to be connected to them. A more uniform treatment of such off-balance-sheet leverage would allow investors to better assess the relative profitability and risks of global financial institutions.

Pricing of Government Guarantees

The provision of implicit deposit insurance is now ubiquitous, and in most cases—up to some threshold level of deposit amount—explicit. Suppose, however, that deposit insurance guarantees are priced differently across countries. Say, for example, deposit insurance is priced fairly for banks in the United States but their commercial banking counterparts in the United Kingdom do not have to pay any premium whatsoever (as has been the practice so far, although it is now under reconsideration). Under such circumstances the UK banks, all else being equal, would be able to offer higher deposit rates, attract a greater base of deposits, and more generally face a lower effective cost of funding. This would affect the competitiveness of the U.S. banks—at least relative to those UK banks that are global players. If the disadvantage to the U.S. banks becomes sufficiently large, lobbying by American banks would soon attempt to induce the U.S. regulators to underprice deposit insurance as well. As we have argued earlier,[2] this will generate moral hazard at commercial banks all over the world. The excessive risk taking by commercial banks could, in turn, be transmitted to unregulated parts of the financial sector as they deal with insurance companies, investment banks, and hedge funds.

Next, consider the bailout packages put in place in October 2008. The U.S. package, as we have discussed,[3] has adopted one-size-fits-all pricing for the loan guarantees involved, charging 75 basis points per annum for protection offered to all banks. In contrast, the UK package relies on market prices, charging 50 basis points plus the median five-year CDS spread for the institution in question in the 12 months up to October 7, 2008. The resulting difference in the cost of loan guarantees can be substantial. In fact, for some institutions, the difference between the two pricing schemes is as high as 125 basis points per annum for a period of at least three years. Not surprisingly, this competitive distortion immediately led to the UK banks lobbying the UK regulators to soften the terms of their bailout package, although from the standpoint of sound and fair pricing, the UK scheme is the more desirable of the two approaches.[4]

Treatment of Over-the-Counter Derivatives

Next, consider dealing with the counterparty risk externality from centralizing clearing of credit derivatives.[5] Assume the United States sets up a centralized clearing platform for over-the-counter (OTC) credit derivatives, while regulators in Europe fail to enforce such a requirement. It may be tempting for one country's regulators to create a credit haven so as to attract a large number of institutions and jobs. Large players in credit markets would then simply move their credit desks to this European country and enjoy the benefits accorded by opaqueness and weaker collateral arrangements in OTC trading. The result would be that the lack of transparency that manifested itself as a counterparty risk externality in the current crisis would be an issue once again when a crisis hits the financial sector in future.

Lender of Last Resort Policies

Lender of last resort (LOLR) policy is one area where better coordination— at least among the largest central banks—could produce substantial improvements. Suppose the Federal Reserve adds conditionality, explicitly or implicitly, to its terms for lender of last resort facilities, requiring that highly leveraged institutions raise capital in order to be eligible for borrowing against illiquid collateral.[6] But suppose at the same time a central bank in another part of the world does not require such criteria. Then, a global player, based primarily in the United States, could simply access liquidity from these other central banks, rendering ineffective the purpose of conditionality in the Fed's LOLR policies, delaying its capital issuances, and imposing a cost on the entire financial sector.

It appears that Lehman Brothers might have been an example of such a situation; Lehman borrowed heavily from the European Central Bank against illiquid collateral during the subprime crisis, substantially weakening the position of the Federal Reserve in persuading its top management to either find a suitor or issue more capital (which was costly for management due to dilution costs). Coordination among central banks in getting Lehman Brothers to reshape its balance sheet *before* it could be deemed eligible for LOLR support might have altered history.

Regulation of Systemic Risk Due to Large, Complex Financial Institutions

Similarly, if large, complex financial institutions (LCFIs) are subject to a systemic risk charge,[7] then some jurisdictional coordination is necessary. How would a national regulator acquire the right to tax a financial entity that is not formally a part of its jurisdiction? The only reasonable outcome is that all significant national financial sectors have a LCFI regulator and they agree on the set of institutions that should be subject to the systemic risk tax. If each country implements some form of LCFI tax on its systemically large players, the outcome would lead to far fewer distortions in the form of gaming of regulatory guarantees through pursuit of the too big to fail (TBTF) status.

Regulating Bank Scope: Demise of the Glass-Steagall Act

A classic case of a regulation that had to be repealed eventually due in part to lack of international coordination is the separation of commercial and investment banking activities in the United States. It is useful to rewind history to 1933, when the passage of the Glass-Steagall Act in the United States set up the Federal Deposit Insurance Corporation (FDIC) and introduced the separation of commercial and investment banking activities. One aim of the Glass-Steagall Act was to avoid the conflicts of interest that characterized the granting of credit to a borrower and the provision of investment and underwriting services in securities of the same borrower. The investment banking activities were also deemed too risky to be put under the same functional umbrella as a commercial bank—the Glass-Steagall Act deemed it important to protect depositors' interests and limit the risk exposure of the FDIC. However, with the exception of a few countries such as China and Japan, such mandatory separation of banking activities has not been implemented elsewhere. The norm in other countries has always been the universal bank with both banking and securities activities under a common umbrella in institutions that generally also have access to deposit insurance.

The passage of the Glass-Steagall Act clearly shaped the financial arena in the United States in the years that followed, leading to the separation of Morgan Stanley from JPMorgan and restricting commercial banks from investments and trading in nongovernment securities. From 1933 until 2007, the world witnessed a growing supremacy of U.S. investment banks—they expanded dramatically, set up worldwide operations, and became the institutions most coveted for jobs by finance (and indeed any other discipline's) graduates. Protected from commercial banks by regulation, the U.S. investment banks were able to innovate in order to grow their business in commercial paper, fixed income, equities, mergers and acquisitions, cash management accounts, and other banklike products, and then rolled many of them out globally to confront the European universal banks head-on—to the point that a disproportionate share of intra-Europe investment banking fees (as high as 70 percent) went to the U.S. investment banks in the late 1990s and early 2000s.

As the U.S. investment banks thrived, the purely commercial banks in the United States felt at a disadvantage. Commercial banks wished to but could not underwrite and trade instruments such as mortgage-backed securities (MBSs) and collateralized debt obligations (CDOs) and could not establish structured investment vehicles (SIVs). They complained about the lack of a level playing field with the commercial banks from abroad, which were all universal banks and could underwrite and trade instruments. They also complained about the lack of a level playing field given the many regulations they were subject to compared with the unregulated investment banks. Lobbying efforts followed, and the Glass-Steagall Act was repealed by the Gramm-Leach-Bliley Act of 1999. In fact, the Glass-Steagall restrictions were effective in both letter and spirit only until 1963, when a series of successful challenges commenced that ultimately allowed commercial banks to underwrite and deal in nongovernment securities. In 1987 commercial banks were allowed to establish the so-called Section 20 subsidiaries, which in turn led to the 1999 Gramm-Leach-Bliley Act repealing Glass-Steagall altogether. It was hoped that the U.S. depository institutions would now be able to compete with the universal banks of other countries, that enforcement of Chinese walls between lending and investing activities of universal banks would prevent any conflicts of interest, and that management of the new financial conglomerates was sufficiently capable to manage the resulting complexity and avoid turning banks into casinos.

Many academics had long questioned the Glass-Steagall Act on the basis of supposed synergies between lending and underwriting activities. In hindsight, it appears that the period from 1933 to the 1960s featured far greater financial stability than the period from the 1970s to date. Even without the hindsight, from a pure design standpoint, it seems that a financial architecture where deposit insurance is provided *only* to commercial lending and not to the highly risky securities activities—one of the intended but largely overlooked purposes of the Glass-Steagall Act—has several advantages: (1) such separation limits the scope of regulation to commercial banking or direct credit intermediation, which is ultimately the main linkage from the financial sector to the real economy; (2) in the process, it limits the scope of regulatory follies to commercial banking as well; (3) it also limits linkages from the unregulated financial sector to the regulated sector and reduces the counterparty risk externality that can affect economy-wide credit intermediation; and (4) it reduces ex-post pressure on regulators to bail out even unregulated institutions by rendering them systemically less important (i.e., no longer too interconnected to fail).

It is not surprising that, given the adverse role played by linkages from the unregulated sector to the regulated/insured one, a similar separation of financial activities as originally enforced by the Glass-Steagall Act is again being revisited at the Bank of England, and more generally in Europe, as a possible way of insulating the payments and settlements system from securities activities. The point here is that such separation may be untenable in a global financial architecture without coordination among national regulators, as the separated entities will most likely be less profitable than their universal counterparts, and a chain of events that will lead ultimately to the repeal of any such separation will soon follow. Nevertheless, there is an uneasy sense that casinos and massive TBTF financial utilities do not cohabit well.

18.2 ADDRESSING REGULATORY EXTERNALITY

All these examples suggest that a "beggar thy neighbor" competitive approach to regulation in different countries—or even the failure to coordinate without any explicit competitive incentives—will lead to a race to the bottom in regulatory standards. This will end up conferring substantial guarantees to the financial sector, giving rise to excessive leverage- and risk-taking incentives in spite of substantial regulation in each country. Such an outcome should be avoided. The problem is once again one of externalities, and the case for coordination is therefore a compelling one. It is imperative, in our opinion, for national leaders, preferably central bankers of countries with large financial markets (the G8, for example), to agree on a broad set of principles that all countries will adopt and implement.

National regulators do not like to give up their independence and discretion. Indeed, it may not be possible to agree on every detail of each issue pertaining to regulatory implementation. It appears to us, however, that the key is to agree on the big reforms. Overarching principles—such as (1) treatment of off-balance-sheet leverage in a fair and consistent manner by standardizing definitions, disclosure, and accounting practices; (2) pricing guarantees and bailouts fairly; (3) requiring transparency in OTC derivatives that connect financial institutions; and (4) avoiding provision of liquidity to insolvent institutions—should be reasonably convincing to most regulators as desirable principles to follow. Once agreement on adopting such broad principles in their individual approaches to regulation is reached, it is possible that different countries will proceed to implement slightly different variants of each principle. But, the constraints imposed by adopting sensible overall principles will minimize the arbitrage that financial institutions can engage in by shopping for the most favorable jurisdiction. This, in turn, will ensure that desired objectives of each individual country's financial stability plans are not seriously compromised.

Will such coordination necessarily arise? And, if yes, what form will it take? It is useful to start with some history of efforts at such coordination.

18.3 HISTORY OF INTERNATIONAL COORDINATION EFFORTS

As with the current crisis, global economic problems in the past have often called for global solutions with international policy coordination. However, nations do not have a very good track record of creating international policy institutions and rules with significant cross-national powers. In finance, the history goes back to the Bretton Woods conference in 1944. With the end of the Second World War in sight, it was clear that the international financial structure should be reconfigured to avoid a return to "beggar thy neighbor" policies of the prewar period. Lord John Maynard Keynes, the dominant intellectual figure at the conference, proposed that exchange rates be fixed to an international currency (the "bancor") issued by an international central bank or global lender of last resort. Perhaps inevitably, the idea of a supranational authority proved far too radical at the time, and the International Monetary Fund (IMF) system that emerged had limited lending authority. Nevertheless, Bretton Woods was a dramatic success because memories of the prewar economic disaster lingered and the dawn of a new era provided an unprecedented opportunity to start afresh. So the shared determination to reform led to an important restructuring of international financial relationships that served the global economy well until the system broke down in the 1970s.

The original Bretton Woods agenda also called for the establishment of a trade organization to coordinate trade policies and reduce impediments to free trade based on two simple but compelling principles—reciprocity and most favored nation treatment (nondiscrimination). However, global trade policy coordination from the establishment of the General Agreement on Tariffs and Trade (GATT) in 1947 and running to its successor, the World Trade Organization (WTO), has had important problems of compliance and enforcement. The WTO operates without any international enforcement powers and relies on consensus among all member nations to establish policies consistent with the agreed rules. Lack of enforcement often makes compliance problematic, and agreements to reduce trade barriers can only be reached after endless rounds of negotiation such as the currently ongoing Doha round. Progress has been made but, in the absence of any supranational authority, it relies on very gradual consensus building.

In the aftermath of the 1997–1998 Asian crisis, there were many proposals to strengthen the IMF by giving it the ability to discipline irresponsible countries or put them into a form of receivership. These proposals would have required countries to give up sovereign powers, and it was quickly clear that neither the U.S. nor other governments would take external intervention on this scale seriously. Moreover, the conditionality imposed by the IMF on debtor countries led to substantial resentment of the institution in emerging markets. Partly as a result, the IMF has not played a significant coordinating role in the international response to the current crisis, although its sovereign lending facilities are once again being utilized. The IMF does, however, play an important role in collecting and disseminating information about national economies and their financial systems. Its Financial Sector Assessment Program (FSAP) does a thorough job of monitoring and evaluating national financial sector stability. However, FSAP reviews are conducted only with the permission of national authorities, who have the final say on the release of findings to the public. Importantly, the United States has never agreed to be the subject of an FSAP review.

Within the European Union, all barriers to trade in financial services and restrictions on cross-border activities of banks were eliminated in 1992 when the Single European Act took effect, and the creation of the euro in 1999 reduced uncertainty due to exchange rate fluctuations among the participating countries. Nevertheless, the adoption of the euro was controversial in many countries and rejected by several EU members, notably the United Kingdom, that wanted to retain sovereign control of monetary policy. The euro area is now a well-integrated financial sector—financial markets have caught up with product and services markets. Although the EU does a great deal of community-wide regulation in the real sector, financial sector regulation and supervision remain under the purview of national authorities. On occasion, the European community has been able to prevent some egregious bailouts from going through, even in the financial sector (for example, French recapitalization of Credit Lyonnais in the 1990s was subject to several EU-imposed constraints).[8] Even today there is some perception that cooperation on financial sector regulation represents an undesirable surrender of national sovereignty of individual member countries.

There are some examples of international coordination of economic and financial policy, but these are usually ad hoc responses to crises without any mechanism for improving the overall picture. For example, the Plaza Agreement in 1986 among the world's five largest economies led to a period of coordinated currency interventions and domestic policy alignment. Similarly, in the current crisis, there has been significant cooperation among central banks in creating almost unlimited currency swap arrangements. However, such instances of coordinated policy are not common and have become more difficult as the number of large economies has increased. In recent years, attempts to coordinate exchange rate policy with China, for example, have been notably unsuccessful.

Coordination Is Key, Not Centralization

While these examples do not inspire a great deal of confidence in the prospects for creating an international regulator—or even achieving significant international coordination after the current crisis—there is some silver lining. In mid-October the British prime minister, Gordon Brown, made a dramatic call for a new Bretton Woods conference to establish a "global way of supervising our financial system." He called for turning the IMF into an international central bank and for placing financial supervision in the hands of an international body. His bold proposals were met with some halfhearted support, notably in Europe, but there has been no noticeable movement toward forming his suggested meeting of world leaders. Nevertheless, his exhortation appears to be an important initiative, in principle.

We concede that it is highly unlikely that an international financial sector regulator with power over markets and institutions will emerge in the foreseeable future; countries are simply not willing to surrender authority. It remains unrealistic to expect that an international central bank will be able to close down a large part of the financial sector of a country, or determine monetary or fiscal policy for a country, or that international civil servants will supervise or inspect national financial institutions.[9]

Instead, improvements in the regulatory structure will have to come through increased coordination and an understanding that a more closely aligned and consistent approach is in each nation's best interest. Basel capital requirements provide an important precedent for this approach. The ostensible purpose of the Basel Accord of 1988 was to level the playing field by eliminating the funding cost advantage conferred to the Japanese banks by their regulators.[10] No matter what one thinks of the end result of the Basel initiative, the process itself was important. The Basel Committee crafted an international consensus with a common set of rules for applying prudential capital requirements on all banks. Countries were then expected to adhere to these rules, although the decision to apply them or tweak them or use them at all remains country specific. The Basel Committee has no way of imposing the agreement on countries or penalizing noncooperation. It was participation in the negotiations that formed the consensus and created a commitment to the outcome.

The Bank for International Settlements (BIS)—which houses the Basel Committee—has made several attempts to standardize rules and definitions in financial institutions. For instance, it has set standards for the collection and dissemination of financial sector information. There is also a new player on the scene. The Financial Stability Forum (also housed at the BIS) was established in 1999 by the G7 countries. It has issued several reports detailing specific recommendations for strengthening and standardizing financial regulation. Specifically, its April 2008 report provided specific benchmarks for (1) strengthening prudential oversight, (2) enhancing transparency and valuation, (3) changes in the role and uses of credit ratings, and (4) strengthening the authorities' responsiveness to risks and providing robust arrangements for dealing with stress in the financial system. None of these suggestions have the force of law, nor can the BIS compel countries to act. However, the BIS looks like the most promising venue for an international consensus to develop, and the fact that the Financial Stability Forum is taken seriously (for now) means that meaningful cooperation and coordination might emerge.

18.4 RECOMMENDED STEPS TO ACHIEVE INTERNATIONAL COORDINATION

What is in store for the future? Will a new Bretton Woods produce a new and powerful international regulator? We view this as unlikely and unrealistic, particularly in the midst of the current crisis. Instead, world leaders need to express a commitment to forge a regulatory consensus on a sensible blueprint for the overall global financial architecture. Our recommended steps to achieve such international coordination are thus as follows:

- Central banks of the largest financial markets (say the G7) should convene first and agree on a broad set of principles for regulation of banks. As advocated in this book (and possibly elsewhere), these principles should cover the following themes:
  - Each central bank should carve out a dedicated role for a powerful LCFI regulator that is in charge of supervising and managing the systemic risk of large, complex financial institutions.

- The supervisory and control apparatus of each LCFI regulator should feature:
  - Coordination with financial sector firms to provide long-term incentives to senior management and traders and other risk-taking employees.
  - Fair pricing of explicit government guarantees such as deposit insurance, and, where implicit government guarantees are inevitable, limiting their scope by ring-fencing activities of guaranteed entities.
  - Standards for transparency and accounting of off-balance-sheet activities and centralized clearing for large OTC derivatives markets to reduce counterparty risk externality.
  - Imposition of a systemic risk tax on LCFIs that is based on aggregate risk contribution of institutions rather than their individual risk exposures.
  - Agreement on overall objective and design of lender of last resort facilities to deal in a robust manner with liquidity and solvency concerns.
  - Agreeing on a set of procedures to stem systemic crises as and when they arise based on clear short-term policy measures (such as loan guarantees and recapitalizations that are fairly priced and impose low costs on taxpayers) and long-term policy measures (such as the shutting down of insolvent institutions, providing fiscal stimulus, and addressing the root causes of financial crises—e.g., mortgages in this case).
- Next, central banks should present their joint proposal with specific recommendations to their respective treasuries or national authorities, seek political consensus for an international forum such as the Financial Stability Forum or a committee of the BIS to coordinate discussion and implementation of these principles, and monitor their acceptance and application.

A commitment to such a process will generate a willingness to take the outcome seriously and, it is to be hoped, pave the way for international coordination on well-rounded policies that balance growth with financial stability as efforts get under way to repair national financial architectures.

NOTES

1. See Chapter 2, "How Banks Played the Leverage Game."
2. See Chapter 7, "Corporate Governance in the Modern Financial Sector."

3. See Chapter 15, "The Financial Sector Bailout: Sowing the Seeds of the Next Crisis?"
4. It should be noted that there could also be an improvement in overall regulation due to such lobbying. For instance, the U.S. package has more or less *forced* all banks to participate in its loan guarantee scheme, whereas the UK package gives banks the *option* to do so. The latter has allowed the better banks in the United Kindom such as HSBC to signal their quality to markets by opting out of government support. The healthier banks in the United States have since lobbied for such optionality too, which is in fact a move in the right direction for the U.S. package (though unlikely to come about).
5. See Chapter 10, "Derivatives: The Ultimate Financial Innovation," and Chapter 11, "Centralized Clearing for Credit Derivatives."
6. See our recommendation in Chapter 14, "Private Lessons for Public Banking: The Case for Conditionality in LOLR Facilities."
7. Say a capital charge for systemic risk, as recommended in Chapter 13, "Regulating Systemic Risk."
8. See Acharya (2003), especially pages 2767–2770, for a discussion of attempts by participating countries in a cooperative arrangement such as the EU to be forbearing toward national banks.
9. The limited capability of existing institutions is often recognized. Timothy Geithner noted in a speech in 2004 that the IMF developed a "financial mission that had some of the characteristics of a lender of last resort ... but without mechanisms to constrain risk-taking behavior."
10. Even then, unsurprisingly, Japanese regulators counteracted any harmful effect of the level playing field created by the Basel Accord of 1988 on the Japanese banks by relaxing their non-Basel policies. Wagster (1996) and Scott and Iwahara (1994) provide supporting evidence for the implied difficulty in achieving a truly level playing field through adoption of Basel capital requirements.

REFERENCES

Acharya, Viral. 2003. Is the international convergence of capital adequacy regulation desirable? *Journal of Finance* 58 (6):2745–2781.
Scott, Hal S., and Shinsaku Iwahara. 1994. In search of a level playing field: Implementation of Basel Capital Accord in Japan and U.S." Occasional Paper No. 46, Group of Thirty, Washington, D.C.
Wagster, John D. 1996. Impact of the 1988 Basel Accord on international banks. *Journal of Finance* 51:1321–1346.

About the Authors

Viral V. Acharya, Professor of Finance, has research expertise in the regulation of banks and financial institutions, corporate finance, credit risk and valuation of corporate debt, and asset pricing with a focus on the effects of liquidity risk. Professor Acharya is at NYU Stern School of Business and London Business School.

Edward I. Altman, Max L. Heine Professor of Finance, has research expertise in corporate bankruptcy, high yield bonds, distressed debt, and credit risk analysis.

David K. Backus, Heinz Riehl Professor of International Economics and Finance, has research expertise in international business cycles, foreign exchange, fixed income securities, and currency and interest rate derivatives.

Menachem Brenner, Professor of Finance, has research expertise in derivative markets, hedging, option pricing, volatility indexes, inflation expectations, and market efficiency.

Stephen J. Brown, David S. Loeb Professor of Finance, has research expertise in hedge funds, mutual funds, Japanese equity markets, empirical finance and asset allocation, and investment management.

Andrew Caplin, Professor of Economics at New York University's School of Arts and Science, has research expertise in economic fluctuations, macroeconomic theory, microeconomic theory, and housing markets.

Jennifer N. Carpenter, Associate Professor of Finance, has research expertise in executive stock options, fund manager compensation, survivorship bias, corporate bonds, and option pricing.

Gian Luca Clementi, Assistant Professor of Economics, has research expertise in corporate finance, firm dynamics, contract theory, and macroeconomic effects of imperfections in financial markets.

Thomas F. Cooley, Richard R. West Dean and Paganelli-Bull Professor of Economics, has research expertise in macroeconomic theory, monetary theory and policy, and the financial behavior of firms.

Robert F. Engle, Michael Armellino Professor of Finance, has research expertise in financial econometrics and market volatility, and is the recipient of the 2003 Nobel Prize in economics for his work in methods in analyzing economic time series with time-varying volatility (autoregressive conditional heteroskedasticity [ARCH]).

Stephen Figlewski, Professor of Finance, has research expertise in derivatives, risk management, and financial markets.

Xavier Gabaix, Associate Professor of Finance, has research expertise in asset pricing, executive pay, the causes and consequences of seemingly irrational behavior, and the origins of scaling laws in economics and macroeconomics.

Dwight Jaffee, Visiting Professor at NYU Stern; Willis Booth Professor of Banking, Finance, and Real Estate; and Co-Chair, Fisher Center for Real Estate and Urban Economics, has research expertise in finance and real estate.

Kose John, Charles William Gerstenberg Professor of Banking and Finance, has research expertise in corporate governance, corporate bankruptcy, executive compensation, and corporate disclosure.

Marcin Kacperczyk, Assistant Professor of Finance, has research expertise in institutional investors, empirical asset pricing, mutual funds, socially responsible investing, and behavioral finance.

Alexander Ljungqvist, Research Professor of Finance, has research expertise in financial intermediation, investment banking, initial public offerings, entrepreneurial finance and venture capital, corporate governance, and behavioral corporate finance.

Anthony W. Lynch, Associate Professor of Finance, has research expertise in asset pricing, mutual funds, and portfolio choice.

Lasse H. Pedersen, Professor of Finance, has research expertise in liquidity risk, margins, short selling, spiral effects, liquidity crisis, and the valuation of stocks, bonds, derivatives, currencies, and over-the-counter (OTC) securities.

Thomas Philippon, Assistant Professor of Finance, has research expertise in macroeconomics, risk management, corporate finance, business cycles, corporate governance, earnings management, and unemployment.

Matthew Richardson, Charles Simon Professor of Applied Financial Economics, and Director, Salomon Center for the Study of Financial Institutions, has research expertise in capital market efficiency, investments, and empirical finance.

Nouriel Roubini, Professor of Economics and International Business, has research expertise in international macroeconomics and finance, fiscal policy, political economy, growth theory, and European monetary issues.

Stephen G. Ryan, Professor of Accounting, has research expertise in accounting measurement, accounting-based valuation and risk assessment, and financial reporting by financial institutions and for financial instruments.

Anthony Saunders, John M. Schiff Professor of Finance, has research expertise in financial institutions and international banking.

Philipp Schnabl, Assistant Professor of Finance, has research expertise in corporate finance, financial intermediation, and banking.

Roy C. Smith, Kenneth Langone Professor of Entrepreneurship and Finance, has research expertise in international banking and finance, entrepreneurial finance and institutional investment practice, and professional conduct and business ethics.

Marti G. Subrahmanyam, Charles E. Merrill Professor of Finance and Economics, has research expertise in valuation of corporate securities, options and futures markets, asset pricing (especially in relationship to liquidity, market microstructure, the term structure of interest rates, and fixed income markets), family business, and real option pricing.

Rangarajan K. Sundaram, Professor of Finance, has research expertise in agency problems, executive compensation, corporate finance, derivatives pricing, and credit risk and credit derivatives.

Stijn Van Nieuwerburgh, Assistant Professor of Finance, has research expertise in finance, macroeconomics, general equilibrium asset pricing, and the role of housing in the macroeconomy.

Paul Wachtel, Professor of Economics, has research expertise in monetary policy, central banking, and financial sector reform in economies in transition.

Ingo Walter, Seymour Milstein Professor of Finance, Corporate Governance, and Ethics, has research expertise in international trade policy, international banking, environmental economics, and economics of multinational corporate operations.

Lawrence J. White, Arthur E. Imperatore Professor of Economics, has research expertise in structure, conduct, and performance of financial intermediaries and risk management in financial firms.

Robert E. Wright, Clinical Associate Professor of Economics, has research expertise in the history of banks and banking, securities markets, corporate finance and governance, government debt, and insurance.

Eitan Zemel, W. Edwards Deming Professor of Quality and Productivity, has research expertise in supply chain management, operations strategy, service operations, and incentive issues in operations management.

Index